Diaspora and Migration Studies Series
No. 11

Basques in Cuba

Edited by
William A. Douglass

Translated by Aritz Branton

Center for Basque Studies Press
University of Nevada, Reno

This book was published with generous financial support from the Basque Goverment.

Basque Diaspora and Migration Series, No. 11
Series Editor: Xabier Irujo

Center for Basque Studies
University of Nevada, Reno
Reno, Nevada 89557
http://basque.unr.edu

Book design by Daniel Montero

Library of Congress Cataloging-in-Publication Data

Names: Douglass, William A., editor. | Branton, Aritz, translator.
Title: The Basques in Cuba / edited by William A. Douglass ; translated by
  Aritz Branton.
Other titles: Vascos en Cuba. English
Description: Reno : Center for Basque Studies, University of Nevada,
Reno,
  2016. | Originally published in Spanish under title: Vascos en Cuba.
  Vitoria, Spain : Servicio de Publicaciones del Gobierno Vasco, 2015. |
  Includes bibliographical references and index.
Identifiers: LCCN 2016017479 | ISBN 9781877802980 (pbk. : alk. paper)
Subjects: LCSH: Basques--Cuba--History. | Pais Vasco
  (Spain)--Relations--Cuba. | Cuba--Relations--Pais Vasco (Spain)
Classification: LCC F1789.B37 V3713 2016 | DDC 305.899/9207291--dc23
LC record available at https://lccn.loc.gov/2016017479

We dedicate this book to the memory
of the great Bascologist,
Jon Bilbao

Contents

Acknowledgments

The eleventh International "Basque Country Mugaz Gaindi" (Beyond the Frontiers of the Basque Country) Seminar was held in Havana on January 12–14, 2015, and focused on the subject of the Basques in Cuba. The vast majority of these articles are based on papers read at that event and subsequently amended. We also commemorated the fortieth anniversary of the publication of *Amerikanuak: Basques in the New World* by William A. Douglass and Jon Bilbao.

We would like to thank all the sponsors of the event in Havana. It was organized by the Basque government (Eusko Jaurlaritza) and the Center for Basque Studies at the University of Nevada, Reno, Havana's Colegio Universitario de San Gerónimo, Fundación Fernando Ortiz, the Grupo de Investigación País Vasco y América: Vínculos y Relaciones Atlánticas of the University of the Basque Country EHU/UPV, USAC-University Studies Consortium, and La Asociación Vasco-Navarra de Beneficencia de la Habana. Asier Vallejo Itsaso of the Basque government, Fernando Ortiz Foundation, William A. Douglass of the Center for Basque Studies, Felix Julio Alfonso López of the Colegio Universitario de San Gerónimo, and Renato García Egusquiza, president of the Asociación Vasco-Navarra de Beneficencia de la Habana, gave the words of welcome and the farewell speeches. The director and staff at the Palacio de Conde de San Esteban de Cañongo were excellent hosts. The audience showed great interest and respect. All the speakers were highly professional and contributed their best efforts. I would like to conclude with a personal note of thanks. I had to organize the event based at Reno, Nevada and this—partly because of the lack of normal relations between Cuba and the United States—gave rise to many difficulties. I do not know what would have happened without the help of Daniel A. Durán at the Fundación Fernando Ortiz. He took charge of all the details connected with the event—publicity, venues, logistics. He was in charge of editing this book in Spanish.

—William A. Douglass

Preface

The Basques are linked to the Cuban historical process from its beginning. There were Basque mariners in Columbus's ships when he arrived in the Antilles on his first voyage and, afterward, Basque surnames have been abundant and outstanding throughout Cuban history.

If it is true that Basques were present in disproportionately small numbers, it is undeniable that, on the other hand, they have been significant protagonists in terms of their actions.

When, in the mid-eighteenth century, Havana resisted fiercely attacks by the British, who by then had begun to dominate the seas, Basques were among those who led the combat against the redcoats of the British sovereign George III.

Examples of Basque surnames in the historical vanguard of Cuba are repeated in many other areas of the social, economic, and cultural life of the largest of the Antilles.

Consequently, we encounter Basques first throughout the colonial adventure and later in the struggle for independence; there are Basque slavers, owners of sugar mills, whose surnames still evince pride among the descendants of the slaves of those old plantations (and, while it might seem paradoxical, with affection as well).

We also find other Basques, founders of libraries and businesses, as well as bishops and benefactors, fomenters of scientific research and art, of neoclassical architecture, for example, that is so common in Havana.

It is in the nineteenth century, when the great economic, political, and social changes converted the island into one Spain's most prosperous and appreciated colonies, that we must pause. For it is in the nineteenth century that the Enlightenment arrives in Cuba with its ideas regarding historical progress, utopia, and social transformation. Here, too, there are outstanding Basques: illustrious promoters of economic and development and ecclesiastical modernizers of education and social welfare.

—María Ángeles Elorza Zubiria
General Secretary of Foreign Affairs
Eusko Jaurlaritza/Basque Government

Editor's Note

The Spanish version of this work, *Vascos en Cuba*, appeared in the autumn of 2015 in time for a book presentation at the Congress of Basque Collectivities in the World held that October in Vitoria-Gasteiz. The present volume is a somewhat liberal, rather than literal, version of *Vascos en Cuba*. As editor I have made certain modifications to the translated texts for several reasons. First, literal translation from Spanish to English (and vice versa) is never totally satisfying. Proper academic prose in Spanish can be stylistically florid, with sentences running on through a series of clauses qualified by sub-clauses. In my many years of translating between the two languages I have even encountered whole Spanish paragraphs consisting of a single sentence. While it does have its own elegance, for the Anglo reader that style can become not only off-putting but rather confusing. In English academic prose sentences tend to be far briefer and more concise. Therefore I have taken the liberty to Anglicize this version of the book by dividing some sentences in the original into two or three in this translation. I have, of course, given each of the authors the opportunity to approve (or not) the changes.

Second, there is the issue of intended audience. None of the participants in the Havana seminar are native English speakers and all wrote their contributions in Spanish at my request. Implicitly, then, they were addressing a Hispanic readership that shared with them certain background knowledge. We could cite the two nineteenth-century Cuban Wars of Independence (1868–1878; 1895–1898) as a prime example. Our Cuban contributors know about them in great deal; our European ones possibly somewhat less so but they are still a part of their own history. Conversely, the average North American reader knows little about them. References to these conflicts are present, even when only in passing, in almost all of the articles in this collection. Therefore, whenever I thought it necessary, I have added an explanatory sentence within the text when not a footnote to it.

Bibliography

Douglass, William A., ed. *Vascos en Cuba*. Vitoria-Gasteiz: Servicio de Publicaciones del Gobierno Vasco, 2015.

Introduction

The idea of organizing the Mugaz Giandi on Basques in Cuba was a result of my naivety in 2013. Let me explain. Many years ago, around 2000, I was in touch with Lola Valverde, a historian at the University of the Basque Country. She had spent two years in Havana doing research on Cuban women and, of course, this led to her coming into touch with Basque-Cuban people. Over several months we exchanged ideas about collaborating on research into Basques in Cuba, believing it to be virgin territory. She was to work the archives and I, as a social anthropologist, would conduct the fieldwork.

And then lightning struck. The book *El roble y la ceiba: Historia de los vascos en Cuba* (The Oak and the Ceiba: The History of the Basques in Cuba) by Cecilia Arrozarena (a person of whom we were unaware) was published. It was a descriptive compendium of Basque activities in Cuba throughout the island's history. From Columbus's first journey to the beginning of the third millennium. Its aim was not to be excessively analytical, from a social scientific perspective viewpoint there can always be further research into any subject, but now we thought that, in many ways, our project would do little more than restate much of what had already been published in that book. So we desisted.

Even so, I still wanted to visit Cuba. I am also an enthusiastic bonefisherman and the island is famous for them. Many of my angler colleagues—all of them Americans—used to ignore the boycott and go fishing in Cuba which, of course, was illegal as far as our government was concerned. I resisted the temptation for decades, until I turned seventy.

But then I seemingly saw that I wasn't going to be on the planet for long enough to be able to witness political changes and decided to enter Cuba via Cancun. When hearing of this, a colleague in the Basque Country insisted on giving me Cecilia's contact details and arranged for us to meet up in the bar of a hotel in Havana. In fact, Cecilia didn't show but, to tell the truth, it didn't bother me much because it was to have been a mere courtesy encounter without any agenda.

The following year I went back, once more to go fishing. And it was then that I actually did meet Cecilia. We became great friends and discussed in detail our various intellectual projects. She told me that she had a lot of new information about the Basques in Cuba that she had gathered herself or been sent by readers of her book. And it was then that I made a suggestion. How about working together on the second edition of her book, using the new information and analyzing it in anthropological terms? And she declined. She had started three novels and hadn't been able to work on them for some time. She also had some unpublished poems that she wished to rewrite. In other words, she wanted to spend all her time on literature without other distractions and commitments, so she gave me all the data and insisted that I should publish it.

The truth is I didn't feel very comfortable with that arrangement. I started to work on some of the subjects thinking that there would be some way to get her involved in the project later. But then I began to realize that I was being naive once again because as I proceeded I kept coming across specialists—both European and Cuban (one was even Uruguayan)—who were researching different facets of the subject of the Basques in Cuba. Once more I was doing something which had already been done. I soon realized that I was a novice in the subject, even though I had been the coauthor of *Amerikanuak: Basques in the New World*.

As I was in my seventies, it didn't make much sense for me to try to reinvent myself. And then I had the idea of organizing the seminar instead of trying to write a book which was supposedly mine, but in which I would be using other people's material. At the same time, the seminar would encourage the training of serious researchers, most of them young, and their papers would be a contribution to our knowledge of Basque history in Cuba. And so it happened.

Thanks to the commitment of the Basque government and the Center for Basque Studies at the University of Nevada, Reno, the results of the seminar were published in two languages, English and Spanish. The Spanish edition appeared in time for the Congress of Basque Collection in the world held in Vitoria-Gasteiz in October 2015, this English edition appearing in June 2016.

I would like to finish on a personal and emotional note. Forty years ago, in 1975, the book *Amerikanuak: Basques in the New World* was published in English by the University of Nevada Press. It was the result of a collaboration between a historian, Jon Bilbao, and a social anthropologist, myself. At that time little work had been done on Basque emigration and its outcomes in the various diasporas around the world. The book was well received and I don't think that it is vainglorious of me to say that it has become an iconic work among investigators who research the causes and effects of Basque emigration. In 2015 some of them organized an international commemoration of the fortieth anniversary of its publication with a series of seminars and publications at universities in events in Latin America, the United States, Iceland, and the Basque Country. All of the events, as well as the various publications, including this book, will bear an *Amerikanuak* commemorative logo.

I think that launching the cycle of events in Havana with the international seminar in January was perfect. Jon Bilbao's first book was *Vascos en Cuba: 1492–1511,* published in 1958 by Ekin publishing house in Buenos Aires. Jon was married to Havanan Marta Saralegui and, during the fifties, worked for his father-in-law in Cuba. In fact, he spent more time researching his book and putting together a library at the Havana Basque Center than he gave to his salaried job.

I met Jon in 1967 at the annual meeting of the American Anthropological Association held in October of that year in Washington, DC. At that time I had only been coordinator of the of Basque Studies program at the University of Nevada for a few months. I invited Jon to Reno and he gave a lecture on the Basque language the following spring. It was so well received that we hired him as a faculty member and, for the following decade, his academic career was based at Reno, before his retirement and return to his beloved Basque Country. He had been raised there at the house named Osabene near Getxo, purchased by his parents after they made their fortune as merchants in Cayey, Puerto Rico (Jon's birthplace).

During his time in Reno, Jon and I collaborated closely and put together the Basque Studies Program and a large Basque library. Jon's presence—he had already established himself as the most important Basque bibliographer in the world—gave us instant credibility. His complete dedication to his work on the Basques was legendary and unquestionable. Jon was always in his office until nine at night and during the weekend too. Over the years, our joint research produced our book *Amerikanuak.* But more than just a colleague, Jon was one of the best friends I've ever had—he was almost a brother.

Last year (2014) was the centenary of Jon's birth and there were various commemorative events held in the Basque Country. They included press and academic articles about his enormous contribution to Basque culture. At the University of Deusto a seminar was held in his honor and there was an exhibition about his career. And Deusto, the Etxepare Institute and the Center for Basque Studies at Nevada founded a research fellowship for the study of Basque emigration in Jon's name. All well deserved. We dedicated the international seminar on Basques in Cuba to Jon Bilbao. Both of the publications of our results bear this dedication. *Eskerrik asko* Jon.

—William A. Douglass

1

A Poem to a Basque Immigrant,
by Agustín Acosta

Félix Julio Alfonso López

Agustín Acosta Bello (Matanzas, 1886–Miami, 1979) was one of the best poets during the first half century of the Republic of Cuba.[1] He was educated in line with Modernist aesthetics and was author of a collection of poems considered emblematic in terms of social protest, *La Zafra* (1926), which anthropologist Fernando Ortiz said all Cubans should read. His poetry was praised by Rubén Martínez Villena, José Antonio Portuondo, Max Henríquez Ureña, and Cintio Vitier, who wrote that "His work . . . as a whole, is strictly personal, intrinsically from the Cuban provinces in its tone (open, frank), with subtle *guajira* malice running right through it and the factual, straightforward, unvarnished way in which he puts down the words and says things, though with a soft, smiling, persuasive touch."[2] This paper's aim is to examine one of Acosta's sonnets, "A Basque," which, after what seems to be a descriptive anecdote, gives profound insight into the human condition. The first thing that draws your attention in the poem is the subject. Unlike the Canarians, Galicians, and Andalusians, who emigrated in huge numbers during the colonial centuries and who projected their own collective image on the island that gave rise to many literary characters, the Basques have tended to be "invisible" in Cuban literature. Even so, Basques in the island's literature can be proud of the formidable Farraluque, "a mixture of semi-titanic Basque and languid Havanan,"[3] whose erotic exploits shake up the pages of *Paradiso*, José Lezama Lima's

---

1. Cabrera Galán's biographical study of him, *Agustín Acosta Bello* is remarkable.

2. Vitier, *Lo Cubano en la poesía*, 358.

3. Lezama Lima, *Paradiso*, 264.

great novel. But now let us read Acosta's poetic text, and we will then give
a brief interpretation of its possible meanings.

Un vasco
Usa boina de paño y bebe el vino en bota.
La báquica alegría en su tráquea repica.
Resume en cesta y cancha su juego de pelota,
Y ama la sombra histórica del árbol de Guernica.

En su español gracioso su verbo se complica
Cuando el lenguaje éuscaro con la razón agota.
Él mismo es como un árbol en cuya savia rica
Sueña la tierra áspera de Vizcaya remota.

No ceja a la esperanza de posibles retornos.
Es un lingote férreo fraguado en altos hornos,
Que como un estandarte romántico enarbola

Un corazón de niño de todo mal ayuno.
Sabe de Iparraguirre, del Gernikako arbola,
¡y no sabe quién es don Miguel de Unamuno![4]

[A Basque
He wears a cloth beret and drinks from a wineskin.
Bacchanal happiness is unending in his windpipe.
summed up in jai alai his pelota game,
And he loves the historical shadow of the Tree of Gernika.

He muddles the verb of his gratuitous Spanish
When the Basque language reaches the limits of its (capacity for)
logic.
He's like a tree himself whose rich sap
Dreams of the rough land of distant Bizkaia.

He doesn't give up on the hope of going back there.
He's an iron ingot forged in tall furnaces,
Which, like a romantic standard is raised

He holds up the heart of a child forced to fast.
He knows about Iparragirre and the Tree of Gernika,
But he doesn't know who Miguel de Unamuno is!]

We do not know when the poem was written or who inspired it, but
chronology and the model taken are not important here. The use of the
indefinite article "a" shows that Acosta's Basque is, rather than a poetic

---

4. Acosta, *Poemas Escogidos*, 193. Unless otherwise stated all translations of quotes in this
book are by the translator.

exercise in local color, a text with a thesis. Let us look at the reason for this. At the start of the poem, the character is shown as an archetypal immigrant from the Iberian Peninsula with ethnic traditions such as his "cloth beret," the difficult art of drinking from a wineskin, and his enthusiasm for playing pelota rather than baseball or American handball. However, this rather folklore-based view becomes more penetrating when it says "he loves the historical shadow of the Tree of Gernika," which is the way Basques express their idea of political freedom.

The second quatrain tells us about nostalgia, memories, and the longing to return. The telluric metaphor of the tree is invoked once again and something else which is fundamental for the Basque people is added: their language. Phrases and sentences in his mother tongue are the most intimate way to express things, in contrast to his "peculiar Spanish," which is the voice of reason, and, in dreams, he sees the far-off coast of his country. However, after these clichés about melancholy, Acosta uses a surprising comparison: the Basque in his poem is "an iron ingot forged in tall furnaces," but who has "the heart of a child forced to fast." Being a person with feelings for both his land and the island, his spirit has the strength of steel and the goodness of his soul. So, to sum up, a hard man who is also, perhaps, a little sad, but also good.

However, it is at the end of the poem that this likeable man's enigma is uncovered. His secret is to be found in a confession which is no less revealing for being unexpected: he is aware of José María Iparragirre, the great Romantic bard, and remembers the lines of the patriotic hymn "Gernikako arbola" (The Tree of Gernika), written in Basque, but does not know who Miguel de Unamuno is. What does this statement mean? Is it to point out the illiteracy of rural Basques? An ingenious resolution to the poem, full of irony? We think not and offer the following interpretation of the final statement. As is well-known, these are two opposite emblematic figures in Basque culture. Iparragirre led an adventurous, bohemian life, fought in the last Carlist War and was exiled for many years in France, Switzerland, Germany, Uruguay, and Argentina, while Unamuno, who was born in Bilbao, studied at the University of Madrid, where he received a doctorate in philosophy and letters, his thesis being titled "Crítica del problema sobre el origen y prehistoria de la raza vasca" (Critique of the problem regarding the origin and prehistory of the Basque race, 1884), in which he first put forward views that were going to be contrary to Sabino Arana's Basque nationalism. He wrote most of his work, which is existentialist in character, while he was a lecturer in Greek and the rector of the University of Salamanca.

It is impossible to imagine two more different views of life and it is this detail—in spite of the poet's feigned reproach in the exclamation mark—which reveals the poem's deepest meaning. Agustín Acosta's Basque is not an educated man; he is a worker who rejects one of his most famous countrymen. But this humble man, who could be from any farmstead, knows his roots and is the bearer of his ancestors' culture, taking the author of "Agur Euskalerriari" as his singer and poet, greatly preferring him to the pro-Spanish Salamanca professor, whose poems and philosophical treatises were always centered around the destiny "of Spain." We believe that this version of the Basque national drama—which is explicit in the Iparragirre-Unamuno antinomy, and its affectionate portrayal of the Basque-speaking immigrant, who, deep down, he forgives for not knowing about the author of *Niebla,* in spite of him being a great writer—means that Agustín Acosta's sonnet shows affection for its subject, a singular sign of profound caring for the Basque Country, its history, and people.

Bibliography

Acosta, Agustín. *Poemas escogidos.* Selected, prologue, and notes by Alberto Rocasolano. Havana: Editorial Letras Cubanas, 1988.

Cabrera Galán, Mireya. *Agustin Acosta Bello: Aproximación a su vida y obra.* Havana: Editorial de Ciencias Sociales, 2009.

Lezama Lima, José. *Paradiso.* Havana: Ediciones Unión, 1966.

Vitier, Cintio. *Lo cubano en la poesía.* Havana: Letras Cubanas, 1970.

2

The Ceiba and the Templete:
The History of a Polemic

Félix Julio Alfonso López

Stop a moment, walker: a tree adorns this place, a leafy ceiba tree, a memorable sign of patience and the growing religiousness of a young city. Under its shade the Creator of our salvation was worshipped and the Council met for the first time. However, the tree protected by eternal tradition gave way to time. So take care that the good faith of Havana does not perish in the future. Today you see this image carved into the stone on the last day of November, 1754.

—Inscription on Cagigal Column, Havana Templete, 1754.

Monuments play a most essential part in the history of each country: but they would be dumb and lifeless . . . if the reasons behind them had not been illustrated by written history.

—Ramón de Palma y Romay, "The Pavilion," 1838.

The small, modest neoclassical building known as El Templete (The Shrine) is on one side of the Plaza de Armas in Old Havana and is overshadowed architecturally by the neighboring Castillo de la Fuerza, Palacio del Segundo Cabo, and the impressive Palacio de los Capitanes Generales, all of which were major symbols of Spanish power in Cuba during the colonial period. However, the building's enormous symbolic weight in the history of the past and the city's present is as proud as ever with its solid columns, topped with pineapples[1]—"la airosa piña de esplendor vestida/la pompa de mi patria" (the successful pineapple dressed in splendor/the pomp of my homeland) as hallucinating poet Manuel de Zequeira y Arango saw it (1964)[2]— and its magnificent ceiba tree tree—"the Briareus, which, with a hundred open arms, seems to threaten the skies eternally," as polygraph Esteban Pichardo put it[3]—and the monumental buildings around it. Generations of Cubans have gone there on November 16 in the secret hope of making their most intimate desires come true.

---

1. The pineapples on the top of the large pillars are of the greatest interest for analyzing the symbolism of the Templete. As architect Felicia Chateloin puts it: "It is with this detail that the Templete seals the assimilation of overseas art with its own connotations, giving our neoclassical architecture a new dimension: the tropical." Felicia Chatelein, *Havana de Tacón*, 55–56.

2. Zequeira y Arango, "Oda a la piña," 9–10.

3. "Seiba," in Esteban Pichardo, *Diccionario provincial casi razonado de vozes y frases cubanas*, 547. We should make clear at this point that the word "seiba" is indigenous and so, according to Pichardo, should never be written with a "c". Bachiller y Morales and Mariano Aramburo's authoritative criteria back him up. The plant's scientific name is *Ceiba pentandra* (L.). See Bisse, *Árboles de Cuba*, 85. In this paper we are using the modern spelling: "ceiba."

Is this confluence of vegetable on stone, mixing together desires and dreams yet to come true, a metaphor for the island itself? Is its small, classical nature—compared with baroque exuberance—an allegory for the radiant poverty which José Lezama Lima talked about in contrast to opulence without historical meaning? What is so singular and disturbing about this tiny church, with its Doric columns and Attic base in whose narrow confines the painter Vermay lies, accompanied by his oil paintings? In fact, dozens of illustrious historians, architects, and researchers into Havana traditions have discussed the place's origins and the real meaning of its symbols,[4] a subject in which, as so often in history, the real and the mythical meet, a story which has come down to us being that of the first Mass held to consecrate the city at the foot of a leafy ceiba tree[5] that was later replaced by the Cagigal Column, built where the original tree is said to have been.[6]

But this search into the past to illuminate the present has become torturous and at times the real meaning of the Templete and the ceiba tree beside it have been the center of violent controversies that usually moved away from a literal interpretation of the constructed heritage and led to the arena of political struggles and symbolic disputes. Perhaps the first person to question the Templete's symbolism—and with obvious political motives—was the Villa Clara historian and patriot Antonio Miguel Alcover (1875–1915) in a text published in the magazine *Cuba y América* during the American military occupation (1899–1902).[7] Alcover's arguments, full of nationalist passion, aim to correct certain "historical mistakes," all connected with Spanish traditions and which, after the war of '95, had to

---

4. The texts written by Ramón de Palma y Romay—"El Templete," published in the magazine *El Álbum,* Havana, 1838—are examples of this, as is Antonio Bachiller y Morales' "El Templete," an article illustrated with an engraving by Federico Mialhe in his *Paseo pintoresco por la Isla de Cuba* (Picturesque journey around the island of Cuba), which was published in Havana in 1842. The Countess of Merlín also wrote a few paragraphs about it in her *Viaje a la Habana* (Journey to Havana), published in Madrid in 1844, a time at which the monument was "covered in waves of dust . . . relegated to a corner of the Plaza de Armas, continually hit and undone by the mules and wheels that move around it during the promenade."
5. There are various records of this custom, such as one saying that "In the language spoken in Hispaniola Ceyba is the name of one of the biggest trees to be found in these Indies . . . these trees are usually planted in the Indian villages' squares because of their great beauty, and even in some Spanish squares. I saw one in Panama in front of the convent of San Francisco which had been there for many years." Cobo, *Historia del Nuevo Mundo,* vol. 2, 124. There are also records of a carpenter from neighboring Puerto Rico, called Pantaleón, drilling into the trunk of a giant ceiba tree around 1582 and putting inside it a chapel dedicated to the saint for whom he felt he most devotion. See Cadilla de Martínez, *Costumbres y tradicionalismos de mi tierra,* 111.
6. "In 1754 Caxigal ordered that a pyramid be raised where the vegetable monument had been. Joseph Yantete, second city engineer, was commissioned to design it and the building work was entrusted to Manuel Felipe Arango, the head Syndic representative. The cost of the pyramid, which the council was to pay for, was "605 pesos and 7 r". AHN, Consejo de Indias, file 21467, quoted by Marrero in *Cuba: Economía y sociedad,* vol. 8, 250.
7. Antonio Miguel Alcover, "La Misa, la ceiba y el templete." Extract from Colección Facticia, no. 107, Havana City Museum Library.

be removed from Cuban archetypes.[8]

One such "mistake" in tradition was the idea that the ceiba tree had died a natural death when, in fact, Alcover tells us, following José María de la Torre's lead,[9] it had been governor Cagigal—"a highly orthodox man and a profaner of historical monuments"—who had had it cut down and, in its place, left "a cruel theft of identity, an unspeakable swindle." Taking this imposture into account, Alcover believes that Cubans should not revere an apocryphal ceiba tree, in whose shade "despots such as Tacón, Balmaceda and Weyler knelt down, without any faith or noble feelings, and trod upon and bloodied our land; but the gentle founders of our city, which is now the capital of Cuba, never did . . . they held the first Mass and council in the real city of Havana beneath a beautiful, leafy tree."[10]

Another fallacy that Alcover refutes is the presence of Diego Velázquez in Vermay's paintings, which, in his opinion, could not have happened because Velázquez was in Santiago de Cuba in 1519, as Jacobo de la Pezuela[11] and Pedro José Guiteras also stated.[12] Finally, the historian from Sagüa La Grande says that Cubans should not carry on celebrating Saint Christopher's Day on November 16, as they had done during the colonial period, in order not to overload the festivity of Santiago, patron saint of Spain, held on the same day, and suggested that instead "let us pay homage to the truth, opening the doors of the Templete on the same day recorded in 1515, which is what Havanans should celebrate as they did not take part in the wars against the Arabs shouting '¡Santiago y Cierra España!'"[13]

A similar approach to the above—one of also being suspicious of the ceiba in terms of it being a symbol to which to pay homage—is advocated by the erudite Manuel Pérez Beato, undoubtedly one of the people who has carried out most research into the history of Havana. Pérez Beato starts from the hypothesis that neither the date nor the actual event of founding the city "are definitely demonstrable, and the deeply held belief in the tradition is due to official confirmation of it given by the raising of the pillar with its commemorative inscription and the building of a Templete which was inaugurated with a parody or simulation of what was supposed to have happened there in the year mentioned."[14] Like Alcover, Pérez Beato rejects the idea of the ritual around the tree, but for different reasons: he is not concerned by the nonexistence of the original ceiba tree—something to be expected after four centuries—but rather by the ominous connotation he sees in it, that of being a "public pillory" or "tree

8. For further information, see Iglesias, *Las metáforas del cambio en la vida cotidiana.* In particular, commonly held ideas about removing the symbols of colonial power.
9. Torre, *Lo que fuimos y lo que somos o Havana antigua y moderna.*
10. Alcover, "La Misa, la ceiba y el templete."
11. Pezuela, *Historia de la isla de Cuba.*
12. Pedro José Guiteras, *Historia de la Isla de Cuba.*
13. Alcover, "La Misa, la ceiba y el templete."
14. Pérez Beato, *Habana antigua, apuntes históricos,* 36.

of infamy" because "they used to whip criminals tied to the ceiba tree when they had committed particular crimes, which removes any respect for a tree honored by tradition and the holding of a Mass at such a sublime moment for the city fathers."[15]

In fact, the people whipped were not strictly speaking "criminals" but rather creole or African slaves caught carrying arms[16] or stealing cassava bread to sell or eat and then sentenced to a hundred lashes tied to the enormous tree trunk; this was doubly painful as such trees are held to be highly sacred in religions of African origin.[17]

However, this was not the only ceiba tree to be "stigmatized": the many successors after Cagigal's decision fared no better, the Council also deciding before building the Pavilion to "cut down the ceiba tree because of the problems its roots cause and because it is not necessary." In the council meeting held on December 14, 1827, councillor José Francisco Rodríguez reasoned that "the damage caused to the building of the monument by the ceiba being there, its roots not only preventing the work from being solid in nature, but also destroying the walls to an extent, are the reasons it was believed that tree should be cut down, as explained, and as the ceiba had been planted some seventy years ago and, so, another one or more could be planted as fitting the place," and, finally, the city council decided "there was no real, effective need to replace that ceiba, the monument preserving the memory of the first Mass held there and the first council meeting."[18]

As we have seen, the early inhabitants of Havana were quite pragmatic when it came to ecology, not bothering too much if there was one or various ceibas there, or if there were none at all. After all, there was a rumor (which was later proved to be false) that the wood chips of the original ceiba tree had been sold to museums in Washington and London. As part of this utilitarian point of view, an interesting interpretation of the changes in the Plaza de Armas between 1754 and 1829 mentions "a process of making the existing symbols sacred. Firstly, replacing the supposedly

---

15. Ibid. Emilio Roig de Leuchsenring said in an issue of *Habana*, "While for some historians the old ceiba tree was something to be venerated, others thought it something to be ashamed of because of the way the people of the city were horrified by it as the place they could be whipped for any reason." *Habana* (March 1939): 10–15.

16. "No black slaves may bear swords, or knives, or any other type of arms, even if they are with their masters, unless with their masters at night, and not otherwise, or in the countryside in daytime with their master, or they will lose those arms the first time and, the second, lose the arms and and be give 20 lashes on the ceiba or pillory or at the prison gates," *Ordenanzas de Cáceres* (1573), quoted in Hortensia Pichardo, *Documentos para la Historia de Cuba*, vol. 1, 111–12.

17. As is well-known tree worship, dendrolatry, is practiced world wide and has been recorded in different periods and cultures, from the Middle East to America, the Mediterranean civilizations and West Africa. For information about magical and religious properties attributed to the ceiba tree in Cuba, see the classic study by Cabrera, *El Monte*.

18. "Acuerdos sobre el templete y la ceiba de los supuestos primeros cabildo y misa de la villa de Havana, en cabildo de 14 de diciembre de 1827" (Agreements about the Templete and the Ceiba of the Supposed First Council Meeting in the Meeting Held on December 14, 1827), in Colección Facticia, no. 107, Havana City Museum Library.

foundational ceiba tree with three new trees and an allegorical monument . . . as a gesture to reconfirm the city's existence," which is interpreted as being "sacrilege" against secular customs "which represent the dominant commercial spirit in the Antilles: in Havana . . . everything is bought and sold."[19]

In addition to these accusations leveled at the ceiba in terms of it being an impure tree which did not deserve to be remembered, there is another reasoning that, if not taken into account, makes any discussion of the issue invalid. It was given by one of the most authoritative experts on the subject, doctor Emilio Roig de Leuchsenring, official historian of the city between 1935 and 1964,[20] when he states: "the important event of founding Havana, which could have been celebrated with a Mass and a commemorative council meeting, *did not take place at Carenas Port,* but, rather, on the third occasion on which the City was moved, possibly, as suggested above, after some months and even years and, consequently, there was no ceremony of any type."[21]

Likewise, Roig reminds us that the *Plaza de Armas* was moved at least three times between 1559 and 1577, all dates after the supposed consecration, which means that "we cannot be sure that there had been a ceiba tree in the place where Cagigal had the pillar built, and still less that that ceiba tree was the one chosen beneath which to hold Mass and the first council meeting," which are events, in any case, whose authenticity is not proven by any documents.[22]

Finally, another factor that seems to round off the "dark legend" surrounding the ceiba tree and the Templete is the fact that that building was constructed during the government of Captain General Francisco Dionisio Vives (1823–1832)[23] with clear political and colonial objectives. On the one hand, celebrating Queen Josefa Amalia's saint's day and, as recorded in the capitulary acts, commemorating Fernando VII's invasion of Catalonia to crush the liberal faction there. An allegorical medal was coined to this end and later hung under one of the columns in the Templete.[24]

In practice, the political effect went beyond a rite of submission to the absolute monarch: Governor Vives sent a report to the Court making clear his intention to distract the people of Havana from the events of libera-

---

19. Segre, *La Plaza de Armas de La Habana*, 14.

20. On July 1, 1935, doctor Emilio Roig de Leuchsenring (1889–1964) was named Official Historian of Havana, and in 1938 the City Historian's Office was set up to support his work, being a public institution and an autonomous municipal organization.

21. Roig de Leuchsenring, *Havana: Apuntes históricos*. Second edition, considerably enlarged, vol. 1, 60.

22. Roig de Leuchsenring, "La Ceiba y el Templete," in *Gran Mundo*, June 1947.

23. Vives's government, the first to have absolute power, stood out for its suppression of separatist movements and tolerance of vice in the colony. As a popular saying had it: "Si vives como Vives, vivirás" (If you live like Vives, you'll live).

24. "Informe sobre el Templete y la ceiba por José Manuel Ximeno, 20 de diciembre de 1827" in Colección Facticia, no. 107, Havana City Museum Library.

tion in continental America, where, in 1827, a late Bolivarian attempt to promote freedom for the island was taking place, and, at the same time, emphasize the Cubans' loyalty to the Crown, as explicitly stated on the inscription of the Templete's tympanum: "During the reign of Don Fernando VII, with Don Francisco Dionisio Vives President and Governor, *the most loyal, religious and peaceful city of Havana* erected this simple monument to commemorate the place where, in 1519, the first Mass and council meeting were held in the city. Bishop Don Juan José Díaz de Espada conducted this august sacrifice on the nineteenth of March, eighteen forty-eight."[25]

Emilio Roig writes about the inaugural ceremony, which was "solemn and full of pomp":

> There was a Mass read by Bishop Espada attended by the *Capitán General* and the ecclesiastical, civil and military authorities in the city, as well as distinguished citizens. Espada gave a speech to them all which Pezuela described as being erudite. Decorations and lights were hung up and the city's people celebrated the inauguration of the monument—one of the few in Havana of a historical nature—for three days.[26]

At the same time, Vermay's oil paintings—both the ones off to the sides, which are historical and commemorative in character, and the ones occupying the central area, which are contemporary with these events, in spite of their neoclassical look—reinforce colonial symbolism by representing the Havanan oligarchy in all its connivance and arrogance seated beside the representative of the Spanish monarchy.

However, at the ceremony there was a character who was to stimulate a new layer of interpretation of the events we are examining. I am referring to the presence of the Basque bishop Juan José Díaz de Espada y Fernández de Landa[27] at the Templete ceremonies—both as a project with civil implications and with its religious consecration—a factor which completely changed the negative interpretations which some historians had been putting forward. The person who started this radical change from seeing

---

25. Author's emphasis.

26. Emilio Roig de Leuchsenring, "La Plaza de Armas y el pavilion," in Colección Facticia, No. 107, Havana City Museum Library.

27. Juan José Díaz de Espada y Fernández de Landa (1756–1832) was born at Arroiabe, a village in the Basque province of Araba. He was bishop of Havana from 1802 until his death and carried out extensive ecclesiastical, social, and teaching reforms and, in thought, went far beyond the limits of his bishopric, his influence being particularly felt at San Carlos Royal and Municipal Seminary, San Ambrosio, and the Friends of the Country's Economic Society. His disciples included Félix Varela and José Martí remembered him with great affection. He was a liberal, illustrated, modern man, and his influence in the first half of the nineteenth century is of enormous relevance in practical terms in religion and philosophy. For discussion of his contribution to Cuban culture, see César García Pons, *El Obispo Espada y su influencia en la cultura cubana*; Eduardo Torres-Cuevas, *Obispo de Espada*; and Rigoberto Segreo Ricardo, *De Compostela a Espada*. Consolación Fernández Mellén's research is more recent, *Iglesia y poder el Havana*.

the ceiba tree and the monument as an emblem of public punishment and Spanish oppression to the complete opposite—in other words, the emblem of the citizens of Havana's liberty—was the wise Cuban ethnologist Fernando Ortiz and a fundamental part of his argument is the figure of Espada and the traditions of the Basque Fueros, which many had missed.

Ortiz published his theory about the Templete for the first time in 1928, on the monument's centenary, as a note in Mario Lescano Abella's commemorative book titled *El primer centenario del Templete, 1828–1928*. In Ortiz's opinion, and in contrast to the tradition that had been prevalent since Arrate, the ceiba tree's symbolism was not mostly religious and "was, in itself, and because it was consecrated, more than just a historical event." He then contradicts Pérez Beato's view that the ceiba tree had to be abominated and states forcefully:

> No. We believe that the ceiba tree at the Pavilion was the emblem of the City of Havana and is the oldest, most permanent emblem of citizen's liberty which we have in Cuba. The people of Havana should visit the ceiba tree in pilgrimage whenever their liberties are curtailed.[28]

It might be thought, after reading this statement, that it was highly contemporary in that at that moment the dictator Gerardo Machado was trying to remain in power using a spurious constitutional reform, but Ortiz's historical reflection goes deeper than that, and he points out that his idea is not a "rushed opinion, perfumed by the romantic" but rather "a documented interpretation based on the history of Castilian and American municipalities, which local historians and historians who have dealt with Cuban municipalities have forgotten."[29]

However, having said this, Ortiz adds that: "This is not the right moment to explain this point. But let me state my thesis here for the first time: *the Templete's ceiba tree is Havana's symbol of municipal freedom, the historical municipal census of its justice and freedom.*"[30]

Finally, Don Fernando says that he owns a hand-colored polychrome print, bought in a bookshop in Leipzig, in which there is a ceiba tree which is "leafy and emblematic, like Bizkaia's venerated Gernika Tree,"[31] from much earlier than the building of the Templete, and promises to publish about it. It should be noted here that Ortiz's explanation legitimized the Havanan ceiba tree as a reflection of civil liberties not only in comparison with Castilian and American traditions but also that of the Gernika oak tree, beneath which Spanish monarchs had to swear loyalty to the traditional fueros of the people of Bizkaia. It is obvious, although Ortiz does not mention it specifically in this text, that Bishop Espada's part in the building of the Templete is behind his analogy, and he interprets it as a type of allegory of the Gernika Assembly House.

---

28. Fernando Ortiz, "Bibliografía," 287.
29. Ibid., 258.
30. Ibid.
31. Ibid.

On examining the *Archivos del Folklore Cubano* we have not come across the explanation which Ortiz promised, but he did refer to it repeatedly on later occasions, particularly during the visit to Havana of José Antonio Aguirre (the President of the Basque government-in-exile)'s visit to Havana and in his speech during the commemorations of the 150th anniversary of the Friends of the Country's Economic Society. Lehendakari Aguirre spoke at the Hispano Cuban Institute of Culture on October 20, 1942, about "The social sense and liberty of nations at the present time," and was praised by Ortiz in a speech in which he mentioned the contributions of the most important Basque people in the history of Cuba. He particularly mentions Bishop Espada "who is to be thanked for the Havana Templete, built behind the ceiba tree which represents Havana's communal liberties, which brought to mind the Gernika Tree (a symbol of freedom) in front of the Captain General of Cuba's palace."[32]

A few months later, on January 9, 1943, during a commemoration of the 150 years of the Friends of the Country's Economic Society, Ortiz read a paper titled "The Enlightenment's Cuban Daughter" and in it made reference to the relationship between enlightened Basque culture (as seen in the Basque Royal Society of Friends of the Country, founded in 1764) and the origins of the city of Havana, emphasising the figures of Don Luis de Las Casas y Aragorri and the Araban bishop. Talking about the latter, he reminds us of Aguirre's words and adds the following:

> While mentioning him (Espada), I remembered how the Basque bishop had got one over the *Capitán General* by building the Templete beneath the legendary ceiba tree for the city, a sign and record of the jurisdictional freedom of the city of San Cristóbal de La Habana, opposite the island's Government Palace and as an approximate reproduction of the Gernika Tree and its Assembly House, which symbolize his people's national freedom.[33]

Thus far Ortiz's arguments, whose main thesis he had already put forward in 1928 and then developed until the conclusion quoted above. In other words, the ceiba tree was already linked with the citizens before the construction of the Templete and, taking advantage of that, and in analogy with his homeland, Espada decided to give the place a new meaning by adding a neoclassical pavilion, his own favorite style and one so deeply rooted in his home region,[34] at the same time as he carried out a

---

32. Fernando Ortiz, "Conferencias," 340.

33. Fernando Ortiz, "La hija Cubana del iluminismo," 55.

34. The foundational document of the neoclassical style, so different from baroque exuberance, is Frenchman Laugier's 1753 proposal, *Essay on Architecture*, in which he puts forth primitive cabins as the model and reference for good architecture because of their nakedness and simplicity, which bring them close to nature. In the Basque Country: "Nature is seen as the ideal, and also as the origin of architectural forms, . . . by referring to tree trunks as the origin of columns." Further on: "houses and their organization were so closely connected with the earth and nature itself that Basque architecture, particularly in Bizkaia and Gipuzkoa, when for public use, was surprisingly severe." Cenicacelaya and Saloña, "Neoclasicismo,

subliminal, subversive interpretation of it which undermined the original, absolutist intentions of the building of the Pavilion.[35]

Ortiz's theory, so convincing in its arguments and apparently obvious as an analogy, was immediately and enthusiastically taken up by Emilio Roig, who wrote in 1947: "This is, *without any doubt* [my italics], the exact meaning of the ceiba tree which the Templete preserves, and this is confirmed by Cagigal de la Vega's building the column in 1754 which is still there today: a census, pillory or stone roll." And Roig adds: "With Dr. Fernando Ortiz we are writing a book about this fascinating historical subject which is to be published immediately with this title: *La Ceiba, del pavilion, de la Villa de San Cristóbal de Havana.*"[36]

Roig's sentence, which anticipates an "immediate publication," suggests that the text had already been written, which seems a reasonable conjecture bearing in mind that they had both been working on the subject separately for various years. However, there is no book with any such title in either of the two researcher's bibliographies, although there is a considerable archive of Ortiz's held in the archive of the Friends of the Country's Economic Society, and with a large number of unpublished works, including a file titled "Ceiba and Templete." Could this be Ortiz's unpublished research work? Why was the book never published?[37]

Leaving these enigmas to one side and to be investigated at a later date, Ortiz's theory is still passed on and accepted, mostly by biographers of Bishop Espada, although they offer slight variations on it. Among the first is César García Pons, who mentions Ortiz's thesis in his biography of the prelate, although with some reservation, stating that:

> The bishop took an active part in the building of the Templete. Nothing happened in Havana without him taking part, and it was

---

dilemas y equilibrios," 17–19.

35. Ortiz supposed that Bishop Espada's liberal ideology was expressed in the Templete of Havana, which is a legitimate supposition bearing in mind Espada's considerable liberal agenda during his years on the island, and Ortiz also sees a conceptual similarity between the building and that which houses the Basque Fueros at Gernika. However, it should not be forgotten that the people behind the new Fueros building in the Basque Country were the leaders of the "royalist" party, who were later known as the Carlists and who fought against the liberals. As is well-known, during the 1812 and 1820–1823 constitutional periods, the Foralist Constitution was abolished, only to be restored under Fernando VII's absolutist rule. So the head of the provincial government, Pedro Novia de Salcedo, promoted the new building for foralist power in Bizkaia to have a physical symbol in a building which represented the power of the representative Basque assembly. The paradox was that it was royalist, antiliberal thinkers who had promoted the building of a parliamentary chamber to represent Bizkaia. My thanks to Joseba Aguirreazkuenaga for drawing my attention to this important point.

36. Roig de Leuchsenring, "La ceiba y el Templete."

37. We have examined this file of Fernando Ortiz's and it includes—along with Emilio Roig's *Havana Antigua: La Plaza de Armas* and Mario Lescano Abella's *El primer centenario del Templtete* (signed copy)—many bibliographical cards and typewritten contents, mostly about the subjects of sacred trees and tree worship in different cultures and periods of human history. There is also a smaller number of press cuttings and photographs of the Templete. All of which leads us to believe that this material had been gathered to be used in a future book that Ortiz never actually wrote.

too big a matter for him not to get involved and lend it his good taste. Espada promised a bust of Columbus and paintings of the first Mass. Some people go beyond that and say he was also involved with the architecture and where the building should be from a political point of view.[38]

García Pons is not completely convinced by Ortiz's explanation and he paraphrases the paper the latter read at the Friends of the Country's Economic Society, which is why he uses the expression "some people go beyond that" when talking about political motivation, but he also adds something new, which complements Ortiz's ideas to an extent: according to García Pons, "whatever Espada's intentions were, the project was his idea, he commissioned José de O'Campo to draw up the plans and paid him for his work. After the bishop's death, O'Campo said that the prelate had liked them."[39]

Who is this José de O'Campo, whom the bishop seems to have trusted so much, even trusting him with this project? He is not mentioned in the considerable bibliography about the Templete and García Pons does not tell us where he got this information either. The person who has always been thought to have been in charge of planning the monument is Havanan military engineer Antonio María de la Torre y Cárdenas, Vives's political secretary, and the original idea for the building has always been attributed to the latter and not to Espada. The great researcher into Cuban colonial architecture Joaquín Weiss writes:

> In 1827 general Francisco Dionisio Vives suggested building . . . a commemorative monument . . . The plan for the new building, the Templete, was the responsibility of colonel of engineers Antonio María de La Torre . . . The Templete was built over the short period of four months and, although ten thousand pesos were budgeted for it, the final cost was twice that.[40]

More recently, architect Roberto Segre and historian Eduardo Torres-Cuevas have taken up Ortiz's theory from the points of view of town planning and the history of ideas. Segre's opinion is to be found in a monographic study into the Plaza de Armas along the borders of which—he tells us—there are avatars of "the events of Cuban history: the ancient fort, civil and spontaneous architecture in eighteenth century housing, the 'roll' and the original ceiba tree, representing metropolitan political power. Unable to achieve an integrated design for the surroundings, other features were added, *expressing the contradictions between the ideologies in force*."[41]

Segre believes that "the tree expresses what is stable, unchangeable, everlasting, which is also the city's objective: to be permanent through-

---

38. García Pons, *El Obispo Espada y su influencia en la cultura cubana*, 129.
39. Ibid., 130.
40. Weiss, *La arquitectura colonial cubana*, 387.
41. Segre, *La Plaza de Armas de Havana*, 21.

out history, a human trace of definitive possession of space,"[42] while the Templete, initially placed opposite the statue of Fernando VII, emblem of tyranny, "symbolizes Cuban independence fighters' struggles."[43] To be true to history, we think that this conclusion, which tries to link the neo-classical Templete with the fight for independence at such an early date as 1828, is excessive: a statement that moves away from Ortiz's original thesis that does mention citizens' liberty in connection with the ceiba tree, and Espada's liberalism in connection with the Pavilion, but does not mention any attempt to separate from Spain.

I believe historian Torres-Cuevas' arguments to be more plausible: following Ortiz, he explains the Basque prelate's social and family origins and how they affected his later thinking:

> His family and regional surroundings seem to be decisive in order to understand some facets of the character of the man who was to become the Bishop of Havana . . . His social surroundings, the Basque Country . . . impregnated his thinking with a sincere love of regional freedom which was symbolized by the Gernika Tree, before which the kings of Spain had to swear to respect the Basque Fueros. Many years later, in 1828, in the middle of King Ferdinand's absolutist rule, the bishop built a reproduction of the Gernika Temple, known as the Pavilion, by the ceiba tree where the city had been founded *in order to express the iron opposition of his anti-absolutist ideas and as a sign of respect for the freedom of Havana.*"[44]

In another text, Torres-Cuevas states that Bishop Espada "made a gesture in those difficult years, *which seems to have been his way of leaving a political will for* future generations of Cubans" and then lays out the above ideas about the "symbolic seal" of enlightened thought to be seen in the Templete, and adds a subtle reflection: "It was work done under and against absolutism."[45]

So much for the historiographical controversy, which has been going on for more that a century, about this small building in Havana, and about which all the signs are that there is now consensus regarding Fernando Ortiz and his followers' thesis. In any case, a comparative examination of the Pavilion in Havana and the Assembly House shows enormous similarity in terms of style, the two buildings being almost identical; as stated above,

---

42. Ibid., 6.

43. Ibid.

44. Torres-Cuevas, *Félix Varela*, 65.

45. Torres-Cuevas, *Obispo de Espada*, 124. Finally, professor Torres Cuevas talks in an interview for the magazine *Opus Habana*, directed by doctor Eusebio Leal Spengler—disciple and continuer of the work which doctor Roig had started to rescue Old Havana in historical and cultural terms—about visiting Gernika and seeing there the validity of Ortiz's theories in that Espada had "deliberately put one by Ferdinand VII by dedicating a shrine in Havana to him which was like the one in the Basque Country symbolizing its autonomy from Spain" and gives his opinion that, deep down, referring to things with a double meaning is typically Cuban, something which Espada must have taken in very well during his three decades on the island. Calcines, "Eduardo Torres-Cuevas por el filo del cuchillo," 27.

the one in Havana dates from 1828 and the plans for it and the Basque building from 1827, built by architect Antonio Etxebarria.[46] In both cases, the severely bare neoclassical style creates unusually perfect buildings, and the tree is decisive as part of the architectural whole, but safeguarding freedom or the Fueros and being a symbol of permanence throughout time.

I would like these reflections to be a tribute to these two great masters of our culture, Fernando Ortiz Fernández and Emilio Roig de Leuchsenring, and their rich, Cuban intellectual friendship. I would also like them to be another sign of the mutual attraction and support between the Cuban and Basque peoples, who know that trees may fall due to the passage of time or men's negligence, but the liberty they symbolize will never be extinguished.

Bibliography

Agirreazkuenaga, Joseba, et al. *Historia de la Diputación Foral de Bizkaia: 1500–2014*. Bilbao: Diputación Foral de Bizkaia, 2014.

Alcover, Antonio Miguel. "La Misa, la ceiba y el templete, Cuba y América." *Colección Facticia, Havana City Museum Library*, no. 107 (1900).

Basurto, Nieves. "La arquitectura de las sedes de la Diputación de Bizkaia: De la Casa de Juntas de Gernika al Palacio de la Gran Vía de Bilbao." In *Historia de la Diputación Foral de Bizkaia, 1500–2014*, edited by Joseba Agirreazkuenaga, J. R. Urquijo, S. Serrano, and M. Urquijo, 481–512. Bilbao: Diputación Foral de Bizkaia, 2014.

Bisse, Johannes. *Árboles de Cuba*. Havana: Editorial Científico-Técnica, 1988.

Cabrera, Lydia. *El Monte*. Havana: Ediciones CR, 1954.

Cadilla de Martínez, María. *Costumbres y tradicionalismos de mi tierra*. Puerto Rico: Imprenta Venezuela, 1938.

Calcines, Argel. "Eduardo Torres-Cuevas por el filo del cuchillo." *Opus Habana* 6, no. 2 (2002).

---

46. Here I follow Doctor Nieves Basurto in her documented research into the architecture of Bizkaian provincial government buildings and, in particular, the new regional parliament home. The plan in neoclassical style for the new chamber for the regional parliament at Gernika was signed by architect Antonio Etxebarria on September 26, 1827. The platform for the monarchs to swear their loyalty—known as the Tribune or Patriarchs' Pavilion—had not been included in the original plan, in the place of honor beneath the oak tree for presiding over the opening of the regional parliament's sessions. In fact, Basurto points out: "As the oak tree could not be included in the way which Etxebarria had wanted at first, it was separate from the pavilion. Furthermore, the work on the foundations damaged the tree's roots irreparably and, in 1859, a shoot had to be planted in front of the Patriarch's Pavilion. The old tree, which was in very poor condition and threatened by the modifications to the building carried out in 1897, was initially surrounded by an iron and glass structure as if it were a relic. This covering was replaced in 1929 by the current, circular pavilion." Finally, on July 5, 1831, the regional parliament was able to hold its first session in the new installations, three years after Bishop Espada had inaugurated the Havana Templete. See Basurto, "La arquitectura de las sedes de la Diputación de Bizkaia," 481–512.

Cenicacelaya, Javier, and Iñigo Saloña. "Neoclasicismo, dilemas y equilibrios." In *Arquitectura neoclásica en el País Vasco*. Bilbao: Departamento de Cultura y Turismo del Gobierno Vasco, n.d.

Chateloin, Felicia. *Havana de Tacón*. Havana: Editorial Letras Cubanas, 1989.

Cobo, Bernabé. *Historia del Nuevo Mundo*. 4 volumes. Sevilla: Sociedad de Bibliofilos Andaluces, 1891 [1652].

García Pons, César. *El Obispo Espada y su influencia en la cultura cubana*. Havana: Publicaciones del Ministerio de la Educación, 1951.

Iglesias, Marial. *Las metáforas del cambio en la vida cotidiana*. Havana: Editorial Unión, 2003.

Guiteras, Pedro José. *Historia de la Isla de Cuba*. New York: J. R. Lockwood, 1865–1866.

Marrero, Levi. *Cuba: Economia y sociedad*. Volume 8. Havana: Madrid: Editorial Playor, 1980.

Ortiz, Fernando. "Bibliografía," *Archivos del Folklore Cubano*, July–September 1928.

———. "Conferencias." *Ultra: Cultura Contemporánea* 9, no. 76 (December 1942).

———. "La Hija Cubana del Iluminismo." *Revista Bimestre Cubana* 51, no. 1 (January/February 1943).

Palma y Romay, Ramón de. "El Templete." *El Álbum*, 1838.

Pezuela, Jacobo de la. *Historia de la Isla de Cuba*. Madrid: Imprenta de Bailly-Bailliere, 1868.

Pichardo, Esteban. *Diccionario provincial casi razonado de vozes y frases cubanas*. Havana: Editorial de Ciencias Sociales, 1976.

Pichardo, Hortensia. *Documentos para la Historia de Cuba*. Havana: Editorial Pueblo y Educación, 1984.

Pérez Beato, Manuel. *Habana antigua, apuntes históricos: Toponimia*. Habana: Seoane, Fernández y Cía, 1936.

Roig de Leuchsenring, Emilio. "La Ceiba y el Templete." *Gran Mundo*, June 1947.

———. *La Habana: Apuntes históricos*. Second edition. Volume 1. Havana: Editora del Consejo Nacional de Cultura, 1963.

Segreo Ricardo, Rigoberto. *De Compostela a Espada: Vicisitudes de la Iglesia Católica en Cuba*. Havana: Editorial de Ciencias Sociales, 2000.

Segre, Roberto. *La Plaza de Armas de Havana: Sinfonía urbana inconclusa*. Havana: Editorial Letras Cubanas, 1995.

Torres-Cuevas, Eduardo. *Félix Varela: Los orígenes de la ciencia y conciencia cubana*. Havana: Editorial de Ciencias Sociales, 1997.

———. *Obispo de Espada: Papeles*. Havana: Imagen Contemporánea, 1999.

Weiss, Joaquín E. *La Arquitectura Colonial Cubana: Siglos xvi al xix*.

Second edition. Havana: Instituto Cubano del Libro, 2002.

Zequeira y Arango, Manuel de. "Oda a la piña." In *Cantos a la naturaleza cubana del siglo XIX*, edited by Samuel Feijóo, 9–10. Santa Clara: Universidad Central de Las Villas, 1964.

3

Basques in the Caribbean Slave Trade (Eighteenth and Nineteenth Centuries)

Urko Apaolaza Ávila

The objective of the current paper is to consider Basque participation in the slave trade from the mid-eighteenth century until the end of the nineteenth century, in other words, the period in which there was mass trafficking to the Caribbean and, in particular, to Cuba. This article begins by examining the commercial companies in which there were Basque interests that tried to enter the slave trade directly, but had little success in doing so. It concludes by describing how some prominent Basque emigrants became involved in illegal trafficking and colonization projects in the nineteenth century, to the extent of becoming major players in the business.

The Basques wove a vast commercial network between ports on the Iberian Peninsula and the Spanish colonies, and many of them undoubtedly took part in the transatlantic slave trade from the very start. So, although the Portuguese were supreme in the business during the sixteenth century, there are examples of Basques who acquired Lisbon licenses to take part in the trafficking. The case of the Urrutias of Balmaseda is well-known and has been researched;[1] they obtained permission in 1523, by royal certificate, to transport forty-five black slaves to the pearl operations on the Caribbean island of Cubagua.

Until well into the seventeenth century, most slaves were introduced into the viceregal economies of Mexico and Peru, where they were used for a variety of jobs and activities as the agricultural model shifted to large plantations. It was from the eighteenth century onward that the greatest

---

1. Gómez Prieto, "Una familia vizcaína en los inicios de la trata de negros en el siglo xvi," 191–202.

demand for forced workers moved to areas which had previously been on the periphery, in particular the Caribbean.[2] Sugar plantation agriculture expanded in Cuba. The English, French, and Dutch Antilles were developed early on and were the great promoters of the sugar trade[3]—the seed of Cuban inventiveness in the nineteenth century—which created excellent conditions there for large-scale slave trafficking. According to some estimates, the British alone brought between 2.5 and 3 million slaves to the Caribbean as a whole.[4]

As part of the Treaty of Utrecht (1714) the English got their coveted royal permit for trafficking in slaves with the Spanish colonies. The South Sea Company held a monopoly until its contract was cancelled in 1743. It was from then on that the Basques entered the slave trade, first as part of the already constituted Basque royal commercial companies and later in a more explicit way.

The Role of Basque Royal Companies in Slave Trafficking

La Real Compañía de la Habana, founded in 1740 by Gipuzkoan shareholders, obtained privileges for supplying black slaves to the island of Cuba between 1741 and 1765. According to the Espinola y Subiza study, it was Martín de Ulibarri y Gamboa who signed the contract "to import 1,100 units [of slaves] with the obligation to pay 33 pesos for the right to do so, and this led to further contracts."[5] A report written by Martín de Arostegui, one of the company's prime movers, shows that between 1743 and 1747, 3,263 slaves were imported in Havana,[6] a relatively low figure compared with the enormous quantities of human merchandise that the English were moving. This company was never able to meet the needs of the emerging Cuban oligarchy which at that time was moving toward sugarcane production through the use of a cheap workforce. Another report from 1752 drawn up at the request of the Consejo de Indias (Indies Council)[7] deals with the citizens of Cuba's request for a "supply of black people" to the Spanish colonies in the Americas saying that "the Compañía de la Habana had not made them available." The alternative they suggest is to buy them from foreign traders, to which the Consejo was completely opposed because it would "open up huge possibilities for smugglers." This report mentions a proposal from Nicolás de Guilisiasti, a citizen of Donostia-San Sebastián, to bring slaves "straight from the coast of Guinea." The Consejo saw this as a difficult mission, but approved the request

---

2. Klein and Vinson, *African Slavery in Latin America and the Caribbean*, 48–49.
3. Mariñez, "Esclavitud y economía de plantación en el Caribe," 87.
4. Madrigal, *Human Biology of Afro-Caribbean Populations*, 7.
5. Espinola y Subiza, *Tratado elemental de instituciones de hacienda pública de España*, 527.
6. Informe de Martín de Arostegui, La Havana, 27 de febrero, 1751: Archivo General de Indias (AGI—Indies General Archive), 2209 in Tornero (1984: 125)
7. Informe surtir de negros las provincias de América, 1 de abril de 1752. Archivo General de Simancas (AGS), Secretariat of the War Office, 6799, 36.

and even allowed him to sail under a French flag.

La Real Compañía Guipuzcoana de Caracas also dealt in slaves, although with limited success. In 1756 it had to import 291 black people to the province of Caracas "as per its permit and contract."[8] A year earlier, however, when the company had wanted to move a batch of slaves from Martinique to Caracas, the French governor of the island forbade it because the ships were under Spanish flags.[9] In both La Guipuzcoana and the Real Compañía de la Habana the traders were closely interconnected and even took part in the same projects. This was so for the mentioned Arostegui, from Arantza, who got involved in La Guipuzcoana's maritime commercial projects very early on and was also a leading player in setting up the Compañía de la Habana.[10]

All attempts to start trafficking in human beings were fruitless. In spite of this, in the 1760s there were traders from Cádiz, of Basque origin, trying to obtain specific permits for slave trafficking, some of them even being closely connected with the companies mentioned. Bernardo Goycoa from Gares, for instance, reached Cuba in 1763 along with his brother Juan José, the official custodian of silver on the *San Fernando*, to take charge of the Compañía de la Habana's business;[11] shortly afterward, Juan José invested part of his fortune in shares of the recently founded Compañía Gaditana de Negros, one of the least known and researched commercial companies of the eighteenth century in Basque historiography. One of the few exceptions to this lack of knowledge about the Compañía de Negros—as it was usually known—is the work carried out more than forty years ago by Bibiano Torres.[12]

Nuestra Señora de Aranzazu alias "La Venganza"

La Compañía Gaditana de Negros operated between 1765 and 1779, experiencing considerable setbacks and problems. Its main warehouse was in Puerto Rico and, by licensed contract, was obliged to sail under Spanish flag and supply Cartagena and Portobelo with 1,500 slaves every year: 400 for Honduras and Campeche; 1,000 for Cuba; 600 for Cumaná, Santo Domingo, Trinidad, Margarita, Santa Marta; and 600 to Puerto Rico.[13] After various years of proposals and counterproposals—the first request had been made in 1760 and the second in 1763—its royal license was granted on July 14, 1765. Shortly afterward, at the King of Spain's insistence,

---

8. Data extracted from the compilation drawn up by the Company itself in 1765: Real Gipuzkoan Caracas Company, *Real Gipuzkoan Caracas Company*, 173.

9. López Rodríguez, "Trata de esclavos y País Vasco," 227.

10. Garate Ojanguren and Blanco Mozo, "Martín de Arostegui (1698–1756)."

11. Record of information and licence of passenger Martín José Alegría y Egües—manager and administrator of the *Real Compañía de la Habana*, in Havana, to the Indies with the following people: Bernardo Goycoa, manager and administrator of the company: AGI, Contratación, 5506, N.1, R. 7.

12. Torres Ramírez, La Compañía Gaditana de Negros.

13. Ibid., 38.

the first ship left Cádiz for the coast of Guinea in order to take on board at least six hundred black people. The ship was the frigate *La Venganza*, whose official name, *Nuestra Señora de Aranzazu*,[14] is an indication of the Company's close relationship with the powerful Basque-Cádiz community. So it could be said that the first company in the peninsula to work exclusively on large-scale slave trafficking was Basque.[15]

Miguel de Uriarte Herrera—or Errea, according to the source consulted—was in charge of requesting the permit. This citizen of Cádiz was son of Juan de Uriarte e Ibieta, a merchant born in Elorrio who moved to Quito and married María Josefa Herrera. Miguel was born and the family finally settled at Puerto de Santa María. Miguel de Uriarte had tried importing slaves in Venezuela previously, but La Guipuzcoana had taken over his license.[16] During the previous years he had worked mostly on exchanging products with Peru,[17] and he then became the main shareholder of Compañía Gaditana de Negros. In any case, Miguel de Uriarte was no more than a useful person for the real power at Cádiz: he had no real wealth and was not trusted at the Casa de Contratación. There are several documents recording his debts with various traders. Pablo Olabide, judge at the Court of Lima, stated in 1763 that Uriarte "is in a serious state, having signed insolvency papers."[18]

The real main players in the company at first were Lorenzo de Ariztegui and Francisco de Aguirre. The former, from Oñati in Gipuzkoa, was one of many brothers who started working in trade at a very young age. He reached Cádiz toward 1732 and, from 1737 onward, had an interesting career at the consulate there. In 1749 he went to Cartagena de Indias "to gain profit from and sell different goods."[19] By that time he was widower to María de Robín; he married off one of the daughters of the marriage, María Pascuala Ariztegui Robín, to Juan Bautista Uztariz,[20] a member of an influential Basque family in Cádiz with whom he had a close relationship. The second, Francisco de Agirre, was from the village of Uztarrotze in the mountains of Navarra, and he was married to Ana Ramírez Ortuño, sister of another shareholder in the company, José Ramírez Ortuño.[21]

---

14. Registry de la ida a Puerto Rico: AGI, Contratación, 1457. As recorded in the register, *Nuestra Señora de Aranzazu* sailed for Puerto Rico for the first time in 1766 and went annually until 1769; Roberto Jeffryes was captain and master.

15. In addition to the shareholders, there were workers, masters, and managers of Basque origin. One such was Vicente Zabaleta, agent in Puerto Rico, another the ship's master on the *San Rafael* Juan Antonio Zabaleta. Torres Ramírez, *La Compañía Gaditana de Negros*, 196.

16. Martínez Del Cerro González, *Una comunidad de comerciantes*, 160.

17. Pastor Rey de Viñas, Historia de la Real Fábrica de Cristales de San Ildefonso durante la época de la ilustración, 435.

18. Debts of Miguel de Uriarte, in Leganés, July 6, 1763: Archivo Histórico de Protocolos de Madrid, 32619, 101–104, in Domínguez Aparicio and Domínguez de Castro, *Leganés en el Archivo Histórico de Protocolos*, 170.

19. Lorenzo Ariztegui: AGI, Contratación, 5490, N. 2, R. 13

20. Report of tests for María Pascuala Ariztegui Robín Lizarralde y Marisol to marry Juan Bautista Uztariz: Archivo Histórico Nacional (AHN), OM, Casamiento/Santiago, file 10010.

21. Martínez del Cerro González, *Una comunidad de comerciantes*, 163.

La Compañía de Negros had difficulties from the start to enter trafficking because of its lack of knowledge of the trade, which meant that it had to make use of intermediaries. By 1770, it had already losses of 1 million pesos,[22] and in 1772 it was almost bankrupt. From that year onward there were changes in license conditions which improved its fortunes temporarily. It was now no longer a requirement to go through the Puerto Rico warehouse, which meant that Havana became more important, but the decline was unstoppable and the company was dismantled in 1779.

The assumed debts, however, had not been satisfied, and this gave creditors, and even the latter's heirs, numerous problems until well into the nineteenth century. In 1837 the Power brothers—soldiers in the Spanish army whose ancestors were Irish and who lived in the slave port of Bordeaux until they moved to Bizkaia[23]—claimed the debts which were still unpaid. Their father, Joaquín Power, had gone to Puerto Rico as an agent of the Compañía del Asiento de Negros. According to his descendants, he had had disagreements when the books had been closed and had taken legal action on several occasions: "Nothing was enough, he was unable to get anything because the company was broken up and there was nothing left of it for him to reach an agreement with."[24]

In spite of La Compañía Gaditana de Negros's terrible economic straits, it brought no fewer than ten thousand slaves into Cuba during the Company's first period and, in the last years, a total of eighteen thousand to various places in the Caribbean, mostly Havana, Cartagena, Puerto Rico, and Portobelo.[25] In fact, they even tried to use all the means at their disposal, and their royal privilege, to control the market, opposing other trafficking enterprises even when the main players were their Basque countrymen. In 1773 Julián Martínez de Murguía, from Manurga in Araba, who reached Cádiz at the young age of fifteen in answer to the call of his uncle, the powerful trader Andrés Martínez de Murguía,[26] tried to obtain a ten-year contract to bring black people straight from the Gold Coast. Juan José Goycoa—who, as mentioned, was a shareholder in the Compañía de Negros—protested against this request immediately. According to Goycoa, Martínez de Murguía was acting on behalf of foreigners.[27] Julián Antonio de Urcullu's project to acquire the rights to traffic with black people in Río de la Plata met the same fate.[28]

---

22. Torres Ramírez, *La Compañía Gaditana de Negros*, 71.

23. Chinea, "Irish Indentured Servants, Papists and Colonists in Spanish Colonial Puerto Rico," 176.

24. Joaquín Power was agent of the company from 1770 to 1778. Petition to re-examine the sentence on José Power and his three brothers in 1837 arguing that the company was debtor to his father. AHN, Ultramar, 2020, file 2

25. Torres, *La Compañía Gaditana de Negros*, 103, 174.

26. Garmendia Arruabarrena, "Los Martínez de Murguía, comerciantes con las Indias."

27. Torres Ramírez, *La Compañía Gaditana de Negros*, 104.

28. Ibid., 171.

The Slave Trader from Baiona, *L'Utile*

In 1760 the French colonies, led by Haiti, were the leading sugar producers, eighty thousand tons annually, while Cuba was only producing five
thousand.[29] To produce such figures required a considerable slave workforce. According to research, from the mid-seventeenth century until the
nineteenth century there were 4,220 slaving voyages from France—1,714
from Nantes, and 419 from the nearby port of Bordeaux.[30] However, other
ports under French rule also took advantage of the situation, although to
a lesser extent, and we will focus here on the Basque city of Baiona.

According to Jean Mettas, in his seminal work on the French slave
trade, such expeditions left Baiona between 1713 and 1792.[31] One example
is the ship *Le Junon*, property of Baiona resident Jaqeues Montz, who
launched a voyage in March 1741 to the coast of Guinea to traffic in black
people, landing at Martinique in March 1742 and returning to Baiona in
November of the same year.[32] As another example, in 1765 a ship called
L'Heureuse (The Happy Ship), captained by Pierre Dolhonde, took 249
black slaves to the port of Saint Marc in Haiti.[33]

The best-known case in connection with Baiona is probably the transatlantic slave voyage of the "forgotten slaves of Tromelin," which is being
archaeologically researched under UNESCO sponsorship.[34] We know that
the ship which started that fateful journey, *L'Utile,* was built at Baiona
between 1758 and 1759,[35] and that it was commissioned for the voyage by
Jean-Joseph d'Laborde, the agent of the Compagnie des Indes Oriental-
es in Baiona. After shipwrecking in the middle of the Indian Ocean, far
from Madagascar, its captain Jean Lafargue ordered the crew to build an
emergency craft and left the slaves they were carrying on that tiny island.
According to genealogist Bernard Harnie-Cousseau, who is working with
the team that is investigating the tragedy, many of the crew were Basque.[36]

Free Trading of Slaves in Spanish Colonies

After the royal decrees of February 28, 1789, free trading of slaves at the
ports of Havana and Santiago—in the latter, only for Spanish traders—
was legalized.[37] This measure had been called for by a Basque, Donostian
Luis Casas Aragorri, governor and captain general of Cuba from 1790 to

---

29. Moreno Fraginals, *El ingenio*, 29.
30. Data published in the *Memorial de la Abolición de la Esclavitud de Nantes* on its website
(www.memorial.nantes.fr/) and also provided by Saugera, *La traite de Noirs en 30 questions*.
31. Mettas, Répertoire des expéditions négrières françaises au XVIIIe siècle, 9.
32. Cauna and Graff, *La traite bayonnaise au XVIIIe siècle*, 95.
33. Chambre de commerceet d'industrie de Bayonne (CCI Bayonne), 064 , H38.
34. All the information about archaeological expeditions in recent years can be found at
www.archeonavale.org
35. Anso Blanco, "'Los esclavos olvidados' comienzan a desvelar algunos de sus secretos."
36. *Bayonne Magazine*, "De 'L'Utile' à 'La Providence.'"
37. Espinosa Fernández, "Una aproximación a la trata esclavista en Cuba durante el período
1789–1820," 182.

1796. During his term of office Casas promoted the importation of slaves for the island, extending the period of free trading and setting up companies for "the allocation of muzzled blacks."[38]

From that date until 1820—which is when the agreement with Great Britain to halt the slave trade was signed—around 225,000 slaves were brought into Cuba according to the official records of the Havana Customs.[39] Moreno Fraginals states that at the start of the nineteenth century, there were as many as twenty creole-Spanish firms grouped together in five large companies.[40] The Basques were well represented. Juan José Zangroniz, Martín de Zavala, Francisco de Bengoechea, and Salvador Martiartu all imported slaves into Cuba. The González-Larrinaga and Pérez de Urria families were also connected. But the most prominent Basque of all was the rich landowner Domingo Aldama Arechaga. The stories of this Bizkaian, and his son Miguel Aldama, are closely connected with slavery and its abolition on the island, as we will see below.

By that time the abolitionist movement was already afoot. France outlawed trafficking during the Revolution—and then restored it during the Napoleonic period; England abolished it in 1807. There was increasing pressure put on the other participants, and in 1815 an agreement was signed in Vienna for international abolition, which lead to the treaty which Spain and Great Britain signed in 1817.

The Hunter Hunted: *El Cazador Santurzano* and the *Feliz Vascongada*

But trafficking continued illegally with the Spanish Crown's knowledge—in spite of the Royal Navy, which wanted to control all the seas. The new treaty of 1835 did not manage to do away with the slave traders either, even by making it a criminal offence to transport devices or food which could be used in trafficking. Researchers agree that this illegality makes it difficult to calculate the number of slaves taken to Cuba in the mid years of the nineteenth century. One of the few sources are the British government's reports about the capture of slave ships published in *Parliamentary Papers,* from which the conclusion may be drawn that more than 350,000 black slaves entered Cuba between 1821 and 1860.[41] The Basque connection can also be found in these sources and it is also possible to see the extent to which we Basques were involved in the slave trade.[42]

---

38. Anakabe Ansutegi, "Kubako euskal jatorriko hiztegi biografikoa," 553.

39. Espinosa Fernández, "Una aproximación a la trata esclavista en Cuba durante el período 1789–1820," 185.

40. Moreno Fraginals, *El ingenio,* 219.

41. Ibid., 225.

42. Herbert S. Klein and Philip D. Curtin drew up a list of the ships which were tried for illegal slave trafficking between 1817 and 1843. There are up to thirty Basque surnames among the captains of these ships: Aresti, Aurteneche, Igartua, Oleaga, Zurbano, Inza, Tellaeche, and so on. Curtin and Klein, *Records of Slave Ship Movement between Africa and the Americas.*

In 1834 José Antonio Ybarra, from the famous banking family, partnered with a trader from Cádiz and sent the brigantine *Cazador Santurzano* on an illegal slave expedition to Sierra Leone. He obtained considerable profits from taking 681 "items" to Cuba and did so again in 1836.[43] But this time the ship was captured after being pursued by the British brigantine *Water Witch*. The slave ship was captained by Ángel Elorriaga and heading toward the Kingdom of Whydah (Xwéda), in the Benin area. The Spanish and British had agreed to constitute mixed courts to deal with such cases. So, in one of the reports issued by the British government, there is a list of the Spanish ships captured between 1835 and 1836 which were tried by the Sierra Leone court.[44] Among 37 cases, more than a quarter—including the above-mentioned *Cazador Santurzano* belonging to the Ybarra family—were captained by sailors with Basque surnames. Examples included:

- On November 27, 1835, the brigantine *Buzzard* captured the Spanish schooner *Norma*, commanded by Tomás Etxeberria. The ship had left Havana for the island of São Tomé on a legitimate commercial voyage, but "instead of going to that island, it went straight to the River Bonny" and loaded 234 slaves. Of whom 218 survived and were freed when the schooner was intercepted.

- The schooner *Tres Tomasas*, under the command of Nicholas Echeandía, was stopped by the Royal Navy one hundred miles from Sierra Leone on December 19, 1835 with illegal equipment which was going to be used for transporting slaves. Echeandía complained about the case brought against him, but his complaint was not admitted because the evidence presented by his captors was considered valid. The ship was confiscated.

- José María Arrarte was in command of the schooner *Matilde* when it was stopped by a Royal Navy ship on February 5, 1836. He was heading for São Tomé with the necessary equipment for transporting slaves, in violation of the 1835 treaty.

- The brigantine *El Explorador* was also captured because of the article about equipment in the Anglo-Spanish treaty. The ship was under the command of its first officer when it was stopped by the British schooner *Fair Rosamond*, and he stated that the captain, Ignacio de Aldegoa [sic], was on shore and that he did not know where the ship had come from or where it was going.

- On February 9 the British ship *Forester* was off the coast of Loango with the brigantine *Golondrina*, a slave ship captained by Juan Domingo de Zavala.

- On January 28, 1836 the sloop *Trinculo* captured a schooner called *Feliz Vascongada*, which was under the command of

43. Díaz Morlan, "Los Ybarra contra el 'sindrome de Buddenbrooks,'" 284.
44. *British Foreign State Papers*, "Abstract of the Proceedings in British and Spanish Court of Mixed Commission," 56–71.

Thomas de Olaguibel. According to the captors, the ship's official route was from Havana to São Tomé, but the master had headed for Africa, "to the well-known slave depot in the River Bonny."

- *María Manuela,* a brigantine sailing along the coast of the River Bonny, was stopped on January 28, 1836. It was under the command of captain Tomás de Ugarte.

- In June 1835 the schooner *Joven María,* "one of the numerous slave ships from the port of Havana," left Príncipe under the command of José Garay. Eight months later, on March 13, 1836, it was captured near the African kingdom of Whydah by the same ship which had caught the *Cazador Santurzano,* the impeccable brigantine *Water Witch*, armed with ten cannons.

- A day later, the same British ship captured another schooner at the port known as Little Popo (currently Anehó, Togo). This time it was the *Galana Josefa,* captained by Francisco Antonio Sarrico. According to the ship's reports, there were "clear indication of the intention to take part in the slave trade, as on other ships from Havana in recent times."

This short examination gives an idea of Basque participation in illegal trafficking at the time. This list may be highly relevant bearing in mind that it was in the years immediately after the 1835 treaty when the greater number of ships were captured.[45] With regards to the Sierra Leone mixed court, the year we have taken for our sample (1836) is the second highest peak in terms of ships adjudicated.[46]

Basques at the "Peak" of Cuban Slave Trading

The peak of transatlantic slave trafficking to Cuba was in the 1850s, in 1859 precisely, when no fewer than 30,473 black slaves and 8,549 Chinese slaves were brought to the island.[47] Hugh Thomas states that there must have been around a hundred thousand slaves imported in Cuba between 1858 and 1862, most of them brought there by Julián Zulueta.[48]

The well-known slave trader Julián Zulueta y Amondo, born in the small Araba village of Anuntzeta, was a particular prototype of the Peninsula traders who appeared once the Cuban oligarchy began to diversify after 1820. These traders bought land and sugar mills, breaking the duality which had been in force until then of Creole producers and Spanish traders. So they made up a powerful new elite which, together with the traditional large sugar magnates, gained economic and political power

---

45. Hugh Thomas, in his excellent work on the subject, states that the Royal Navy was more efficient after the treaty. While between 1830 and 1835 British ships captured ten slave ships per year, between 1835 and 1839 this figure rose to thirty-five. Thomas, *The Slave Trade,* 655).
46. Arnalte Barrera, Luis Arturo. "El tribunal mixto anglo-español de Sierra Leona."
47. Moreno Fraginals, *El ingenio,* 238.
48. Thomas, *The Slave Trade,* 642.

and controlled everything to do with the island, also influencing Spanish colonial policies extraordinarily with their ultraconservative ideas, among other things because of their enormous dependence on the slave trade.[49] Many of these families, which interacted at the Casino Español, were of Basque origin, such as Manuel Calvo y Aguirre from Portugalete, an important trader, banker and landowner who was also involved in the slave trade.[50] But perhaps the best-known and most influential member of the club was Julián Zulueta.

It is difficult to determine the number of slaves Zulueta imported, a la Thomas, but there has been recent research into this important figure.[51] He was closely connected with the London firm Zulueta and Co., had connections with the Malaga trader Pedro Blanco and also had his own fleet of slave ships as shareholder in the company Expedición por África. Zulueta set up companies, built railways, mechanized sugar mills, was the first person to vaccinate slaves and even had a business in which he rented them out. He is a representative of a system of slavery at the service of capital, a type of modernity which, however, was always essentially limited: it depended on a slave workforce and, consequently, on illegal trafficking.

This was the contradiction permanently hanging over the Antillan elite—as it was in opposition to the leading economic doctrines of the day. There was also a fear that a racial imbalance would lead to an insurrection. The Cuban slave owners were very much aware of the Haitian catastrophe of 1791.[52] This fear can be seen, for instance, in the reaction of the colonial governors after a slave mutiny on Domingo Aldama's property in 1841.

Domingo Aldama Arechaga was an outlaw from Gordexola, Bizkaia, who had arrived in Cuba at the beginning of the nineteenth century. The owner of sugar mills and slaves, he became involved in numerous businesses with his father-in-law, including the railways.[53] In 1836 he was the fourteenth richest man in the colony, according to the Development Board.[54]

---

49. Rodrigo y Alhajilla, "¿Hacendados versus comerciantes?" 653–57.

50. Ramos Martínez, "Manuel Calvo y Aguirre."

51. For historiography about Julián de Zulueta, see Apaolaza Avila, "Un análisis sobre la historiografía en torno al alavés Julián de Zulueta y Amondo." For information about his relationship with Zulueta and Co. in London, and capital transfers, see Bahamonde Magro and Cayuela Fernández, *Hacer las Américas*; and Cayuela Fernández, "Transferencia de capitales antillanos a Europa." For information about Zulueta's political influence: Agirreazkuenaga Zigorraga, "Los vascos y la insurrección de Cuba en 1868." The only biography written can also be consulted—Marrero, *Julián de Zulueta y Amondo*—and there is the film documentary *Zulueta* directed by Angel Katarain as part of the project *Semillas en el tiempo (Seeds in Time)* (www.semillaseneltiempo.com).

52. Gonzalez-Ripoll, Dolores, Naranjo Orovio, Ferrer, García Rodríguez, and Opatrny, *El rumor de Haití en Cuba*.

53. Aldama took part in the building of the Habana-Güines railway, the first one in Cuba, in 1830. The Alfonso-Aldama clan became the main shareholder and creditor of the railways. According to Zanetti, they were owed 1,700,000 pesos. Zanetti Lekuona and García Álvarez, *Caminos para el azúcar*, 44, 107).

54. Anakabe, "Kubako euskal jatorriko hiztegi biografikoa," 507.

This fortune allowed him to build a great mansion outside the walls of Havana in which slaves of his worked.

On October 9, 1841, while working on the luxurious building, there was a slave rising which led to the deaths of six blacks and the wounding of ten others. The event sounded the alarm bells and the secretary of state sent the island's governor, Captain General Gerónimo Valdés, to find out what had happened and "double up control over colored people who might not be trusted." The result was a series of investigations that produced is considerable documentation. According to the report kept in the National Historical Archive,[55] Domingo Aldama rented out twenty-five to thirty black people of the Lucumi ethnic group so that they could work on the Guanabacoa railway,[56] which they refused to do. According to the overseer, "they only wanted to go and earn a daily wage,"—to which Aldama answered that "they should not insist because slaves have to do what their master orders." The record also includes the declarations of several of the slaves that had rebelled, who had argued that they had been sure they were not going to be taken to the railway but "to the countryside" because some shackles had been brought to the factory. Be that as it may, Aldama ordered a squad of soldiers to open fire and use bayonets on his slaves with the abovementioned results. The interrogators insistence on finding out whether the slaves' attitude had been due to external agitators is of particular interest. The captain general concluded that there was no doubt that it "had been an isolated incident" and that "fortunately it is a small number of black people and they can be put down at the start."

Figure 3.1. Current view of the Aldama mansion in Havana. Source: Urko Apaolaza.

55. AHN, Ultramar, 8, file. 10

56. Renting slaves was one of the main systems used for building the railways due to their experience at building paths and roads. Zanetti Lecuona and García Álvarez, *Caminos para el azúcar*, 124.

Colonization Project: Coolie Slaves on the *Oquendo* and the *Bella Vascongada*

The reaction to the small uprising at the Aldama mansion reflects the growing tension the authorities were under with regards to the part of the African slave population which "gives frequent signs of bloody sedition in its acts of uprising."[57] This, together with the growing abolitionist trend and, above all, the serious workforce shortage, explains why there were so many efforts during the nineteenth century to find alternatives—such as colonization and immigration schemes in which the Basques also took an active part.

In fact, an example of this can be seen with Miguel Aldama himself, Domingo's son and an openly declared abolitionist, who worked to introduce a contingent of Basques—or, as he put it, "my Bizkaians"—in 1844.[58] Another trader of Basque origin, Domingo de Goicuria, a soldier who later became a separatist and was executed for that reason,[59] promoted immigration projects from other communities such as the Canary Islands, Galicia, and Cantabria; many of the people were transported in wretched conditions and ended up working as semi-slaves.[60] Goicuria even started up another company—Zangróniz y Hermanos—which imported Yucatecans from Mexico. By the first quarter of 1855, 416 natives of Yucatan had already been transported.[61] There was a complaint about this traffic from the British ambassador in Mexico, Mr. Doyle: these trading companies from Havana had asked the Mexican government to supply a force of two hundred soldiers to "make war on the Indians, keeping for their own use all the Indians taken prisoner, also paying the Mexican government 15 pesos for each one of them."[62]

Bizkaians, Canarians, Yucatecans, Irish, Turks, Abyssinians, and more were recruited. There were numerous attempts to colonize, but they were all in vain. However, there was one which worked: trafficking with coolie slaves. Once more it was a Basque, this time Julián Zulueta, who was the prime mover behind this Asian colonization. He arrived in Havana on June 3, 1847 on board the frigate *Oquendo* with a cargo of 206 Chinese people brought from the port of Amoy; a few days later a cargo of a

---

57. Ibid.

58. They only managed to import ten Bizkaians out of a total of eighty-five, after which they desisted because of the high recruitment cost. Letter from Miguel de Aldama to Domingo Delmonte from Havana (February 9, 1844), in Irigoyen Artetxe, *La Asociación Vasco-Navarra de Beneficencia y otras entidades Vasco-Cubanas*, 38.

59. Arrozarena, *El roble y la ceiba*, 186.

60. There are also signs of trafficking with minors from the Peninsula. In 1846, when he was given a permit to transport colonists, Goicuria embarked 317 colonists at Santander and other places and "during the voyage, 46 underage children unfortunately died of measles." The ship was put in quarantine and the Havanan Basque trader protested about medical treatment of the other colonists "being charged to the contractor." *Contrato para trasladar colonos de la península a Cuba*: AHN, Ultramar, 19, file 23.

61. Moreno Fraginals, *El ingenio*, 260.

62. Quejas por un contrato para llevar a Cuba presos yucatecos AHN, Ultramar, 93, file 45.

further 365 slaves arrived. The ships had been contracted by Zulueta from Matía, Menchacatorre and Co., which belonged to a countryman of his, the Araban José Matía Calvo. The latter, who was from Laudio, had a fleet of ships which plied the Cádiz-Manila route and he had become involved in transporting Chinese people from Macau to Cuba and Peru from the start. In 1851 it was his intention to take no fewer than twenty thousand colonists to the Americas, reaching an agreement with the Scottish firm Tait & Co. to do so.[63] At that time the Panamá Railroad Company was building the railway that was to cross the Isthmus of Panama and revolutionize transport between the two oceans. To do so, thousands of Irish and then Chinese workers were needed. Matía Calvo also supplied Chinese laborers to this company and sent a thousand coolies on the famous frigate *Bella Vascongada* in 1854.[64] This ship is connected with the Barojas, being piloted by the famous sailor Justo Goñi, a maternal relative from Donostia of the writer's family, and the man who inspired Pío Baroja to write *Las inquietudes de Shanti Andia* and *Pilotos de Altura*, two of his best-known books about the sea.

Figure 3.2. Chinese "coolies" embarking at Macao. Source: Caminos para el azúcar.

In a report written in 1874 for the Cuban Landowners' Association, Julián de Zulueta gave a brief description of the effect of the importation of the Chinese labourers from 1847 until that year.[65] According to the Araban's calculations, around 58,000 Chinese had been imported in Cuba during those years, of whom only 32 were women—Moreno Frag-

63. Ibarzabal Aramberri, "La ruta Cádiz-Manila de José Matia Calvo," 89.

64. Apaolaza Avila, "Bella Vascongada."

65. "Expediente general de colonización asiática" (General Report about Asian Colonisation), AHN, Ultramar, 87, files 6, 20.

inals talks about around 160,000 over the whole of the nineteenth centu-ry.[66] The Asian colonization must have been met with enthusiasm by the abolitionists because it was a step toward a free labor market. But, in fact, according to the statistics in the report, only half of the Chinese people imported were still on the island in 1872. Zulueta admits that many of them were fugitives and that the rate of arrests was larger than that among white and black people. The transport and working conditions, which practically amounted to slavery, cannot have been very attractive for those people. In Zulueta's view, however, the norms for the colonists were cor-rect: the problem was that those imported came from an area, Kwantung, in which there was a lot of "the vice of masonry, which allows the Chinese to become lazy." He died with this same blinkered view four years later, taking with him the title of having been the last great slave trader.

Brief Conclusions

While we lack definitive data—this being only an approximation—we can suggest some hypotheses about the Basques' participation in transatlantic slave trading.

Trafficking had stopped being a sporadic activity by the second half of the eighteenth century and had become a promising line of business. Participation in it was to increase. In the nineteenth century Basque trans-porters became very important in the worldwide slave trade due to some of them having joined the Cuban elite; Julián de Zulueta was exemplary.

It could also be said that the first Basque attempts to structure the trade and bring slaves straight from the coast of Africa were not fruit-ful and did not produce the desired results, above all due to their lack of knowledge of the trade. So they had no choice but to use intermediaries. But from the liberalization of trading in Cuba in 1789, and during the nineteenth century, Basque transporters began to be successful in the slave trade and, furthermore, they were pioneers in starting to use new, more sophisticated ways of obtaining cheap workforces, for instance by setting up colonization schemes of communities other than blacks.

Bibliography

Agirreazkuenaga Zigorraga, Joseba. "Los vascos y la insurrección de Cuba en 1868." *Historia Contemporánea* 2 (1989): 139–64.

Anakabe Ansutegi, Carmelo. "Kubako euskal jatorriko hiztegi bi-ografikoa." *Vasconia* 38 (2012): 495–643.

Anso Blanco, Martín. "'Los esclavos olvidados' comienzan a desvelar al-gunos de sus secretos." *Gara,* February 12, 2007.

Apaolaza Avila, Urko. "Un análisis sobre la historiografía en torno al ala-vés Julián de Zulueta y Amondo." *Sancho el Sabio* 18 (2003): 121–40.

---

66. Moreno Fraginals, *El ingenio,* 261.

———. "Bella Vascongada: Txinatar esklaboen heriotzarako bidea." *Argia* 2024 (2006).

Arnalte Barrera, Luis Arturo. "El tribunal mixto anglo-español de Sierra Leona (1819–1874)." Ph.D. disseration, Universidad Complutense de Madrid, 1992.

Arrozarena, Cecilia. *El roble y la ceiba*. Tafalla: Txalaparta, 2003.

Bahamonde Magro, Ángel and José Gregorio Cayuela Fernández. *Hacer las Américas: La élites coloniales españolas en el siglo xix*. Madrid: Alianza Editorial, 1992.

Bayonne Magazine. "De 'L'Utile' à 'La Providence.'" 134 (December 2004–January 2005): 26–27.

British Foreign State Papers. "Abstract of the Proceedings in British and Spanish Court of Mixed Commission, and in the British and Spanish Mixed Court of Justice, in the Period from the 1st January, 1836, to the 1st January, 1837." Pages 56–71. London: James Ridgway and Sons, 1853.

Cauna, Jacques and Marion Graff. *La traite bayonnaise au XVIIIe siècle: Instructions, journal de bord, projets d'armement*. Pau: Éditions Cairn, 2009.

Cayuela Fernández, José Gregorio. "Transferencia de capitales antillanos a Europa: Los patrimonios de Pedro Juan de Zulueta y Ceballos y de Pedro José de Zulueta y Madariaga (1823–1877)." *Estudios de Historia Social* 44-47 (1988): 191–212.

Chinea, Jorge L. "Irish Indentured Servants, Papists and Colonists in Spanish Colonial Puerto Rico, ca. 1650–1800." *Irish Migration Studies in Latin America* 5, no. 3 (2007): 171–82.

Curtin, Philip D. and Herbert S. Klein. *Records of Slave Ship Movement between Africa and the Americas, 1817–1843*. New York: Columbia University, 1973.

Díaz Morlan, Pablo. "Los Ybarra contra el 'sindrome de Buddenbrooks': El éxito de seis generaciones de empresarios." In *Fortuna y negocios: Formación y gestión de los grandes patrimonios (siglos xvi–xx)*, coordinated by Ricardo Robledo Hernández and Hilario Casado Alonso, 275–300. Valladolid: University of Valladolid, 2001.

Domínguez Aparicio, Jesús and Santos Domínguez de Castro. *Leganés en el Archivo Histórico de Protocolos*. Madrid: Visión Libros, 2007.

Espinola y Subiza, Ramón. Tratado elemental de instituciones de hacienda pública de España, Madrid: NP, 1859.

Espinosa Fernández, José Manuel. "Una aproximación a la trata esclavista en Cuba durante el período 1789-1820." *Segundo Simposio de la Asociación Española de Americanistas: Medina del Campo, 1999*, 181–92. No place: Asociación Española de Americanistas, 2001.

Garate Ojanguren, Montserrat and Juan Luis Blanco Mozo. "Martín de Arostegui (1698–1756), fundador de la Real Compañía de la Habana," *Revista Hispano Cubana* 2 (1998): 73–79.

Garmendia Arruabarrena, José. "Los Martínez de Murguía, comerciantes con las Indias," *Boletín de la Real Sociedad Bascongada de Amigos del País* 44, no. 3–4 (1998): 425–51.

Gómez Prieto, Julia. "Una familia vizcaína en los inicios de la trata de negros en el siglo xvi: Los hermanos Urrutia." In *Comerciantes, mineros y nautas: Los vascos en la Economía americana*, edited by Ronald Escobedo Mansilla, Ana de Zaballa Beascoechea, Oscar Álvarez Gila, 191–202. Vitoria-Gasteiz: University of the Basque Country, 1996.

Gonzalez-Ripoll Navarro, María Dolores, Consuelo Naranjo Orovio, Ada Ferrer, Gloria García Rodríguez, and Josefa Opatrny. *El rumor de Haití en Cuba: Temor, raza y rebeldía (1789–1844)*. Madrid: Consejo Superior de Investigaciones Científicas, 2004.

Ibarzabal Aramberri, Xabier. "La ruta Cádiz-Manila de José Matia Calvo." *Boletín de la Real Sociedad Vascongada de Amigos del País* 1, no. 58 (1998): 87–95.

Irigoyen Artetxe, Alberto. La Asociación Vasco-Navarra de Beneficencia y otras entidades Vasco-Cubanas. Vitoria-Gasteiz: Eusko Jaurlaritza, 2014.

Klein, Herbert S. and Ben Vinson III. *African Slavery in Latin America and the Caribbean*. Oxford: Oxford University Press, 2007.

López Rodríguez, Josune. "Trata de esclavos y País Vasco: ¿Participó la sociedad vasca en el comercio trasatlántico de esclavos?" *Boletín JADO* 24 (2013): 217–33.

Madrigal, Lorena. *Human Biology of Afro-Caribbean Populations*. Cambridge: Cambridge University Press, 2006.

Mariñez, Pablo A. "Esclavitud y economía de plantación en el Caribe." *Sotavento* 1, no. 2 (1997): 83–102.

Martínez Del Cerro González, Victoria Eugenia. Una comunidad de comerciantes: Navarros y Vascos en Cádiz (segunda mitad del siglo xviii). No place: Junta de Andalucía, 2006.

Mettas, Jean. *Répertoire des expéditions négrières françaises au XVIIIe siècle*. Paris: Societé Française d'Histoire d'Outre-Mer, 1984.

Marrero Cruz, Eduardo. *Julián de Zulueta y Amondo: Promotor del capitalismo en Cuba*. Havana: Ediciones Unión, 2006.

Moreno Fraginals, Manuel. *El ingenio*. Barcelona: Crítica, 2001.

Pastor Rey de Viñas, Paloma. Historia de la Real Fábrica de Cristales de San Ildefonso durante la época de la ilustración. Segovia: Fundación Centro Nacional del Vidrio, 1994.

Rodrigo y Alharilla, Martín. "¿Hacendados versus comerciantes? Negocios y práctica política en el integrismo cubano."In *Octavo Congreso Internacional de Historia de América (AEA)*, coordinated by Francisco Morales Padrón, 647–63. Las Palmas of Gran Canaria, Cabildo de Gran Canaria, 1998.

Ramos Martínez, Jon Ander. "Manuel Calvo y Aguirre: Se Portugalate a Havana, pasando por Madrid (1817–1904)." *Euskosare*, January 4, 2009.

Real Gipuzkoan Caracas Company. *Real Gipuzkoan Caracas Company: noticias historiales prácticas* . . . Madrid: NP, 1765.

Saugera, Eric. *La traite de Noirs en 30 questions*. La Crèche: Geste Éditions, 1998.

Thomas, Hugh. The Slave Trade: The Story of the Atlantic Slave Trade, 1440–1870. New York: Simon and Shuster, 1999.

Tornero Tinarejo, Pablo. *Andalucía y América en el siglo xviii*. Sevilla: Consejo Superior de Investigaciones Científicas, 1984.

Torres Ramírez, Bibiano. *La Compañía Gaditana de Negros*. Sevilla: Escuela de Estudios Hispano-Americanos de Sevilla, 1973.

Zanetti Lecuona, Oscar and Alejandro García Álvarez. *Caminos para el azúcar*. Havana: Editorial de Ciencias Sociales, 1987.

4

The Leadership of Manuel Calvo y Aguirre in the Spanish Party and among Basques and Navarrese in Cuba

Juan Bosco Amores Carredano and Jon Ander Ramos Martínez

Manuel Calvo y Aguirre, born in Portugalete, Bizkaia, in December 1816, was one more Peninsular Spaniard—most of them were from the Bay of Biscay and Catalonia—who emigrated to Cuba to seek his fortune during the first decades of the nineteenth century.[1] They were driven by the extraordinary economic growth of the Antilles in sharp contrast with the poverty on the Peninsula, which was a consequence of the turbulent reign of Ferdinand VII and the later Carlist War.[2] From among these emigrants, most of whom were of very modest origin, businessmen emerged and they, during the 1830s, were to control much of the island's economy and trade—including the slave trade, which was the starting point of many of their fortunes—and a large part of the Cuban sugar industry.

At the end of the 1830s the Spanish government's Cuba policy underwent profound changes, peninsular liberalism putting an end to the long-lasting arrangement between the metropolis and the Cuban elites which had been advantageous to both. Over the following decades, in the mid-century period, Spanish metropolitan governments tried to regain control of relations with the island and restore its colonial exploitation

---

* This paper is part of the work carried out by the Basque University System Research Group, "Basque Country and the Americas: Links and Atlantic Relationships" (GIC 10/48), and that of the University of the Basque Country Training and Research Unit: Europe and the Atlantic World" (UFI 11/02).

1. Pérez Murillo, *Aspectos demográficos y sociales de la isla de Cuba en la primera mitad del siglo xix*, 121–22.

2. Santamaría García, "Reformas coloniales, economía y especialización productiva en Puerto Rico y Cuba."

of Cuba by reinforcing the political and administrative power that almost completely excluded Cubans. It would privilege the interests of the island's Spanish businessmen in order to keep Cuba as a captive market for the Peninsular economy.[3]

This change, which was to have considerable influence on the relationship between the metropolis and the great Antillean colony, coincided with the natural demise of Arango y Parreño (1765–1837), the main architect of that successful colonial pact. He was succeeded by a new generation, educated in ideas of romantic liberalism and strongly attracted by the political, social, and economic model of the United States. It began to seriously question Spanish domination of the island.

So in the 1840s, there were two factions: the creoles, who favored first annexation of Cuba by the United States and, later, autonomy; and the irredentist, ultraconservative Spaniards, ready to do anything in order to keep Cuba within Spain's sphere of influence (although there were also some creoles who sympathized with the latter and Spaniards who were in favor of greater autonomy). The Creole faction was represented by the Club de La Habana, whose most influential members were the great landowners Miguel Aldama, José Luis Alfonso, Cristóbal Madan, the Iznagas, and the Count of Pozos Dulces, and who were openly in favor of the island being annexed by the growing power to the north, an agenda opposed by their political and intellectual leader, José Antonio Saco.[4]

This attitude inevitably led to a hardening of the centralist, authoritarian policies of the colonial authorities, best represented by General Gutiérrez de la Concha during his second term of office on the island (1854–1859). This period also saw the consolidation of their control of the economy by the Spanish Antillean business elite who were also, or at different times, slave traders, merchants and financiers, and owners of large sugar mills and shipping and transport companies. Outstanding among them were Julián de Zulueta y Amondo,[5] Suárez Argudín, Salvador Samá, the Count of Casa Lombillo, José Baró, José Eugenio Moré, and the future Marquis of Comillas, Antonio López.[6] The economic power of this Spanish Cuban group, which had direct contacts with Spain, such as those of Juan Manuel de Manzanedo—who had earned his fortune as a slave trader in Cuba—and Antonio López with his Catalonian links, was behind the political rise of the Unión Liberal. It was the party of the "overseas" generals—thus known because of their close connection with Cuban interests, as well as many of them having been captain generals of the island. The Unión Liberal dominated Cuban national politics between

---

3. On the development of the political system, see Alonso Romero, *Cuba en la España liberal*. On colonial relationship and the predominance of Spanish Cuban business elites, see Bahamonde and Cayuela Fernández, *Bahía de ultramar*.

4. Opatrný, *José Antonio Saco y la búsqueda de la identidad cubana*.

5. Marrero Cruz. *Julián de Zulueta y Amondo*.

6. Rodrigo Alharilla, *Los marqueses de Comillas*.

1856 and 1863.[7] This Antillean Spanish group was a real Spanish Party on the island. Led by Julián de Zulueta, the founder of Cuba's Spanish Voluntary Corps and the Casino Español in Havana, the Party's political club that soon spread its influence to Cuba's most important cities and towns.[8] The leaders of this Spanish party were an effective lobby that, in close collaboration with the authorities on the island, used colonial politics in their own interests and in favor of maintaining the status quo. Manuel Calvo y Aguirre was to become an active member of this lobby.

Calvo's Career as a Spanish Immigrant Who Made Good on the Island

Thanks to Cuban historian Carmen Barcia and the documentation in the Cuban National Archive, we know quite a lot about Manuel Calvo's career as a Spaniard who made good in Cuba. He arrived in 1833, at the age of just seventeen, to work as a shop assistant at his uncle Juan Calvo's ironmongers, one of the types of businesses that Basques used to run on the island.[9] He must have had good personal qualities because very soon, by the end of the 1830s, Manuel was already associated with Antonio López in trade in Santiago de Cuba, where López had began to make his own fortune. At the start of the following decade, Manuel was already working for himself with a coastal fishing trade and as a moneylender.[10] In 1841 he requested a license for a steamship he owned, the *Cubano*, to sail on the San Diego and Coloma Rivers in the Pinar del Río region.[11] There is no doubt that he was a rich man by the end of the decade when he requested a license to rebuild his house on the corner of Calzada del Monte and Ángeles Street, one of the prime residential districts in Havana.[12]

According to Barcia, in 1848 Calvo founded a Compañía de Navegación Trasatlántica (Transatlantic shipping company) with Antonio

---

7. Cayuela Fernández, *Bahía de Ultramar*.

8. Marrero Cruz. *Julián de Zulueta y Amondo*, 128–29, 141.

9. Barcia, *Élites y grupos de presión*, 15–24. Juan Calvo writes from Cuba to his brother Matías asking for Manuel: "My dear brother Matías. To confirm my previous letters, which I'm sure you received, I would now like to tell you that I have decided that your son and my nephew Manuel Aparicio should move here as soon as possible as I have a position for him and if, as I hope, he is hardworking and well-behaved, he will soon make his fortune, which will be a great comfort to you later on. Don't delay in sending him: I promise to make him a man of worth. No more than that: please send my regards to Maripepa and know that your brother thinks of you": Archivo Histórico Nacional (AHN), Ultramar, 364, N. 46, July 3, 1833.

10. Among others: Archivo Nacional de Cuba (ANC), Escribanía de Salinas, 1844: autos seguidos por D. Manuel Calvo contra D. Benito Henríquez en cobro de pesos en tercería por el curador de Da. Josefa Jústiz de Fuente; ANC, Tribunal de Comercio, 1847: Manuel Calvo, contra la sociedad anónima Caridad de la Victoria, en cobro de pesos de suministros hechos en el ramo de la ferretería; ANC, Gobierno Superior Civil, 1848: expediente manifestando D. Manuel Calvo que D. Fernando Ignacio Maresi le adeuda 70 000 pesos.

11. ANC, Escribanía de Ortega, 1841.

12. ANC, Licencias de fábrica, 1849: file provided by Manuel Calvo for the rebuilding of his home.

López. Six years later, along with his partner José Caneda, he registered two limited companies called Empresa de Navegación y Comercio de la Costa Sur (South Coast Shipping and Trading Company) and Fomento de la Costa Sur (South Coast Initiatives), which housed the transport, trade, and shipping activities that they had been carrying out along the Pinar del Río coast for some years.[13] This activity was approved with the license he was given to build a bridge over the River Hondo, in the Pinar del Río region—and in association with the successors of the famous manufacturer of Partagás tobacco—to take a considerable part of the tobacco from the Consolación del Sur region, in the western part of the island, to the coast; he later got the government to authorize him to set up a toll station there in order to recover the money he had invested.[14]

When the Banco Español de La Habana was built in 1856 at General Gutiérrez de la Concha's iniciative, Calvo was one of the first shareholders, along with all the great Cuban and Spanish Cuban businessmen who consituted the island's economic and trading elite at the time.[15] He was already co-owner of a sugar mill at Sagua la Grande.[16] At the start of the 1860s—in addition to his ceaseless trading activity, reflected in mercantile and notarial documents—he is recorded as being the owner of a stud farm at San José de las Lajas, near Havana.[17] That estate was to be where Portugalete sugar mill was built, founded by Calvo in 1862–1863, and at the same time as he built a road from the sugar mill to the main highway between San José and Havana.[18]

At the end of the 1850s he was a "privileged person" as a supplier to the public finance office and, at the start of the following decade, was working as an assistant to the Emancipation Board Secretariat, where he probably acted as a spokesman for the interests of Cuban slave dealers who, in connivance with the authorities, had made nonsense of the emancipation regulations. This is why he was removed from the position

13. ANC, Tribunal de Comercio, 1855: José Caneda y Reventó and Manuel Calvo asking for the foundation of two limited companies to be approved. Also Barcia, *Élites y grupos de presión*, 15–16.

14. Archivo Histórico Nacional (AHN), Ultramar, 191, file 12 for 1870. The bridge, made of iron and some thirty meters long, was at the place called Marcos Vázquez and cost thirty-one thousand pesos to build.

15. Marrero Cruz, *Julián de Zulueta y Amondo*, 270–78). In 1857, which was a year in which there was an international financial crisis, the government of the island had to request a large loan through the Banco: Calvo contributed fifty thousand pesos. About Gutiérrez de la Concha's activities and his relationships with the great Spanish Cuban businessmen see Cayuela Fernández, *Bahía de Ultramar*, 127–35.

16. Barcia, *Élites y grupos de presión*, 16.

17. ANC, Gobierno General, 1863. Report drawn up following the instructions of Manuel Calvo Aguirre about taxation on his stud farm, Feliz Casualidad, in the San José area. There are a dozen ANC documents from the Tribunal de Comercio y Escribanías that are Calvo's cases against various debtors, some of them for several thousand pesos, such as the case against the Levy company and brothers, which went on for several years, and the case against López Trapaga and Co.

18. See http://rveloz.cubava.cu/2015/02/el-central-portugalete-de-san-jose-de-las-lajas/ (accessed April 25, 2015).

when the Unión Liberal government initiated a policy—indeed an effective one—for ending the trafficking and gradually abolishing slavery.[19]

Figure 4.1. Portugalete sugar mill. Engraving from La Ilustración Americana, *1889.*

Having become a sugar magnate and joined the inner group of businessmen who were fierce defenders of the island's colonial status quo, in 1876 Calvo ended up replacing the powerful Samá y Sotolongo group as the Cuban agent for Compañía Trasatlántica with a new company which he founded in equal partnership with López.[20] Five years later, the two shipping lines—Calvo's Vapores and López's Trasatlántica—amalgamated and became the Empresa de Vapores Correos Trasatlántico (Business for Transatlantic Postal Steamships), with Calvo as vice chairman.[21] That same year, in 1876, the first board meeting of the Banco Hispano Colonial de la Isla de Cuba—the successor of the Banco Español de La Habana—was held: Calvo was one of the leading shareholders, his last great success as an important businessman on the island. Both the Banco Español de La Habana and the Hispano Colonial were private entities that served and were protected by the government of Cuba—in reality, they were fundamental in financing the Spanish administration of the island—but they were also the means of controlling colonial relationships.[22]

---

19. ANC, Intendencia General de Hacienda, 1857, copy of Manuel Calvo being given special rights. AHN, Ultramar, 4700, file 14, about the removal of Manuel Calvo as assistant to the Emancipation Board Secretariat, 1864–1866. About the Emancipation Board Secretariat, see Roldán de Montaud, "En los borrosos confines de la libertad."
20. About A. López' Compañía Trasatlántica see Hernández Sandoica, "La Compañía Trasatlántica Española," and Rodrigo Alharilla, "Entre Barcelona, Cádiz y Ultramar."
21. Rodrigo Alharilla, *Los marqueses de Comillas.*
22. Roldán de Montaud, "El Banco Español de Havana," and Rodrigo Alharilla, "El banco Hispano Colonial y Cuba."

According to his biographers, Calvo's fortune was a relief for his whole family and for his hometown, Portugalete, where he made considerable investments, as well as for everyone who formed part of his life, according to his biographers.

Calvo, Key Member of the Spanish Party in Cuba

In September and October 1868, with just a few weeks in between, Isabella II was deposed and the first Cuban war of independence broke out (known as the Great War or the Ten Years' War). More than by this conflict, the powerful Spanish-Antillean group and their Peninsular partners felt that their interests were seriously threatened by the proposals for colonial policy reform being put forward by people who supported the provisional government in Madrid—above all, the political groups which emerged during the Glorious Revolution of progressive thinkers and republicans—which included the abolition of slavery.

This is when Manuel Calvo enters the stage, at the same time as the Revolution. He went to Madrid from Paris and founded, with the direct economic support of his Spanish Cuban partners in the Liga Nacional, an authentic pressure group. Its purpose was to carry out—directly and through a network of Centros Hispano Ultramarinos (Overseas Spanish Centers) set up in the main cities in Spain—an intense, efficient public opinion campaign to influence the Spanish parliament, government, and the general public against conceding any sovereignty to the island. In particular, it opposed the republican-progressive's projects to abolish slavery. Among other things, in 1870 Calvo managed to have Manuel Becerra replaced as head of the Overseas Ministry; he was then highly influential in getting Moret's Freedom of Womb's Law (emancipating the offspring of slaves) passed, which made certain that abolition was going to be delayed. He was in close contact with most of the main politicians of the day, from unionists such as Cánovas to radicals such as Ruiz Zorrilla and including liberals such as Moret. It seems that he was also behind the choice of Amadeo of Savoy as constitutional king, but two years later he described him as an "imbecile" and told his allies in Cuba he was leaving the country.

Calvo also worked directly to have Spanish troops sent to the island to put down the Cuban uprising.[23] In his intense correspondence from Madrid with his allies in Havana during these years (1869–1874), Calvo always seems sure of achieving what is best for the group's interests.[24]

---

23. Roldán de Montaud, *La Unión Constitucional y la política colonial de España en Cuba*, 66–67; and Barcia, *Élites y grupos de presión*, 16–22.

24. ANC, Donativos y remisiones, file 616, folder 11, 1869–1874. A file including Manuel Calvo's correspondence to the chairmen of the Casino Español de La Habana, Segundo Rigal, Mamerto Pulido and others (among others, Julián de Zulueta). For example, on December 3, 1872, he wrote to Zulueta: "My dear friend, we continue with our work and the Liga Nacional is beginning to make the government fear certain things and regret having committed itself to the reforms."

As can be seen in the Havana newspaper *El Amigo del Pueblo: Periódico sin Careta* (The people's friend: An unmasked newspaper), on January 23, 1869, Calvo's work in Madrid was familiar in Cuba.

> To Traders in Human Flesh. We have been informed by reliable sources that Manuel Calvo is carrying out invaluable work in Madrid with regards to these outrages in order to keep the Always Loyal (island of Cuba) as one with the metropolis.[25]

When he traveled to Havana at the end of 1870, he was received as a hero by the Spanish Volunteers and the members of the Casino Español, who organized an act of homage to him. The same year, the captain general of Cuba obtained the Gran Cruz de Isabel la Católica award for him, Julián de Zulueta, and other main members of the Spanish faction.[26]

After the death of his old friend and partner Julián de Zulueta in 1874, Calvo—who was living between Madrid and Havana—consolidated his position as the political representative of the Spanish Cuban bourgeoisie's interests and, for this reason, he became the main figure in maintaining the colonial status quo in the last two decades of Spanish domination of the island. The fundamental means of carrying out this task was the Banco Hispano Colonial, through which this powerful group of businessmen controlled colonial administration in practical terms. A long letter from Manuel Cancio Villamil, the director of the island's tax office, to Julián de Zulueta, makes it quite clear how the colonial government absolutely depended on this Spanish Cuban oligarchy in economic and financial terms.[27] The Banco was the means of financing the war so that, from that point onward, its shareholders controlled Cuba's debt and customs revenue, which meant that they had direct influence over the island's fiscal policies.[28] Calvo continued to secure the sending of Spanish troops to Cuba, right up until the final group sent under General Martínez Campos.[29]

However, after the Pact of Zanjón, which put an end to the Great War in 1878, internal conditions changed in Cuba because of the political reforms which Martínez Campos introduced and the increasing pressure from the US government. The United States had become the main de facto market for the island's products in spite of Madrid's protectionist policies. One of the consequences of these changes was that the previously united Spanish Party began to splinter; with a considerable group of businessmen

---

25. *El Amigo del Pueblo*, January 23, 1869 (Library of Friends of the Country's Economic Society, Havana).

26. AHN, Ultramar, 4725, file 16.

27. ANC, Donativos y remisiones, Box 448-A, no. 4. Copy of the letter signed by Mariano Cancio Villamil, sent to Julián de Zulueta, chairman of the Casino Español. Havana. With regards to the political and economic situation of the island of Cuba. Havana, March 12, 1874.

28. Roldán de Montaud *La Hacienda en Cuba durante la Guerra de los Diez Años*.

29. AHN, Diversos. Títulos-Familias, 2543, no. 17. "Letter from Manuel Calvo to Antonio Cánovas del Castillo, the reinforcement battalions which must be sent to Cuba" September 29, 1876.

increasingly questioning Calvo's leadership more and more and, above all, the Banco Hispano Colonial's monopolist and exploitative practices.[30] This questioning is well expressed in the following text, published in the Havana newspaper *La Discusión* in 1882:

> The island of Cuba belongs to the *Colonial* (bank), to López and Calvo. There is a cry which has been taken up by the people: "Oh, to be López!" People also say "Oh, to be Calvo!" Calvo is the *Banco Colonial*. And Calvo represents the *Colonial* and López. Some ill-intentioned people used to say: "Oh, to be López with Cánovas as prime minister!" But those same people now say: "Oh, to be López with Sagasta as prime minister!" For López everyone is as good as Cánovas. Every day Calvo receives 33,500 pesos in customs through the *Colonial*. Cuba is not López. López is a Spanish province. He is more than Cuba. The government is more López than Cuban.[31]

A small example of Calvo's power and influence over the main authority on the island is the creation, following his request for armed protection of his sugar mill Portugalete, of a company of rural, municipal, and private guards.[32]

In any case, the historiography has made quite clear the considerable influence of the Spanish Antillean oligarchical group, then led by Manuel Calvo, on Spanish politics from the Restoration until the loss of the colony in 1898.

The Peculiar Ethnic Leadership of Calvo among the Basques and Navarrese of Cuba

Manuel Calvo was also at the forefront of what we can take to be the first example of Basque ethnic and regional associationism in Cuba, the Asociación Vasco Navarra de Beneficencia, founded in Havana in 1877.[33] Following the Catalans' earlier iniciative—their mutual aid association—and with the support of the partial implementation of the Spanish Constitution of 1876 after the Pact of Zanjón which, among other things, permitted welfare societies on the island for Spanish residents from different regions. These associations' statutory aims were exclusively welfare-related, assisting the members in the greatest need. In spite of this, until 1898 they were inevitably connected with the social and political activities promoted by people who defended Cuba remaining in the Spanish sphere of influence, whose specific organization was the Unión Constitucional party.

In contrast to what had happened in the American republics, the different regional communities of Spanish immigrants in Cuba had weak

---

30. Barcia, Élites y grupos de presión, 59–70.
31. "¡Quién fuera López!" cited in Bizcarrondo and Elorza, *Cuba/España*, 124.
32. AHN, Ultramar, 154, file 17. Report on the creation of rural, municipal and private guards, 1883–1884. Calvo's request, 1881.
33. Amores Carredano, "Presencia de los navarros en Cuba al final del período colonial," 249–53; and Ramos Martínez, "La asociación Vasco-Navarra de Beneficencia de la Habana."

ethic differentiation and specific characteristics. They shared with the Cubans the same political community. Furthermore, marriage between Spanish immigrants and Cubans had been the custom for generations. In connection with other Spaniards, the Cuban war of 1868 had consolidated their identity as "Spanish." A further, no less important, factor was the shared social class to which most of the immigrants from the Peninsula belonged during these decades. Finally, all being immigrants brought them much closer together than their regional or even ethnic differences might have separated them.

However, there was an important qualifier in the case of the Basques and Navarrese. There was the movement among them favoring restoration of their fueros abolished by the Spanish Constitution of 1876. So the weekly coverage of news of the Basque Country in the magazine *Laurac Bat* (The four are as one), which was the Asociación de Beneficencia's official publication until 1896, was followed with the greatest interest. In this regard, the editor's ideology was openly conservative and his usual source of news was the pro-fueros *La Unión Vasco-Navarra*. But when the Cuban War of Independence began, the magazine's pro-fuero leanings gave way completely to the sentiment of being Spanish. The editor and manager of *Laurac Bat* was Calvo's nephew, Faustino Díez Gaviño, journalist, poet, and leading member of the Basque community in Havana until his death at the start of the War of Independence in February, 1895.[34]

Manuel Calvo, who was the honorary president of the Asociación de Beneficencia, was described by it as being the "*patriarca de la colonia euskara*" (patriarch of the Basque-speaking colony).[35] Calvo is also all over the association's bulletins and year books: it is striking that one of the bulletins is almost exclusively about a fire at Portugalete in 1895, part of the sabotage campaign which the Cuban Mambises carried out before the start of the War of Independence the same year.[36] Manuel Calvo is also mentioned in the Association's board minutes as the representative of the Compañía Trasatlántica, which ran the island's steamboat mail service, and the discount in prices for its ill members, for which the association thanked him.

So the question is to what extent Calvo can be considered to have been the ethnic leader of the Basques and Navarrese in Cuba? And, if so, what type of leadership he gave?

Even today, with abundant research work into migration, there is no clear position with regards to the nature of ethnic leadership within groups of emigrants. Some people believe that ethnic leaders acted as intermediaries in the inevitable process of the immigrants' cultural assim-

---

34. Ramos Martínez, "Faustino Díez Gaviño e a primeira empresa xornalística en Cuba," and "Los inicios de la prensa vasca en Cuba"; and Amores Carredano, "Presencia de los navarros en Cuba al final del período colonial," 251–52.

35. *Laurac Bat* of La Habana, September 29, 1895.

36. *Laurac Bat* de La Habana, January 13, 1895. *Mambises* was the term used for all rebel fighters of whatever their background in both of the Cuban Wars of Independence.

ilation in the receiving society; others, in contrast, see them as catalysts and agents for communicating a more or less latent ethnic consciousness among these migrant groups.[37]

Of course, it is in the multicultural United States that a great number of studies have been carried out and it was in the 1940s that the concept of ethnic leader became a precise theoretical category, above all after John Higham's work *Ethnic Leadership in America* (1978). Later there were many research projects into very diverse groups—and not only in terms of leadership—which could be incorporated in a generic way into the analysis of the economic and social networks which arise within them.

Subsequently, and following the lead of US historiography, studies of ethnic leadership have been carried out in Argentina, Uruguay, and Brazil, above all. However, the US context is very different from that of the Latin American countries, as Higham pointed out.[38] While in Anglo-Saxon North America racial discrimination—which favors the development of leaderships in connection with protest, struggle, or compromise—and the ghetto experience were crucial factors, in Latin America this did not happen and, in fact, it was generally quite the opposite. In other words, in Latin America there was a continual process of integration, mixture, and assimilation between new immigrants and the receiving societies. Obviously, this was particularly true when it came to Spanish immigrants, who shared much of a culture in common with the receiving societies as a consequence of many centuries of the metropole's influence in the development of Hispanic American societies.

Calvo's leadership of the Basque people in Havana is, then, clearly subordinate to his role as leader of the Spanish Party on the island. This fact also defines the type of influence he exerted over members of the group, the Basques in this case. Specifically, he used his influence more to soften the group's identity—just at a time when it was gaining strength due to the Spanish Restoration government's anti-fueros' policies. It was something which had to be overcome in order to achieve greater unity, defending all things Spanish against the threat of Cuban separatism and its potential ally, the US's expansionist interests. So when in March, 1895, after the death of Díez Gaviño, *Laurac Bat* starts what it describes as its "second phase," it is apparent that matters connected with the war take up most of the publication, the matter of the Fueros and Basque liberties occupying a very modest second place; there is no doubt that the pro-fueros feeling gave way to feeling Spanish given the immediate and real danger of a Spanish defeat.

Finally, if we ask of what leadership consisted in Calvo's case, the inevitable conclusion is that it was not based on personal charisma, nor did it stem from previous leadership experience within the ethnic group. It was, above all, his personal and professional relationship with the per-

---

37. Núñez Seixas, "Modelos de liderazgo en comunidades emigradas."
38. Higham, "La movilización de los immigrantes."

son who had preceded him, Julián de Zulueta, the first individual who managed to bring all the Spaniards in Cuba together in a network of centers, the Casinos Españoles, from which he exerted social and political influence over Spaniards on the island, seeking unity in order to face up to the separatist threat. When, from 1878 onward, it is the Unión Constitucional party which officially represents these interests in both Cuba and the Spanish parliament, Manuel Calvo does no more than direct or directly represent Spanish Cuban businessmen. So the generic origin of his leadership is to be found in his privileged economic position within the small circle of Spanish Cuban interests—which are closely dependent on the Madrid government's trade and customs policies—and financial support for Spanish administration on the island through the Banco Hispano Colonial.

However, Manuel Calvo's leadership in the Basque community in Cuba can also be seen as a strategy of adaptation by the ethnic group in its social, economic, and political context. It was a matter of putting the person with the greatest chance of obtaining resources—above all, economic resources—at the forefront of the group in order to achieve Basque objectives.

Clearly, the situation changed after Cuba became independent. The Centro Euskaro, was founded in Havana in 1908 as a recreational and cultural society for the Basques and Navarrese in Cuba, following a pattern set in other capital cities in the Americas. One Cuban particularity was that Havana's Spanish welfare associations survived independence, including the Basque one. It would play an important role in receiving immigrants during the republican era and looking after its members.

In any case, after independence the Spanish groups in Cuba and their leaders identified more with the new republic's interests than with their country of origin. As the Spanish government's representative in Havana, Pablo Soler, bitterly complained to his superior, Minister of State Allendesalazar, in 1909 the Spanish colony on the island "calls itself Spanish but is as Cuban as the Cubans themselves because all their roots and interests are here."[39]

Bibliography

Alonso Romero, María Paz. *Cuba en la España liberal (1837–1898): Génesis y desarrollo del régimen autonómico.* Madrid: Centro de Estudios Políticos y Constitucionales, 2002.

Amores Carredano, Juan Bosco. "Presencia de los navarros en Cuba al final del período colonial." In *Las migraciones vascas en perspectiva histórica (siglos xvi-xx)*, edited by Óscar Álvarez Gila and Alberto Angulo Morales, 235–58. Bilbao: University of the Basque Country, 2002.

---

39. Otero Abreu, *La diplomacia de los vencidos*, 202.

Bahamonde, Ángel and José G. Cayuela Fernández. *Bahía de ultramar: España y Cuba en el siglo xix. El control de las relaciones coloniales.* Madrid: Siglo XXI, 1993.

Bizcarrondo, Marta y Antonio Elorza. *Cuba/España. El dilema autonomista, 1878–1898.* Madrid: Editorial Colibrí, 2001.

Barcia, María del Carmen. *Élites y grupos de presión: Cuba 1868–1898.* Havana: Editorial de Ciencias Sociales, 1998.

Cayuela Fernández, José G. *Bahía de Ultramar: España y Cuba en el siglo xix. El control de las relaciones coloniales.* Madrid: Siglo XXI, 1993.

Hernández Sandoica, Elena. "La Compañía Trasatlántica Española: Una dimensión ultramarina del capitalismo español." *Historia Contemporánea* 2 (1989): 119–64.

Higham, John. "La movilización de los immigrantes." *Estudios Migratorios Latinoamericanos* 4 (1986): 461–87.

Marrero Cruz, Eduardo. *Julián de Zulueta y Amondo: Promotor del capitalismo en Cuba.* Havana: Ediciones Unión, 2008.

Núñez Seixas, Xose Manoel. "Modelos de liderazgo en comunidades emigradas: Algunas reflexiones a partir de los españoles en América (1870–1940)." In *De Europa a las Américas: Dirigentes y liderazgos (1880–1960),* edited by Alicia Bernasconi and Carina Frid, 17–42. Buenos Aires: Biblos, 2006.

Opatrný, Josef. *José Antonio Saco y la búsqueda de la identidad cubana.* Praga: Editorial Karolinum, 2010.

Otero Abreu, Hilda. *La diplomacia de los vencidos: Cuba y España 1898–1931.* Pamplona: Ediciones Eunate, 2012.

Pérez Murillo, María Dolores. *Aspectos demográficos y sociales de la isla de Cuba en la primera mitad del siglo xix.* Cádiz: Servicio de Publicaciones de la Universidad, 1988.

Piqueras Arenas, José Antonio. "Grupos económicos y política colonial: La determinación de las relaciones hispano-cubanas después del Zanjón." In *La nación soñada, Cuba, Puerto Rico y Filipinas ante el 98,* edited by Consuelo Naranjo Orovio et al, 333–46. Madrid: Doce Calles, 1998.

Ramos Martínez, Jon Ander. "La asociación Vasco-Navarra de Beneficencia de la Habana (1877–1902)." *Sancho el Sabio: Revista de Cultura e Investigación Vasca* 33 (2010): 97–118.

———. "Los inicios de la prensa vasca en Cuba. *Laurac Bat* de Havana (1886–1895)." In *Organización, identidad e imagen de las colectividades vascas de la emigración (siglos xvi–xxi),* coordinated by Óscar Álvarez Gila, 195–206. Bilbao, University of the Basque Country, 2010.

———. "Faustino Díez Gaviño e a primeira empresa xornalística en Cuba." *Estudos migratorios: revista galega de análise das migracións* 4, nos. 1-2 (2011): 85–104.

Rodrigo Alharilla, Martín. "Entre Barcelona, Cádiz y Ultramar: La Compañía Trasatlántica (1862–1932)." In *Catalunya y Andalucia en el siglo xix: relaciones económicas e intercambios culturales*, 105–26. Cornellá de Llobregat: Segundo Congreso de Historia Catalana-Andaluza, Fundació Gresol, 1998.

———. *Los marqueses de Comillas, 1817–1925: Antonio y Claudio López*. Madrid: LID, 2001.

———. "El banco Hispano Colonial y Cuba, 1876–1898." *Illes i Imperis: Estudios de Historia de las Sociedades en el Mundo Colonial y Post-Colonial* 4 (2001): 49–70.

Roldán de Montaud, Inés. *La Hacienda en Cuba durante la Guerra de los Diez Años (1868–1880)*. Madrid: ICI- Instituto de Estudios Fiscales, 1990.

———. *La Unión Constitucional y la política colonial de España en Cuba (1868–1998)*. Madrid: Universidad Complutense de Madrid, 1991.

———. "El Banco Español de Havana (1856–1881)." *Revista de Historia Económica* 2 (1995): 281–310.

———. "En los borrosos confines de la libertad: el caso de los negros emancipados en Cuba, 1817–1870." *Revista de Indias* 71, no. 251 (2011): 159–92.

Santamaría García, Antonio. "Reformas coloniales, economía y especialización productiva en Puerto Rico y Cuba, 1760–1850." *Revista de Indias* 65 no. 235 (2005): 70.

5

The Parliamentarians Elected in the Basque Country's Cuban Connection, 1812–1939

Joseba Agirreazkuenaga

Jon Bilbao's book *Vascos en Cuba, 1492–1511*, published in 1958, examines the Basque presence on the island during the initial transatlantic exploration period and is the predecessor of this volume. Although there is information about the Basques in Cuba during the colony's first centuries, particularly in Havana, it was not until the mid-eighteenth century that certain prominent men whose origins were directly connected with the Basque Country made their mark on the island's society. Some of them stood out as landowners and in mercantile ventures, but the greatest example of the degree of the connections between Cuba and the Basque Country is civil associationism during the Enlightenment. No small number of these "illustrious" Havanans had their origins in the Basque Country. They stood out as landowners and in mercantile ventures, in administrative roles and in work connected with the Catholic Church and have been the subject of many research projects. Fully 75 percent of the founders of the Real Compañía Económica de los Amigos del País (Friends of the Country's Economic Society) in Havana had connections with the Basque Country.[1] The foundation of the Real Compañía de Comercio de La Habana (Royal Company of Trade of Havana) in 1740 by an important group

* I would like to thank doctor Hilda Otero for her help in obtaining the information and data for the writing of this paper and her suggestions regarding the archives and history of Cuba.
1. The figure multiplies when you take into account that most of the Cuba's partners were also descended from Basques. Moreno Fraginals and Moreno Masó, "La Real Sociedad Económica de Amigos del País a través de sus socios en Havana," 189–91. A study on the Friends of the Country's Economic Society of Havana has been undertaken by Álvarez Cuartero, *Memorias de la Ilustración.*

of Basque traders led to it obtaining a monopoly on commerce between the Peninsula and Cuba. Colonial items such as sugar and, above all, tobacco were exported from the island, while merchandise and manufactured goods were imported from Spain.[2]

From the eighteenth century there was a considerable volume of trade between the Basque coast and the largest island in the Antilles, and this left its mark on Creole society, all of which has been researched more or less. At Basque ports, Cuban influence could be seen in the amount of tropical products being traded, in particular because in 1728 La Real Compañía Guipuzcoana de Caracas (the Gipuzkoan Royal Caracas Company)[3] further strengthened the connection between Basque society and its economy and the overseas territories. The networks of Basque traders—first in Seville and then in Cádiz—ensured Basque participation in the importation of products from the Americas could be shipped and this gave rise to successful careers on both sides of the Atlantic. In 1756 Manuel Larramendi, in *Corografía de Gipuzkoa,* was the first to underline the importance of America in the economic flourishing of towns along the Basque coasts. During the nineteenth century the links between Havana and Bilbao grew, as we have stated in other research.[4]

The wealth of the Spaniards who made good in the Americas and who went back to their homes with large fortunes left its mark in the collective imagination, but they were the exceptions. Most immigrants were employed in hard agricultural work or in small-scale trade. More modest "Cuban" savers sometimes went back to their home towns and bought land there, or paid off mortgages on their family homes—"etxea" or "etxeauntza" in Basque. The dwelling, and the relationships that constituted the household, are the nodal factors in the Basques' worldview of the past and the future, the house itself representing their communication with ancestors and successors, as well as the nexus of union and the continuing present. So Basque emigrants felt closely duty bound—even though the Atlantic separated them—to the people who, along with them, make up the household and loyalties to it through moral obligations.

The cultural trace of the Basques on the island has been considerable for various centuries in spite of the relatively small size of the Basque colony in Cuba.[5] On examining recent historiography about Cuban society and its economy during the colonial period, Basque captain generals, bishops, superintendents, and major titles of nobility stand out.

---

2. See a monograph on this company in Gárate Ojanguren, *Comercio ultramarino e ilustración.*

3. Larramendi, *Corografía de Guipúzkoa o descripción general de la muy noble y muy leal provincia de Guipúzcoa.* Originally written in 1756.

4. Agirreazkuenaga, "Los Vascos y la insurrección de Cuba" and "Las instituciones representativas vascas frente a la insurrección de Cuba en 1868."

5. On the demographical influence of the Basque colony on the island, see Angulo Morales and Álvarez Gila, coordinators, *Las migraciones vascas en perspectiva histórica siglos XVI–XX,* 235–58.

By marriage or for professional reasons, the activity of Basques in the Americas led them to succeed in business, or prosper professionally in the Basque Country and within the structures of the Spanish monarchy. So Cuba was the place where men of future import on the Spanish political scene started their careers and met; underlining this connection may be of interest when researching the political events which shook up Spanish parliamentary history.

Parliamentarians Elected in the Basque Country

In this article we focus on the parliamentarians who were elected to the Spanish parliament for the Basque Country. From 1837 until 1923, elections were organized within the legal framework of a parliamentary monarchy—except for during the interregnum of the First Republic, 1873–1874—and elections were held on a regular basis. Elections were also called during the periods 1810–1814, 1820–1823, and 1931–1936. Until 1877 there were also representative assemblies in Araba, Bizkaia, and Gipuzkoa that were made up of local representatives and that evolved toward a process of political modernization by adapting parliamentary practices and customs. These assemblies chose their own governments which held effective political and administrative power in their respective chartered foral territories. In this way, between 1839 and 1877, as part of the Spanish constitutional system, representatives for each representative assembly were chosen in Araba, Bizkaia, and Gipuzkoa; the assemblies then named the government in each foral territory; and parliamentarians were chosen for these same territories to be sent to the Spanish parliament. The foral governments had a decisive influence in the choice of the representatives in the Spanish parliament until 1877. In Navarra, the members of the regional government were chosen by district, as were the representatives for the Spanish parliament.

However, there had been no systematic research into the origin and careers of the governing Basque elite and their connection with Cuba. If we start by examining the *Diccionario Biográfico de Parlamentarios de Vasconia* (Biographical dictionary of parliamentarians from the Basque Country, edited in 1993) and the *Diccionario Biográfico de Parlamentarios Vascos* (Biographical dictionary of Basque parliamentarians, edited in 2007),[6] we can see that of the 610 parliamentarians elected in the Basque Country/Navarra from 1808 to 1936, 51 of them had connections, to a greater or lesser extent, with the island of Cuba. This figure increases if we add members of the foral governments and the regional parliaments.

For the moment, our research is limited to the parliamentarians elected between 1808 and 1939, thirty-eight parliamentarians excluding the

---

6. Agirreazkuenaga, Urquijo, Serrano, and Urquijo, *Diccionario biográfico de the parliamentarians de Vasconia 1808–1876*, 1080; and Agirreazkuenaga, Alonso, Gracia, Martinez, and Urquijo, dirs., *Diccionario biográfico de Parlamentarios de Vasconia, 1876–1939*, 2834.

thirteen military personnel who are analyzed by Mikel Urquijo in his article in this volume.

Of these thirty-eight, most of them were elected in the nineteenth century, in the period between 1812 and 1898. In relation to all of the parliamentarians elected throughout the period, they represent around 10 percent of the total. During the twentieth century there were still some Basque family and trade connections, but they are neither as significant nor as striking.

Biographical Dictionaries about Basques and Cuba

Drawing up biographical dictionaries requires precise methodology in order to systematically organize people in their settings. Biography is an intersection of historiographical challenges. It is indispensable in order to obtain complete historical knowledge and to explain the processes and events which help to overcome mechanistic interpretations because if we do not take human intervention into account plausible explanations are beyond our reach. All fields of research—political history, social history, historical anthropology—need to make use of biography in order to validate and verify the results which they aim to achieve. The stakeholders and people who are the subjects of the historical discourse of any problem offer a vision which is otherwise unobtainable. Their situations within places and periods reflect inevitably reciprocal relationship between biography and context. Life and history are not a game of abstractions and doctrines but, rather, a stage on which there are men and women in continual social exchange and negotiation. The objective is not to interpret history simply in terms of individuals, but rather to be able to process peoples' contributions, both as individuals and in groups, as a source for thinking about social phenomena in historical terms.

The course of life, as part of a scientific experiment, is a necessary source, a component in a complex situation in a precise time and place. Any new social, political, or cultural history with an anthropological orientation requires the contribution of the systematic analysis of biographical sources. They are a source for history which is always provisional and open-ended, subject of endless possible debates as well.

Dictionaries often offer objective documentary material that differs compared with other sources. If, in future works, we wish to go further and look for keys for interpretations and behaviors and for forming subjective approaches that condition actors when intending to take political or social action within their immediate surroundings, dictionaries present primary evidence. So there is a point to carrying out a prosopographic analysis and evaluation of the scale of the Basque Country's political elites' Cuban connections in personal, professional, and business terms. To do so, we suggest drawing up a biographical dictionary of politicians and intellectual and economic elites in Cuba who developed connections with the Basque Country that went beyond the merely genealogical.

The concept of Basqueness that we are going to use is similar to that posited by a man born in Havana, Jesús de Sarria, when he began to publish a magazine about art and thought—*Hermes*—in Bilbao in 1917. He believes that Basqueness incorporates all persons who live and carry out their activity in connection with the Basque Country, independently of their birthplace or official residency or the census they may be in.[7] In these times of globalization in which Basqueness has taken on a dimension that goes beyond the original territories by the Bay of Biscay and in the Western Pyrenees, Sarria's reflection seems contemporary. I will say no more regarding this Cuban Basque about whom we published a symposium in the magazine *Bidebarrieta,* along with an extensive piece on the magazine *Hermes* and its director J. Sarria.[8] Although I must admit that on that occasion we missed the opportunity to underline his Cuban dimension and experience and his Havanan family surroundings.

A Cuban-Basque dictionary was published by Karmelo Anakabe, written in Havana in 2000 and published by Eusko Ikaskuntza-Sociedad de Estudios Vascos in the magazine *Vasconia.*[9] We, however, are going to concentrate on the parliamentarians elected in the Basque Country given that Cuba was the first reference for many of them and, on occasion, the necessary starting point for political, bureaucratic, or business careers. Recognition of their activity there let them take part in political life as parliamentarians. Professional and business links were reinforced by family connections, strengthening links of continuity with the island. However, with some exceptions, they did not take part in parliamentary debates regarding Cuba. After political independence in 1898, a Cuban connection continued to give political advantages in parliament, albeit that this began to weaken without ever completely disappearing.

Our objective is not to offer biographies systematically but, rather, to find common points or links within this group and, in the first place, we must emphaze the importance of Cuban women in the consolidation of social advancement and the political careers of members of the elected parliamentary elite in the Basque Country.

---

7. "People who have come or are going to come to our country cordially and to become long-term participants in our fate, whether favorable or poor, are one with us. All nationalities link with the things which are injected into them. Nor is it true that nationalism rejects the Castilians who have come to our country. People who have come or are going to come to our country cordially and to become long-term participants in our fate, whether favorable or poor, are one with us. All nationalities link with the things which are injected into them. We link ourselves with whoever comes with warmth to Basque lands and wishes to become one with us. We want to march together and, as far as we nationalists are concerned, whatever other people may decide, our decision is final: we are going to work for everybody . . . Basque nationalism neither hates nor rejects. It loves, loves a lot, no more than that. And its arms are always open, and its heart even more so." Sarria, *Oligarcas y ciudadanos,* 16–17.

8. *Bidebarrieta* 7, (2000), See www.bidebarrieta.com/revista/7. Agirreazkuenaga, *Hermes.* Agirreazkuenaga, "De periodistas a emprendedores de la comunicación de masas en la 'fábrica' de Bilbao."

9. Anakabe, "Kubako euskal jatorrizko hiztegi biografikoa." A copy can be obtained from at the website www.euskomedia.org/PDFAnlt/vasconia/vas38/3804950643.pdf.

Elected Parliamentarians and Their Connections with Cuba

On examining the biographies of Basque parliamentarians with links with Cuba, there are two main groups:

1. Parliamentarians whose main links are to colateral and affinal relatives, children or parents, which also lead to notable social, professional, and economic relationships in Cuba: Eduardo Ramón Alonso Colmenares, Joaquín Calbetón Legarra, Fermín Calbetón Blanchón, Manuel Allendesalazar y Muñoz de Salazar, Ángel Allendesalazar y Muñoz de Salazar, Alberto Aznar Tutor Marqués de Zuya, Eduardo Aznar Tutor Marqués de Bérriz, Luis Díez de Ulzurrum López de Ceriain, Eduardo Díez de Ulzurrun y Alonso Marqués San Miguel de Aguayo, Eduardo Dato Iradier, Casimiro Egaña Oquendo, José Elósegui de Aparicio, José Gaytán de Ayala y Brunet, Ramiro Maeztu Whitney, Manuel Gómez de Acebo Modet, Martín Garmendía Lasquíbar, Pedro Lemonauria Puch, Joaquín Sánchez de Toca Calvo, Eduardo Victoria de Lecea Arana, and Eusebio Zubizarreta Olavarría.

2. Parliamentarians whose main ties are economic and business. Julián de Zulueta led most of his professional life in Cuba. Others, however, directed their businesses from the Peninsula after their Cuban experiences or, like M. Arrotegi, from places like Liverpool. The list of parliamentarians in this group includes: Manuel de Aróstegui Sáenz de Olamendi, José Manuel Collado Parada, Manuel Echeverría Peralta, Tomás José Epalza Zubarán, Luis Mariátegui Vasallo, José María Musquiz Callejas, Federico Solaegui Mugica, Gregorio Alzugaray y Azcovereta, Manuel Arrotegui Amunategui, Joaquín Arteaga Echagüe, Marqués de Santillana, José Ma. Rodríguez de Ubago Rodríguez, Bernardo Rengifo Tercero, Enrique Satrustegui Barrie, Veremundo Ruíz de Galarreta, and Julián de Zulueta Amondo.

Jacinto Ma. Martínez Sáez was also a parliamentarian in periods in which ecclesiasts were allowed to be political representatives. Lastly, republican leader and member of the Basque government in 1936, Ramón Ma. Aldasoro Galarza, died suddenly in Havana. He was a political exile.

Among the elected parliamentarians, Julián de Zulueta stands out as a Cuban leader who was equally influential in Basque politics because of his defense of the fueros in the Senate when the law of the July 21, 1876. was being debated and passed. Paradoxically, his posture then was the opposite of what he defended for Cuba when he was in Havana. During the monarchist restoration of Alfonso XII after the republican experience of 1873, the Cubans had considerable political influence because they contributed money for buying political and military support.[10] A person of

---

10. Espadas, *Alfonso XII y los orígenes de la Restauración*.

equal importance was Manuel Calvo Aguirre from Portugalete who, although not an elected parliamentarian, had political influence that went beyond Cuba and also reached the Basque Country.[11]

Others used their time in Cuba to obtain experience and notoriety: university lecturer and member of parliament for Donostia-San Sebastián Joaquín Calbetón Legarra was public prosecutor in Havana between 1855 and 1861. His son Fermín Calbetón Blanchón, a distinguished politician during the Restoration, followed his father's professional and political footsteps, first as a lawyer and lecturer at the University of Havana and then as a member of parliament for Matanzas on two occasions, in 1884 and 1886, and then from Colón in 1893,[12] becoming minister of finance. Chronologically, Calbetón Legarra alternated his time in Cuba with parliamentarian Eduardo Alonso Colmenares.[13] The latter was public prosecutor in Havana between 1859 and 1861 and, after a short period in Santo Domingo, he was back in Cuba between 1864 and 1866. He was removed that year, but continued to work as a lawyer in Havana until 1868. His daughter Eladia Alonso Morales de Setién married on the island to the senator for Iruñea, Luis Díez de Ulzurrum, the first Marquis of San Miguel de Agüayo.[14] Alonso Colmenares continued his political career on the Peninsula and was elected member of parliament for Tutera in 1871.

Some men's social rise was crowned by marrying well on the island. Matrimonial alliances consolidated businesses, titles of nobility, and political careers

Cuban Women and Marriage Strategies

Matrimonial alliances were used to consolidate businesses and titles of nobility in Peninsular society and in Basque society in particular. When property and inheritance laws were liberalized in the nineteenth century in Spain, matrimonial alliances became important. Until the development of liberal society of the first half on the nineteenth century, a title in the nobility could mean more than the money. But this was to change over the century.[15]

The above statement above is valid in the analysis of several large Cuban fortunes that, once repatriated to the Peninsula, were then consolidated through affinal kinship, particularly during the second half of the century. In their relationships with Madrid, the "Spanish circle" on the island, close to the captain general's authority, reached the highest political

---

11. Barcia, *Élites y grupos de presión*.

12. Agirreazkuenaga, Alonso, Gracia, Martinez, and Urquijo, dir., *Diccionario Biográfico de Parlamentarios Vascos 1876–1939*, vol. 1, 724.

13. Agirreazkuenaga, Urquijo, Serrano, and Urquijo, *Diccionario biográfico de the parliamentarians de Vasconia 1808–1876*, 103–7.

14. Agirreazkuenaga, Alonso, Gracia, Martinez, and Urquijo, dir., *Diccionario biográfico de Parlamentarios de Vasconia, 1876–1939*, vol. 1, 921.

15. Carmona Pidal and Fernández Delgado, "La tradición moderna," 595–611.

spheres in the metropolis, putting their interests to work for them within the highest levels of colonial relationships. This group's inbreeding led to the consolidation of connections between members of the Cuban and Peninsular elites.[16]

We will now examine some cases in which the Cuban women's contribution was significant in terms of consolidating newly married couples' economic status.

Eduardo Aznar de la Sota (born in Seville but directly descended from Bizkaian families) married Luisa Tutor Fuentes from Matanzas, Cuba, and his son Eduardo Aznar Tutor was a member of the Basque financial elite and elected to the Spanish parliament for the Bizkaia district.

Eduardo Dato, parliamentarian for Vitoria-Gasteiz, later prime minister, got married at the age of twenty-two, on November 10, 1879, to Carmen Barrenetxea Montequi (or Montagugi) of Havana, descended from a family from Bidania, Gipuzkoa. Casimiro Egaña married Concepción Aranzabe Alpizar from Matanzas and widow of Labaien. They lived in Madrid, separating at the start of 1884. Eduardo Victoria de Lezea Arana married Carmen San Pelayo Basozabal of Havana on July 16, 1843.

Joaquín Sánchez de Toca Calvo born in Madrid on September 24, 1852, married María Ballester y Bueno, of Cuban family. They had two children, Joaquín and María, the latter marrying the Marquis of Lema, the secretary of state in Dato's first government. Sánchez de Toca was the owner of a sugar factory in the Guantánamo area, and he managed it himself from Madrid via the Confluence Sugar Company, founded in Bergara in 1906.

Ángel Allendesalazar Muñoz de Salazar, from Lumo, was the son of Manuel Allendesalazar Loizaga Conde de Montefuerte and Ángela Muñoz Salazar Martorell. Ángel married María del Carmen Zaragoza y Ayllón in 1879, who had been born in Havana, daughter of Francisco Javier Zaragoza Aznar (from Borja, Zaragoza), brigadier of engineers, and Nicanora Ayllón Hernández, from Madrid. Ángel and María del Carmen had two children Ángela (Madrid, November 7, 1884—September 5, 1975) and Juan (Gernika, August 23, 1882–1938), the latter being a renowned art critic and member of the San Fernando Fine Arts Academy.

In other cases, although the wife was not Cuban, if the wedding was held in Cuba then it could also serve to consolidate the link between Cuba and the Basque Country.

Eduardo Díez de Ulzurrun, his parents were Luis Díez de Ulzurrun López de Zeriain (born in Navarra) Marquis of San Miguel de Aguayo and Eladia Alonso Morales de Setién (born in Corella) married in Havana in March 1867. In 1886 Luis Díez de Ulzurrun was co-owner, along with Bizkaian Francisco Ibáñez, of the Compañía Territorial Cubana, which

---

16. The family stories of the main leaders of the pro-Spanish faction in Cuba are dealt with in Portela Míguelez, *Redes de poder en Cuba, en torno al Partido Unión Constitucional (1878–1898)*.

owned seven sugar estates.[17] The Díez de Ulzurrun family saga acquired its links with Cuba in the next generation. Eduardo Díez de Ulzurrun married Hortensia del Monte Varona.[18] The marriage was held in Havana on April 8, 1897.[19] After the independence of Cuba, Eduardo Díez de Ulzurrun kept part of his Cuban sugar business. He was one of the few Spanish nobles to maintain a permanent base on the island and was a reference for the rest of the Basque and Spanish colony.

Isabel Falguera Moreno Lara y Moscoso de Altamira, Countess of Santiago was born in Madrid, only daughter of José Falguera Lara, born in Havana, and Eloísa Moreno Moscoso, born in A Coruña. Isabel married the Marquis of Santillana, Joaquín Arteaga Echagüe, who was elected to the Spanish parliament for Zumaia, Gipuzkoa.

Rafael García Goiena, son of the lawyer Florencio García Goiena García, was in the Puerto Rico court in 1852, and then its president until his death in 1861. He married Mercedes Boza Agramante, from Puerto Príncipe, Cuba, daughter of Manuel Boza Corona y de Cruz Agramante Arteaga, from Puerto Príncipe.

On May 1, 1877, Martín Garmendía Lasquibar, married María Josefa Larrañaga Larrañaga, born in Azpeitia and daughter of Ignacio Larrañaga Galdós, founder and owner, along with his brother, of a large tobacco factory in Havana. They moved to Rome to live near the Vatican, but finally returned to Bilbao.

Senator for Navarra (1876) Gregorio Alzugaray Azkobereta married Casimira Vega Rodríguez, from Herencia, Ciudad Real, niece of Tomasa Gómez Morejón, business partner of Gregorio Alzugaray. Casimira brought properties inherited from her aunt to the marriage: a house in Iruñea valued at three hundred thousand pesetas, a house in Hernani, Gipuzkoa, and a sugar estate in Cuba.[20]

Among the thirty-eight parliamentarians listed, we will give a short biographical profile of the only elected politician to be born in Cuba.

Gumersindo Vicuña Lazcano was born in Havana on January 13, 1840, and died at Portugalete, Bizkaia, on September 10, 1890. His father Millán José de Vicuña Ondategi, from Eskoriatza, Gipuzkoa, had the surname García de Vicuña, and was from Ullibarri, Araba, but dropped the

---

17. Archivo Nacional de Cuba, fondo Secretaría de Hacienda, file 473, folder 58.
18. Eduardo Díez de Ulzurrum's biographical information in Agirreazkuenaga, Alonso, Gracia, Martinez, and Urquijo, dir., *Diccionario biográfico de Parlamentarios de Vasconia, 1876–1939*, vol. 1, 914.
19. Diocese Archive at Havana Cathedral, Bishop of Havana, Provisor and Vicar General's Records. Marriage license between Don Eduardo Díez de Ulzurrum, son of the First Marquis of San Miguel de Aguayo, and María Hortensia del Monte Varona, from Havana, of the parish of Espíritu Santo. Born in Havana on September 21, 1872, son of Guillermo del Monte, from Havana, and Mercedes Varona, born in Puerto Príncipe.
20. Torre, "Orígenes, expansión y crisis de la empresa harinera Alzugaray y Compañía, 1840–1888." Also see the entry for Alzugaray in Agirreazkuenaga, Alonso, Gracia, Martinez, and Urquijo, dir., *Diccionario biográfico de Parlamentarios de Vasconia, 1876–1939*, vol. 1, 914., vol. 1, 308.

surname García. We do not know what he did in Cuba, but he is listed as a merchant, his mother, Rosa de Lazcano, was from Santurtzi, Bizkaia. At the age of three he went to Santurtzi with his maternal grandparents to start school and later studied in Bilbao at the Colegio e Institución Vizcaíno.[21] His brother Félix was born in Bilbao in 1848 and the next child, Gregorio, was born in Portugalete in 1857, which is where the family finally settled.

Later on, between 1856 and 1862 he studied mechanics at the Royal Institute of Industrial Engineering in Madrid. He furthered his studies in Great Britain, Belgium, and France. From 1866 he was supernumerary professor of mathematical physics at Madrid—where he wrote a paper on imaginary quantities and another work on algebra—and became a full professor in July 1871. He had an impressive academic and intellectual career and founded the magazine *La Semana Industrial* (1882).[22] His career took a turn when he was elected to the Spanish parliament for Balmaseda, Bizkaia, and he was a parliamentarian until his death, holding various important administrative and political posts.

Member of the Partido Conservador led by Antonio Cánovas del Castillo, even so Vicuña opposed the law of July 21, 1876. He also spoke out against the decree to abolish the regional parliament of Bizkaia and the foral regional government of Bizkaia, issued by the Spanish government, on May 5, 1877. In 1878 he was sent to Cuba as a member of the army administrative corps, but he only stayed there a few months. In 1880 he was named director general of agriculture, commerce and industry. Before winning back his seat at Balmaseda in April 1884, he was named director general of stablized income at the finance ministry, from which he resigned in December 1885. In 1876 the regional parliament of Bizkaia gave him the honorary title of "Father of the Province for his Defense of its Fuero."

He represented Balmaseda, Bizkaia in the Spanish parliament. His first term as member of parliament was the result of elections held on January 20, 1876—or at a time when the Carlist War had not yet finished and only candidates loyal to the royal dynasty could stand—and ended ten years later, in 1886. He turned out to be an active parliamentarian, involved with industrial, mining, and railway interests. He was described as an "eloquent, fluent orator, and highly educated," presenting many initiatives and often taking part, in contrast with abstentions of most Basque parliamentarians.'At the 1879 elections he stood for Balmaseda as an Independent supporter of self-government, but the intransigent "euskalerriaco" supporters of self-government, led by Fidel Sagarminaga believed him to be at the behest of the Conservative Party. He won his race in 1879 against the "euskalerriaco" candidate, but by a small margin, and there

---

21. Velasco, "Excmo Sr. D. Gumersindo de Vicuña, ingeniero industrial y catedrático de la Facultad de Ciencias," 203–4.
22. For an interpretation of his academic and scientific activities, see Anduaga, "Gumersindo Vicuña Lazcano." Also, Anduaga, *Scientia in Vasconia*, 257–59.

were accusations of election rigging. He lost the election against rising political leader and industrial innovator Victor Chavarri in 1886, and there were reports of serious irregularities and misconduct.

Figure 5.1. Gumersindo Vicuña Lazcano, the member of parliament born in Cuba. Source: La Ilustración Española y Americana. *October 8, 1890, 216.*

Among his speeches are the ones he gave in the Spanish parliament against the law of July 21, 1876, which was to abolish the self-governance of the political and legal fuero regime and the regional parliaments. In his speeches are references to Cuba and he stated his opposition to its slave regime, in which he was supported by the prime minister, A. Cánovas. In his opinion, the law of July 21, 1876, was not a regular law because its contents were about the political and administrative issues connected with the Spanish nation-state. G. Vicuña spoke in favor of dual loyalty and dual patriotism "to the Basque Provinces" and to the "Spanish Nation": "I do not defend the Provinces when their excesses make them like another state within the other state, I am not as mad as that . . . I do not know what prevails in me, my affection for the Basque Provinces or my affection for the Spanish Nation."[23]

He does not understand the need for a law to reform and abolish political-administrative system, let alone consider it to be just. And in this context he makes a comparison of the Basque provinces with slavery in Cuba: "However, you think that slavery cannot be removed immediately in Cuba because that might cause disturbances which must be foreseen and avoided . . . Can you dare to find any similarity between the abominable institution of slavery and the existence of the fueros?" Finally he offers

---

23. These quotes are take from his parliamentary speeches. *Diario de Sesiones del Congreso de Diputados,* July 1876.

a reflection about the unity of Spain: It will not be achieved through the method of abolishing rights and he is afraid that in the future this may produce the opposite of the intended effect, "if you want to achieve the unity of Spain in this way, try not to let this question cause the Fatherland any serious disturbances."

But his disagreement was even sharper when A. Cánovas abolished the Bizkaia representative assembly and, consequently, the regional parliament, and then ordered the abolition of the regional foral governments by decree on May 5, 1877. In the debate held on May 8, 1877,[24] with Prime Minister A. Cánovas del Castillo he denounced the fact that such measures had not been included in the law of July 21, 1876, and denounced the prime minister for exceeding his authority and, consequently, gave his opinion that the decree was not legal: "the decree published in yesterday's *Gazette* is the abolition of the internal regime of the Basque Provinces and the decree is clearly against the law." In his opinion the government had acted hastily because it had prevented the regional parliament of Bizkaia—the institutional synonym for a representative assembly with parliamentary characteristics—from reaching an agreement about the two sentences being discussed by the fueros commission: "the unusual clumsiness with which the Ministry and its delegates have worked on dissolving the regional parliament in Bilbao . . . the government takes over the roads of Bizkaia, most of which have been built using private funds . . . an attack on property." In conclusion, "what the decree has done has not been to reform the internal organization of Bizkaia but to brutally repress it." According to A. Cánovas, the fueros' authorities had been an obstacle to the observance of the law and, so, the fueros' laws had to be replaced with others.

In short, G. Vicuña, born in Havana, who had lived in Bilbao but mostly in Madrid, was an outstanding academic and scientist who was involved in industrial and mining development and in the administration of the Spanish state. In the Spanish parliament he tried to maintain dual loyalty, on the one hand to the Bizkaia regional parliament and, on the other, to the Spanish nation as represented by the central government. Consequently, he opposed the law of July 21, 1876 and also took advantage of the moment to denounce the slave regime in Cuba. In 1877 he spoke against the abolition of the fueros' or self-government of Bizkaia and suggested that such measures would not contribute to the unity of Spain, rather the opposite. In fact, his nephew and godson Ramón Gumersindo Vicuña Nepali (1885–1935), lawyer, ship builder, and ceaseless traveler, became a supporter of Basque nationalism at a young age and a main leader of the Basque Nationalist Party, becoming its president in 1931. In 1933 he was elected member of the Spanish parliament and defended autonomy for the Basque Country.

---

24. Diario de Sesiones del Congreso de Diputados, May 8, 1877.

Conclusion

Cuba is part of the lives of a significant number of the parliamentarians elected for the Basque Country and their connections with the island are with social and political groups that worked in favor of it remaining Spanish and governed from Madrid. However, they defend the political and administrative self-government of the Basque foral territories against the "one nation" homogenizing policies of political leaders in Spain after the restoration of the monarchy in 1876.

Bibliography

Agirreazkuenaga, Joseba. "De periodistas a emprendedores de la comunicación de masas en la 'fábrica' de Bilbao: Kazetari azkarrak, komunikazio enpresen sortzaile, industringintza garaiko gizartean: Juan Eustaquio Delmas (Bilbao 1820–Madrid 1892), Manuel Echevarria (1842–1917), Jesús Sarria (1887–1922)." In *De la sociedad industrial a la sociedad de la información*. Bilbao: Asociación de historia de la Comunicación, 2009.

———. *Hermes: Revista del País Vasco y Bilbao 1917–1922: La ciudad, el hombre, la revista. Hiria, gizona, aldizkaria*. Bilbao: Bidebarrieta Kulturgunea-Ayto de Bilbao, 2000.

———. "Las instituciones representativas vascas frente a la insurrección de Cuba en 1868: La formación del 'Tercio de voluntarios vascongados' o Legión vasca" por las Diputaciones Forales de Araba, Bizkaia y Gipuzkoa." In *Patria y libertad: Los vascos y las guerras de independencia de Cuba (1868–1898)*, coordinated by Alexander Ugalde. Tafalla: Txalaparta, 2012.

———. "Los Vascos y la insurrección de Cuba." *Historia Contemporánea* (1989): 139–64.

———. *The Making of the Basque Question: Experiencing Self-Government 1793–1877*. Reno: Center for Basque Studies, 2011.

Agirreazkuenaga, J., E. Alonso, J. Gracia, F. Martinez, and M. Urquijo, directors, *Diccionario biográfico de Parlamentarios de Vasconia: 1876–1939*. 3 volumes. Vitoria-Gasteiz: Eusko Legebiltzarra-Parlamento Vasco, 2007.

Agirreazkuenaga, J., J. R. Urquijo, S. Serrano, and M. Urquijo. *Diccionario biográfico de los parlamentarios de Vasconia, 1808–1876*. Vitoria-Gasteiz: Eusko Legebiltzarra-Parlamento Vasco, 1993

Álvarez Cuartero, Izaskun. *Memorias de la Ilustración: Las sociedades económicas de Amigos del País (1783–1832)*. Madrid: Departamento de Publicaciones Real Sociedad Bascongada de Amigos del País, 2000.

Anakabe, Karmelo. "Kubako euskal jatorrizko hiztegi biografikoa." *Vasconia* 38 (2012): 495–643.

Anduaga, Aitor. "Gumersindo Vicuña Lazcano," In *Auñamendi Eusko Entziklopedia*. At www.euskomedia.org/aunamendi/142286.

———. *Scientia in Vasconia: Ochenta biografías de científicos e ingenieros vascos*. Donostia-San Sebastián: Ttartalo, 2008.

Angulo Morales, Alberto and Óscar Álvarez Gila, coordinators. *Las migraciones vascas en perspectiva histórica siglos XVI–XX*. Vitoria-Gasteiz: University of the Basque Country, 2002.

Barcia, María del Carmen. *Élites y grupos de presión: Cuba 1868–1898*. Havana: Editorial de Ciencias Sociales, 1998.

Bilbao, Jon. *Vascos en Cuba, 1592–1511*. Buenos Aires: Editorial Ekin, 1958.

Carmona Pidal, Juan and Javier Fernández Delgado. "La tradición moderna: La política matrimonial de los grandes de España (1800–1923)." In *La sociedad madrileña durante la Restauración (1876–1931)*, edited by Ángel Bahamonde and Luis E. Otero. Madrid: Comunidad de Madrid-Alfoz, 1989.

Espadas, Manuel. *Alfonso XII y los orígenes de la Restauración*. Madrid: CSIC, 1990.

Gárate Ojanguren, Monserrat. *Comercio ultramarino e ilustración: La Real Compañía de HavanaI*. Donostia-San Sebastián: RSBAP, 1993.

Larramendi, Manuel. *Corografía de Guipúzkoa o descripción general de la muy noble y muy leal provincia de Guipúzcoa*. Buenos Aires: No publisher, 1950 [1756].

Moreno Fraginals, Manuel and José J. Moreno Masó, "La Real Sociedad Ecónomica de Amigos del País a través de sus socios en Havana." In *La Sociedad Bascongada y América: III Seminario de Historia de la Real Sociedad Bascongada de los Amigos del País*. Bilbao: Fundación BBVA, 1992.

Portela Míguelez, María José. *Redes de poder en Cuba, en torno al Partido Unión Constitucional (1878–1898)*. Cádiz: University of Cádiz, 2004.

Sarria, J. *Oligarcas y ciudadanos*. Bilbao: Editorial Vasca, 1919.

Torre, Joseba. "Orígenes, expansión y crisis de la empresa harinera Alzugaray y Compañía, 1840–1888." *Geronimo Uztaritz*, no. 14–15, (1999): 179–99.

Velasco, Eusebio. "Excmo Sr. D. Gumersindo de Vicuña, ingeniero industrial y catedrático de la Facultad de Ciencias." *La Ilustración Española y Americana*, no. 37 (1890): 203–4.

6

The Tragic End of a Colonial Adventure: the Life and Death of the Basque Units in Cuba, 1869–1873

Óscar Álvarez Gila

Forming the Basque Units

Throughout the nineteenth century, Cuba became one of the places in America to which Basques most emigrated, Río de la Plata being the only more attractive destination. Among the many reasons that have been mentioned to explain this process, there are economic factors (in particular the take-off and expansion of sugar cultivation on the island in a context of growing international demand), social factors (the progressive decline of the slave trade, which had supplied the workforce for agriculture and the sugar industry), and political ones (the island being a colony only made it easier for the emigrants to move there from the metropolis and furthermore also that this immigration was protected and promoted by the colonial authorities).[1] Numerous initiatives were taken to encourage emigration during the nineteenth century, including offers made to Basques to immigrate,[2] to which unsolicited, spontaneous immigration along migratory networks must be added. In sum, it has been calculated that around three quarters of a million immigrants from the Peninsula settled in Cuba during this period.[3]

In opposition to attempts to guarantee political control of the colonial territories—which included efforts to give public administration wid-

---

* This chapter is part of the work of the consolidated research group "*País Vasco y América: Vínculos y Relaciones Atlánticas*" (IT822-13).

1. Amores Carredano, "Presencia de los navarros en Cuba al final del período colonial," 235–36.

2. Irigoyen Artetxe, *La Asociación Vasco Navarra de Beneficencia de Havana y otras entidades vasco-cubanas*, 36–38.

3. Maluquer de Motes, *Nación e inmigración: Los españoles en Cuba*, 49–54.

er powers, control the economy and make Cuba's population whiter[4]—
movements calling for different political statuses for the island appeared
very early on and soon focused on three alternatives: autonomy within
Spain; annexation by the United States; and, in the second half of the
century, independence.[5] The Ten Years' War, which started with Carlos
Manuel de Céspedes's independentist proclamation on October 9, 1868,
ended in a military defeat for the patriots, but in political terms it saw the
consolidation of Cuban national identity in opposition to the survival of
the Spanish colonial model on the island.

The scale of the military operations and the progress of the war in
various areas of Cuba led the Spanish government formed after the 1868
revolution to reinforce its troops billeted on the island and, at the same
time, raise a series of volunteer regiments, recruited mainly from among
the Spanish immigrant population, and principally in urban areas: the
chapelgorris. From the start, many Basques took part in setting up and
recruiting for these volunteer battalions.[6] This atmosphere of Spanish
national fervor also reached the Basque Country, and it was "one of the
critical moments of demonstrating Spanish patriotism during the nineteenth century."[7] The regional governments—the main organs of government and political representation—soon responded to this climate and,
using manifestos and other types of propaganda, joined the many voices
calling for the Spanish government to give a direct, forceful response to
the separatist challenge. However, there was a peculiarity in the provinces
of Araba, Bizkaia, and Gipuzkoa compared with the rest: the survival of
the foral system—which gave them considerable political autonomy and
their own tax institutions—meant that the people born there were not
obliged to do military service in the Spanish army. The regional governments' response was to form a series of volunteer battalions, collectively
known as the Tercios Vascongados (Basque units), which were managed
and financed by the Basque institutions as their contribution toward the
Spanish army's needs in Cuba.

Initially, the regional governments' objective was to recruit one thousand men as quickly as possible, 50 percent from Bizkaia, 37.5 percent
from Gipuzkoa, and 12.5 percent from Araba.[8] This decision was based
on the lesson learned from the previous founding of units for the fighting
in Morocco, which had been delayed because of the time it had taken to
recruit and train the promised three thousand soldiers. However, not even

---

4. This included using the Catholic Church as a political instrument for controlling con-
sciences by bringing Spanish religious to the colonial territories and setting up missionary
school after the concordat of 1853. Amores Carredano, "La Iglesia en Cuba al final del período colonial," 70.

5. Ibid., 68.

6. Amores Carredano, "Presencia de los navarros en Cuba al final del período colonial,"
255; and Amores Carredano, *Cuba y España*, 82–84.

7. Agirreazkuenaga Zigorraga, "Los vascos y la insurrección de Cuba en 1868," 154.

8. This distribution had been established in the criteria agreed by the regional governments
of Bizkaia and Gipuzkoa on March 3, 1869. Agirreazkuenaga Zigorraga, "Las instituciones
representativas vascas frente a la insurrección de Cuba en 1868," 314.

these limited projections for Cuba could be met and only 556 soldiers were sent at first: 113 from Araba, 200 from Gipuzkoa, and 243 from Bizkaia.[9]

The first volunteers reached Havana on board the steamship *Guipúzcoa* on June 2, 1869, and were given a reception by—according to the records of the time—the most distinguished members of the Basque community in the city.[10] The names mentioned included Julián de Zulueta,[11] Ramón María de Araiztegui, and José Arcocha, who were the unofficial leaders of the Basque community, which had not yet been organized institutionally, but which took advantage of such a striking act to show itself in public. So there was no lack of symbols of Basque identity such as the units parading beneath the banners of their respective provinces, flags of which were hung up in the Templete (shrine) next to which the ceremonial speeches were given beside a ceiba tree that served as a Caribbean alter ego for the Gernika oak tree.[12] The very use of Basque in the welcoming speech, given by Joaquín Calbetón (an official at Havana Court who was from Donostia-San Sebastián), reinforced the image of dual patriotism (Basque-Spanish) in harmony and with shared interests.

Negotiations between the regional governments for organizing, recruiting, and sending a second contingent started immediately, the process being well advanced by October 1869[13] and lasting into December. It was no more successful than the first one: in spite of calls from the Basque oligarchy in Cuba (represented by Julián de Zulueta) "to make new sacrifices, this second recruitment did not meet its objective (409 volunteers compared with the projection of 600)."[14] Altogether, 965 soldiers joined the units. The units—which were incorporated into the Spanish army's organizational structure and chain of command—were divided into six battalions, four with soldiers from the first contingent and the other two with soldiers from the second.

Death in the Cuban Countryside

In 1998 we had the opportunity to access documents of particular interest in the General Military Archive at Segovia. It was a report about the sol-

---

9. Ibid., 316; Álvarez Gila y Tápiz Fernández "La formación de los Tercios Vascongados para la Guerra Grande de Cuba."

10. *Álbum Vascongado,* 1869; Arrozarena, *El roble y la ceiba,* 182.

11. Cayuela Fernández, "Comportamientos inversos de la élite económica antillana en Europa"; Agirreazkuenaga Zigorraga, "Los vascos y la insurrección de Cuba en 1868," 142–54; Apaolaza Ávila, "Un análisis sobre la historiografía en torno al alavés Julián de Zulueta y Amondo"; Marrero Cruz, *Julián de Zulueta y Amondo*; Ramos Martínez, "Manuel Calvo y Aguirre, una eminencia en la sombra"; Barcia Zequeira, *Élites y grupos de presión.*

12. Arrozarena, *El roble y la ceiba,* 182.

13. ATHA, DH 90-1, "Telegrama del Diputado de Guipúzcoa al de Álava," Tolosa, October 13, 1869. The second in "Informe sobre la recluta de un segundo Tercio," Vitoria, October 1869.

14. Ugalde Zubiri, "Los vascos ante las guerras de independencia de Cuba," with reference to Agirreazkuenaga Zigorraga, "Las instituciones representativas vascas frente a la insurrección de Cuba en 1868."

diers in volunteer Basque units' final payslips.[15] The procedure when one
of the soldiers in the Tercios died was similar to that applied to the regular
units in the Spanish colonial army. First, their personal effects were gathered, particularly their clothes, and sold to the highest bidder, the proceeds
from which were added to their unpaid wages. Apart from some cases in
which soldiers were buried in their own clothes, or in which the clothes
were in such a poor state that there were no takers, people who had died
from infectious diseases were excluded from this process, their clothes and
other belongings being incinerated for health reasons. The deceased's pos-
sessions were then added up, including any wages that were owed, but sub-
tracting indebtedness for food rations, clothes supplied, money advances
given in Havana (mostly on leave days), for misconduct fines levied by officers in keeping with military regulations, funeral expenses, an allowance
for the chaplain who held the funeral, and even the stamp used on the
envelope sent to inform the family of the death.

What was left went to the heirs, either having been included in the
deceased's will or being the legally established successors. In fact, only one
of the volunteers who died had written a will; he did so in Cuba and in it
he left some money to a nurse who had looked after him in the hospital.

The reports that have been conserved date from between June 1869
and December 1873. The first to die was Roque Aragolaza Alberdi, from
Bergara, just twenty-two days after the units reached the port of Havana,
on June 24, at Villa Clara Hospital, diagnosed as having "fever." The last
registered death is that of Juan Imaz Badiola, from Hernani, on Christmas
Day 1873, at Manzanillo Hospital, of "harmful fever." Altogether, a total
of 476 died during this period, which means that total mortality (assuming that no more died in action or after the latter date) is around half the
volunteers (precisely, 49.33 percent) in just three years. We have not had
access to the specific mortality rates from the 1869–1879 war, but there are
studies about the last Spanish-Cuban colonial one. Rozalén Fuentes and
Úbeda Vilches, for example, write about the latter conflict:

> The mortality rate in the colonial army was high, among other
> things, because of the soldiers' youth, most of them being under 22;
> the poor food, which was usually a few dried biscuits and fruit they
> found along their way; the hygienic conditions they had to cope with,
> having to walk for days on end, semi-naked and carrying their rifles
> along jungle paths and in fields full of mud because of the continual
> rain, soaked in water and with mud up to their knees, fully exposed
> to the torrid sun and in danger of catching tropical fevers, and suf-
> fering from nervous complaints which increased their physical and
> moral fatigue.[16]

---

15. These documents were referenced, when we examined them, as Archivo General Militar
[AGMS], Segovia, 6th–8th, 9-J, 7th Div., file 95.
16. Rozalén Fuentes and Úbeda Vilches, "Nuestros soldados fallecidos y repatriados,"
293–94.

	Bat. 1	Bat. 2	Bat. 3	Bat. 4	Bat. 5	Bat. 6	Totals
Araba	25	17	17	21	21	24	125
Bizkaia	25	11	17	28	18	25	124
Gipuzkoa	44	40	30	23	30	27	194
Navarre	2	3	1	–	1	–	7
Spain	5	2	4	6	2	3	22
Others	1	–	1	–	–	–	2
Unknown	–	1	1	–	–	–	2
	102	74	71	78	72	79	476

*Table 6.1. Number of deaths in the Basque units by battalion
and province of birth.*

Records about the casualties, bearing in mind the high percentage of
the volunteers who died, allow us to deduce some general characteristics
about their recruitment, for example their provinces. In table 6.1 there are
totals (by battalion and for all the units) of deaths, classified by place of
origin. The data in figure 6.1, show, first, a high number of Gipuzkoans;
assuming that there was no reasonable cause for the Gipuzkoan death rate
to be higher than that for soldiers from the other two provinces, it may be
supposed that what this data reflects is that the different recruitment drives
were much more successful in Gipuzkoa.[17]

Furthermore, if we also apply a correction on the recruitment rate
based on the differences of population between the three provinces,[18] the
efforts made in Bizkaia compared with in the other two provinces are clear.
As has been pointed out on numerous occasions, it was never possible to
fill the quota of volunteers called for in Bizkaia (half of the total), and it
had to make up the shortfall by recruiting in other provinces and assuming

---

17. In any case, the recruitment data we have does not seem to reflect that difference with
regards to volunteers for Cuba. According to the figures that Agirreazkuenaga Zigorraga
gives in "Las instituciones representativas vascas frente a la insurrección de Cuba en 1868,"
214–15, the distribution of recruiting per province was as follows:

Province	First recruitment	Second recruitment	Total (%)
Araba	113	141	254 (26.32)
Bizkaia	117	243	360 (37.31)
Gipuzkoa	151	200	351 (26.32)

However, these figures should be treated with caution because while the data for the first
recruitment shows the volunteers' places of birth, the second show the regional governments
which organised it (and not the volunteers' place of birth). So it is quite possible that many of
the soldiers consigned to the Bizkaian contingent were, in fact, from other provinces.
18. The census closest in time to the recruitment of the units is the 1857 one, which provides the following population data. Araba, 96,398 inhabitants; Bizkaia, 160,597; Gipuzkoa,
156,493. These figures were the basis on which the quota of volunteers for the units to be
sent to Morocco was set. Cajal Valero, "Discrepancias entre las tres 'Provincias Hermanas,'"
73–74.

that cost.[19] To a large extent, this small contribution in terms of volunteers was the same as had happened ten years earlier, although we do not know whether on this occasion too, as Cajal Valero points out, Bizkaia was able to make up a substantial part of its quota using economic incentives to recruit "Gipuzkoans, Arabans, and others."[20] The only really noticeable difference, in any case, was that on this occasion it was Gipuzkoa, not Araba, which made the greatest contribution to the units in absolute and relative terms. This tendency is confirmed by the list of towns with the greatest number of casualties (table 6.2) which, apart from the provincial capitals, are mostly in Gipuzkoa.

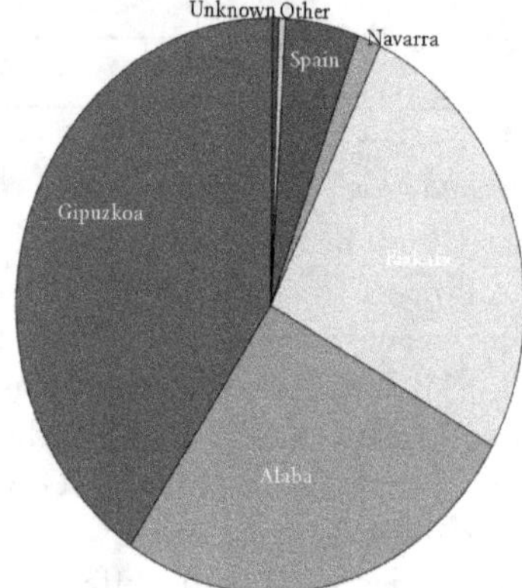

Figure 6.1. Total deaths (1869–1973) by province of birth.

Town (province)	No. casualties	Town (province)	No. casualties
Vitoria-Gasteiz (A)	32	Irun (G)	9
Bilbao (B)	30	Aiara (A)	7
Tolosa (G)	29	Urkabustaiz (A)	7
Donostia-San Sebastián (G)	22	Oiartzun (G)	7
Begoña (B)	14	Oñati (G)	7
Hernani (G)	13	Abando (B)	7
Azpeitia (G)	10		

Table 6.2. Towns with the greatest numbers of casualties.

In any case, this data with the casualties listed by towns allows us to deduce how representative the results are with greater accuracy as reflection of the recruitment itself, if we compare it with the only sample of series of data which exists, that of the recruits in Bizkaia (given that, as Agirreazkuenaga Zigorraga says, "there is no such precise statistical information for the others"). In this sample "around 55 percent" are "residents

---

19. Agirreazkuenaga Zigorraga, "Las instituciones representativas vascas frente a la insurrección de Cuba en 1868," 214, 216.
20. Cajal Valero, "Discrepancias entre las tres 'Provincias Hermanas,'" 84.

of Bilbao and neighboring towns: Begoña, Abando and Deustu";[21] in other words, a picture very similar to that given by the data for casualties.

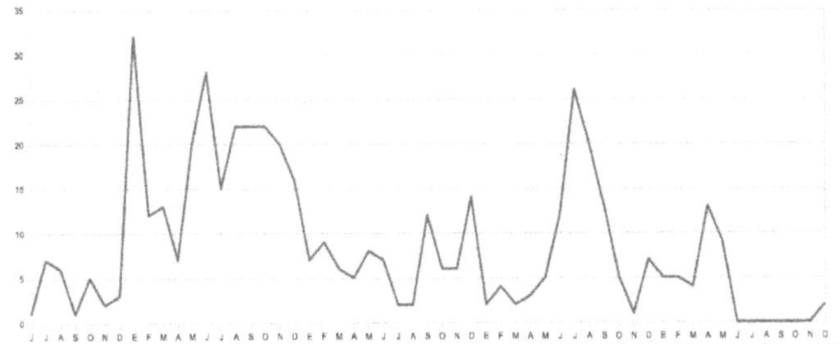

Figure 6.2. Total number of deaths by month (June 1869–December 1873)

The presence of soldiers who were not from these three Basque provinces was nothing new (others from elsewhere had been allowed to join in 1859), but on this occasion there were many fewer of them: while in 1859 the soldiers from "the general territory" (of Spain) made up 11.21 percent of the recruits, on this occasion they were 6.5 percent of the casualties, in other words, a reduction of almost 50 percent. It is possible that the central government's reluctance in 1859 for men who had been born in provinces in which they could be called up to do obligatory military service to be recruited into this volunteer corps[22] led to a certain self-limiting of this practice in 1869. In any case, the place of origin of these non-local soldiers was the same, in order of importance Navarra, Burgos, and La Rioja.[23] It should be taken into account that the reverse happened. In other words, people from these three Basque provinces who, in spite of not being obliged to do military service, were recruited and fought in regular battalions of the Spanish army throughout the war. For example, according to the records of a single battalion (the Cazadores de Chiclana), there were seven soldiers from Araba, Bizkaia, and Gipuzkoa who died between 1870 and 1873.[24]

However, the most striking point about this analysis of the list of the casualties is the causes (and place) of death, about which the source offers

---

21. Agirreazkuenaga Zigorraga, "Las instituciones representativas vascas frente a la insurrección de Cuba en 1868," 318.

22. Cajal Valero, "Discrepancias entre las tres 'Provincias Hermanas,'" 80–82.

23. In one case, the volunteer had been born in Cuba; in another in the French Basque Country. Nevertheless, data about the soldiers' places of birth should be qualified given that various references in the reports lead one to think that they lived in the three Basque provinces, or at least had family connections there, but had not been born there. In two cases, the "place of birth" box includes the clarification that they had been born outside the Basque Country "by accident."

24. AGMS, Sect. 6th/8th. Office 9-J, 4th división, file 11 "Fallecidos 1871–1884. Relaciones filiadas de los fallecidos del Batallón de Cazadores de Chiclana." Specifically, the following soldiers: Miguel Echavarría Veistegui, from Elgoibar (G): July 13, 1871. Nicanor Gutiérrez Bastida, from Bilbao (B): May 17, 1871. Eduardo Alfonso Alonso, from Vitoria-Gasteiz (A): November 7, 1871. Pablo Humedes Arana, from Vitoria-Gasteiz (A): November 7, 1871. Gabriel Betolaza López, from Monasterio (A): July 9, 1872. Felipe Zabala Iriarte, from Sarria (A): March 18, 1872. Antonio Elezpuru Arese, from Otxandio (B): January 3, 1873.

more information. Only 10 of the 476 casualties (2.1 percent) died, according to the records, for reasons directly connected with the war (bullet wounds, in six cases, while in another three they died "while fighting with the enemy" or "in action").[25] The greatest number of deaths in battle happened on April 2, 1873, at the Moja-Casabe, in which three soldiers died, from units 1, 4, and 5 respectively.

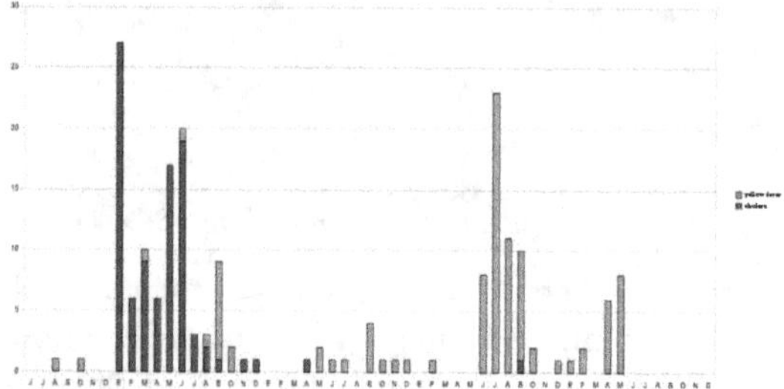

Figure 6.2. Death due to yellow fever and cholera (June 1869–December 1873).

While not wanting to underestimate the independentist army's resistance to the Spanish colonial troops, it was not in vain that the Basque units were attacked by "the most cruel of natures" from the moment they arrived in Cuba[26] in terms of the impact of the climate and, above all, illnesses. In fact, the fragmentary information we have about the causes of the volunteers' deaths, such as that provided by Agirreazkuenaga Zigorraga, demonstrates the abysmal difference between the casualties for reasons of war and those who fell victim to illnesses. Different lists of the deaths during some months of 1869, 1870, and 1872 hardly mention death due to wounds received in battle compared with the battering received by different epidemics and illnesses.[27] This was something which those analyzing developments in the Cuban war theater and the behavior of Spanish colonial troops, both in this war and in that at the end of the century, became aware of very early on. During this period it was a commonplace among sources close to the military that "the most terrible enemy" was not the Cuban patriot given that:

If the rebels groups were the only plague on that land, the campaign would have been as difficult as a parade on a parade ground for the Spanish soldiers. But the endemic illnesses on the island—vomiting, fever, illnesses connected with adapting to the climate, the natural fatigue brought on by marching back and forth in marshy, inhospitable terrain were the main causes of death in our army.[28]

Our objective here is not to underestimate the role carried out by the independentist armies during the conflict, an idea that may be behind this

25. To these we must add one case of disappearance ("he got lost") on the battlefield.
26. Arrozarena, *El roble y la ceiba*, 183.
27. Agirreazkuenaga Zigorraga, "Las instituciones representativas vascas frente a la insurrección de Cuba en 1868," 325.
28. "La guerra en Cuba," *Blanco y Negro*, Madrid, November 2, 1895, quoted by Esteban Marfil, "Los médicos y la guerra de Cuba," 65.

type of justifications and that seems to be an attempt to justify patriotic pride; however, it must be admitted that Cuban natural surroundings and not having adapted to the climate, environmental conditions, and immunity factors with regards to local endemic illnesses, played a very considerable role in weakening the Spanish military force.

The importance of the illnesses can be seen in their impact on the changes in the deaths over the period recorded, which are shown in figure 6.2. As can be seen from it, there is no seasonal pattern to the deaths, but nor is there any connection with the periods of fighting and the battles in which the units fought and any increase in the number of casualties. It is the illnesses and, more specifically, the moments of greatest virulence of two particular ones—yellow fever and cholera—which mark the casualty rate and changes in deaths (figure 6.3). These two illnesses were responsible for 196 deaths (in other words, 41.18 percent of the total), and could be greater because some imprecise diagnostics may also have been given for casualties caused by these two illnesses.

Illnesses	Appropriate Diagnosis	No. casualties
Cholera		98
	"Diarrhoea" (unspecified)	8
Yellow fever		98
	"Fevers"	53
	"Temperatures"	38
	"Harmful fevers"	13
Dysentery		21
Tuberculosis		20
Typhus		10
	Typhoid fevers	4

Table 6.2. Diagnoses and casualties.

In general, the data provided by the diagnostics on the deaths of the volunteers in the Basque units are very similar to that obtained in other research into the deaths of Spanish soldiers in Cuba, in both the 1869–1879 and 1895–1898 wars. With regards to the latter, for instance, we have a sample provided by Pascual which summarizes the causes of casualties using the lists of deaths published throughout the war in the *Diario Oficial del Ministerio de Guerra* (Official Ministry of War newspaper). According to this sample, out of a total of 44,389 identified casualties, 4.57 percent happened on the battlefield (2,032), 2.41 percent in hospitals as the result of battle wounds (1,069) and the rest were the result of various illnesses (infectious or not) and accidents.[29]

Among the illnesses, yellow fever—also known as "black vomit," or just "vomit"[30] was undoubtedly the one which led to the greatest number of casualties. Between 1895 and 1898 the same data used by Pascual states that almost 37 percent of the soldiers in the Spanish army died as

---

29. Pascual, "La prensa de España, Cuba, Puerto Rico y Filipinas y las guerras de independencia."

30. Toledo Curbelo, "La otra historia de la fiebre amarilla en Cuba," 221.

a result of this illness.[31] For example, estimates published in the Spanish press during the first year of the war attributed more than 82 percent of the causalities until then to this reason.[32] Toledo Curbelo estimates that this illness was responsible for around twenty thousand casualties during the 1869–1879 war.[33]

> The significance of this endemic illness in Cuba at the time . . . was not just because of the clinical picture it created, with high temperatures, cephalea, jaundice, serious prostration and black, coagulated vomit—which is why it was also called "black vomit" or just "vomit," but also because there was no treatment to cure it, only alleviating measures were available, and so the mortality rate was high, between 15 and 60 percent depending on the virulence of the outbreak.[34]

With regards to cholera, the other great cause of death in the Basque units, its concentration in a single period leads us to examine the effects of the known pandemics of this illness in Cuba. While cholera had been known in previous periods, it was not until the start of the nineteenth century that it became a virulently contagious disease, spreading in a series of large-scale pandemic outbreaks in different parts of the world, its spread being made easier by more efficient and frequent uses of means of transport.[35] In 1863 and 1875 one of these pandemics reached Cuba and other countries in the Americas;[36] as far as the Basque units were concerned, the epidemic hit hardest in the first half of 1870, later becoming less lethal and almost disappearing. Although the theories of the day had not yet identified the origin and transmission of the disease—which was still believed to appear and spread due to miasmal and telluric causes—measures of hygiene were known to prevent contagion,[37] which makes it very clear that the barracks and other installations in which the colonial army was billeted in the hurry of the first year of the war of independence had shortcomings in this respect.

Epilogue

The Basque units—beyond their significance in the political debates between the Basque provinces and the central government, or their involve-

---

31. Pascual, "La prensa de España, Cuba, Puerto Rico y Filipinas y las guerras de independencia." A total of 16,328 casualties.

32. *La Crónica Meridional*, February 29, 1896, quoted by Rozalén Fuentes and Úbeda Vilches, "Nuestros soldados fallecidos y repatriados," 294.

33. Toledo Curbelo, "La otra historia de la fiebre amarilla en Cuba," 225.

34. Esteban Marfil, "Los médicos y la guerra de Cuba," 66.

35. Batlle Almodóvar and Dickinson Meneses, "Notas para una historia del cólera en Cuba durante los siglos xix, xx y xxi," 3-4.

36. Pérez Ortiz y Madrigal Lomba, "El cólera en Cuba."

37. Carlos J. Finlay, the first person to identify the mosquito *Aedes Aegyptis* as the vector of transmission for yellow fever also made some observations about cholera. Batlle Almodóvar and Dickinson Meneses, "Notas para una historia del cólera en Cuba durante los siglos xix, xx y xxi," 5.

ment in the question of the relationship between the old fueros and the new, liberal state, or even in their links with questions of Spanish nationalism and patriotism and how wide-spread they were in the provinces—also had a side connected with the volunteers' experiences, expectations of a short war that quickly became a difficult long one attrition in a hostile natural and unyielding human environment. Many of the volunteers, seduced by the incentive bonus offered by the contracts ended up not finding an easy way to build an economic foundation for a better life in the future but, rather, a premature end to their days. The documents with the reports about closing the deceased volunteers' accounts provide a picture of the gap which always exists in conflicts between the rearguard and the people who suffer at the front.

Bibliography

Agirreazkuenaga Zigorraga, Joseba. "Los vascos y la insurrección de Cuba en 1868." *Historia Contemporánea* 2 (1989): 139–64.

———, ed. *La articulación político-institucional de Vasconia: Actas de las Conferencias firmadas por los representantes de Álava, Bizkaia, Gipuzkoa y eventualmente de Navarra (1775–1936).* 2 volumes. Bilbao, Diputación Foral de Bizkaia, 1995.

———. "Las instituciones representativas vascas frente a la insurrección de Cuba en 1868: La formación del 'Tercio de voluntarios vascongados' o 'Legión vasca' por las Diputaciones forales de Álava, Bizkaia y Gipuzkoa." In *Patria y Libertad: Los vascos y las guerras de independencia de Cuba (1868–1898),* coordinated by Alexander Ugalde Zubiri, 285–326. Tafalla: Txalaparta, 2012.

Álbum Vascongado. Relación de los festejos públicos hechos por la Ciudad de Havana en los días 2, 3 y 4 de Junio de 1869 con ocasión de llegar a ella los tercios voluntarios enviados a combatir la insurrección de la isla por las M.N. y M.L. provincias de Álava, Guipúzcoa y Vizcaya. Havana: Imprenta de J.M. Eleizegui, no date.

Álvarez Gila, Óscar and José María Tápiz Fernández. "La formación de los Tercios Vascongados para la Guerra Grande de Cuba (1869)." In *Cuba y Puerto Rico en torno al 98,* coordinated by Cecilia Parcero Torre and María Emelina Martín Acosta, 83–93. Valladolid: Universidad de Valladolid, 1998.

———. "Propaganda y actitudes ante la independencia cubana: los Tercios Vascongados (1869)." In *De súbditos del rey a ciudadanos de la nación,* 8–9. Castelló: Centro de Investigaciones de Latin America—Universitat Jaume I, 2000.

Amores Carredano, Juan Bosco. *Cuba y España, 1868–1898: El final de un sueño.* Iruñea-Pamplona: Eunsa, 1998.

———. "La Iglesia en Cuba al final del período colonial." *Anuario de Historia de la Iglesia* 67 (1998): 67–83.

————. "Presencia de los navarros en Cuba al final del período colonial." In *Las migraciones vascas en perspectiva histórica (siglos xvi–xx)*, edited by Óscar Álvarez Gila and Alberto Angulo Morales, 325–38. Bilbao: University of the Basque Country, 2002.

Apaolaza Ávila, Urko. "Un análisis sobre la historiografía en torno al alavés Julián de Zulueta y Amondo." *Sancho el Sabio* 18 (2003): 235–58.

Arrozarena, Cecilia. *El roble y la ceiba: Historia de los vascos en Cuba.* Tafalla: Txalaparta, 2003.

Barcia Zequeira, María del Carmen. *Élites y grupos de presión: Cuba, 1868–1898.* Havana: Ed. de Ciencias Sociales, 2003.

Batlle Almodóvar, María del Carmen, and Félix Orlando Dickinson Meneses. "Notas para una historia del cólera en Cuba durante los siglos xix, xx y xxi." *Revista Anales de la Academia de Ciencias de Cuba* 4, no.1 (2014): www.revistaccuba.cu/index.php/acc/article/viewFile/195/153

Cajal Valero, Arturo. "Discrepancias entre las tres 'Provincias Hermanas': El reclutamiento de los Tercios Vascongados para la Guerra de África (1859–1860)." *Sancho el Sabio* 35 (2012): 121–40.

Cayuela Fernández, José G. "Comportamientos inversos de la élite económica antillana en Europa: la progresión patrimonial de don Pedro Julián de Zulueta, 1834–1874." *Estudios de Historia Social* 44–47 (1988): 8–9.

Echegaray, Carmelo. *Compendio de las instituciones forales de Guipúzcoa.* Donostia-San Sebastián: Imprenta de la Diputación, 1924.

Esteban Marfil, B. de. "Los médicos y la guerra de Cuba (1895–1898)." *Seminario Médico* 53 (2001): 48–67.

Irigoyen Artetxe, Alberto. *La Asociación Vasco-Navarra de Beneficencia de Havana y otras entidades vasco-cubanas.* Vitoria-Gasteiz, Eusko Jaurlaritza, 2014.

Maluquer De Motes, Jordi. *Nación e inmigración: Los españoles en Cuba (siglos xix y xx).* Gijón: Ed. Júcar, 1992.

Marrero Cruz, Eduardo. *Julián de Zulueta y Amondo: Promotor del capitalismo en Cuba.* Havana: Ed. Unión, 2006.

Martínez-Antonio, Francisco Javier. "Lost in Colonialism: La sanidad española en Cuba antes y después de la Guerra de los Diez Años." *Scripta Nova: Revista Electrónica de Geografía y Ciencias Sociales* 16, no. 418 (2012): www.ub.es/ geocrit/sn/sn-418/sn-418-20.htm.

Pascual, Pedro. "La prensa de España, Cuba, Puerto Rico y Filipinas y las guerras de independencia (1868–1898)." Paper presented to the VI *Congreso de Latinoamericanistas Españoles*, Madrid 1997, at http:// pendientedemigracion.ucm.es/info/cecal/encuentr/areas/historia/3h/ prescuba.htm.

Pérez Ortiz, Letier and Ramón Madrigal Lomba. "El cólera en Cuba: Apuntes históricos." *Revista Médica Electrónica* 3 no. 7 (no date): http://scielo.sld.cu/scielo.php?pid=S1684-18242010000700002&script=sci_arttext.

Ramos Martínez, Jon Ander. "Manuel Calvo y Aguirre, una eminencia en la sombra." *Guregandik* 4 (2008): 210–27.

———. "Los immigrantes en Cuba, de región a nación (1880–1902)." In *200 años de Iberoamérica (1810–2010)*, edited by Eduardo Rey Tristán and Patricia Calvo González, 1041–50. Santiago de Compostela: USC, 2010.

———. "De toros y romerías: Fiesta e identidad: la Asociación Vasco Navarra de Beneficencia y las fiestas en honor de la Virgen de Begoña en Havana (1883)." *Sancho el Sabio* 36 (2013): 29–46.

Rozalén Fuentes, Celestina and Rosa María Úbeda Vilches. "Nuestros soldados fallecidos y repatriados (1895–1898)." In *La crisis de fin de siglo en la provincia de Almería: El desastre del 98*, 293–300. Almería: Instituto de Estudios Almerienses, 2004.

Toledo Curbelo, Gabriel José. "La otra historia de la fiebre amarilla en Cuba, 1492–1908." *Revista Cubana de Higiene y Epidemiología* 38, no. 3 (2000): 220–27.

Ugalde Zubiri, Alexander. "Los vascos ante las guerras de independencia de Cuba." *Calibán: Revista Cubana de Pensamiento e Historia* 10 (2011): www.revistacaliban.cu/articulo.php?numero=10&article_id=107.

7

The Cuban War (1895–1898) in Gipuzkoa: A Critical Reading of Regional Government Acts

Haizpea Abrisketa

The Cuban War of Independence (1895–1898) had an unquestionable impact on Basque society. Around 700 Gipuzkoans, a similar number of Bizkaians, 1,200 Navarrese, and 400 Arabans were buried in Cuba.[1] In 1897, these four Basque provinces had a total population of 885,118.[2] With fewer than a million people, the death of three thousand young people abroad is an unusually high statistic. It is hard to imagine that there would not have been unease over this in Basque society.

It is not known how many Basque soldiers went nor how many came back and in what state. Of the 220,285[3] soldiers from the Spanish state who left,[4] 53,000 died in Cuba,[5] one in every five soldiers.

In order to find out about the repercussion of the Cuban War of Independence in Basque society we will examine references to the war from the minutes of the Gipuzkoa regional government between 1895 and 1903, compare them and complement them with the press from those years. In this way we hope to uncover certain information and have a slightly better

1. In 1999 General Raúl Izquierdo Canosa carried out a census of all the Spanish soldiers buried in the provinces of Cuba in *Viaje sin regreso*, 347. The War Ministry also published the official list of casualties in the *Official Bulletin*; it is from there that we have taken data about the Basque provinces. We are merging, comparing, and correcting both sources. Up to now we have counted around three thousand Basque soldiers. This is still a provisional total.
2. Basque Country database: www.datutalaia.net. Aztiker, Gaindegia, KAM.
3. According to Manuel Moreno Fraginals's data, it was the largest army to be transported by sea before World War II.
4. Moreno Fraginals and Moreno Masó, "La última migración armada."
5. *Diario Oficial del Ministerio de la Guerra*, Biblioteca del Senado, Madrid. *Signature RA91.* We have counted all the casualties published there.

understanding of society's reaction to the war.

We will analyze the Gipuzkoan regional government's relationship with the government of Spain, on the one hand, and with the citizenry, on the other, and the limitations and contradictions it was faced with in order to understand what attitude to the war in Basque society.

The Regional Government's Relationship with Central Power

At the start of the Cuban war, the government, through the Ministry of War, organized the recruitment of soldiers and their transport to Cuba and back and used local authority to administer economic aid and prepare to defend the territory. This, basically, was what the Gipuzkoa regional government did during the war. The relationship between the Spanish and Gipuzkoan administrations was based on collaboration and communication through the use of protocols. Formal communication was restricted to sending notes of mutual thanks, congratulating Spanish generals on their deeds, underlining the Gipuzkoans' patriotism, and sending telegrams of condolence when there were casualties.

The Government's Subordination and Lack of Confidence

The first mention of troops going to the war is in the regional government's minutes from April 4, 1895.[6] There is a request for the minutes to mention thanks sent by the national government to the regional government for the help it had given. But the government does not always take the regional government into account when providing news of its initiatives. The first expedition left Donostia-San Sebastián on March 6, 1895, and nobody from the regional government went to bid it farewell. The members of the Gipuzkoan parliament explain in the influential republican newspaper *La Voz de Guipúzcoa* that because they were unaware of the scheduled departure they had not gone to bid the soldiers farewell.[7]

On March 7 the arrest of four arms manufacturers from well-known families in Eibar caused great concern in the town.[8] They were accused of selling arms to the rebels and ran the risk of being executed at any moment. Furthermore, one of them was a son of Juan José Larrañaga, a former

---

6. Gipuzkoa, Diputación Provincial, "Registro de las sesiones celebradas por la Diputación Provincial de Gipuzkoa durante el segundo período semestral del año económico de 1894 a 1895," 43.

7. "It is clear, but not surprising, that people were not as excited as when Valencia marched to Malaga to go to Melilla a little over a year ago. Yesterday the departure of our soldiers was unknown. Some people found out about it thanks to the echo of the happy music. The weather, too, was frightful." "Crónica del día/Valencia y Sicilia (Instantánea)," *La Voz de Guipúzcoa*, March 6, 1895.

8. In the newspaper *La Voz de Guipúzcoa* (http://liburutegidigitala.donostiakultura.com) there is information about this almost every day.

mayor of the town.[9] On March 9, according to *La Voz de Guipúzcoa*, the governor of Gipuzkoa announced that he would only deal with the Spanish government about this subject, leaving the regional government out of the loop, and the regional government answered that it knew nothing about it.[10] So the regional government asked the Asociación Vasco-Navarra de Beneficencia—a mutual assistance association for Basques in Cuba—for information. What we see here is a certain lack of trust between the two administrations when it came to sharing information.

The Regional Government's Patriotism and Commitment

In its plenary session held on April 25, 1896, the only decision that the council took about Cuba was to send thanks to the Spanish military governor of the island for the help he was giving Gipuzkoans there. At the start of the war, the regional government expressed its patriotism time and again, underlining the Gipuzkoans' loyalty. During the plenary session on April 3, 1897—with the situation in Cuba deteriorating and more than two hundred Gipuzkoans dead—the regional government agreed to send a telegram of congratulation to General Polavieja, the Spanish army general in the Philippines.[11]

The regional government demonstrated continual collaboration and commitment. It made the decision to defend the Cuban coast, taking the initiative to raise funds, showing its patriotic determination, and not questioning any of the subscriptions organized by the Spanish government.[12]

During the plenary session of April 2, 1898, the province of Gipuzkoa took the initiative to collaborate actively in the war and suggested raising funds for defense.[13] During the plenary session of April 29, 1898, the regional government replied to the national government's request for financial assistance. It was unanimously decided to make the contribution urgently. The meeting also became an opportunity for the Gipuzkoan members of the Spanish parliament to show their loyalty and support for central authority.

> Everybody will realize what a sacrifice this agreement means for Gipuzkoa where—due to its limited area and the hard, unyielding nature of its land—children are fed thanks to continual, persistent and truly huge effort. But neither this truly important consideration,

---

9. Gipuzkoa, Diputación Provincial, "Registro de las sesiones celebradas por la Diputación Provincial de Gipuzkoa durante el segundo período semestral del año económico de 1894 a 1895," 53–54.

10. *La Voz de Guipúzcoa*, March 9, 1895.

11. Gipuzkoa, Diputación Provincial, "Registro de las sesiones celebradas por la Diputación Provincial de Gipuzkoa durante el segundo período semestral del año económico de 1896 a 1897," 28–31.

12. The government organized subscriptions through the regional governments to raise money for the war. It was the way of raising money from the people.

13. In 1898, due to the threat of intervention by the United States, the regional government answered the government's request to raise funds without making any objections.

nor the challenging days which are to come, have been enough to change the Gipuzkoa regional government's traditions, always believing itself to be noble and having feelings of unbreakable loyalty to Mother Spain . . . Gipuzkoa has always been the supporter of national honor and interests . . . Since then living conditions in this country have changed, and we lament the loss of the civil institutions which, in other times, brought our prosperity; but what has not changed, and never will, because it is passed on from generation to generation in blood, is the love of Spain which we wear as a badge and always will in days of plenty and times of hardship . . . The regional government passed it [the motion] unanimously.[14]

But the problem of the fueros is latent in the minutes and, as a whole, the regional government is in favor of them being brought back into effect. The Basque liberals supported the fueros and did not accept the measures that Madrid had taken against them after the Carlist War.[15]

Contradictions

When the war was lost, the regional government only sent a telegram expressing its sorrow on July 6, 1898. However, the Gipuzkoan council's unease was apparent. Behind the protocol gesture in reaction to Spain's disaster, the regional government seems to be more worried about its own people. This brings into question the admiration that it had expressed for the national government until then. According to our data, no Gipuzkoans died in the sea battle at Santiago de Cuba on that date.[16]

> Mr. President . . . thinks it best to send His Majesty's Government a telegram expressing the Gipuzkoans' sharing of the great sorrow which Spain is suffering from . . . Mr. Pavía . . . , said that among the brave sailors who have been victims of the catastrophe, there are undoubtedly many sons of the most noble land of Gipuzkoa . . . which is why we request that . . . a list of the casualties, wounded and prisoners from this province during the catastrophe be drawn up.[17]

By that time Gipuzkoa had lost almost six hundred soldiers in Cuba. The regional government's desire to collaborate and its patriotism were not the same at the end of the war as at the beginning. Due to the serious-

---

14. Gipuzkoa, Diputación Provincial, "Registro de las sesiones celebradas por la Excma. Diputación Provincial de Gipuzkoa durante el segundo período semestral del año económico de 1897 a 1898," 173–77.

15. In 1877 the central government had dismantled the regional parliaments and abolished the fueros. Gipuzkoa had lost its foral rights and become a provincial administration like any other in Spain.

16. Among the casualties published in the *Diario Oficial del Ministerio de la Guerra* and those recorded by General Izquierdo Canosa, we have not come across any Gipuzkoans who died in the summer of 1898 at Santiago de Cuba.

17. Gipuzkoa, Diputación Provincial, "Registro de las sesiones celebradas por la Excma. Diputación Provincial de Gipuzkoa durante el segundo período semestral del año económico de 1897 a 1898," 265–66.

ness of the situation and the citizens' obvious unease, the regional government's difficulties became more apparent.

The support for central war policy among the citizenry dwindled and the regional government—caught between the two—found it difficult not to contradict itself. Five years after the conclusion of the war regional governments were asked again for money to build a monument in the Retiro Park in Madrid. This time, however, it was decided to exhaust bureaucratic procedures in order to delay[18] when, earlier, economic support had been given unquestioningly and quickly. It is apparent that the regional government could not afford to spend more money on the war when its citizens had not yet received the compensation to which they were entitled.

No Criticisms of the Government's Policy

However, the regional government made no reference to the national government's policies. There is a great contrast between the regional government's attitude and what is published in the press. In *La Voz de Guipúzcoa,* March 7, 1895, the Spanish government is sharply attacked:

> The reasons behind these problems and the protocols they are based on are apparent. The leaders—splendidly paid and rewarded in Zanjón—have no real reason not to do what they have done again, and people who aspire to lead—who are to be found in each new generation—have no real reason not to follow the example of people who have gone before them . . .
>
> The Minister for War has said that all the Spanish infantry will go to Cuba if necessary . . .
>
> But is Cuba burning from one end to another? . . .
>
> If that is not the case, if it is just (as can be gleaned from the Minister of War's own speech) a matter of two or three rebels leaders wandering around at the head of two or three bands, let us take care of our wretched soldiers and not send them to die on hospital beds without having even seen the bandits from afar.
>
> Fortunately, we are not the only people who think this way. Many very important newspapers make similar observations and Mr. Cánovas still believes that sending so many thousands of soldiers to Cuba is a mistake.[19]

As the war continued, more and more recruits were sent to the front; the first patients reached the hospital at Santander in February 1896. During the same period—after the failure of Martínez Campos's policies—Valeriano Weyler was named commander in chief in Cuba in order to strengthen the war effort. Meanwhile, *La Voz de Guipúzcoa* continued to publish news and comments:

---

18. Gipuzkoa, Diputación Provincial, "Registro de las sesiones celebradas por la Excma. Diputación Provincial de Gipuzkoa durante el primer período semestral del año 1903, 79–80.
19. "Crónica del día," *La Voz de Guipúzcoa,* March 7, 1895.

> if the war goes on, as it threatens to, for a couple of years, where will
> the Government find economic resources? . . . If Cuba cannot handle
> the bills, will the Peninsula have to? . . . asking for eighty or ninety
> thousand men for active service, doubling the usual contingent, forc-
> ing a multitude of families to make enormous sacrifices with their
> sons and removing strength from national work . . . Can proceedings
> like this become the norm? Can this be done for two or three more
> years? Where will it end?[20]

However, the regional government's minutes make no mention of this
matter.

On the one hand, there was superficial communication and a certain
lack of trust; on the other, the need to express the Gipuzkoans' loyalty
and will to the Spanish authorities. Gipuzkoa regional government had
to manage conflicts in the short and long term, for instance the matter of
the fueros. Gipuzkoan regional government, along with the other Basque
regional ones, was trying to have the law of 1876—which had removed
their fueros—repealed. Criticizing the war in Cuba and creating difficulties would not help their campaign to have the Basque fueros restored. By
showing loyalty to Spain, Gipuzkoa and its sister provinces felt they had
greater legitimacy to demand what they were owed—their fueros.

The Regional Government and the Gipuzkoans

> While it is the duty of all Spaniards to give support, to the extent
> they are able, in achieving the objective of the Government of the
> Nation, which is to keep that colony for the Motherland, it is also
> the province's duty to give support to the families of those serving
> who, having left their homes, children and lands, have lost their lives
> carrying out their most sacred obligations. Session of the February
> 21, 1896.[21]

The above text tells us of the Gipuzkoan regional government's dual commitment: keeping up a good relationship with the national government
and answering the Gipuzkoans' needs, which are pressing as a consequence
of the war. It had to face this dichotomy continually.

"To the Extent They Are Able To . . ."

The soldiers were the regional government's main worry in connection
with Cuba, although their first initiative with regards to the Gipuzkoan
soldiers was merely symbolic. In order to emphasize that the fallen Gipuzkoans were not forgotten, in the meeting held on November 18, 1896, it
was suggested that the names of the casualties be written on a board in the

---

20. "¡A Cuba!" *La Voz de Guipúzcoa.* April 4, 1895.
21. Gipuzkoa, Diputación Provincial, "Registro de las sesiones celebradas por la Diputación
Provincial de Gipuzkoa durante el primer período semestral del año económico de 1895 a
1896," 99–102.

main meeting room. France was to do the same with its own after World War I.

By this time some Gipuzkoans had already come back from the front in critical condition and around 170 had died. There was an attempt to justify the institution's limitations in these minutes. People who stay at home are obliged to help the soldiers, but always "to the extent that their strength permits them to."[22] They repeat what had been said in the meeting on February 21, 1896: "to the extent they are able to." The repetition of this qualification shows that the regional government had very limited resources. One of the members of parliaments' objectives is to not worsen the conflicts they have with the Spanish government, in particular with reference to restoring the fueros, while, at the same time, explaining their limited capacities to the people of Gipuzkoa.

Even so, the regional government did all it could to ensure young people not go to the war or to limit the number that did. It made a special effort to protect those who had the legal option not to go. It did what it could to see that the law of April 2, 1895, is respected.[23] This was decided in the meeting held on April 18, 1896:

> Mr. Machinbarrena asked to speak and said that he was aware that Mr. Vice Chairman of the province's civil commission had received the Royal Decree issued in keeping with the clauses of the law passed on April 2, 1895, about Basque volunteers being exempt from military service,[24] that Royal Decree recognizing the mentioned exemption for the sons of volunteers whose names are on the list published in the *Gaceta de Madrid,* whose exact copy exists thanks to the data held in the regional government's offices, and, with regards to Gipuzkoa, it was appropriate, in his opinion, to validate them because, as has been observed, there are mistakes in the Bulletin which must be corrected because the provincial commission must give certificates granting this exemption. And, for this reason, suggested a scrupulous examination of the lists, a list of the mistakes in them, which must be sent requesting the scrupulous attention of Mr. Home Secretary.[25]

In order to request the exemption permitted by this law, the list of Basques who had fought on the liberal side published in *La Gaceta de Madrid* on March 17, 1896, had to be used. This was one year after the law had been passed. There is no doubt, seeing how much attention the re-

---

22. Gipuzkoa, Diputación Provincial, "Registro de las sesiones celebradas por la Diputación Provincial de Gipuzkoa durante el primer período semestral del año económico de 1896 a 1897," 142–43.

23. *La Gazeta de Madrid* (published April 3, 1895). This law—based on the abolition of the fueros in 1876—made it possible for those who had fought for "the legitimate king" and their children to be exempt from military service.

24. *Basque volunteer* means those who fought against the Carlists in the previous Carlist War.

25. Gipuzkoa, Diputación Provincial, "Registro de las sesiones celebradas por la Diputación Provincial de Gipuzkoa durante el segundo período semestral del año económico de 1895 a 1896," 15–16.

gional government paid to it, that this matter had led to many complaints. The repeated use of the word "scrupulous" is striking.

If the regional government could not stop the young men from going, it could take steps to reduce their number. As mentioned in the plenary session held on January 7, 1898, administrative problems had led to two sons from some families being sent to war; the regional government took steps to prevent that from happening *to the extent it was able.*

These measures taken by the regional government seem anecdotal taking into account the scale of the problem, but they also demonstrate the regional government's frustration.

In Favor of the Gipuzkoan Soldiers

The regional government's main responsibilities with regards to the war effort was to organize the soldiers' reception in Cuba and arrange for economic support. Soldiers coming back from Cuba were in a difficult situation. Most returned with disabilities or suffering from the consequences of some epidemic, so they had to spend time in hospitals near the ports where they landed. For Gipuzkoa, that was Santander. However, the Spanish government's lack of support and bureaucractic impediments between provinces prevented soldiers from being properly received. In November 1895, it was necessary to build a hospital in Santander to accept patients arriving from Cuba, and the Santander regional government asked for economic support.[26] It took two years—to the soldiers' detriment—to solve this problem. By the meeting held on April 2, 1897, the issue had not been resolved as yet. At the plenary session this irresponsibility was blamed on bureaucracy.[27]

In August, 1898, when the four-year war ended the four Basque provinces at last reached an agreement about how to receive the returning soldiers.[28]

Even so, the regional government's only power was to administer economic support. Unfortunately, this power was very limited. There was little money and, as we will see below, it was very badly managed.

In February 1896, the regional government presented a new program for support and subsidies.[29] Funds were raised to help the families of sol-

26. Gipuzkoa, Diputación Provincial, "Registro de las sesiones celebradas por la Diputación Provincial de Gipuzkoa durante el primer período semestral del año económico de 1895 a 1896," 78.

27. Gipuzkoa, Diputación Provincial, "Registro de las sesiones celebradas por la Diputación Provincial de Gipuzkoa durante el segundo período semestral del año económico de 1896 a 1897," 15–16.

28. Gipuzkoa, Diputación Provincial, "Registro de las sesiones celebradas por la Excma. Diputación Provincial de Gipuzkoa durante el segundo período semestral del año económico de 1897 a 1898," 302.

29. Gipuzkoa, Diputación Provincial, "Registro de las sesiones celebradas por la Diputación Provincial de Gipuzkoa durante el primer período semestral del año económico de 1895 a 1896," 99–102.

diers who had died in Cuba: as the minutes state, there were no previous provisions for these cases. There were a considerable number of young men who did not come back and this had direct economic consequences for their families. The regional government had to deal with this.

Difficulties

People had great difficulties receiving their pensions. At the plenary session held on November 6, 1897, the case of Agustín Elorza, who had been denied his pension for more than two years, was mentioned.[30]

Citizens did not know that they had the right to receive a pension from the regional government. On November 8, 1897, Mr. Rafael Barnabé Bats from Deba made a formal request to the council asking for citizens to be informed in the Official Bulletin that they had the right to receive these pensions.[31] Knowing that the economic support project had been agreed at the meeting on February 21, 1896, it is surprising that Mr. Bats should make such a request a year later and not even settle the matter once and for all until the meeting of November 10, 1898! Former liberal member of parliament Barnabé Bats's[32] insistence was not a matter of chance but, rather, an example of the great difficulties that people had in obtaining this support. This must have led to penury and anger among the population.

There were even problems with municipal councils: at Bergara, there was a complaint because the economic support had not been given out. Furthermore, we know that this was not the first time. The cases of Bergara residents Santiago Gabilondo and Matías Urcelay were examined at the regional government meeting on November 8, 1898, the war having ended the prior August.

At the meeting the negligence of the Bergara town council was criticized. Two members of parliament opened the debate. Apparently, Bergara was not conforming to the regional government's recommendations, while other municipal authorities had helped soldiers.[33]

However, the reports examined in the Gipuzkoa General Archive about soldiers from Bergara tell a different story.[34] Official notification of the death of reservist Cecilio Ibarzabal reached the Bergara town council

---

30. Gipuzkoa, Diputación Provincial, "Registro de las sesiones celebradas por la Diputación Provincial de Gipuzkoa durante el primer período semestral del año económico de 1897 a 1898," 35.

31. Ibid., 42–43.

32. Barnabé Bats became famous when he said that the conservative party had been responsible for abolishing the fueros. The liberal and conservative parties allied against Carlism and it was easy to identify defending the fueros with Carlism.

33. Gipuzkoa, Diputación Provincial, "Registro de las sesiones celebradas por la Excma. Diputación Provincial de Gipuzkoa durante el primer período semestral del año económico de 1898 a 1899," 47–49.

34. *Vergara Expediente del reservista Cecilio Ibarzabal. (Expedentes relativos al cobro de haveres de soldados fullecidos en UHramar. 1989–192") Cecilio Ibarzabal* ("Reports about payments to soldiers deceased abroad. 1898–1902"). AGG-GAO JDIT1995a.

five months after his death (he died on September 2, 1896, but notification from the ministry of war did not arrive until February 4, 1897). On January 16, 1897, not having received any official identification, the town council asked the regional government if he could continue to receive his pension. Four days later, the regional government's mixed commission replied as follows: "may Josefa Aguirrebeña y Aldazabal, the lad's mother, continue to receive the pension while we confirm officially that reservist Cecilio Ibarzabal has died." One year later—during which time the town council had received notification from Madrid—the regional government having said that it had received no information about the matter, stopped payment of the pension on January 1, 1898, and, on February 7, asked the town council about it. The Bergara town council replied three days later: "it is my honor to inform you that this town council told you on February 9, 1897: 'This town council has received a certificate issued on the 4th of this month . . . stating that soldier . . . Cecilio Ibarzabal y Aguirrebeña died on September 2 (1896) at Sagua (Santa Clara) of yellow fever.'" The Bergara town council had informed the regional government at the time, but the latter had not received the information.

In fact, examining the documents from Bergara we can see that negligence was not one-directional and that pension management was affected by multiple administrative problems. Even so, it is striking that, without receiving any official communication, the mother of Cecilio Ibarzabal received a pension from the regional government for fifteen months, from September 1896 to January 1898. So the problem was more complicated than might first appear.

The regional government took very few initiatives for the province. Its reaction to the massacre taking place was to manage economic support and justify the war in some way. This situation demonstrated this administrative organization's incapacity and limitations.

The Cuban Question, the Fueros, and a Basque Cultural Renaissance

In the Basque Country at this time there was a resurgence of Basque culture. As part of this, the floral games which Antoine D'Abbadie had created at Urruña (Iparralde—the north Basque Country on the French side of the frontier) some years earlier began to be held in the south of the country (Hegoalde) as well. With the patronage of the members of parliament in Gipuzkoa, the Council of Basque Floral Games was founded and, in 1896, the Basque festivities or floral games were organized in Arrasate.[35] The council's chair was Alfredo Laffitte, a member of the Gipuzkoan par-

---

35. At the floral games, or Basque festivities, there was a livestock competition and a literary competition in Basque. The literary competition was for written prose and poetry and had to cover subjects chosen by the council. First they were handwritten, then presented for the competition and, finally, the winning texts were printed and published.

liament at the time. In the plenary session held on April 21, 1896, these games were mentioned, praised and supported.[36]

One of the subjects chosen for its poetry competition was the war in Cuba. Pedro María Otaño and José Artola won and their verses were published in the commemorative book *Fiestas Vascas en Mondragón 1896*. At least nine poems about the war in Cuba were presented. They were hand-written and only the winners' ones were printed. The first prize was won by Pedro Mari Otaño with his verses titled *Kubako gure anayai* (To our Cuban brothers).[37]

The objective behind the floral games was the renaissance of Basque culture and writing. The illustrious people who took part in these festivities were in favor of the fueros and so used the former to praise the latter. With regards to the war in Cuba, what they wanted at that time was to underscore the importance of the soldiers' actions, praise them to the glory of Spain, and emphasize the Basques' loyalty to Spain.

The following year, when the floral games were held at Oiartzun and carried the name Nekazaritza, ganaduen billaldiya eta euskal-festak Oyartzun-en, 1897 (Farming and Livestock Parade and Basque Festivities, 1897), Cuba was not one of the subjects for the poems, but peace was. This is significant because at that moment the war in Cuba had become more difficult than expected. In political terms, the strong measures taken by Weyler were not giving the expected results and in Madrid there was increasing opposition to the way the war was being conducted. It was expensive in economic and human terms. There were thousands of deaths and the threat of an attack from the United States was ever closer. The provincial government's minutes did not mention these festivities.

Pepe Artola won the poetry competition about the subject of peace. The poems were published in the magazine *Euskal-erria: Revista Bascongada*.[38] He wrote eight poems praising peace and comparing it with the harm brought about by war. In the second poem he writes about the pain of having to fight abroad: "How much men suffer/when there's a war/ when they have to leave/their beloved home and country." There can be no doubt that Artola was thinking about the soldiers going to Cuba.

In 1898 the Basque festivities were held at Zestoa and, although Cuba was not mentioned in the poems, it was in everybody's mind: the festivities were almost cancelled because of the war. In April, in response to some illustrious people in the town, it was decided to cancel them. But the subject was discussed again on July 1 and finally it was agreed to hold the livestock

---

36. Gipuzkoa, Diputación Provincial, "Registro de las sesiones celebradas por la Diputación Provincial de Gipuzkoa durante el primer período semestral del año económico de 1896 a 1897," 27–28.

37. See www.armiarma.com.

38. Artola, "Bedeikatua izan dadilla beti ta beti pakea." His poems were reprinted in the magazine *Euskal-erria* during World War I in Artola, "Bedeikatua izan dadilla beti ta beti pake."

competition and to celebrate mass.[39] During the plenary session of August 24 it was also decided to hold the floral games. This time the matter was not discussed, so an agreement had been reached previously.

> The request from Benito González and others—all residents in Zestoa—that a literary-musical competition be held was read . . . It was agreed to grant the request . . . to hold the agriculture and livestock competition and hold a religious ceremony . . . but not the banquet, which is cancelled this year.[40]

In the monograph *Fiestas Vascas en Zestoa* written by Luzia Alberro mentions that Antonio Arzak[41] had given a conference titled: "*Recuerdos y Esperanzas (Oroitz eta Esperantzak* [Memories and Hope]).[42] When it was published in the magazine *Euskal-erria*, it is stated in a footnote that it had been read during the official lunch organized by the town council on August 18.[43] We have found no other reference to this lunch, but it does seem that in the end—and contrary to what is written in the provincial government's minutes—there was lunch and a festive atmosphere at Zestoa.

The author analyzes this matter with precision. The initial decision to cancel the festivities at Zestoa had led to protests and, consequently, in the end both the fair and the games were held. As Alberro demonstrates, Arzak's conference shows the atmosphere at the time and feelings about the war in Cuba.

> Please forgive me, ladies and gentlemen, if my last words are sad: they are for the young men we have in mind and have lost in far-off lands. Oh, the mothers and wives of the fields whose tears have doubtless increased the water level of the rivers between those mountains; their crying has joined with the birdsong in the trees in whose shade lambs used to play, but who were later taken to the slaughterhouse! Poor boys! And the ones who come back . . . I don't want to say the state they're in. The most excellent provincial government succours their unfortunate families, but that is not enough: mothers who have lost their sons, houses which have had their strength removed . . . here we see the people who were those young men's friends, their neighbours, who worked in these fields to build their houses, because mutual help and above all help for those who need it is, and will always be, the finest of all Basque customs.
>
> Weapons have shone like shafts of sunlight in the hands of our young men for a long time now, but there would be no graves with

---

39. Gipuzkoa, Diputación Provincial, "Registro de las sesiones celebradas por la Excma. Diputación Provincial de Gipuzkoa durante el segundo período semestral del año económico de 1897 a 1898," 236–40.
40. Ibid., 309–10.
41. Antonio Arzak, director of the magazine *Euskal-erria* (1884–1904), writer, and musician was involved with Basque culture. He was the secretary of the Floral Games Council. The chair was Alfredo Lafiotte. Both were members of the Gipuzkoan provincial government.
42. Alberro Goikoetxea, *Fiestas Vascas en Zestoa*, 35–37.
43. Arzak, "Oroitz eta Esperantzak."

their names on them if shovels and forks not had shone! Today this is what I ask Our Lord for so that our land can be happy.[44]

And the Fueros

Vindications of the fueros appear time and again. Gipuzkoa, Bizkaia, Araba, and Navarra refer to each other as "sister provinces" and petition the Spanish government together for restoration of their fueros. The minutes for the meeting of the Gipuzkoan council on November 22, 1898, after discussing war issues, turns to the fueros. The discussion and formal statement of the council's position sum up the wishes of the Gipuzkoans clearly:

> we demand from the public authorities recognition for the administrative autonomy of the Basque Provinces—in other words, its provincial governments and municipal authorities—as a complement to their economic autonomy, re-establishing the organisms of the foral regime with only the modifications required by the country's current needs and present circumstances.
>
> 2nd. For greater solemnity and strength for the previous agreement, we request that the sister regional governments be linked together, inviting them to share management of the common good in order to achieve the aspirations mentioned and which are the ideal for all good Basques.
>
> [...]
>
> It being Mr. Echeverria's turn to speak . . . he returns to a subject on which Gipuzkoa regional government has previously expressed its unanimous opinion and has, on several occasions, requested the return to foral government.
>
> The proposition presented is unanimously accepted for consideration.[45]

So, along with requesting the return of the fueros, Basque literature and culture underwent a renaissance during this decade. Basque nationalism, too, took its first steps into a stormy future.

Conclusions

The war in Cuba and its tragic consequences have to be placed in the context of deep changes. The industrial revolution, above all in Bizkaia; the loss of economic interests in Cuba; the flourishing of Basque culture; the attempt to recover the fueros; the rise of new ideologies; Basque nationalism and socialism. And, in opposition to all of that, there were the militaristic police force in Madrid, 220,000 young men in Cuba from all over

---

44. Arzak, "Oroitz eta Esperantzak."

45. Gipuzkoa, Diputación Provincial, "Registro de las sesiones celebradas por la Excma. Diputación Provincial de Gipuzkoa durante el primer período semestral del año económico de 1898 a 1899," 176–77.

Spain; 53,000 casualties there, including 3,000 Basques. And Cuba was one of the main issues in the local, state, and international press. Poetry about the war was sung in every Basque town and village.

That Basques had to go to Cuba as Spanish soldiers was considered to be a result of having lost the fueros. At the same time, the Basque ruling class needed to justify the war as part of a strategy for restoring them. But how could they justify young men having to go to die in that war side by side with the people who had removed the fueros? The regional government, as we have seen, often had to deal with harsh local reality and with policies that were difficult to manage.

Full of contradictions, the war led to a change of mentalities and reflected the tensions which existed between Spanish nationalism and the Basque institutions asking for greater self-government. We can suppose that Basque nationalism, too, would feed off these contradictions.

Bibliography

Alberro Goikoetxea, Luzia. *Euskal Festak Zestoan 1898*. Lankidetzan 27. Donostia: Eusko Ikaskuntza, 2003.

Artola, José. "Bedeikatua izan dadilla beti ta beti pakea." *Euskal-erria: Revista Bascongada* no. 37 (1897): 54–55.

———. "Bedeikatua izan dadilla beti ta beti pake." *Euskal-erria: Revista Bascongada*, no. 75 (1916): 451.

Arzak, Antonio. "Oroitz eta Esperantzak." *Euskal-erria: Revista Bascongada* 39 (1898): 212–13.

Gipúzcoa, Diputación Provincial. "Registro de las sesiones celebradas por la Diputación Provincial de Gipuzkoa durante el segundo período semestral del año económico de 1894 a 1895." Donostia-San Sebastián: Imprenta de la Provincia, Fondo Gorkeak, Bilblioteca KM, 1895.

———. "Registro de las sesiones celebradas por la Diputación Provincial de Gipuzkoa durante el segundo período semestral del año económico de 1895 a 1896." Donostia-San Sebastián: Imprenta de la Provincia, Fondo Gordeak, Bilblioteca KM, 1896.

———. "Registro de las sesiones celebradas por la Diputación Provincial de Gipuzkoa durante el primer período semestral del año económico de 1895 a 1896." Donostia-San Sebastián: Imprenta de la Provincia, Fondo Gordeak, Bilblioteca KM, 1896.

———. "Registro de las sesiones celebradas por la Diputación Provincial de Gipuzkoa durante el segundo período semestral del año económico de 1896 a 1897." Donostia-San Sebastián: Imprenta de la Provincia. Fondo Gordeak, Bilblioteca KM, 1897.

———. "Registro de las sesiones celebradas por la Diputación Provincial de Gipuzkoa durante el primer período semestral del año económico de 1896 a 1897." Donostia-San Sebastián: Imprenta de la Provincia, Fondo Gordeak, Bilblioteca KM, 1897.

————.“Registro de las sesiones celebradas por la Excma. Diputación Provincial de Gipuzkoa durante el segundo período semestral del año económico de 1897 a 1898.” Donostia-San Sebastián: Imprenta de la Provincia, Fondo Gordeak, Biblioteca KM, 1898.

————.“Registro de las sesiones celebradas por la Diputación Provincial de Gipuzkoa durante el primer período semestral del año económico de 1897 a 1898.” Donostia-San Sebastián, Imprenta de la Provincia, Fondo Gordeak, Bilblioteca KM, 1898.

————.“Registro de las sesiones celebradas por la Excma. Diputación Provincial de Gipuzkoa durante el primer período semestral del año económico de 1898 a 1899.” Donostia-San Sebastián: Imprenta de la Provincia, Fondo Gordeak. Bilblioteca KM, 1899.

————.“Registro de las sesiones celebradas por la Excma. Diputación Provincial de Gipuzkoa durante el primer período semestral del año 1903.” Donostia-San Sebastián: Imprenta de la Provincia, Fondo Gordeak, Bilblioteca KM, 1903.

Iparragirre, Gotzon. “Eibar.” In *Eibar 1346–1996: Ekarpen historikoak: Aportaciones históricas.* Lankidetzan 14. Donostia-San Sebastián: Eusko Ikaskuntza, Eibarko Udala, 1999.

Izquierdo Canosa, Raúl. *Viaje sin regreso.* Havana: Verde Olivo, 2001.

Moreno Fraginals, Manuel and José J. Moreno Masó. “La última migración armada.” In *Guerra, inmigración y muerte (el ejercito español en Cuba como vía migratoria).* Colombres Asturias: Ediciones Jucar, 1993.

Sáez García, Juan Antonio. “La Batería del astillero Para la defensa del puerto de Pasajes (Gipuzkoa) en la Guerra hispano americana.” *Bilduma Ayuntamiento de Renteria* no. 15 (2001): 173–86.

8

The Cuban Connections of Military Personnel Elected in the Basque Country for the Spanish Parliament, 1808–1939

Mikel Urquijo

The importance of the island of Cuba[1] in the politics, society, and the economy of the kingdom of Castile, and later in that of Spain, is a commonplace. The building of the Castilian empire from the sixteenth century, and its influence on the process of progressive globalization[2] of the world, is unquestionable. Christopher Columbus opened a new horizon for Europeans to the west just as Marco Polo had to the east. The small "European peninsula on the Eurasian continent"[3] opened out upon a wider world which would be completed over the following centuries with expansion in Africa, Asia, and Oceania.

During the globalization of this world, the new territories "discovered" and exploited by the Europeans meant new political and economic opportunities for them. In the Spanish empire and the post-imperial kingdom there were four main routes to rapid political, economic, and social ascent:[4] a military career, an administrative one, entrepreneurial activity in the new territories, or royal favor. Often these routes converged rather than running in parallel. Colonial civil servants combined their public employment with economic activities and soldiers sold pro-

---

1. For more information about the importance of Cuba and, especially, the city of Havana as a bridge between the Peninsula and the Spanish empire in America see Sorhegui, *Havana en el Mediterráneo americano*, 168ff.
2. Eriksen, *Globalization*, 1–3 and 102–4.
3. Coudenhove-Kalergi, *Pan-Europa*, 33.
4. There is an analysis of the relationships between creoles, soldiers, and nobles in Moreno Fraginals, *Cuba/España: España/Cuba: Historia común*, 137–44.

tection to businessmen—and all of them depended upon royal favor, for which they were grateful.[5]

The connections between the main Spanish-Cuban businessmen and civil servants and soldiers were well known. Havana newspaper *La Tribuna* said: "What is it about Mr. Calvo[6] that makes all the superintendents *like him* so much and so quickly?"[7]

In this context, the importance of the crown's American territories, in general, and of Cuba,[8] in particular, must be examined in detail when analyzing the biographies of soldiers, politicians, and businessmen and, especially, their professional careers. They were stepping stones for promotion, as well as times of consolidation, in their political-military careers. It should not be forgotten that the highest authority in Cuba was the captain general, a political-military post held by the generals most trusted by the Spanish governments of the day.

At the same time, the loss of most of the Spanish empire in America at the start of the nineteenth century made Cuba the most highly valued territory in what was left of the empire because of its symbolic and economic value. The balance of trade shows this well,[9] favoring the Peninsula throughout the nineteenth century in spite of growing US participation in Cuban business.[10]

Who Have We Researched?

In this case we have examined a triangle: the Parliament, the Army, and Cuba. We have researched military personnel who had been in Cuba at some point of their careers and who were elected to parliament for the Basque provinces between 1808 and 1939. There are thirteen people who meet these three criteria.

Some Methodological Premises

Our work about the people mentioned above is based on previous biographical analysis carried out in various research projects which use the concept of collective biography and prosopographic methods.[11]

---

5. Piqueras, *Cuba, emporio y colonia*, 13–15.

6. Manuel Calvo was one of the most important businessmen in Cuba; see Barcia, 1998: 15-24.

7. Quoted in Barcia, *Élites y grupos de presión*, 74.

8. J. Casanovas described Cuba as a "colony of exceptional importance in the Spanish empire" in *¡O pan, o plomo!*, 2.

9. Balance of trade in Zanetti, "Las relaciones comerciales hispano-cubanas en el siglo XIX," 116.

10. Ibid., 95–117.

11. The basis for thes approaches can be seen in Stone, *The Past and the Present*; Sotinel, "Prosopographie et biographie"; Bulst, "Prosopography and the Computer"; Schijvenaars, "Computerized Prosopographical Research"; and Keats-Rohan, "Prosopography and Computing."

Person	Time in Cuba	Parliament
Azcarraga Palmero, Marcelo	Head of General Staff (1857–1865)	Member of Parliament for Morella (Castellón), 1876–1877 Senator for Castellón, 1879–1881 Senator for Navarra, 1884–1886 Senator for life, 1891–1912 Senator in his own right, 1912–1915
Castillo Gil de la Torre, Ignacio María	Captain General of Cuba (1883–1884)	Senator for Bizkaia, 1876–1878, 1886–1887 Senator for life, 1887
Dabán Ramírez de Arellano, Antonio	Regimental captain (1869–1871)	Member of Parliament for Santiago de Cuba, 1879–1884 Member of Parliament for Tafalla (Navarra), 1884–1890 Senator for life, 1897–1902
Ezpeleta Enrile, Joaquín	Captain General of Cuba (1838–1840)	Representative for Navarra, 1834–1836 Senator for life, 1845–1854, 1857–1863
Gándara Navarro, José de la	Commander–Governor of Puerto Príncipe (1842–1848) Returned to Cuba with the rank of colonel (1848–1856)	Senator for Navarra, 1871–1872 Member of Parliament for Iruñea (Navarre), 1872–1873
González Goyeneche, Zacarías	Senior Regimental Major (1864–1874)	Senator for Navarra, 1891–1893
Hera la Puente, José Santos de la	2nd Corporal for the Island of Cuba (1831–1832) Governor and General Commander of the Western Region (Santiago de Cuba) (1832–1834)	Member of Parliament for Toledo, 1839 Senator for Toledo, 1839–1843 Senator for Bizkaia, 1843–1844 Senator for life, 1845–1854, 1857–1859
Lersundi Ormaechea, Francisco	Captain General of Cuba (1866) Captain General of Cuba (1867–1869)	Member of Parliament for Bergara (Gipuzkoa), 1850–1853 Senator for life, 1853–1854, 1857–1868
Miguel Mauleon, Fructuoso	Major (1858–1865) Lieutenant Colonel / Head of the General Staff (1868–1869)	Member of Parliament for Lizarra (Navarra), 1876–1883
Modet Eguia, Juan	Captain and Major (1856–1859) Inspector General of Public Works on the Island of Cuba (1866–1867) Colonel (fought in the Cienfuegos war) (1869)	Member of Parliament for Lizarra (Navarra), 1859–1865
Nardiz Alegría, Venancio	Navy Lieutenant (1895–1898)	Member of Parliament for Gernika (Bizkaia), 1920–1923
Olave Díez, Serafín	Lieutenant Colonel (wounded in combat) (1869)	Member of Parliament for Oltza (Navarra), 1872–1874
Torre Mendieta, Nemesio	Second lieutenant (resigned) (1859–1860)	Member of Parliament for Gernika (Bizkaia), 1873–1874

Table 8.1: Military parliamentarians who had been in Cuba: Azcarraga Palmero, Marcelo (Agirreazkuenaga, Alonso, Gracia, Martinez, and Urquijo, Diccionario biográfico de parlamentarios de Vasconia, 1, 543–56, and military report in AGMS, Sec. 1, file A-2687); Castillo Gil de la Torre, Ignacio María (Agirreazkuenaga, Urquijo, Serrano, and Urquijo, Diccionario biográfico de parlamentarios de Vasconia, and Agirreazkuenaga, Alonso, Gracia, Martinez, and Urquijo, Diccionario biográfico de parlamentarios de Vasconia, 1, 780–88); Dabán Ramírez de Arellano, Antonio (Agirreazkuenaga, Alonso, Gracia, Martinez, and Urquijo, Diccionario biográfico de parlamentarios de Vasconia, 1, 870–80); Ezpeleta Enrile, Joaquín (Agirreazkuenaga, Urquijo, Serrano, and Urquijo, Diccionario biográfico de parlamentarios de Vasconia, 386–88, and Urquijo, Diccionario biográfico de parlamentarios españoles); Gandara Navarro, José (Agirreazkuenaga, Urquijo, Serrano, and Urquijo, Diccionario biográfico de parlamentarios de Vasconia, 421–23); Gonzalez Goyeneche, Zacarías (Agirreazkuenaga, Alonso, Gracia, Martinez, and Urquijo, Diccionario biográfico de parlamentarios de Vasconia, 2, 1231–35); Hera la Puente, José Santos de la (Agirreazkuenaga, Urquijo, Serrano, and Urquijo, Diccionario biográfico de parlamentarios de Vasconia, 460–63, and Urquijo, Diccionario biográfico de parlamentarios españoles); Lersundi Hormaechea, Francisco (Agirreazkuenaga, Urquijo, Serrano, and Urquijo, Diccionario biográfico de parlamentarios de Vasconia, 545–52, and Urquijo, Diccionario biográfico de parlamentarios españoles); Miguel Mauleón, Fructuoso (Agirreazkuenaga, Urquijo, Serrano, and Urquijo, Diccionario biográfico de parlamentarios de Vasconia, 622–23, and Agirreazkuenaga, Alonso, Gracia, Martinez, and Urquijo, Diccionario biográfico de parlamentarios de Vasconia, 2, 1706–11); Modet Eguia, Juan (Agirreazkuenaga, Urquijo, Serrano, and Urquijo, Diccionario biográfico de parlamentarios de Vasconia, 626–29); Nardiz Alegría, Venancio (Agirreazkuenaga, Alonso, Gracia, Martinez, and Urquijo, Diccionario biográfico de parlamentarios de Vasconia, 2, 1769–75); Olave Diez, Serafín (Agirreazkuenaga, Urquijo, Serrano, and Urquijo, Diccionario biográfico de parlamentarios de Vasconia, 728–35); Torre Mendieta, Nemesio (Agirreazkuenaga, Urquijo, Serrano, and Urquijo, Diccionario biográfico de parlamentarios de Vasconia, 854–55).

Our approach differs from bringing together a series of biographies without any previous methodological criteria or planning.[12] First, collective biography[13] is taken to be work that starts by defining the object of study using parameters which can be established objectively. In this work, the objects of study are the Basque military parliamentarians who had been posted in Cuba. Second, our analysis also examines all the people using the same scheme, which will allow us to later compare them by answering the same questions. Thirdly, each person's entire biography is taken into account in order to see each subject in full context. This involves examining each person's family circle, education, social and cultural surroundings, economic background, and political activity. Fourthly, primary sources must be used in order to guarantee the veracity of the information. All of this will allow us to obtain an overall understanding of the person under study and, then, a prosopographic analysis will take us from the individual to the collective.

The previous writing of the biographies—dealing with only what we call collective biography—allows us to take a quantitative approach to these parliamentarians and also provides information about their entire lives.[14] In some prosopographic work we have seen that the authors limit themselves to a quantitative analysis of their database; in others, the lack of previous biographical study and the use of secondary material provides results which are not as reliable. So this previous research is essential in that it allows us to reach solid conclusions about the careers of the group under study.

The empirical information on which this work is based is taken from biographies published in four different works. *Diccionario biográfico de los parlamentarios de Vasconia (1808–1876)*, *Diccionario biográfico de los parlamentarios de Vasconia (1876–1939)*, *Diccionario biográfico de los parlamentarios españoles (1810–1814)*, and *Diccionario biográfico de los parlamentarios españoles (1820–1854)*. These works include biographies of all the parlamentarians (members of parlament and senators) who were elected for the Basque Country between 1808 and 1939. The biographies published in these works cover their entire lives: their family circles, social and cultural environment, and political networks.[15]

Families—including families by marriage—are examined exhaustively, including the people associated with them and who are significant in the development of each subject's political or professional career. It is also important to look at parents' and grandparents' careers in order to discern any family traditions in politics or any of the subject's other activities. In the social and cultural context we examine each subject's upbringing, both

12. For information about this, see Keats-Rohan, "Prosopography and Computing."

13. On this concept see Urquijo, "Prosopografía parlamentaria a partir de la biografía colectiva."

14. This qualitative method of research can also be found in legal analysis, Hespanha, "L'étude prosopographique des juristes."

15. For information about the concept of biography and surrounding circles, see Caro Baroja, *Biografías y vidas humanas*, 9–37.

formal and informal, their involvement in cultural associations, Atheneums, et cetera. We also analyze their writings in the press, in books, and so on. By material context we refer to their means of livelihood. This can mean a professional activity, exploiting rural or urban property, or receiving returns on investments. Lastly, the political context refers to the subject's activities in institutions and political organizations. In this section particular attention is paid to the subjects' parliamentary activity, looking at their election to parliament, interventions, participation in government, and parliamentary commissions.[16] The objective is to provide an analysis of each person covering all such facets of his life and placing him in context. Work was carried out to complete the same scheme for each person in the most complete way possible.

The question we try to answer is: What was the significance of their time in Cuba in terms of their military and political careers? Several variables are examined in order to answer this:

- Their age when they joined the forces and family professional tradition;
- Military experience previous to their time in Cuba;
- Their time in Cuba and participation in colonial wars;
- The development of their professional careers, both military and political, paying particular attention to their parliamentary activity.

Person	Age upon joining the military	Military family
Azcarraga Palmero, Marcelo	17	No
Castillo Gil de la Torre, Ignacio María	18	Yes
Dabán Ramírez de Arellano, Antonio	13	Yes
Ezpeleta Enrile, Joaquín	12	Yes
Gándara Navarro, José de la	12	Yes
González Goyeneche, Zacarías	10	No
Hera la Puente, José Santos de la	18	No
Lersundi Ormaechea, Francisco	16	Yes
Miguel Mauleon, Fructuoso	16	No
Modet Eguia, Juan	19	No
Nardiz Alegría, Venancio	18	No
Olave Díez, Serafín	18	Yes
Torre Mendieta, Nemesio	20	Yes

Table 8.2: Age of joining the army and family tradition. Source: see table 8.1.

Analysis of the Characters

Nine of the people examined joined the military between the ages of sixteen and twenty. The remaining four did so even younger and in periods in which there were no wars. This allows us to draw the conclusion that their joining the army was not determined by the need for soldiers for Spain's numerous wars throughout the nineteenth century, among others the colonial wars in America. We believe that family tradition was more important

---

16. For a more detailed explanation of this model, see J. Agirreazkuenaga, E. Alonso, J. Gracia, F. Martinez, and M. Urquijo, dirs., *Diccionario biográfico de Parlamentarios de Vasconia: 1876–1939*, vol. 1, 48–51.

in their choice of profession than other factors as seven of the thirteen were sons of soldiers and some of them, such as Ezpeleta, had a family military history going back to the eighteenth and nineteenth centuries.

Person	Years of previous military experience	Role in Cuba	Years in Cuba	Participation in the wars
Azcarraga Palmero, Marcelo	7	Military	8	No
Castillo Gil de la Torre, Ignacio María	48	Political-military post	2	No
Dabán Ramírez de Arellano, Antonio	11	Military	3	Yes
Ezpeleta Enrile, Joaquín	38	Political-military post	2	No
Gándara Navarro, José de la	10	Military	14	No
González Goyeneche, Zacarías	33	Military	10	Yes
Hera la Puente, José Santos de la	21	Political-military post	4	No
Lersundi Ormaechea, Francisco	33	Political-military post	3	Yes
Miguel Mauleon, Fructuoso	10	Military	14	Yes
Modet Eguia, Juan	12	Military	6	Yes
Nardiz Alegría, Venancio	6	Military	3	Yes
Olave Díez, Serafín	20	Military	1	Yes
Torre Mendieta, Nemesio	1	Military	2	No

Table 8.3: Time in Cuba. Source: see table 8.1.

Examining their time in Cuba, we see that they went there after they had some military experience, except for Nemesio Torre Mendieta, who left the forces for unknown reasons.

With regards to their time in Cuba, there are two groups: those who went to the island as officers in the army or the navy (nine of them) and those who were given political appointments to senior military posts (four of them). The members of each group can be seen in table 8.1 and table 8.3.

In the first group, all but three had at least a decade of military experience and were officers when they went to Cuba, being captains at least. The time of their stay on the island varied. Of the nine people who had military postings—rather than political ones—four stayed in Cuba for fewer than three years; three between six and eight years; three for ten years; and one for fourteen years. Of these nine, six fought in colonial wars (1868–1878, 1895–1898) and three did not. Taking this into account—and that most of them were promoted during their time in the Caribbean—we can draw the conclusion that being posted to Cuba was undoubtedly a route to promotion, as was usual in all the colonies, especially in wartime. Nor did they have to spend long periods there in order to be promoted, as can be seen in Antonio Dabán Ramírez de Arellano's case (he spent only three years).

Person	Rank on going to Cuba	Rank on returning to the peninsula
Azcarraga Palmero, Marcelo	Major	Lieutenant Colonel
Castillo Gil de la Torre, Ignacio María	Lieutenant General	Lieutenant General
Dabán Ramírez de Arellano, Antonio	Captain	Major
Ezpeleta Enrile, Joaquín	Lieutenant General	Lieutenant General
Gándara Navarro, José de la	Major	Colonel
González Goyeneche, Zacarías	Lieutenant Colonel	Colonel
Hera la Puente, José Santos de la	Field Marshall	Lieutenant General
Lersundi Ormaechea, Francisco	Lieutenant General	Lieutenant General
Miguel Mauleon, Fructuoso	Major	Lieutenant Colonel
Modet Eguia, Juan	Captain	Major
Nardiz Alegría, Venancio	Navy Lieutenant	Navy Lieutenant
Olave Díez, Serafín	Lieutenant Colonel	Colonel
Torre Mendieta, Nemesio	Second Lieutenant	Second Lieutenant

Table 8.4: Promotion in Cuba. Source: see table 8.1.

The second group is made up of four men who were politically appointed to high military ranks. Three of them were captain generals of Cuba—Ignacio Ma. Castillo Gil de la Torre, Joaquín Ezpeleta Enrile, and Francisco Lersundi Ormaechea—and the fourth, José Santos de la Hera la Puente, was second in command of the island and general commander of the Eastern Region (Santiago de Cuba). In all four cases they had considerable military experience before they reached the island, between twenty-one and forty-eight years. Three of them spent shorter periods in Cuba—around two years—and the fourth spent four years there. General Lersundi was captain general first for less than a year and later for two years. General José Santos de la Hera was second in command for two years and governor and commandant general of the Eastern Region for a further two years. Of the four, the only one who took part in the war was Lersundi, the conflict starting during his term of office. After his return from Cuba José Santos de la Hera was promoted to lieutenant general. The other three were not promoted because they were already lieutenant generals, the highest rank a soldier could aspire to at the time. This was not the same as for officers posted to Cuba. Captain generals of Cuba did not attain the post militarily, it was a matter of being trusted and appointed by the government. At the same time, given the relationships between political-military power and economic power on the island, being Captain General of Cuba was a "prize" given the possibilities for becoming wealthy. M. Bizkarrondo and A. Elorza classify the system of government in colonial Cuba as "a type of military despotism, based on administrative corruption and economic exactions,"[17] that unquestionably led to considerable wealth for the people who received an appointment.

PERSON	PRESENCE
Azcarraga Palmero, Marcelo	After
Castillo Gil de la Torre, Ignacio María	Before and after
Dabán Ramírez de Arellano, Antonio	After
Ezpeleta Enrile, Joaquín	Before and after
Gándara Navarro, José de la	After
González Goyeneche, Zacarías	After
Hera la Puente, José Santos de la	After
Lersundi Ormaechea, Francisco	Before and after
Miguel Mauleon, Fructuoso	After
Modet Eguia, Juan	Before and after
Nardiz Alegría, Venancio	After
Olave Díez, Serafín	After
Torre Mendieta, Nemesio	After

Table 8.5. Presence in Parliament. Source: see table 8.1.

These peoples' political careers are a matter of interest. Nine of the thirteen were parliamentarians after their time in Cuba and four served both before and after being on the island. Three of the latter four were the Captain Generals I. M. Castillo, J. Ezpeleta, and F. Lersundi, who had had significant military and political careers on the Peninsula before going to Cuba. Juan Modet Eguia met both conditions because he was a member of parliament after his first period in Cuba, although he went back to the island for two further periods.

17. Bizkarrondo and Elorza, *Cuba/España*, 15.

The posts held in addition to being in parliament are a second facet of professional, military, or political advancement to be analyzed. Of the thirteen people studied, six held political posts in the government (two were prime ministers and ministers, two were simply ministers, one was undersecretary at the ministry of war, and another was director general of security and director of the civil guard), four held high military positions (captain generals, commanders of the navy, assistants to the King's Order, and high officers of the war and navy tribunals), and only three held no outstanding positions. Two of the latter were republicans, which made it hard for them to advance in politics—except during the first republic—as they were not trusted by the royal governments. The other, J. Modet, was a member of parliament for six years. In summary, it seems that their time in Cuba was a significant factor for all these military personnel.

PERSON	
Azcarraga Palmero, Marcelo	Prime Minister (1897, 1900–1901, 1904–1905)
	Minister of War (1878, 1890–1891, 1895–1897, 1899–1900)
	Navy Minister (1904–1905)
Castillo Gil de la Torre, Ignacio María	Minister of War (1886–1887)
	Captain General of Granada (1874)
	Captain General of Valencia (1874)
	Captain General of Madrid (1882–1883)
	Captain General of Navarra (1885–1886)
Dabán Ramírez de Arellano, Antonio	Director General of Security (1886)
	Captain General of Extremadura (1889–1890)
	Captain General of Valencia (1890–1892)
	Captain General of Puerto Rico (1892–1897)
	Director General of the Civil Guard (1889–1901)
Ezpeleta Enrile, Joaquín	Minister of War (1852)
	Navy Minister (1852)
	Advisor on Foreign Affairs (1851)
	Vice–president of the Military High Court (1854)
Gándara Navarro, José de la	Captain General of Santo Domingo (1862)
	Captain General of Philippines (1866–1869)
	Captain General of Old Castile (Restauración)
González Goyeneche, Zacarías	Captain General of Aragon (1884–1886)
	Captain General of Baleares (1887–1888)
	Captain General of New Castile (1888–1889)
Hera la Puente, José Santos de la	Captain General of Baleares (1839–1840)
	Member of the Royal Council for Spain and Abroad (1850–1853
	President of the Military High Court (1856–1859)
Lersundi Ormaechea, Francisco	Prime Minister (1853)
	Minister of War (1851–1852, 1864)
	Navy Minister (1856–1857)
	Captain General of New Castile (1852–1853)
Miguel Mauleon, Fructuoso	Undersecretary of the Ministry of War (1876, 1879, 1881–1883)
	Advisor to the Military High Court (1884–1885)
Modet Eguia, Juan	No outstanding posts
Nardiz Alegría, Venancio	Assistant to the King's Order (1911–1918)
	Commandant of Donostia (1924–1929)
	Commandant of the Navy, Bilbao (1930)
Olave Díez, Serafín	No outstanding posts
Torre Mendieta, Nemesio	No outstanding posts

Table 8.6. Political promotion. Source: see table 8.1.

Outstanding Careers

The above analysis confirms the importance of spending time in Cuba as part of the *cursus honorum* of military personnel who held important political and military posts. The presence of some of these people in Cuba at the height of their careers leads us to think that being captain general of Cuba was a coveted position due to the possibilities it offered of becoming rich, without even mentioning questionable business opportunities such as the slave trade.[18]

This interpretation is supported by the careers of two people of special interest: Joaquín Ezpeleta and Francisco Lersundi.

Joaquín Ezpeleta Enrile,[19] Count of Ezpeleta and Tribiana, had been born in Havana because his father, José Ezpeleta Galdeano (1742–1823), a distinguished soldier during the reign of Ferdinand VII, had been governor general of Cuba (1785–1789). He was part of a distinguished military family saga with involvement in politics. Joaquín Ezpeleta's son, Luis Ezpeleta Contreras, reached the rank of division general, the equivalent of the old rank of field marshal. His brother, José María Ezpeleta Enrile, was also a soldier. He reached the rank of lieutenant general and was captain general of Aragón (1832) and later of New Castile, as well as holding other important military posts. His nephew José María Ezpeleta Aguirre-Zuazo did not have a distinguished military rank, only reaching captain, but he was mayor of Iruñea-Pamplona (1856), civil governor of Madrid (1863), second-in-command of the Prince of Asturias's military household (1865), and head of the royal household (1868), which led him to emigrate, along with Isabella II, after the 1868 revolution. In short, it was a family that evolved from its loyalty to absolute monarchy in the eighteenth century and the first decades of the nineteenth century toward the moderate liberalism of the reign of Isabella II. His relationship with Cuba seems to have been significant as his father, José Ezpeleta Galdeano, had been captain general when they achieved political promotion, and he went on to hold other important posts: viceroy of New Granada (1789), after his time in Cuba, and Viceroy of Navarra (1814–1820). Like his father, Joaquín Ezpeleta Enrile was to become captain general of Cuba. He was rapidly promoted in the army, doubtless with his father's help. In 1800 he joined as a cadet in the Spanish royal guard and was a lieutenant colonel by 1836, the highest rank a soldier could achieve at that time. So his time in Havana can be seen as a reward for his fulfilled military career. From then on his trajectory would be political: parliamentarian, minister in the moderate liberal governments, and a golden retirement as senator for life.

---

18. Moreno Fraginals, *Cuba/España: España/Cuba*, 222.
19. See Agirreazkuenaga, Urquijo, Serrano, and Urquijo, *Diccionario biográfico de los parlamentarios de Vasconia, 1808–1876*, 386–88 and Urquijo, *Diccionario biográfico de parlamentarios españoles*.

Another example is Francisco Lersundi Ormaechea.[20] His father, too, had been a soldier, although not as important as Ezpeleta's. He had begun his career as a volunteer during the First Carlist War and reached the rank of lieutenant colonel due to his success in combat. His later promotions came thanks to putting down various uprisings against the moderate government and to taking part in the expedition to Italy in 1849 to assist the Pope. His military career was successful due to his achievements in war and the political protection of moderate governments, he was named field marshal in 1848, rising in just thirteen years from second lieutenant (in 1835) to field marshal (in 1848). Four years later he completed his military career being promoted to the rank of lieutenant general (1852) after a period at the war ministry (1851–1852). The end of his military career overlapped with the start of his political one, his being elected to parliament in 1850. From then on he was given military posts by political designation, such as captain general of New Castile (1852), with political roles such as member of parliament (1850–1853), senator for life (1853), and prime minister (1853). Toward the end of his political career he was captain general of Cuba twice (1866, 1867–1869), named by the O'Donnell and Narváez governments. Together they were the culmination of his political career. The political changes after the 1868 revolution led to radical changes in the political regime which affected him politically and personally. Franscisco Lersundi, after returning to the Peninsula, lived as a private citizen until his death on November 17, 1874.

Conclusion

Analysis of the lives of soldiers posted to Cuba who were also elected to parliament shows two different groups. On the one hand, those who were posted to Cuba as soldiers and, on the other, those soldiers who were given political positions while on the island.

For the first group, their time there meant promotion in their professional careers. Later on they were all to hold distinguished political posts in the Peninsula as members of parliament and other political or political-military posts.

For the second group, their time in Cuba was part of their political career, which—except in F. Lersundi's case—led to holding important military posts or political ones, such as being ministers, when they went back to Spain.

Bibliography

Agirreazkuenaga, J., E. Alonso, J. Gracia, F. Martinez, and M. Urquijo, directors, *Diccionario biográfico de parlamentarios de Vasconia: 1876–*

---

20. See Agirreazkuenaga, Urquijo, Serrano, and Urquijo, *Diccionario biográfico de los parlamentarios de Vasconia, 1808–1876*, 545–52; and Urquijo, *Diccionario biográfico de parlamentarios españoles.*

1939. 3 volumes. Vitoria-Gasteiz: Eusko Legebiltzarra-Parlamento Vasco, 2007.

Agirreazkuenaga, J., J. R. Urquijo, S. Serrano, and M. Urquijo. *Diccionario biográfico de los parlamentarios de Vasconia, 1808–1876*. Vitoria-Gasteiz: Eusko Legebiltzarra-Parlamento Vasco, 1993

Barcia Zequeira, María del Carmen. *Élites y grupos de presión: Cuba, 1868–1898*. Havana: Editorial de Ciencias Sociales, 1998.

Bizkarrondo, Marta y Antonio Elorza. *Cuba/España: El dilema autonomista, 1878–1898*. Madrid: Editorial Colibrí, 2001.

Bulst, Neithard. "Prosopography and the Computer: Problems and Possibilities." *History and Computing* 2 (1989): 13–18.

Caro Baroja, Julio. *Biografías y vidas humanas*. Donostia-San Sebastián: Txertoa, 1986.

Casanovas Codina, Joan. *¡O pan, o plomo! Los trabajadores cubanos y el colonialismo español en Cuba, 1850–1898*. Madrid: Siglo XXI, 2000.

Coudnhove-Kalergi, Richard N. *Pan-Europa*, Madrid: Encuentro, 2010.

Eriksen, Thomas Hylland. *Globalization: The Key Concepts*. London: Bloomsbury, 2014.

Hespanha, Antonio M. "L'étude prosopographique des juristes: entre les 'practiques' et leurs 'représentations.'" In *El Tercer Poder*, edited by J. M. Scholz, 93–101. Frankfurt: Klosterman, 1992.

Keats-Rohan, Katharine S. B. "Prosopography and Computing: a Marriage Made in Heaven?" *History and Computing* 12-1 (2000): 1–11.

Moreno Fraginals, Manuel. *Cuba/España: España/Cuba: Historia común*. Barcelona: Crítica, 1995.

Piqueras Arenas, José Antonio. *Cuba, emporio y colonia: La disputa de un mercado interferido (1878–1895)*. Mexico City: Fondo de Cultura Económica, 2003.

Schijvenaars, Toine. "Computerized Prosopographical Research." In *Prosopography and Computer. Contributions of Mediaevalists and Modernists on the Use of Computer in Historical Research*, edited by Koen Goudriaan, Kees Mandemakers, Jogchum Reitsma, and Peter Stebel, 1–24. Leuven: No publisher, 1995.

Sorhegui D'mares, Arturo. *Havana en el Mediterráneo americano*. Havana: Ed. Imagen Contemporánea, 2007.

Sotinel, Claude. "Prosopographie et biographie." In Problemes & Methodes de la biographie. Actes du Colloque (Sorbonne, May 3–4, 1985). Paris, 149–51.

Stone, Lawrence. *The Past and the Present*. New York: Routledge, 1981.

Urquijo, Mikel, director. *Diccionario biográfico de parlamentarios españoles: Cortes de Cádiz. 1810–1814*. Madrid: Cortes Generales, 2010.

———.*Diccionario biográfico de parlamentarios españoles: 1820–1854*. Digital edition. Madrid: Cortes Generales, 2013.

———."Prosopografía parlamentaria a partir de la biografía colectiva: algunas reflexiones metodológicas." In *Naciones en el estado nación: La formación cultural y política de naciones en la Europa contemporánea*, edited by Joseba Agirreazkuenaga and Eduardo J. Alonso, 57–63. Barcelona: Base, 2014.

Zanetti Lecuona, Oscar. "Las relaciones comerciales hispano-cubanas en el siglo XIX." In *La ilusión de un Imperio: Las relaciones económicas hispano-cubanas en el siglo xix*, edited by Salvador Palazón Ferrando and Candelaria Saíz Pastor, 95–117. Alicante: University of Alicante, 1998.

9

From the Bidasoa Regatta to the Matanzas Plain: American Heritage in the Mansion at Sunbilla

Hilda Otero Abreu

On the banks of the Bidasoa River, half way between Iruñea-Pamplona and France, the village of Sunbilla's beautiful surroundings are impressive. Set in the mountains of so-called Humid Navarra, the place's past is directly connected with emigration. It was after the building of the stone bridge in 1652 that the village became more important, the road over it being used to bring arms from the factory at Eugi and to the port of Pasaia and to France.[1]

It is known that the families in the area—taking advantage of Navarrese influence at court—acquired coats of arms and fortunes during the seventeenthth and eighteenth centuries. The concept of "universal nobility," approved by the Bourbons, made it possible for surnames which had their origins in rural households of middling fortune to reach the highest social levels, similar to that of the old Castilian nobility. Merchants and soldiers completed their rise with titles and medals which perpetuated the legacy and fortune which they had inherited as eldest sons. Part of that success came from America. It is easy to see the connection across the Atlantic even today.[2]

---

1. For information about the bridge at Sunbilla (Sumbilla in Spanish), see Latasa; "Apuntes para la historia del puente de Sumbilla," 185–98.

2. Phillip V and Charles III surrounded themselves with "foreign" advisors and ministers in order to govern with greater freedom from the Castilian nobility. So there were French, Dutch, Irish, and some Navarrese very close to the monarch and they held key positions in the administration. Moving from commerce to the nobility, active men from those valleys ennobled their lineages and put coats of arms above the doors on their façades. Described in the classic essay *La Hora Navarra*, by Julio Caro Baroja, demonstrating that social advancement had its origins in the eighteenth century and the importance of trade with America. See

Assisted by compatriots from the neighboring area of Baztan and other parts of Navarra, outstanding participants from Subilla in Cádiz's transatlantic trade included the Larrain brothers (Juan Francisco, Juan Bautista, and Juan Miguel), and the Ezpeletas, whose fortunes were based on networks of customers in the Peninsula and America. Others had distinguished careers in the army or colonial administration, such as the Oteizas. Some went back to the village, others never did, but favored their countrymen and relatives in business and maintained contact with their land or origin, even if only from a distance.[3]

One particular house in Sunbilla stands out for its age and strong connections with America, particularly with Cuba. It is known simply as the "mansión" (mansion) mentioned in documents as Oteizarena Miarra. It is a family home with three floors, around a thousand square meters, and with an old baroque coat of arms on its facade.[4]

Reconstructing its past involved examining various archives, although the documentation about its first years has been lost. The law suits between the inheritors, testamentaries, and matrimonial contracts allow us to piece together a period in which the splendor of such houses was always implicated with America.

Rise and Fall of a Navarrese Surname

In order to forge a career and make their fortune, the brothers Oteiza left their native Sunbilla in the first decades of the eighteenth century.[5] The eldest, Miguel Antonio Oteiza y Ubiría, opened up the American route for the rest. After a period in Madrid to make contacts at court, he left for America in 1715 where he held various posts in the viceroy of Peru's bodyguard. Years later he married the widow marchioness of Salinas, María Catalina Sojo Olavarrieta, member of a wealthy family from the region of Piura. His rise was crowned with the post of governor of the province of Guayaquil, where he died.[6] The next brother, Pedro Juanchín, spent time in America but returned to his village, where, as the sole heir, he received his parents' property. Their father, Juan Gerónimo Oteyza, chose the inheritor from among his children. He left nothing to his eldest son

---

Imizcoz Beunza; "La hora navarra del xviii," 46.

3. Martínez del Cerro González, *Una comunidad de comerciantes*, 65; Castellano de Gastón and Bosco Amores Carredano, *Entre el valle del Baztan y América*, 97.

4. For a description of the facade, see *Catálogo Monumental de Navarra*, vol. 5, 593–600.

5. The reader will notice that the surname Oteiza is spelled differently there. We have left the spelling as in the document. At the end of the seventeenth century the surname appears as "Oteyza" in documents, being changed a century later.

6. The first Marques of Salinas was José Antonio Echarri e Irurzun, from Gares, Navarra. He had won a reputation with the captain general of Buenos Aires and was gentleman in the king's chamber. He died in Madrid in 1707. Widow María Catalina de Sojo y Olabarrieta married Juan Miguel Oteiza y Ubiría, from Sunbilla, in 1721. See Expediente de información y licencia de pasajeros a Indias, Archivo General de Indias, Casa de Contratación, Pasajeros a Indias, Informaciones y Licencias, November 11, 1715.

because—as he puts it in his will—"Juan Miguel is at the Court in Madrid and much has been spent to help him there."[7]

Figure 9.1. The coat of arms on the current facade of Oteizarena Miarra at Sunbilla. Baroque coat of arms from the eighteenth century with a helmet crest and a bishop rampant, flanked by lions and infants on a quartered background. The first quarter shows a mermaid with a mirror and comb (the arms of Bertizarana) over a fleur-de-lis between two golden roundels; the second, a tree between two lilies and with a cross above; the third, as in the second but with a Malta cross; the fourth, a tower between two stars with three sashes to the left, three stalks of sugarcane, two wolves two wolves in checkered form and passant pose. These are the symbols of the houses of Echevarría, Garaicoechea, Arburua, Zozayarena, Zubieta, Juangorena, and Lacoizqueta, and the Araníbar mansion in Arantza. Cfr. Catálogo monumental de Navarra, Gobierno de Navarra, *Institución Príncipe de Viana, 1996, vol. 5, 600.*

He had further children from his marriage with Emerenciana Latasa, the daughter of a soldier from Sunbilla, Gerónimo Latasa y Araníbar. The eldest, Juan Domingo, was born in 1697 and inherited his father's property. Still being a minor, his mother administered the houses and income and managed to accumulate some wealth, enough to support the family. Soon Juan Domingo followed in his elder brothers' footsteps and headed for the Americas.[8] At the end of 1737 he was a captain in the halberdiers' company at the viceroy's palace in Mexico City. In 1740 he assumed the command of the twenty-four men in Viceroy Juan Antonio de Vizarón y Eguiarreta's personal bodyguard. In 1749, while he was still in America, the Iruñea-Pampona court opened a case against the coat of arm on the facade of the family home in Sunbilla. He was also a shareholder in the Real Compañia Guipuzcoana de Caracas, which suggests that he was suc-

---

7. Causa de hidalguía de Juan Domingo Oteiza Latasa Araníbar y Ezpeleta. Archivo General de Navarra, hereinafter AGN, Audiencia de Pamplona, Sala 3rd, file 137677.

8. Juan Gerónimo de Oteyza's first wife was Francisca Ubiría: their children were Juan Miguel and Pedro Juachín. It was his descendants from his marriage with Emerenciana Latasas who built the mansion. See the testimony of Juan Gerónimo Oteyza, mayor of Sunbilla in 1704, March 7, 1704, AGN, Audiencia de Pamplona, Sala 3rd, file 137677.

cessful in business, probably with the help of some countrymen.[9]

After obtaining a medium-sized fortune and the title of nobility for his surname, Juan Domingo de Oteiza settled in Sunbilla. His shares in the Gipuzkoan Company doubled in value and, in less than a year, he obtained considerable profits which gave him a comfortable lifestyle.[10]

Using the profits from his businesses, and probably with contributions from his spouses, in June 1780 Captain Oteiza set up an entailed estate with various houses in Sunbilla, Arantza, Errenteria, and shares worth 3,500 pesos in the Real Compañia Guipuzcoana de Caracas.[11]

The mansion, called Oteizarena Miarra, with its surrounding area, is in the street next to the royal highway, and was built at a later date. On founding the entailed estate, he expressed his intention to build "a new house of around 3,600 feet, three floors and a value of 50,000 reals," having already bought the materials needed for its construction.[12]

He died in 1782 and named his grandson Juan Bautista Oteiza Urrujulegui as his heir.[13] His widow, Ana María Usabiaga, died in 1797. Her heiress was her niece, who lived in Azkoitia, and who soon claimed the part of the property contributed to the entailed estate by her aunt, worth approximately 87,600 reals.[14]

The heir, Juan Bautista Oteiza, like his forebears, married twice. He had three children from his first marriage, with Feliciana Aldave. After his death, he married Manuela Antonia Ayesta and had a further two children with her. When he passed away, in 1829, he left six heirs who could claim proportional parts of the entailed estate.

The first effects of liberalism changed the social order in Navarra. The laws passed from 1820–1823 made it possible for an entailed estate to be dismantled and other privileges of the aristocracy in the area were abolished. Activities connected with social advancement—the army, public administration, and trade—were reconfigured in the new liberal setting

---

9. Reaching final judgements about nobility was a long and expensive process. Once the final sentence had been given, all the parties were notified and, at the interested party's request, it was transcribed into the book of royal favors held by the Navarrese Chamber of Accounts. Cfr. *Nobiliario del Reino de Navarra,* vol. I, *Nobleza ejecutoriada en los tribunales reales de Corte y Consejo de Navarra, 1519–1832,* 80.

10. He had a total of thirty shares in the Gipuzkoana according to Gárate Ojanguren's *La Real Compañía Caracas Guipuzcoana,* 92.

11. The properties in Sunbilla were the houses of Tellería and the apple orchard next to it, Simonena, Juanchenea, Arranoiseta Larra, Arranobieta Berea, and Oteyzarena miarra. In Arantza, there was Andresenea, and another building in Errenteria. The total value of the entailed estate was 475,867 reals, with a calculated annual income of 12,845 reals. See the case brought by the inheritors of Ana María Usabiaga. Cfr., AGN, Case number 26545, year 1824.

12. The first references to the Oteizarena Miarra house are in the documents about the lawsuit over the inheritance of the entailed estate; in 1780 it was not yet as large as it would become. Cf. The inheritors of Ana María Usabiaga Juarista, widow of captain Juan Domingo Oteiza, claiming Juan Bautista Oteyza's share of the inheritance. AGN, Case number 94010, year 1797.

13. She was the daughter of Domingo Oteyza and María Bautista de Urrujulegui. We have respected the original spelling of the surname Oteyza with a "y," as in the documents.

14. AGN Case 26545, year 1824.

and this affected the region's daily life.[15]

The region was desolated after the French invasion. The end of the trade monopoly with the colonies, and their later independence, dramatically changed overseas trade. The return of Ferdinand VII opened a new framework of government in the Kingdom of Navarra. They were tough years in which Navarra had to pay from its own funds for the destruction it had suffered during the War of the Pyrenees and the Peninsula War. The valleys had been emptied. Connections with the Americas were important for reconstructing houses and towns but, after the loss of the American colonies, they were depressed for several decades, which also affected local politics.[16]

Income was scarcely able to maintain large families and shares in the Real Compañía Guipuzcoana de Caracas—transformed into the Comercio de Filipinas—produced little profit. The old Oteiza lineage still had some returns: the mansion on the straits and some farming huts and houses of poor quality.

There was little left of the Oteiza's medium-sized fortune, perhaps because there were few male descendants and they were poorly educated. In 1824, Juan Bautista Oteiza requested permission from the Iruñea-Pamplona court to be able to separate a house from the entailed estate in order to give it to one of his daughters as a dowry. By the time he died, in 1829, the law recognized the right of all direct heirs to inherit entailed estate property.

A sentence in 1853 gave Miguel Oteiza, the first son, rights over the rest of the entailed estate which his grandfather had founded. Overwhelmed by gambling debts, old, and sick, he passed the property on to his daughter Ramona Oteiza. She and her husband did not have enough money to pay the notaries for the inheritance deeds and gave up their right in favor of a relative, María Cruz Sarratea Aldave.[17]

In addition to the mansion of Oteizarena Miarra, the entailed estate included that of Echevarría, the house of Yragerieta in Sunbilla, a value of three hundred Navarrese ducats in the house of Lanrabel in Legasa, and the property of the religious institution founded by Pedro Joaquín de Oteiza, vicar of Oronoz, and various bonds worth around four thousand pesos. In 1886 Joaquina Oteiza left the religious institution inherited from the old entailed estate to her son Mariano Ibarra y Oteiza, who lived in Buenos Aires.[18]

---

15. For information about the impact of the deregulation of entailed estate properties, see Martínez López, "Sobre familias, elites y herencias en el siglo xix," 459–61.

16. For information about the solidarity of people from Baztan in Mexico in the reconstruction of houses in the valley, see Castellano de Gastón and Bosco Amores Carredano, *Entre el valle del Baztán y América*, 153–55.

17. The widow Sarratea Aldave had presented a case at Burgos Court claiming her daughters' rights to the returns on a religious institution (*capellanía*) founded in Errenteria in 1640 and of which her late husband, Javier María Iturralde, was heir. They needed money because those lawsuits were expensive and protracted. The whole case can be followed in the notaries' protocols, AGN, Protocolos Notariales José María Elizondo, years 1858–1860.

18. See other deed in AGN Escribanía de José María Elizondo, writ dated October 27, 1859.

Cuba, Destination for Emigration

The Navarrese institutions accepted the legitimacy of Isabella in 1841. Under the authority of a military governor named by Madrid, they sent young men to the army. In 1846 a royal decree stated that no Navarrese man could emigrate without first naming and paying for his substitute to go into the army. Poverty, and the possibility of being called up for military service, drove many young Navarrese to head out for what they supposed would be a better destiny. America was once more on the horizon of Humid Navarra's rural families: in fact, it had never gone away as far as family facilitation of related immigrants were concerned, nor had ties with relatives on the other side of the sea been broken. Navarrese people started once more to emigrate to their traditional destinations: Buenos Aires and Montevideo in South America, and Havana and even Mexico. Fewer went to San Juan in Puerto Rico, or to Caracas and La Guaira.[19]

Always helped by people who had settled these previously, the young Navarrese went to work in Cuba. Some met with better fortune and went back to buy their birth farmstead or the mansions of ruined local nobility. This was what happened to the Sunbilla mansion.

In 1860 Oteizarena Miarra was bought by the married couple Félix Sarratea Aldave and Magdalena Jorajuría Zunda.[20] The new owners were involved in trade, particularly with wine. Having obtained rights to the local weights and measures tax, Sarratea was involved in the retail sale of wine at Doneztebe where he also rented the largest inn. He was the distributor of oil in the town, but the widespread poverty meant that there was no guarantee of return on investment for some years. In 1877 he asked for a loan of 5,600 pesetas from Félix Ibarra Jorajuría, a local trader, who had accumulated some wealth by administering a tobacco plantation in the Pinar del Rio area.[21]

Ten years later Ibarra had still not received the sum he was owed and sold the debt to the trader Gerónimo Arrechea Olazar, who sold it in turn to Miguel Oyarzun y Seminario, who lived at Olagüe and who, too, had just returned from Cuba.[22]

Sarratea died in 1882 without leaving a will, which suggests that he may have died suddenly. Magdalena Jorajuría outlived him by two years. Having no children, the couple's property was inherited by Ángel Albis-

---

19. For information about liberal legislation regulating the departure of Spaniards from the Peninsula, see Idoate Ezquieta, *Emigración navarra del valle de Baztán a América*, 16–20.

20. Iruñea-Pamplona property register, Santesteban, notary Juan Urriza February 25, 1860, entry 148–149, folio 67, vol. 15.

21. Deed signed by Félix Ibarra Jorajuría in Doneztebe, October 4, 1869 in favor of Gregorio del Llano, living at Pinar del Río, for him to administer a tobacco plantation on the island. Cfr. AGN Protocolo Juan de Urriza. Loan deed of Félix Ibarra Jorajuría to the married couple Sarratea-Jorajuría in Doneztebe in the presence of Notary Juan Urriza in Doneztebe, February 24, 1879, Iruñea-Pamplona Property Register, sheet 190 backside, section 86.

22. Deed of Debt Sale signed at Doneztebe on October 28, 1891. Iruñea-Pamplona Property Register, sheet 191 front, section 86.

tur, a nephew who lived in Cuba. He inherited little, the main property being the Oteizarena mansion, valued at 17,500 pesetas, and some smaller items. Almost everything was heavily mortgaged.[23] In May 1884 Albistur granted his brother-in-law, Gerónimo Arrechea, a power of attorney to pay the mortgages on the property he had inherited, being unable to be his late aunt's executor himself because of distance. Albistur was well-known among the Basque emigrants in the Matanzas sugar region. He had been a small-scale trader, stating himself to be the owner of a grocery store in Cuba and mayor of Bolondrón between 1891 and 1898, tough years during the War of Independence.[24]

The Basque Connection with Cuban Sugar

If Liberalism transformed Navarrese society, it did the same to Cuban society in the early nineteenth century. For one thing, the island was modernized thanks to slaves, sugarcane, and coffee. Economic success allowed the rise of a new business elite, while the political reality reduced any real possibility of advancement for creoles. In 1868, at the same time as the what came to known as the Glorious Revolution, landowner Carlos Manuel de Céspedes rose up against Spain. A conflict unfurled and, against all expectations, it would last more than a decade. Fear of war swept across the island in just a few weeks, putting the military garrisons on guard: they were insufficient to stop the hostilities from spreading rapidly. Meanwhile, in Madrid the successful republican revolution diverted military resources and delayed the arrival of reinforcements and military equipment in the Antilles.

Given the large number of African slaves on the island, the fear of a generalized black uprising, as had happened in Haiti, made the military concentrate its efforts on containing the situation in the eastern region. The "Volunteers" forces, raised at the "Spanish Casinos," became unexpectedly important. This paramilitary organization was made up of traders, property owners, and employees who were ready to defend the "Spanishness" of Cuba, not to mention their own interests, to the death. These battalions acted in towns and cities. The violence with which they behaved whipped up anti-Spanish sentiment, the repression involving the seizure of property, imprisonment, and, in many cases, banishment or death.

In Havana the president of the Spanish Casino was the Basque Julián de Zulueta, the first Marquis of Álava and a well-known slave-trader. He was a prosperous, versatile businessman and a key figure in irredentist conservatism. At the end of the 1840s he had bought the sugar mill at Regalado, in the Banagüises area, which he modernized and called Ála-

---

23. Magdalena Jorajuría Zunda was Ángel Albistur's mother's cousin. The will left him Oteizarena house in Sunbilla on March 4, 1884 with property valued at 18,932 pesetas, and debts of 12,217 pesetas. AGN, *Protocolos Juan Urriza*.
24. Ángel Albistur died in Cuba in 1939 at age eighty-six.

va; this sugar mill was to become the most profitable and modern one on the island.[25]

The volunteer forces included the Chapelgorris ("red berets"), Basque volunteers who watched over villages in which they had their businesses in the region to the south of Havana and the current province of Matanzas.

The Chapelgorris of Guamutas protected the Álava factory area, Vizcaya, and Havana mills—all of them belonging the Zulueta family. This battalion watched over the countryside, patrolling and transporting fugitive slaves. In 1868 they were reorganized as an armed body. They were extremely vigilant during the war and reported creoles they suspected of conspiring against Spain.[26]

These units' range of action went from the Caimito area in the west to the foothills in the Vuelta Abajo (now, Pinar del Río) area, to the central Álava area—the region known as San José de los Ramos—and beyond in order to protect the property in central Zaza in Placetas. It was rich, vast sugar region which gave work to people who had recently arrived from Spain, many of them from the Basque Country.[27]

In 1878 the Cubans and Spaniards ended hostilities. Peace favored business. The end of slavery was a reality and the sugar plantation owners set out to replace their slave workers by encouraging Spaniards to immigrate. The profile of some of the Navarrese immigrants who arrived in the last quarter of the nineteenth century fits in here: most of them were country people—fleeing from poverty, avoiding military service, and also wanting to take advantage of the business opportunities on the island, even though the real situation they encountered had little to offer them.

On the island, the modernization of the sugar industry led to a division between industrial and agricultural work, and the rail links between the sugar mills and the large storehouses and the ports increased. Agricultural land was available, as were other means for earning a living. The fact that their countrymen were already settled there attracted more young Navarrese.

Toward the 1870s, and particularly over the following decade, the arrival of cash from Cuba was obvious in towns such as Sunbilla. It was a

---

25. Julián de Zulueta made Álava sugar mill one of the most productive on the island and at one time had eight hundred African slaves on the land around it, each slave producing an average of thirty-two boxes of sugar. For further information about Julián de Zulueta, his family and businesses, see Marrero Cruz, *Julián de Zulueta Amondo.*

26. For a description of the Chapelgorris' activity, see Arrozarena, "Los vascos en las guerras de independencia de Cuba," 39–40. Report to the local judge at San Agustín (town of Batabanó), José Rubira, presented by the officer of the squadron of Chapelgorri cavalry from Bejucal, about the suspect Pedro Osorio from Quivicán. The young man was innocent, but his brother Juan Bautista Osorio had been executed by firing squad a few days earlier for conspiring in favor of independence. Archivo Histórico Nacional, Ultramar, file 4345.

27. For information about the posting of young men to Cuba during the 1868 war, see Agirreazkuenaga, "Las instituciones representativas vascas frente a la insurrección de Cuba. La formación del 'Tercio de Voluntarios Vascongados' o 'Legión Vasca' por las diputaciones forales de Araba Bizkaia y Gipuzkoa," 285–326.

two-way traffic, money was lent on the island or sent to a representative and invested in small businesses or paid for a substitute to serve in the army.[28]

The Legacy of a Life of Work

From a young age Francisco Jorajuría Aldave stood out among the people of Sunbilla.[29]

It is impossible to say exactly when he arrived in Cuba, but he came of age when the Ten Years' War broke out, so joining the army was probably a way out for him. His Basque background linked him with other Basque businessmen settled there. Skillful and enterprising, he spoke fluent Spanish, knew about accounting, and knew how to write, which was a considerable advantage at the time. We know that he was in the Chapelgorria at least during the events of the last War of Independence.

In 1888, after the age of forty, he married Antonia Iribarren Arrechea—who was also from Sunbilla—at the parish of Jesús María at Havana Cathedral; the witness was Julián de Zulueta Ruíz de Gamís, son of the late marquis of Álava. We estimate that by that time he would have spent many years on the island, stating that he had savings of thirty-five thousand pesetas to bring to the marriage. She was twenty-four, the only daughter of a trader who was also a moneylender. A relative who lived in Havana met her in the port and took her to her wedding as soon as she arrived in Cuba.[30]

The enclave Habana Matanzas was well-known for the importance of the sugar industry there, which was associated with Basque immigrants. Francisco Jorajuría administered Álava; in the Perico area, fourteen kilometers away, Gerónimo Astondoa, also from Sunbilla, was in charge of the España factory, very close to Bolondrón, whose mayor was the aforementioned Ángel Albistur. They found a place for the newly arriveds, who worked as machine operators in industry and in agriculture. Fewer of them worked in retail, railway maintenance, carpentry—making boxes for packaging—and jobs which were manual to some extent. Jovellanos and Colón were the nucleus that linked the port of Cárdenas with the railway, and it was from there that sugar was exported to the refineries in the United States.[31]

---

28. This was what happened with Juan Bautista Petrirena, from Sunbilla, who returned from Cuba in 1872, named his brother Francisco—who lived at Macagua and was nicknamed the Tiger—his representative to sell a slave on his property and send him the money. Years later, one of the latter's children was to be mayor of the town. AGN Protocolos Juan Urriza, Santesteban, escritura de poder, Santesteban, August 14, 1872.

29. Francisco María Jorajuría Aldave had been born at Sunbilla on November 21, 1853, and was son of Gerónimo Jorajuria Gamboa and Juana Josefa Aldave Michelena. Iruñea Diocese Archive

30. Marriage certificate dated the November 27, 1888, Havana. Francisco Jorajuría Aldave, forty year-old bachelor, factory administrator and Antonia Iribarren Arrechea, twenty-four, married. Witness: Julián de Zulueta Ruíz de Gamís. Copy of the deed in the Oteizarena Miarra private archive.

31. According to the record of Spaniards in Cuba in 1899, there were twenty-eight people

The War of Independence of 1895 affected the sugar interests in the region. The volunteer bodies were called back into action, the old Chapelgorris accompanying regular troops. In December, 1895, a proindependence column commanded by Antonio Maceo burned the sugarcane plantations at España mill; the administrator had offered to pay a large contribution to the cause, but the rebel army refused the money and the fields were burned.

In February 1896, General Máximo Gómez and his troops attacked the garrison protecting the Álava mill, which was commanded by Jorajuría. As they retired, the Cubans set fire to twenty wagons, destroying all the fields. Álava mill itself was protected by having men quartered there. The troops converted old storehouses and abandoned mills—such as San Martín, in the photograph below—into barracks to resist Cuban rebels' attacks.[32]

Figure 9.2. The abandoned San Martín mill.

According to the family history, Francisco Jorajuría was in charge of defending the Álava estate and tried to prevent its destruction by offering General Máximo Gómez money. He did not succeed, as we have said, and the fields were torched. Public opinion in Navarra paid scant attention to Spain's loss of Cuba, perhaps it was even something of a relief, it being the end of a conflict in which the young had died. The press hardly mentioned the war and there were very few outstanding people from Navarra whose interests were affected by the Cuban conflict. At a more immediate level, in places where families had relatives who had emigrated, the end of the war was seen in a different way. The Sunbilla town council, meeting in the summer of 1898, after Spain had been defeated, unanimously decided that "given the sad circumstances which the nation is facing in the wars in Cuba, Puerto Rico and the Philippines against the rebels and the United

from Sunbilla there, most of them working in agriculture. See Bosco Amores Carredano, "Presencia de navarros en Cuba a fin del período colonial," 243.
32. This incident is mentioned in Marrero Cruz, *Julián de Zulueta Amondo*, 153–54.

States with the spilling of so much blood which has caused the grief of so many families (we will) cancel the festivities in honor of our patron saint, only holding the religious ceremonies."[33]

Francisco Jorajuría returned to Spain with his wife in spite of the offers which the Zulueta family had made him to stay and be in charge of the Álava mill. Unlike other people from Sunbilla who stayed on the island after the conflict had ended, the couple returned to their home town at the start of 1899.[34]

The decision had not been made in haste. Previously, in 1897, Jorajuría, through his brother-in-law, Gregorio Iribarren, had bought the rights to the Sunbilla flour mill, which belonged to the town council. He owned all the rights when he reached the town, an investment which would give him a steady annual income. He bought Oteizarena miarra with its kitchen garden and threshing floor for 13,020 pesetas. The mansion had been closed up since the death of Magdalena Jorajuría in 1884 and was mortgaged, so it had lost value. After the purchase he had it modernized, it was one of the first houses in the town to have running water, toilets, and electric lights. He had learned of these domestic advances in Cuba.

On settling in the town, Jorajuría and his brother were members of the municipal "twenty." Gregorio Iribarren was the greatest property owner and Jorajuría the most significant industrial player in the town. After reaching an agreement with the town council, they brought electricity to the streets of Sunbilla. This initiative later led to founding the Compañía Eléctrica Jorajuría S.A.[35] After taking in her elderly parents, Antonia Iribarren received their property. The married couple became one of the families with greatest purchasing power in the town. He kept some property in Cuba, probably in the Zulueta estates on the Matanzas plain, leaving his countryman Gerónimo Astondoa as his representative there. He died at an advanced age in Sunbilla in 1923. His widow inherited all their property. Their holdings in Cuba had been sold by this time, but their link with the island remained, Francico's younger brother, José María Jorajuría, still being there, along with other relatives and friends.[36]

Living off the income from her properties, Antonia Iribarren faced up to the events of the Spanish Civil War (1936–1939) and the penury which

---

33. Sunbilla Municipal Archive, minutes, July 31, 1898.

34. Of the approximately 65,000 Spaniards registered, 680 were from Navarra, most of them from the Iruñea-Pamplona area, Baztan, Bertizarana, and Bortziriak. Most of the people from Sunbilla worked in agriculture in the area between the towns of Perico and Bolondrón in the Matanzas region. The author states that eleven were from Donamaria, seventeen from Doneztebe, and twenty-eight from Sunbilla as well as people from neighboring villages such as Almandoz, Arezo, and Azkarate. See Bosco Amores Carredano, "Presencia de navarros en Cuba a fin del período colonial," 245.

35. Agreement between Sunbilla Town Council and Mr. Francisco Jorajuría Aldave for public electricity for the town. See Sunbilla Town Council minutes, February 26, 1899. The last rights to the company were sold to Iberduero in the 1970s.

36. The marriage contract between Francisco Jorajuría and Antonia Iribarren was signed at Doneztebe, March 2, 1899. AGN Protocolos Santesteban, year 1898.

followed it, partly thanks to occasional help from Cuba: she was sent small quantities of sugar and coffee which crossed the frontier at Irun. She died at the age of ninety-three in the spring of 1957.

As an Epilogue

It is not possible to write about the house's two hundred years of history without fully addressing this area's "American" link. After decades of splendor, the old nobility hardly survived at all once the Navarrese privileges in trade and colonial administration came to an end. In the Oteizas' case, their marriage policy and business skills did not work and they were unable to save the house from ruin during the nineteenth century. It was to be recuperated by another "Indiano" (person who had made his fortune in the West Indies). This time, they had been people of modest means who had emigrated and returned to the town after prospering in business in Cuba and acquiring the main houses and lands.

Francisco Jorajuría brought with him the entrepreneurial spirit that he had developed in Cuba and, together with others, helped to modernize life in his natal town. There is evidence that he kept in touch with the Zulueta family, who lived in Vitoria-Gasteiz. And he maintained his relationship with Cuba through his younger brother.

The Jorajurías left descendants in Cuba. José María Jorajuría Aldave disembarked in Cuba at the end of the nineteenth century. He settled in land on the Matanzas plain where he raised a sizeable family and was in close connection with other businessmen of Basque origin, and countrymen from Sunbilla and nearby towns. When he died in Cuba, he was one of the most prosperous sugarcane growers in Matanzas province. His eldest daughter, María Josefa, married another man from Sunbilla, Demetrio Oyarzábal, Francisco and Antonia's godson, who worked all his life in Cuba in the laboratories at the Guipúzcoa sugar mill, property of Manuel Arocena, who was from Tolosa. The Cuban Jorajurías currently live in Venezuela and various places in the United States and, whenever they can, they make the pilgrimage back to their ancestors' house at Sunbilla.

Bibliography

Agirreazkuenaga, Joseba. "Las instituciones representativas vascas frente a la insurrección de Cuba: La formación del 'Tercio de Voluntarios Vascongados' o 'Legión Vasca' por las diputaciones forales de Araba Bizkaia y Gipuzkoa." In *Patria y Libertad: Los vascos en la independencia de Cuba*, edited by Alexander Zubiri Ugaldey et al., 285–326. Tafalla: Txalaparta, 2012.

Amores Carredano, Juan Bosco. "Presencia de navarros en Cuba a fin del período colonial." In *Las migraciones vascas en perspectiva histórica*, edited by Óscar Álvarez Gila and Alberto Angulo 235–58.

Vitoria-Gasteiz: University of the Basque Country, 2002.

Arrozarena, Cecilia. "Los vascos en la independencia de Cuba." In *Patria y Libertad: Los vascos en la independencia de Cuba*, edited by Alexander Zubiri Ugaldey et al., 15–160 Tafalla: Txalaparta, 2012.

Caro Baroja, Julio. *La Hora Navarra del XVIII: Personas, familias, negocios e ideas*. Iruñea-Pamplona: Institución Principe de Viana, 1969.

Castellano de Gastón, Gaspar and Juan Bosco Amores Carredano. *Entre el valle del Baztán y América: El indiano Juan Bautista de Echevarría y casa Gastón de Irurita*. Iruñea-Pamplona: Ediciones Eunate, 2014.

Catálogo Monumental de Navarra. Volume 5. Iruñea-Pamplona: Government of Navarra, Institución Príncipe de Viana, 1996.

Gárate Ojanguren, Montserrat. *La Real Gipuzkoan Caracas Company*. Donostia-San Sebastián: Sociedad Guipuzcoana de Ediciones y Publicaciones, 1990.

Idoate Ezquieta, Carlos J. *Emigración navarra del valle del Baztán a América en el siglo xix*. Iruñea-Pamplona, Editorial Príncipe de Viana, 1989.

Imizcoz Beunza, José María. "La hora navarra del xviii: Relaciones familiares entre la monarquía y la aldea." In *Juan de Goyeneche y el triunfo de los navarros en la monarquía hispánica del xviii*, edited by María Concepción García Gainza and Ricardo Fernández Garcia, 45–77. Iruñea-Pamplona: Fundación Caja Navarra, 2005.

Latasa, Francisco Javier. "Apuntes para la historia del puente de Sumbilla." *Revista Príncipe de Viana* 249 (2010): 185–98.

Marrero Cruz, Eduardo. *Julián de Zulueta Amondo: Promotor de capitalismo en Cuba*. Havana, Ediciones Unión, 2006.

Martínez del Cerro González, Victoria E. *Una comunidad de comerciantes navarros y vascos en Cádiz (segunda mitad del xviii)*. Sevilla, Consejo Económico y Social de Andalucía, 2006.

Martínez López, David. "Sobre familias, élites y herencias en el siglo xix." *Historia Contemporánea* 31 (2005): 457–80.

10

Basques and Navarrese People in Santiago de Cuba: Preliminary Notes

María Cristina Hierrezuelo Planas

To Santiago de Cuba on the five hundredth anniversary of its foundation. To the Basques and Navarrese people who contributed to make it a beautiful, prosperous, rebellious, hospitable, and heroic city.

A first approach to the documentation about Basques and Navarrese people in Santiago de Cuba shows that they were not numerous, which reflects of their situation on the rest of the island of Cuba. A demonstration of this is that in 1899 there were 2,453 heads of family recorded in the Register of Spaniards for Santiago, of which 5 percent—approximately 122 people—were Basques and Navarrese.[1] Absolute numbers aside, it is interesting to see the diversity of their activities, particularly during the eighteenth, nineteenth, and twentieth centuries, with special emphasis on the later two. Over these centuries, the city was witness to the work of small traders such as the Gipuzkoan Francisco Pérez y Hernandorena and the Araban Teodoro Echazarra Alegría who were owners, respectively, of the food shops at Victoriano Garzón Street, No. 74,[2] and Estrada Palma Street No. 83;[3] of coachmen such as Asencio Barbará Garallo, from Laudio in the province of Araba.[4] There were also people who spent shorter periods in the city for work; this was the case of "men of the sea" such as José María Arriaza, from Bizkaia, captain of the merchant ship *Pájaro del Océano*,[5] and another Bizkaian, José Rufo de Goicochea, the captain of a Spanish brigantine.[6]

---

1. Arrozarena, *El roble y la ceiba*, 153, 259–60.
2. Archivo Histórico Provincial de Santiago de Cuba (AHPSC). *Protocolos Notariales*. No. 1447, folio 1265, year 1918.
3. AHPSC, *Protocolos Notariales*, No. 1079, folio 298, year 1914.
4. AHPSC, *Protocolos Notariales*, No. 1442, folio 1226, year 1917.
5. AHPSC, *Protocolos Notariales*, No. 292, folio 398 v., year 1862.
6. AHPSC, *Protocolos Notariales*, No. 292, folio 258, year 1862.

The second most important city in Cuba also welcomed people whose work in trade, innovation, and religion, as we will see, were to mark the city's history.

The Human and the Divine: Matías Alqueza, Joaquín Osés de Alzúa, and Valentín Zubizarreta

When speaking about Matías Alqueza it is important to remember that the city ceased to be the capital of the island and lost population because of the expeditions that went to conquer and colonize the American continent at the end of the Encomiendas regime. This had such a negative effect on the social and economic development of Santiago de Cuba, that if, according to Nicolás Joseph de Ribera, in the eighteenth century it was "A large town full of civilized people,"[7] by the end of that century, it had become "the prolongation and axis of the rural life under its jurisdiction."[8]

However, it should be pointed out that by that date the creoles had undertaken a series of initiatives that were to modify the state of affairs and give their city the brilliance and splendor they believed it deserved. This included founding San Basilio Magno Seminary School on April 14, 1722, and setting up the Sociedad Patriótica de Amigos del País in 1787, made up of a large group of property-owning residents that, in spite of its brief existence—it was disbanded in 1792—expressed the local intention to attend to the territory's educational and economic needs.

It was in this context that the Navarrese Matías Alqueza emerged, his being the historical initiative of bringing a printing press to Santiago de Cuba. Juan Bautista Vaillant (1788–1795), was the governor of the Eastern Department at the time and his progressive attitude allowed him to see how important having such technology could be for the city. That was why he responded to Alqueza's proposal by writing a letter to Luis de Las Casas: "It will certainly be very useful to the public, it will work in favor of this poor city which needs help from all sides to grow and shine in the way which I believe it deserves to."[9]

In spite of the captain general's negative reply and the suggestion that the petition should be sent to the monarch, it seems that the press actually began functioning: in 1792 a sermon by Father Veranes was printed on it. Some months later, on October 7, 1793, royal approval was granted. That same year Alqueza published *Letras de los villancicos que se han de cantar en la santa iglesia catedral de Cuba en los maitines del nacimiento de Cristo nuestro señor* (lyrics for the carols to be sung in the holy cathedral of Cuba at matins for the birth of Christ our lord), the first work known to have been printed outside Havana where, seventy years earlier,

---

7. Portuondo Zúñiga and Rovira, *El Colegio Seminario San Basilio Magno*, 140.
8. Portuondo Zúñiga, *Santiago de Cuba desde su fundación hasta la Guerra de los Diez Años*, 99.
9. Ibid., 103.

in 1723, Carlos Habré had printed the famous *Tarifa general de precios de medicinas* (General medicine prices), the first work to be published in Cuba.[10]

Alqueza also published Christmas carols in 1806, 1809, 1811, 1812, 1813, 1815, 1816, and 1817. A further work, which is believed to have been printed in 1807, included "various sonnets and prose dedicated to the celebration of the ascension of the cathedral of Santiago de Cuba to the category of Metropolitan."[11]

Matías Alqueza died in Santiago de Cuba on January 8, 1819.[12] The last thing he printed was from the previous year. The following text is featured on the cover: *For the festivity of His birth, sacred eclogues, put to music and for the holy ceremonies of Christmas Eve in the Holy Metropolitan Church of Cuba by Father Juan Paris and chapel master of the mentioned Holy Church. All licenses granted. Printed in Cuba by Matías Alqueza on December 14, 1818.*[13] There is no doubt that his initiative as a printer had immediate results. At first, Gutenberg's invention was used almost exclusively to publish novenas, sermons, and carols, but in 1806 *El Amigo de los Cubanos,* Santiago's first newspaper, was founded, and this was unquestionably a landmark in the eastern city's cultural history.

Joaquín Osés de Alzúa also hailed from Navarra—born in Iruñea-Pamplona on September, 22 1755—and was named bishop of Santiago de Cuba on November 6, 1791. His term of office was affected by the immigration of thousands of French—after the revolution broke out in Haiti, they settled in this part of the island—and by the work of governors as significant as the aforementioned brigadier Juan Bautista Vaillant (1788–1795), and colonels Juan Nepomuceno Quintana (1796–1798) and Sebastián Kindelán O'Regan (1799–1810), who focused on bringing about the economic and social transformation of Cuba's eastern region and its capital city.

Osés de Alzúa's position—not being prepared to accept certain decisions taken or proposals given by specific public figures in the region, such as Sebastián Kindelán O'Regan—made him a controversial figure in the history of Santiago de Cuba during the last decade of the nineteenth century and the first decade of the twentieth. These measures included prohibiting burials inside churches and building a cemetery outside the urban area. This proposal was based on simple reasons of hygiene but was not accepted, presumably because it would lead to the church losing income.[14]

His attitude toward the French immigrants was also questionable, strongly criticizing their way of life and customs, to the extent of blaming

---

10. *El libro en Cuba,* 11.
11. Leon Estrada, *Santiago literario,* 34.
12. Ibid.
13. Ibid.
14. For more on this matter see María Elena Orozco Melgar, "El nacimiento de la higiene urbana en Santiago de Cuba y el exilio de los muertos," 14–29.

them for the city's young people's lack of interest in religious studies.[15]

However, it must be admitted that Osés de Alzúa was a strong defender of the region's prosperity, which can be seen in actions such as reopening San Basilio Magno Seminary in 1792. In order for the center to revert to its original pedagogical mission, he ordered: "let there be classes of Grammar, Theology, Morality, Ecclesiastical History, Holy Theology, Scholastic Theology, Philosophy and Plain Song."[16] His work in favor of founding a university in the east of Cuba must also be taken into account: at the time, young people in this part of the island who wanted to study had to go to Havana or abroad.

Another thing which demonstrates Osés's initiatives to improve eastern Cuba is the report of November 1794 that he presented to the monarch, Charles IV, and in which he expressed his concern about the backwardness of the region:

> Havana having been helped so much in its growth and grandeur, Cuba has in no way benefited from this,[17] it is sadly annihilated and destroyed, perhaps the people looking after the island's interests have believed that Havana could not win without Cuba losing, in other words, the former could not become rich without impoverishing the latter, lifting itself up whilst ruining the other, without realizing that parts cannot be lost without losing the whole, without taking into account that if one part grows too much, although only its head, if all the blood goes there, and one concentrates on that, the body becomes apoplectic and the whole machine breaks down and dies.[18]

A firm supporter of free trade and small-scale agriculture, a prisoner, like many of his contemporaries, of a "fear of blacks" due to the Haitian revolution, defender of the idea of "populating the countryside with free, white workers,"[19] Joaquín Osés de Alzúa was unable to prevent Cuba and its eastern region from developing slave plantations, and, to his sorrow, the mountains became immense coffee plantations and the plains rippling sugarcane plantations whose production and productivity depended on the martyred backs of the thousands of slaves who disembarked in Santiago Bay every day.

With regards to Bizkaian friar Valentín Zubizarreta, his work in running San Basilio Magno Seminary and the building of the Virgin de la Caridad Sanctuary at el Cobre, in honor of the protector of Cuba and

---

15. Portuondo Zúñiga and Rovira, *El Colegio Seminario San Basilio Magno*, 55.

16. Portuondo Zúñiga, *Santiago de Cuba desde su fundación hasta la Guerra de los Diez Años*, 163.

17. He refers to the jurisdiction that, just like Santiago de Cuba, was generally called by the name of the city.

18. D. Joaquín Osés y Alzúa: "Fomento de la agricultura e industria en la parte oriental de la Isla de Cuba (Primer Arzobispo de Santiago de Cuba, 30 de noviembre de 1794)" in *Memorias de la Real Sociedad Económica de Amigos del País* (Havana, 1880), in Portuondo Zúñiga, *Nicolás Joseph de Ribera*, 160. The original text from the document is not respected.

19. AGI, Ultramar, 387; see Orozco Melgar, *Ana Manuela Mozo de la Torre*, 19.

symbol of our Cuba identity,[20] is enough for him to be recognized as a distinguished figure in the cultural life of Santiago de Cuba. When he arrived in the city, the seminary operated on the ground floor of the bishop's palace; he sold the space to the La Salle Brothers almost immediately with an idea in mind: building a new seminary next to the El Cobre basilica.[21] After six years of hard work, on September 8, 1931, he blessed the new seminary building which, as was to be expected, kept the name San Basilio Magno and was built in the area around the sanctuary "in the shade . . . of the blessed Mother of all Cubans."[22]

With regards to the sanctuary, suffice it to point out that when Zubizarreta began his term the building, while still standing, had its arches, walls, and floors seriously compromised as a consequence of the work incorrectly carried out by The Cobre Mines company on land near the church and in galleries underneath it. This happened in May 1906, and caused so much damage that even if the buildings had been completely restored it would have been almost impossible to make them as solid as they had been originally.[23] The archbishop gave his patronage to the building of the new church. Most of the work was finished in 1927. Multiple donations from the public and from institutions, along with the indemnity paid by the mining company to the church, were used to pay for incurred expenses.

After almost twenty-three years of pastoral work, Valentín Zubizarreta died at the Colonia Española sanatorium on the afternoon of February 26, 1948. His body was taken to Santa Ifigenia cemetery at half past two on the next afternoon. It was not a coincidence that in his funeral address Monsignor Enrique Pérez Serantes, who was bishop of Camagüey at the time, mentioned the most interesting facets of the dead pastor of souls' life: he underlined Zubizarreta's participation in the coronation of the Virgen de la Caridad del Cobre, which had taken place in December 1936; the building of the Archbishop's palace, the National Sanctuary of the Protector of Cuba at El Cobre and the foundation of San Basilio el Magno college at the same place.[24]

Julián Cendoya: A Successful Businessman

After a quick and chronologically fragmented search with regards to the nineteenth and twentieth centuries, we have identified around thirty Basque people whose work was connected with trade, being shop assistants, wine store owners, and members of mercantile partnerships. They include, from both centuries, Manuel Aguirre, Esteban Beola, Francisco

---

20. For the historical basis to this criteria, see Portuondo Zúñiga, *La virgen de la Caridad del Cobre.*
21. Portuondo Zúñiga and Rovira, El Colegio Seminario San Basilio Magno, 154.
22. Ibid.
23. Portuondo Zúñiga, La virgen de la Caridad del Cobre, 234.
24. *Diario de Cuba*, Santiago de Cuba, February 27–29, 1948.

Goya, Eugenio Leisaga, Tomás Larrea, Emilio Sanz, and particularly, Julián Cendoya Echeverría, from Tolosa, Gipuzkoa.

Cendoya arrived in the United States of America at an undetermined date and took out US citizenship. He married Isabel Lane Purcell on June 26, 1889 and—as far as we know—had three children with her: Julián, John, and María. After his wife died on October 9, 1914 in Brooklyn—where they had traveled to take their daughter to boarding school—he married Mary Lane Purcell on July 20, 1916.[25]

By the second half of the 1890s he was already involved in trade in Santiago de Cuba, which was also where he lived. In 1898—the year in which Spanish colonial domination of the island came to an end—he signed a three-year contract—later extended for another year—with trader Eduardo Ramírez Rodríguez, contributing the capital needed to set up a food warehouse. In exchange he received 67 percent of the profits and business operations, the rest going to his partner, who leant his name to the company.[26]

The year 1902 was transcendental in Cuban history. On May 20 the republic was proclaimed and the United States—which had been on the island since intervening in 1898—kept and extended its domination of the island's economy and many of its natural resources. During that year, along with a large group of traders, property owners, and individuals who worked in various activities,[27] Julián Cendoya founded the banking firm La Acumulativa: Compañía Anónima Mutua de Ahorros and became its chairman.

It was capitalized at 350,000 pesos divided into 3,500 shares, each one with a value of 100 pesos, and its objective was to "favor and encourage saving among all social classes using all available means."[28] Documents show considerable activity in giving out mortgages with an annual interest rate of 10 percent. For example, the mortgage given to "José Bueno y Compañía: Sociedad en Comandita" for up to ten thousand pesos with the guarantee (collateral) of three houses.[29] In September of the same year the organization changed its name to Banco de Oriente. Its headquarters and center of operations was still Santiago de Cuba, but it was now able to set up agencies and branches in the rest of the island, and even abroad.[30]

In 1906, in partnership with Enrique Giraudy Faurest, Cendoya founded Enrique Giraudy y Compañía, with capital of twenty-five thou-

---

25. AHPSC, *Protocolos Notariales,* No. 967, folio 743, year 1928.

26. AHPSC, *Protocolos Notariales,* No. 1305, folio 797, year 1902.

27. These businessmen included Eligio Ros Pochet, Amaro Ros Revilla, Gustavo Ros Revilla, Pablo Badell Loperena, and José Vicente Taquechel Miyares, and property owners Laureano Fuentes Pérez and Manuel Boris López de Queralta. Others involved included José Hill Feliú, trade expert; Joaquín García Navarro Kindelán, land owner; and Ana Valiente Portuondo, represented by her husband; pharmaceutical doctor Tomás Padró Griñán. See AHPSC. *Protocolos Notariales.* No. 1103, folio 292, year 1902.

28. AHPSC, *Protocolos Notariales,* No. 1103, folio 292, year 1902.

29. AHPSC, *Protocolos Notariales,* No. 1305, folio 647, year 1902.

30. AHPSC, *Protocolos Notariales,* No. 1305, folio 775, year 1902.

sand pesos, for buying food in general, local produce and making candles. This Gipuzkoan's economic resources were to increase over the following years: he bought and sold houses, plots of land, and made investments in mining and natural resources in Cuba. For example, in December 1917 he acquired six buildings on various streets in the city worth 35,000 pesos;[31] he sold a house on Narciso López Street, built on his own plot of land, both for a total of 21,500 pesos; he owned 48 percent of the one hundred shares of *La Feliz* mine, which had 144 hectares of copper and other minerals;[32] he also owned 25 percent of *La Gloria* magnesium mine, at San Luis, which had forty-nine hectares.[33]

He also managed several trading companies. These included Compañía Azucarera Cendoya S.A. (1919) and Cendoya y Valls Sociedad en Comandita (1925). Some of these he founded in partnership with people from the Basque Country, which can be seen as a countrymen's network. For instance, Julián Cendoya Sociedad en Comandita (1911), Compañía Sanitaria de Santiago (1914), and Ferretería Cendoya S.A. (1925) whose partners included, in the former and the latter respectively, Ángel Badiola, and Tomás Arana, both from Gipuzkoa; and, in the latter, José Liñero Arbaiza, from Bizkaia.

These companies' corporate purposes were as varied as the purchase and sale of coal; importing, buying and selling power plants, electric motors, accessories for them and similar products; taking local sugar and wood to market; sowing sugarcane.

The importance of the latter in the Cuban economy is reflected in Cendoya's involvement in it, particularly during World War I. As is well known, the conflict—which began in 1914—had a considerable impact on European production of sugar beets; its price rose considerably and, as a result, Cuba—a great producer of sugarcane—had a period of economic prosperity known as "the dance of millions" or "the fatted cows." The country was subjected to massive speculation which ended in 1920 with the sudden, resounding fall in prices and the ruin of many investors. In this context, Cendoya was a planter and everything suggests that he was not affected adversely, selling the sugarcane from his plantations under stable conditions during both the boom and the crisis. In 1916, thanks to his agreement with Ermita Sugar Corporation, he guaranteed his sales for the sugar harvests of 1916–1917 until 1920–1921,[34] and in 1922 he reached a similar agreement for the years 1922–1923, 1923–1924, and 1924–1925.[35] The agreement involved Cendoya buying the sugar produced by the Ermita factory.

In the 1910s this Gipuzkoan started to work with his two sons. In 1911 one of them—Julián—was one of the partners of the company Ju-

---

31. AHPSC, *Protocolos Notariales,* No. 1444, folio 2360, year 1917.
32. AHPSC, *Protocolos Notariales,* No. 1422, folio 2548, year 1913.
33. AHPSC, *Protocolos Notariales,* No. 949, folio 1846, year 1924
34. AHPSC, *Protocolos Notariales,* No. 1436, folio 614, year 1916.
35. AHPSC, *Protocolos Notariales,* No. 923, folio 139, year 1923.

lián Cendoya Sociedad en Comandita, which imported, sold, and bought hardware items; in 1918, along with his brother John, he was a partner in Cendoya Sons and Company, which financed ships, exploited docks and warehouses, sugar storage, and exported local wood. This situation certainly made it easier for his sons, and then his grandsons, to carry on his work in business after his death. In 1958 one of his grandchildren, Julián Cendoya Hechavarría, was the owner of a company called Cendoya y Compañía, with its headquarters in Santiago, dedicated to importing and marketing hardware.[36]

A Few Words about Gender and Family

With regards to women, the documents show the presence of a small number of them: their lives, in keeping with the norms of the time, were quite different from those of the men. Women's work was in the home. Rosa Díaz de Irraza y Martínez de Crispín was an example of this, taking care of household matters and only having her own right to do things as simple as buying a house once she was widowed.[37]

Josefa Antonia de Mendizábal's life was similar. She was from Lazkao, Gipuzkoa, and married Antonio María de Guruceaga, from El Ferrol, Galicia, had no children and was widowed in December 1857. In her will she stated that she was the owner of the house she lived in on Santo Tomás Street as well as two flat-roofed buildings on either side of San Pedro Street, one of which housed a stable and a carriage house. She also owned eight shares in the gas factory—which provided lighting for a large part of the city—and four domestic slaves. With the freedom that being a widow gave her, she left part of this property to Ana Perozo, a Creole. It seems they were friends rather than relatives. Initially, Josefa Antonia stated that Ana should be given five hundred pesos after her death and that she should have the use of one of the flat-roofed buildings, the one with the stable and carriage house, for the rest of her life.[38] She later modified this, stating that her friend should be its owner.[39]

José de Mendizábal—father of Josefa Antonia—also emigrated to Santiago de Cuba. Before settling there, he had lived in Maracaibo in Venezuela. That was where Josefa Fernández—his wife and the mother of his two daughters (the aforementioned one and another named Agustina)—must have died. In his will he describes her as deceased after "having emigrated to a foreign country" and describes himself as having "emigrated to this city," which gives the impression that he had arrived not long before.[40] Perhaps this was a reunited family: the father—an old man

---

36. Jiménez, *Los propietarios de Cuba, 1958*, 147.
37. AHPSC, *Protocolos Notariales*, No. 646, folio 1670, year 1906.
38. AHPSC, *Protocolos Notariales*, No. 292, folio 471, year 1862.
39. AHPSC, *Protocolos Notariales*, No. 300, folio 204, year 1870.
40. AHPSC, *Protocolos Notariales*, No. 273, folio 67, year 1843.

of more than seventy—becoming a widower in a foreign land and, trying to escape his solitude, deciding to travel to where his daughter and some of their relatives abide. The documents mention that Manuel de Aguirre Mendizábal and his nephew and nieces—Manuel, Francisca, and Trinidad Beola Aguirre—were present.[41]

This family's links with the loved ones who did not leave their land of birth were never broken. Josefa Antonia's husband, Antonio María de Guruceaga, as his father-in-law's executor, made Ángel Gil de Alcain—a trader in Donostia-San Sebastián—his representative so that he could receive a sum of money from his late father-in-law's will.[42]

The same thing happened with the previously-mentioned Manuel de Aguirre Mendizábal and Francisca, Manuel, and Trinidad Beola Aguirre; the first in his own right and the other three as the legitimate children of the late Trinidad Aguirre Mendizábal de Beola gave powers to José María de Aramburu, who lived in Gabiria, Gipuzkoa, in order for him to give Juana Aramburu the deeds for their gift of a farmstead there. They made this gift because of the particular affection they had for the person receiving it and also because of Antonio Aguirre's recommendation at the time of his death, the latter being the legitimate father of Manuel and grandfather of the other contributors and of Juana Aramburu.[43]

Final Comments

Studying the presence of Basques and Navarrese in Santiago de Cuba allows us to see their active participation in this eastern city's economic, social, and cultural life. As a living memory of this work, a main street there bears the name Valentín Zubizarreta and the square in front of El Cobre sanctuary hosts his portrait as a stone sculpture by artist Fernando Boada Martín. Neither of these homages can be seen as coming exclusively from the Catholic community: they are, rather, recognition of a personality whose work was inextricably linked with the church which houses the image of the Virgen de la Caridad del Cobre, the protectress of Cuba and of all the Cubans who invoke and venerate her as a religious symbol but also of our Cuban nationality. Another homage is to the Navarrese man who first brought printing to Santiago de Cuba. The name of the printer of the city's historical conservation office is Ediciones Alqueza.

Bibliography

Arrozarena, Cecilia. *El roble y la ceiba: Historia de los vascos en Cuba.* Tafalla: Editorial Txalaparta, 2003.

Fornet, Ambrosio. *El libro en Cuba.* Havana: Editorial Letras Cubanas, 2002.

41. AHPSC, *Protocolos Notariales,* No. 117, folio 192 v., year 1867.
42. AHPSC, *Protocolos Notariales,* No. 284, folio 61, year 1854.
43. AHPSC, *Protocolos Notariales,* No. 117, folio 192 v., year 1867.

Jiménez Soler, Guillermo. *Los propietarios de Cuba, 1958*. Havana: Editorial de Ciencias Sociales, 2007.

León Estrada. *Santiago literario*. Santiago de Cuba: Fundación Caguayo-Editorial Oriente, 2013.

Martínez Videaud, Luis. *Las calles de Santiago de Cuba*. 3rd edition. Santiago de Cuba: No publisher, 1965.

Orozco Melgar, María Elena. "El nacimiento de la higiene urbana en Santiago de Cuba y el exilio de los muertos." *Del Caribe* 23 (1994): 14–29.

———, compiled and introduced by. *Ana Manuela Mozo de la Torre: Los acentos de una mujer*. Santiago de Cuba: Editorial Oriente, 2007.

Portuondo Zúñiga, Olga, complied and introduced by. *Nicolás Joseph de Ribera*. Havana: Editorial de Ciencias Sociales, 1986.

———. *Santiago de Cuba desde su fundación hasta la Guerra de los Diez Años*. Santiago de Cuba: Editorial Oriente, 1996.

———. *La virgen de la Caridad del Cobre: Símbolo de cubanía*. Santiago de Cuba, Editorial Oriente, 2011.

Portuondo Zúñiga, Olga and Joan Rovira S. J. *El Colegio Seminario San Basilio Magno*. Santiago de Cuba: Editorial Oriente, 2000.

Veigas Zamora, José. *Escultura en Cuba, siglo xx*. Santiago de Cuba: Fundación Caguayo-Editorial Oriente, 2005.

11

The Basques in the Cienfuegos–Villa Clara Railway Project, 1847–1880

Miliada Hernández García

The contributions to this book have brought to light a wide range of subjects that have been researched or are still to be and which, inevitably, implicate all of the social sciences. Links between the Basques and other migratory groups, their activities connected with and attitudes toward different stages of Cuban history, their participation in the capitalization of the island's economy and of the Basque region, associationism, their contributions to international law, and current Basque-Cuban relations are now coming to light.

In the present case, too, a series of investigations into the regional history of Cienfuegos have proven commulative—adding to the knowledge gained over the last five years thanks to evaluations and quantifications of Basque and Navarrese immigration—that has awakened our interest in certain questions: Was the work of certain Basques in the Cienfuegos's government decisive in its final approval of the railway project? Was Basque participation proportional to their ownership of sugar estates along the line? Are there indications that the Basques' participation in the railway project led to or strengthened any family or economic relationships?

As was to be expected, there are problems when trying to examine the Basque presence in the context of the planning, carrying out and final installation of the Cienfuegos-Villa Clara railway. The first challenge is that the period examined should include both the nineteenth-century project and the use of the completed railway up to the first decades of the twentieth century, or when capitalism was finally consolidated in Cuba. The realization of the project is in itself a demonstration of transition toward a new economic-social order which was to bring with it profound changes in the superstructure and infrastructure of the island: for instance, modifications in the workforce. So the issue of the railways is intertwined with the introduction of Chinese and slave labor in the region and Basque participation in it. Many other issues could be taken into account, but they would go beyond the limits of this article.

Therefore, our proposal—which is in an exploratory phase, since many other variables and Basque surnames may still come to light during more in-depth research into the subject—is to concentrate on the role of the Basques in getting the railway project passed, without examining its actual construction process. May it be said that measuring the importance of Basque partners' participation in this enterprise, and in the networks which were set up then, linking them with some connections with later periods, after the approval of the railway project, was inevitable. All of this has been done in order to confirm the company-capitalism-family syndrome that we have researched in previous works.[1]

This chapter has been based on archive material and some memoirs. The main ones were *Colección de Documentos Florentino Morales* of the provincial museum of Cienfuegos, "Ferro-Carril desde la Villa de Cienfuegos a la de Santa Clara. Reglamento de esta Empresa, aprobado por el Escmo. Sr. Gobernador y Capitán General, en 11 de Enero de 1848" and "Camino de Hierro, Informe de los Ingenieros don Julio Sagebien y don Alejo Helvecio Lanier, sobre el de Cienfuegos a Villa-Clara," both kept in the José Martí National Library. We also made use of texts about regional history by authors such as Pedro Oliver y Bravo, Enrique Edo Llop, Pablo Rousseau, and Pablo Díaz de Villegas, as well as the 1830 census, held at the Cienfuegos Provincial Historical Archive. Sources used to verify the Basque origin of some surnames were also very important.[2]

Various Proposals for a Railway Project between Cienfuegos and Villa Clara: Basques Involved in Its Design

Fernandina de Jagua colony was founded on April 22, 1819, and before two full decades had gone by there was a sugar boom that lasted from 1835 to 1855 and, consequently, many more sugar estates were established. Understandably, the need to transport the sugar led to the idea of improving the roads and building a railway.

1. The company-capitalism-family hypothesis has been developed by English researcher and anthropologist Jack Goody in his work *The Development of the Family and Marriage in Europe*, looking at the direct relationship between companies and family relatives. Cuban researcher Ana Vera's work *El qué, el cómo y el para qué de la historia de la familia* (The what, how and why of family history) deals with the relevance of this hypothesis for economic, local, and social history in general on a family scale. Our previous research includes Hernández García, "Goytisolo y Castaño."

2. In this case we used the documents of the Asociación Vasco-Navarra de Beneficencia de Havana, specifically the association's minutes. We also consulted Arrozarena's *El roble y la ceiba* and the one coordinated by Ugalde, *Patria y Libertad*.

This led to isolated initiatives in the 1830s to construct a railway from Cienfuegos. However, there was no consensus about the route it should take. Some people wanted to link it with the Júcaro railway and others with Villa Clara.

Later, in 1841, during governor Pedro Bassadona's term of office, the railway project was resuscitated and the following year the first plan was drawn up with a more precise idea about the projected route to Villa Clara. The engineer Alejo Helvecio Lanier mapped the trajectory, but the initiative came to nothing. That lack of a clear financial plan limited all of the railway proposals, is clear in all of the texts with regards to the building of the Cienfuegos railway.[3]

The situation changed somewhat when Ramón María de Labra became provincial governor. Around 1844 there were numerous economic and social transformations and he was appointed above all because of his ability, along with his influence with people around him and in the city council. In this regard, we should mention the very wealthy Tomás Terry, Enrique de Zaldo, and the Basque Fermín Gorozabel.

During Labra's four-year term, addressing the railway project became once again a viable matter. One of the main reasons for the failure of the previous projects had been the lack of a budget. With regards to supplementing governmental funds, one of the first initiatives was to raise subscriptions, each subscriber contributing a sum for the founding of a railway company and would later receive a corresponding amount of shares. The Economic Council and Engineers' Headquarters was founded at this time and took charge of planning for the main infrastructural construction, including the railway.[4] However, there remained differences of opinion over the railway's routing. The Basque protagonists, too, took differing positions here.

There are references in various sources to the Basque Juan Pedro Gorozabel as mayor of the city in 1846. On the same date he had been chosen "By the Most Excellent Mr. Superintendent of the Island's Royal Tax Office, inspector of cost appraisals for the city mayor's office."[5]

However, during his term of office as mayor and in spite of the existence of Alejo Helvecio's plan proposing a railway line to Santa Clara, at the end of the year the Economic Council sent a note expressing its disagreement about building a Cienfuegos-Villa Clara railway and specified:

> we believe it is better, for the moment, to take our eyes off that route and look at the Júcaro railway in Laguna Grande or in Pipian, which seems to be the start of a trunk line linked to the Gran Unión, which will reach Cienfuegos bay according to the clarifying report drawn up by civil engineer Manuel Cabrera y Heredia.[6]

3. Edo y Llop, *Memoria histórica de Cienfuegos y su jurisdicción*, 89.
4. Ibid., 110.
5. Rousseau and Díaz de Villegas, *Memoria descriptiva, histórica y biográfica de Cienfuegos*, 94 and 135.
6. Edo y Llop, *Memoria histórica de Cienfuegos y su jurisdicción*, 130.

Until now we have not found any sources which refer to Juan Pedro's position with regards to the two proposals, but when a provisional board met in May of the next year to support and fix the details of the building of the Cienfuegos-Villa Clara line, he was not one of the first subscribers. And the chair of that provisional board was another Basque, Fermín Gorozabel. On that occasion the project to build a line to Villa Clara was presented, backed by ninety-eight subscribers who raised a total of $189,500.[7]

As we have mentioned, there were different criteria among the inhabitants of Cienfuegos about the route the railway should take, and the fact that people at Sagua also brought pressure to bear for the project to start from there made Fermín's work as chair of the board and the support of all the subscribers for the Villa Clara line more important. It should also be noted that the means which the city council brought into play for raising funds were not sufficient for building the project and, because of this, some people said that the connection with Júcaro had to be more economical.

However, the attention that the board, headed by the Basque, paid to the budget and planning of this line was, in our opinion, decisive. Another crucial point was the highly detailed plans and calculations made by engineers Julio Sagebien and Alejo Helvecio Lanier that provided the details about the project's viability and the difficulties involved in the other proposals.[8] At the same time they implemented the successful strategy of having a substantial initial amount of capital, enough to start the construction, and later requesting the support of the Royal Development Board, which was asked to simply assist the project rather than paying for all of it.

The final plan for the railway was completed in 1848. In that year there was published: *Ferro-Carril desde la Villa de Cienfuegos a la de Santa Clara: Reglamentos de esta Empresa aprobado por el Escmo Sr. Gobernador y Capitán General, en 11 de Enero de 1848* (Railway from the City of Cienfuegos to Santa Clara. Company Regulations, approved by the Excellent sir Governor and Captain General, on January 11, 1848). Its introduction states,

> Office of the Most Excellent Mr. Civil Superior Governor to Cienfuegos Council
>
> I have seen fit to pass every part of these regulations for the company for the railway line from this city to Santa Clara and sent them to your Excellence on December 27, the Board being quite able to start work and carry out the project.

The quote ends "Cienfuegos, January 17, 1848—Ramón María de Labra y Fermín Gorozabel, chair of the provisional Board for the railway

---

7. Ibid., 155–58.
8. Biblioteca Nacional José Martí (BNJM), *Camino de Hierro*, 3–14.

between this city and Santa Clara." Fermín died the same year, by which time he was an investor in the railway and, as such, was at the board meeting held on 10th May, 1847 and in the one held in December.

Basque Surnames and Networks in the Cienfuegos-Villa Clara Railway Project

Approval of the railway project depended to a large extent on the contributions of numerous landowners who were interested in it. In 1847, as we have said, there were two board meetings to address the issue and they were crucial in refining the idea. During the first meeting the initial list of subscribers was made known and it included some Basque surnames which we summarize in table 11.1.

It might seem absolutely to be expected that the chair of the provisional board for the railway would be among the first shareholders of the company. However, we believe that his commitment and presence among the project's partners were more influenced by his being a landowner, since

Basque surnames	Capital brought to the company
Fermín Gorozabel	$ 500
Heirs of Joaquín Reyna Capetillo	$ 500
José María Vidaurreta	$ 500
Fermín Olayzola	$ 500
Pedro Irízar	$ 500
Antonio Digat	$ 500
Total: 6	$ 3,000

Table 11.1 Basque surnames amongst the first subscribers to the Cienfuegos-Villa Clara railway (Board meeting held on the 10th of May, 1847). Source: Enrique Edo Llop (1943); Memoria Histórica de Cienfuegos y su jurisdicción, Havana, Úcar, García y Cía, 155–58.

becoming part of the process helped to favor his property.

In 1839, in partnership with Joaquín Reyna Capetillo, he owned the Hormiguero sugar estate,[9] and there are sources regarding their other previous landholdings as well.[10] This property was one of the best positioned sugar mills in relation to the railway planned by Alejo Helvecio Lanier in 1842.[11] On it the engineer stated:

> From Lajitas to the edge of Fermin Gorozábel's sugar mill or Las Cruces circle . . . 2m [miles] 178 y. [yards]. Lajitas stream, Hormigue-

---

9. García Martínez, "Estudio de la economía cienfueguera desde la fundación de la colonia Fernandina de Jagua hasta mediados del siglo xix," 117–69, Annexes.
10. Joaquín Reyna Capetillo is recorded as being an owner from 1831 and Fermín Gorozabel from 1838; although the source does not specify the name of the property, it could have been Hormiguero. Oliver Bravo, *Memoria histórica, geográfica y estadística de Cienfuegos y su jurisdicción.*
11. Ibid., 26–35.

ro stream and two reed banks are in this area.[12]

Later, in the report which was finally approved in 1848, engineers Alejo Helvecio and Julio Sagebien described the modifications to the railway line as follows:

> This straight line continues across some land prepared on a site next to Gorosabel's sugar estate and, a little further on, cuts very obliquely through the first levelling and enters the land of the new Dorticos sugar estate, of course leaving the original line and Villa Clara highway to the south, the highway remaining close as it goes through Fuentes, Acosta, Hernández, Cabezas and Padilla, and by the sources of Grande and Hormiguero streams.[13]

Hormiguero sugar estate was one of the most favored in both railway plans. Its proximity to the new railroad would make transporting its goods cheaper and so increase the business's profitability, which is what actually happened. In later studies about the Cienfuegos economy Hormiguero is mentioned as one of the most productive sugar estates in the region and this was, in part, due to its proximity to the railroad. Furthermore, Basque families clustered together, drawn by this prosperity, and remained in Cienfuegos almost from the foundation of the colony.

In this sense Fermín's marriage with Juana Irady, who was related to the trader Martín Irady, from Donostia-San Sebastián, and who had settled in the city in 1830, was the perfect starting point for a family saga.[14] When Fermín died, his wife inherited Hormiguero and continued to develop it until when, in 1880, she left it in the hands of her heirs, Elías Ponvert and Luisa Maximina Terry Irady. The latter's maternal grandfather was Martín Irady and her father was Antonio Terry.[15]

By that time Luisa's relative, Tomás Terry, had become the main shareholder in the Cienfuegos-Villa Clara railway.[16] In this way one of the oldest networks with Basques in it was formed in Cienfuegos; it would

---

12. Ibid., 33.

13. BNJM, Camino de Hierro, 10.

14. Martín Irady is mentioned in the 1830 census, written down as Martín Hirady, from the Peninsula, without specifying that he was from Donostia-San Sebastián, but we believe he was the same man referred to by Rousseau and Díaz de Villegas and by García Martínez in *Esclavitud y colonización en Cienfuegos 1819–1879*, 25. The latter author places Martín Irady in Cienfuegos in the 1830s as a Basque trader with a business on Gasell Street and whose shop assistant is Tomás Terry. This would explain the family relationship between the Terrys and the Iradys. Also see: AHPC. Pedro Antonio Aragonés, *Padrón de la Villa de Cienfuegos 1830*, 42.

15. Rousseau and Díaz de Villegas, *Memoria descriptiva, histórica y biográfica de Cienfuegos*, 425–32.

16. In 1863 its shareholders were Joaquín Justiniani, Tomás Terry, Gabriel Bachiller, and Pedro Nolasco Abreus, and associated capital included the Sociedad La Hereditaria and the Sociedad de Crédito Industria. Associations of this level led to a concentration of shares which eventually, in 1864, favored Tomás Terry, strengthening the position of his capital financially and commercially and, to a large extent, the supremacy of his interests in the region. Multiple authors, *Síntesis Histórica Provincial: Cienfuegos*.

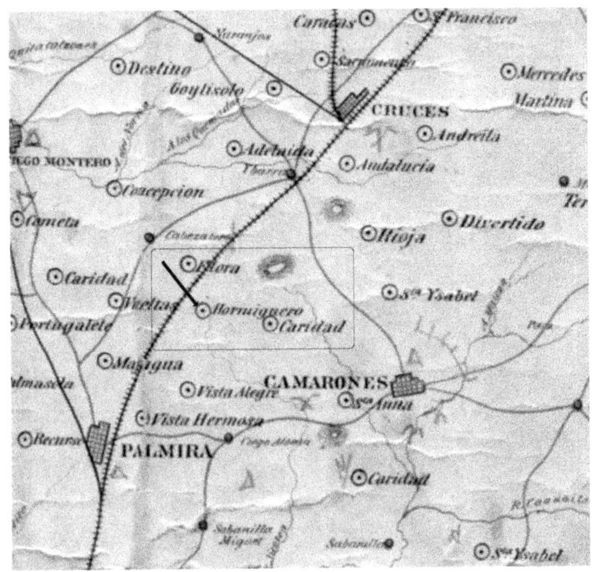

Figure 11.1 (above). Section of the sketch from 1873
showing Hormiguero sugar plantation.
Figure 11.2 (left). Legend on both sketches
Figure 11.3 (below). Section of the 1873 sketch showing
Agustín Goytisolo Lezarzaburu's sugar properties.
Source for all figures: Archivo Histórico Provincial de
Cienfuegos. Esquicio Topográfico de la Jurisdicción de
Cienfuegos, dedicado a las virtudes cívicas e ilustración
del Sr. Dn. Eduardo A. del Camino por Nicolás de
Gamboa. 1873.

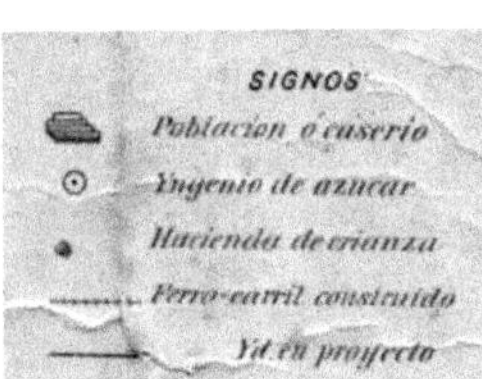

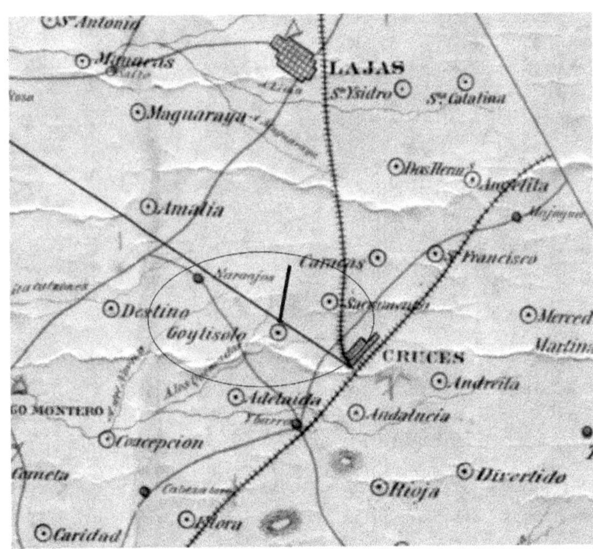

continue to exist while capitalism was firmly established on the island. It is worth pointing out that this transition took place in Cienfuegos based on the consolidation of the sugar estate-railway-port triumvirate.

With regards to networks we could also offer a hypothesis about the origin and later career of Pedro Irízar Clouet, another of the first shareholders of the railway. It seems that both he and his brother Agustín may have been descended from Lorenzo Irízar and one of Luis D'Clouet's nieces, D'Clouet having founded the Fernandina de Jagua settlement.

Cienfuegos historian Orlando García mentions Lorenzo Irízar in Cienfuegos between 1820 and 1830 and also his marriage.[17] And no other inhabitant of the city with the surname Irízar has been found, not even in the 1830 census. Although some other sources have yet to be consulted, our hypothesis would explain Pedro's presence among the city's first economic and political elite, made up of the people closest to the founder and/or people he had helped, particularly taking into account that he was elected financial councillor of Cienfuegos city council in 1849. In 1850 he was named lieutenant in the Batallón de Voluntarios Nobles Vecinos de Cienfuegos and, in 1858, mayor.[18]

Furthermore, both he and his brother were members of one of the economic networks set up by Basque immigrants who settled in Cienfuegos. The Bizkaian Agustín Goytisolo Lezarzaburu was at its center. With regards to the economic relations he had with the Irízar brothers, it was based, among other things, on the trust between immigrants of the same origin or ancestry, as researcher Martín Rodrigo explains:

> The Irízar brothers were closely connected with the Goytisolos, something which would happen again later in Barcelona. So in January 1873 Agustín Goytisolo Lezarzaburu named Pedro Irízar his general representative for his property on the Peninsula, along with Francisco Sola. At the same time, Pedro's brother Agustín Irízar, who lived in Cienfuegos, replaced Goytisolo's son-in-law, the late Miguel Plana, as his main representative on the island along with his son Fabián.[19]

Goytisolo was also related to one of the other initial main shareholders in the railway, Antonio Digat.[20] The marriage between Antonio Digat and Paula Irarramendi, as reflected in the 1830 census, had several children including Estanisláa Digat Irarramendi, who married the aforementioned Agustín Goytizolo in 1846. So it is not surprising that one of the main

---

17. García Martínez, *Esclavitud y colonización en Cienfuegos 1819–1879*, 38.

18. Bustamante, *Diccionario biográfico cienfueguero*, 90.

19. Rodrigo Alhajilla, "Los ingenios San Agustín y Lequeitio (Cienfuegos)," 24.

20. The marriage between Antonio Digat and Paula Irarramendi, as we have seen in the 1830 census, took place prior to their arrival in Cienfuegos, appearing there as a family living on Santa Cruz Street, and some of their children had been born in Trinidad and others in Cienfuegos. However, we have not been able to check the French Basque origin of the family, which researcher Martín Rodrigo mentions, because in the census Antonio Digat and Paula Irarramendi are stated to be from Bizkaia.

property owners in Cienfuegos during the sugar boom period, with his sugar estates—Simpatía and later San Agustín—very close to the railway line,[21] should marry one of the daughters of one of the first subscribers to the project.

Returning to the names in table 11.1, we might consider the Vidaurreta and Olayzola's cases. There are no references to where they were born and they have been included because their surnames are of Basque origin. We have been able to find out more about the latter's interest in the railway project because in 1846 he was the owner of Victoria sugar estate in the Caunao district of Cienfuegos,[22] that the railroad was to go through.

While the last details were being settled, other Basques joined the project in December 1847. Meeting the conditions set by the superior government, businessmen of Basque origin living in other places were enrolled. They included Ramón Larrazabal, José Larralde, and Fernando Echamendía, from Trinidad and Havana, about whom the sources examined to date have given no precise data.

Final Considerations

Starting with the fact that the Cienfuegos-Villa Clara railway company was a local initiative based on subscriptions, the contributions of the first shareholders must be evaluated and analyzed bearing in mind their importance for the project's eventual approval. And this is regardless of the fact that the railway would later be a company whose main financial and commercial capital was contributed by just a few legal residents.

The existence of other proposals for railway projects was useful experience for those interested in the Villa Clara line, but Fermín Gorozabel's skillful management must also be taken into account. Formulating the initial budget, detailed planning and harmonizing the interests of engineers and proprietors were all essential in order for him to be able to complete the project.

Finally, it must be said that the Basques' involvement in the company was fundamentally motivated by their participation in a regional elite and, in Gorozabel's, Capetillo's, and Olayzola's cases, there is an obvious relationship between the railway and their being sugar estate owners. The railway also facilitated family and economic networks which sprang up around the project and contributed to its completion. We should bear in mind that some of these networks, such as those started by Gorozabel and Juana Irady, later consolidated by the Terrys and the Ponverts, persisted thanks to ownership of a sugar estate very well positioned with regards to the railway.

---

21. Hernández García, "La inmigración vasca en Cienfuegos."
22. García Martínez, "Estudio de la economía cienfueguera desde la fundación de la colonia Fernandina de Jagua hasta mediados del siglo xix," 117–69, Annexes.

Bibliography

Alonso Valdés, Coralia. "Consideraciones generales sobre inmigración española: siglo xix." In *Nuestra Común Historia*, 106–16. Havana: Editorial Ciencias Sociales, 1993.

Arrozarena, Cecilia. *El roble y la ceiba: Historia de los vascos en Cuba.* Tafalla: Editorial Txalaparta, 2003.

Bustamante, Luis J. *Diccionario biográfico cienfueguero.* Cienfuegos: Imprenta R. Bustamante, 1931.

Edo y Llop, Enrique. *Memoria histórica de Cienfuegos y su jurisdicción.* 3rd edition. Havana: Imprenta ÚCAR, García y Cía, 1943.

Fernández, Empar and Pablo Bonell Goytisolo. *Cienfuegos 17 de agosto.* Barcelona: Rocaeditorial, 2004.

García Martínez, Orlando. "Estudio de la economía cienfueguera desde la fundación de la colonia Fernandina de Jagua hasta mediados del siglo xix." *Islas (Revista de la University of Las Villas)* 55–56 (1976–1977): 117–69.

García Martínez, Orlando. *Esclavitud y colonización en Cienfuegos 1819–1879.* Cienfuegos: Ediciones Mecenas, 2008.

González Sedeño, Modesto. *Último escalón alcanzado por la plantación comercial azucarera esclavista (1827–1886).* Havana: Editorial de Ciencias Sociales, 2003.

Goody, Jack. *The Development of the Family and Marriage in Europe.* Cambridge: Cambridge University Press, 1983.

Hernández García, Miliada. "La inmigración vasca en Cienfuegos (1860–1898)." Masters thesis, University of Cienfuegos, 2010.

———. "Goytisolo y Castaño: Empresas y familia durante la transformación capitalista en Cienfuegos (siglos xix y xx)." In *América Latina en la turbulencia global: oportunidades, amenazas y desafíos,* coordinated by Alexander Ugalde Zubiri. 525–536. Leioa: University of the Basque Country, 2014. Also available at https://web-argitalpena.adm.ehu.es/listaproductos.asp?IdProducts=UWLGSO8540 percent20 percent20&page=1&IdTopics=011525&Id=&buscapor=&key1=&Avanzada=&IdTopicsgrupos=&arbol=01.

Iglesias, Fe. *Del Ingenio al Central.* Havana: Editorial de Ciencias Sociales, 1999.

Jiménez Soler, Guillermo. *Las empresas de Cuba 1958.* Havana: Editorial de Ciencias Sociales, 2004.

———. *Los propietarios de Cuba.* Havana: Editorial de Ciencias Sociales, 2008.

Le Riverend, Julio. *History Económica de Cuba.* Havana: Editorial Pueblo y Educación, 1974.

Moreno Fraginals, Manuel. *El Ingenio, complejo económico social cubano del azúcar.* Havana: Editorial de Ciencias Sociales, 1978.

Multiple authors. *Síntesis Histórica Provincial: Cienfuegos.* Havana: Editora Historia, 2011.

Oliver Bravo, Pedro. *Memoria histórica, geográfica y estadística de Cienfuegos y su jurisdicción*. Cienfuegos: Imprenta de Francisco Murtra, 1846.

Rodrigo Alhajilla, Martín. "Los ingenios San Agustín y Lequeitio (Cienfuegos): Un estudio de caso sobre la rentabilidad del negocio del azúcar en la transición de la esclavitud al trabajo asalariado (1870–1886)." In *Azúcar y esclavitud: En el final del trabajo forzado*, compiled by José A. Piqueras, 252–68. Madrid, Fondo de Cultura Económica, 2002.

———. "Los Goytisolo: De hacendados en Cienfuegos a inversores en Barcelona," *Revista de Historia Industrial* 23 (2003): 11–37.

Rousseau, Pablo L. and Pablo Díaz de Villegas. *Memoria descriptiva, histórica y biográfica de Cienfuegos 1819–1919*. Havana: Establecimiento tipográfico "El Siglo XX" Teniente Rey 27, 1920.

Santiso González, María Concepción. "Emigración vasca entre 1840 y 1870: Pautas de análisis acerca del éxito vasco en América: cadenas familiares, primeras letras y otras consideraciones." *Boletín de la Asociación de Demografía Histórica* 11, no. I (1993): 83–105.

Ugalde Zubiri, Alexander, coordinator. *Patria y Libertad: Los vascos y las guerras de independencia de Cuba (1868–1898)*, Tafalla, Editorial Txalaparta, 2012.

Vera Estrada, Ana. "Estudiar la familia: Un repaso." *Revista Temas* 31 (October–December (2002): 101–10.

———, compiled by. *La familia y las Ciencias Sociales*, Seminario permanente de Familia, Identidad Cultural y Cambio Social, Centro de Investigación y Desarrollo de la Cultura Cubana Juan Marinello, 2003.

Zanetti, Oscar and Alejandro García. *Caminos para el azúcar*. Havana: Editorial de Ciencias Sociales, 1987.

Documentary Sources

Archivo Histórico Provincial de Cienfuegos. Pedro Antonio Aragonés. *Padrón de la Villa de Cienfuegos 1830*.

Archivo Histórico Provincial de Cienfuegos. *Esquicio Topográfico de la Jurisdicción de Cienfuegos, dedicado a las virtudes cívicas e ilustración del Sr. Dn. Eduardo A. del Camino por Nicolás de Gamboa. 1873*.

Biblioteca Nacional José Martí [BNMJ]. *Ferro-Carril desde la Villa de Cienfuegos a la de Santa Clara. Company Regulations, approved by the Excellent Sr. Gobernador y Captain General, en 11 de Enero de 1848*.

Biblioteca Nacional José Martí [BNMJ]. *Camino de Hierro, Informe de los Ingenieros don Julio Sagebien y don Alejo Helvecio Lanier, sobre el de Cienfuegos a Villa-Clara*, Habana, Imprenta del gobierno y Captainía General por S. M., .1848.

Museo Provincial de Cienfuegos. Centro de Información. Colección de documentos Florentino Morales.

12

French Basques in Cuba: Their Contribution to the Development of Tanning

Beñat Çuburu-Ithorotz

While the quantity of people who emigrated to Cuba from the Basque Country was nothing like that of those who went from Galicia, Asturias, and the Canary Islands, it was still a fundamental contributor to what Cuban society is today.

In the fifteenth and sixteenth centuries the Basques, thanks to their maritime tradition, were among the discoverers and colonizers of Cuba and contributed to the creation of commerical ties between Spain and the New World. During the eighteenth and nineteenth centuries numerous families in the sugar aristocracy were descended from Basques who had settled in Cuba. The amassed immense fortunes were partly repatriated after Cuba became independent and that gave Hegoalde—the southern Basque Country—an important cash infusion. During the twentieth century there was considerable migration to Cuba, but the Basque Country was not one of the regions that provided most immigrants.

It is difficult to give precise data to form an idea of the importance of the Old World–born Basque community—or those with Basque ancestry—at any one particular time, but all sources consulted suggest that together they were less than 5 percent of the total. We can state, however, that it was a highly active group in economic terms and also socially thanks to two of its immigrants' associations: the Asociación Vasco-Navarra de Beneficencia and the the Centro Vasco in Havana.

The Basques were also very well represented in Cuba thanks to Basque pelota.Had not the revolutionary government forbidden betting in the sports world at the start of the 1960s, Havana's pelota court would doubtless have been among the most important venues for international jai alai today.

We should also remember the not inconsiderable number of toponyms and patronyms of Basque origin in Cuba which provide the unquestionable evidence of the influence of long-standing Basque immigration in the country.

The following thoughts are about a very particular type of immigration, that of young Basques from Iparralde—the northern Basque Country—and, in particular, of people from the town of Hazparne. Some of them elected to emigrate to Cuba in the mid-nineteenth century, a destination which most of their countrymen did not choose. They settled throughout Cuba and worked as tanners, which had been their craft in Hazparne before emigrating. They set up a considerable number of companies in which they employed emigrants from their far-off town, whom they went to fetch and eventually transferred to them the tanneries they had set up and developed in Cuba.

After showing how important this industry was in the Cuba and in the Basque Country, we will try to clarify the conditions which favored the departure and settling in Cuba of these emigrants. We will then examine some of the tanneries set up by French Basques, as examples of social success and integration.

Tanning in Cuba

Tanning is the technique used to turn animal skins into leather. Humans have employed leather for footwear, clothes, and other daily objects for centuries. In Cuba, there is no evidence of leather having been used by the aboriginal inhabitants: on the other hand, the conquerers and colonizers needed large quantities of leather and tried to produce it rapidly by introducing domesticated animals to the island early on (bovine, equine, ovine, and porcine livestock). These animals multiplied and there were soon surpluses which could be taken to market, Cuban leather becoming a product that was smuggled and even used as currency.[1]

The production and sale of leather was important during the first colonial phase, during the sixteenth century and the first half of the seventeenth. Livestock farming was developed in order to replace mining, and leather production also supported a craft industry for making everyday objects.[2] At that time, leather was the second most important product in the Cuban economy, after sugar, and large quantities of leather reached Seville from Cuba (sometimes more than fifty thousand units annually between 1561 and 1620).[3] This level of production was maintained throughout the eighteenth century with sixty thousand tanned hides being

---

1. Arrozarena, *El roble y la ceiba*, 45.
2. Sarmiento Ramírez, "La artesanía popular tradicional cubana," 497.
3. Chaunu and Chaunu, *Séville et l'Atlantique*, vol. 6, 1012–13, vol. 8, 561.

exported around 1755,[4] and at the end of the century it was the fourth biggest export after sugar, tobacco, and alcohol (190,459 hides were exported during 1784–1788, above all to European ports such as Cádiz and Barcelona and American ones such as Campeche).[5]

With regard to the number of tanneries in the country, the first data available is from 1820 and tells us that there were nine establishments, mostly in Havana.[6] Another source from 1836 reveals that there were around ten tanneries within the city walls of Havana with twenty-eight tanners, and a further eleven and twenty-three, respectively, outside the walls.[7] The number of tanneries had reached fifty by 1838;[8] they do not seem to have been large companies and were mostly in the western part of the country, where there was more trading activity. In other regions— where the lifestyle was more subsistence-based—peasants used the prime materials they found around them (such as animal skins) to make their houses and everyday objects. The techniques used by the peasants would later be employed by the Mambi Army[9] in the swamps, using the leather they made in the rudimentary tanneries they set up. They used leather for arms (machete scabbards, leather cannons), for architecture (leather for waterproofing roofs and making doors and furniture), and footwear.[10] In 1846 there was a total of fifty-six tanneries in the Sancti-Spíritus region and this had risen to sixty-one in 1860, having moved eastward to the Holguín region given the increases in livestock there.[11]

In the eastern part of the country, where there were craftsmen, crafts products were sold at very low prices; in Remedios tanned leather was sold by weight in the 1860s. Until the 1880s the only large industries on the island were sugar and tobacco; after that there were some small factories, including tanneries, which were considered to be a lesser industry.[12] After the 1880s there was diversification of the economy and immigrants played an important role in it, owning 45 percent of the tanning industry by 1927.[13] Leather and other items, such as wood and clay, were less affected by the technological changes of the industrial revolution; leather was still produced using traditional techniques and this favored the arrival and settling of Basque tanners, as we will see.

In 1898 there were fifty-three tanneries throughout Cuba in the following places (ten of which belonged to French Basque tanners):

4. Marrero, *Cuba: Economía y sociedad*, 215–16.

5. Bosco Amores, *Cuba en la época de Ezpeleta*, 214–32.

6. Langlois, *Géographie universelle, physique, politique et historique*, 933.

7. Fernández de Pinedo Echevarría, *Comercio exterior y fiscalidad*, 355–56.

8. Moreau and Slowaczynski, *Annuaire statistique pour 1838 de l'Europe, l'Asie, l'Afrique, l'Amérique et l'Océanie*, 176.

9. Juan Ethnnius Mambi was a black officer in the Spanish Army who deserted Santa Domingo in 1846 to fight against the Spaniards. Mambises was the term used for all rebel fighters of whatever their background in both of the Cuban Wars of Independence.

10. Sarmiento Ramírez, "La artesanía popular tradicional cubana," 502.

11. Le Riverend, *Historia Económica de Cuba*, 373–74.

12. Vidal Rodríguez, *La emigración gallega a Cuba*, 318–19.

13. Marqués, *Las industrias menores*, 155.

Province	Number of tanneries
La Habana (capital)	7
Havana	6
Matanzas	7
Pinar del Río	3
Puerto Príncipe	5
Santa Clara	14
Santiago de Cuba	11
% of total	53

Table 12.1. Tanneries in Cuba in 1898. Source: Commercial Directory of the American Republics, Government Printing Office, Washington, 1898.

From the Basque Country to Cuba: Leather Professionals

Most of the Basque tanners we are going to consider were from the French Basque town of Hazparne (Hasparren in French), and we will look at the area and its specialized emigration's characteristics.

Hazparne is a Basque town in the province of Lapurdi near Lower Navarre. It has always been one of the most populous towns in Iparralde, reaching its highest total of inhabitants—5,822—in 1886. Agriculture was the main activity in Hazparne, but in the eighteenth and nineteenth centuries working in more than one activity was very common and farm workers were often also tanners, shoe-makers, or cape manufacturers. Hazparne had three things which led to the setting up of tanneries there: tannin, taken from oak trees, was easily available from the surrounding woods; there was water from the numerous streams that come down from the Ursuia Mountain; there was an abundance of livestock from which the hides came. The latter were also imported from Portugal, Holland, Canada, and Uruguay. The Hazparne tanners tanned thick hides which were used for shoe soles and military gear, and also thinner hides for making gloves, for example. The infrastructure the tanner required was rudimentary: a few tools, pits, and a few barrels. In 1831 there were fifty-one tanneries in Hazparne spread throughout all the town's districts, most employing only two or three people.

Tanning was demanding, but most of the people involved were also farmers and they were used to hard work. Working in two activities was almost natural to them as the peasants produced the animal hides which they were later going to tan on their own property. In her study of tanning at Romans, Annie Roche states that it is "the first company in which people agree to work from five in the morning to one o'clock so that they have have the afternoon free for their land."[14] The hides were sold at the local market and in the surrounding areas but, at the beginning of the nineteenth century, the people of Hazparne started to use hides they tanned themselves to make shoes. Producing footwear became so important that

---

14. Roche, *La tannerie romanaise de 1403 à nos jours*, 106.

it emerged on the town's main industry during the twentieth century.

The decline in tanning began in Hazparne in the 1860s due to the oidium epidemic which affected the oak trees in the region, as well as the failure to adapt modern tanning techniques. The censuses carried out during the nineteenth century confirm that shortly before the French Revolution, there were 137 tanners; in 1856 there were 158; 66 in 1881; and there were only 14 left in 1911.[15] Many of those who were left without work decided to emigrate to seek employment in the tanneries set up in Cuba, Mexico, Argentina, Uruguay, and Chile by other people from Hazparne.

Emigration from Hazparne began before the nineteenth century. Immigrants from the town are to be found in French overseas colonies during the seventeenth and eighteenth centuries, and in Spain and the Spanish colonies in America during the eighteenth century.[16] They were also pioneers at that time, opening the way for mass emigration from the 1830s onward. That emigration from Hazparne was sustained and continual for more than a century. The countries of destination can be seen in table 12.2, mostly Argentina, Uruguay (chosen by 60 percent of immigrants), Spain, Cuba, and Chile. France also figures on the list, but to large cities far from the Basque Country such as Bordeaux and Paris.

Destination	Number of emigrants	% of total
Argentina	1,183	42.54
Uruguay	518	18.63
France	287	10.32
Spain	173	6.22
Cuba	162	5.83
Chile	148	5.32
Unknown	114	4.10
United States (California)	58	2.08
America	53	1.90
Mexico	43	1.55
Various*	42	1.51
Total	2,781	100

* (Algeria, 10; England, 2; Belgium, 4, Bolivia, 5; Canada, 7; Ecuador, 3; Madagascar, 1; Morocco, 3; Overseas Territories, 1; Peru, 2; Newfoundland, 2; Venezuela, 2)

Table 12.2. Destination of emigrants from Hazparne (1830–1930). Source: Municipal, provincial, consular, and family archives.

Shoemakers were the most important group of immigrants, which is not surprising taking into account that theirs was the main profession in Hazparne (table 12.3). In spite of local employment opportunities, many prefered to try their luck abroad because there was no guarantee of work in Iparralde and salaries were not high. Tanners were also among the main emigrants to Cuba, Argentina, and Chile, and emigrants from the leather professions made up 35 percent of the total.

This professional specialization was to have repercussions as most of the immigrants pursued their crafts in their adopted countries, some of them founding companies and conserving commercial relations with

---

15. Population censuses from 1804, 1856, 1881, and 1911. Hazparne municipcal archive.
16. Hazparne municipal archive, Register of declaration of Spanish property (I-11-136).

their home town. In fact, during the nineteenth century, immigrants from Hazparne were involved in exporting leather from America to Hazparne and later, in the twentieth century, in selling footwear made in Hazparne in American markets. Furthermore, immigrants who had set up tanning or footwear companies often returned in search of workers and to take advantage of their professional know-how. In this way they managed to dominate these sectors in some countries (tanneries and footwear factories in Chile; tanneries in Cuba).

TRADE	NUMBER	% OF TOTAL
Shoemaker*	788	28.34
Agricultural worker	582	20.93
Tanner	198	7.12
Tradesman**	158	5.68
Carpenter	53	1.91
Servant	52	1.87
Cape manufacturer	35	1.26
Student	29	1.04
Brick layer	27	0.97
Military	27	0.97
Chocolate maker	22	0.79
Baker	22	0.79
Religious	21	0.75
Blacksmith	16	0.57
Cook	13	0.47
Waiter	13	0.47
Milkman	12	0.43
Various or without trade	183	6.58
Unknown	530	19.06
TOTAL	2,781	100

* Shoemaker (775), espadrille maker (9), bootmaker (2), apprentice shoemaker (2).
**Shop clerk (110), shopkeeper (27), trader (15), importer (3), commercial representative (3).

Table 12.3. Jobs of emmigrants from Hazparne (1830–1930). Sources: Municipal, provincial, consular, and family archives.

Tanners from Iparralde in Cuba

There are always some "pioneers" in migratory network processes who open the door for others to enter. Everything points to two brothers, Dominique and Pierre Lorda, having been the earliest French Basque tanners in Cuba. They settled in Santa Clara and San Juan de los Remedios respectively in the 1830s, as reflected in a notarial document.[17] They were both members of the Harriague family through their mother. The Harriagues were famous tanners in Hazparne, and various members of the family emigrated to Galicia where they worked in tanneries and made the industry prosper in that region. We cannot reject the possibility that Dominique and Pierre Lorda emigrated first to Galicia before departing for Cuba, where they both opened tanneries and became prosperous tanners. Dominique Lorda was the father of Antonio Lorda Ortegosa, born in Santa Clara in 1845, who, after having studied to become a medical doctor in France, was a hero in the Cuban war of independence.

Later, in the 1850s, other tanners emigrated to Cuba and opened tanneries. We should also mention Etienne Amespil and Arnaud Jaureito, both born in 1835 and who, fleeing from military service, chose Cuba as their

---

17. Pirineos Atlánticos Provincial Archive—Archives Départementales des Pyrénées Atlantiques (ADPA): http://earchives.cg64.fr/img-viewer/FRAD064003 IR0001/Hazparne/3E7359/viewer.html, pages 54–57.

destiny before attaining the age of twenty. They became partnered to open a tannery at Nuevitas, in the central region of the country,[18] possibly after having worked for the Lorda brothers. Years later, having improved their financial situation, they visited Hazparne and brought other young tanners from the town to work in their tannery and who were later to open their own tanneries:[19] for example, Santiago Heguy in Remedios, the brothers Pierre and Jean Baptiste Etcheverry in Morón, and Graciano Daguerre in Gibara.

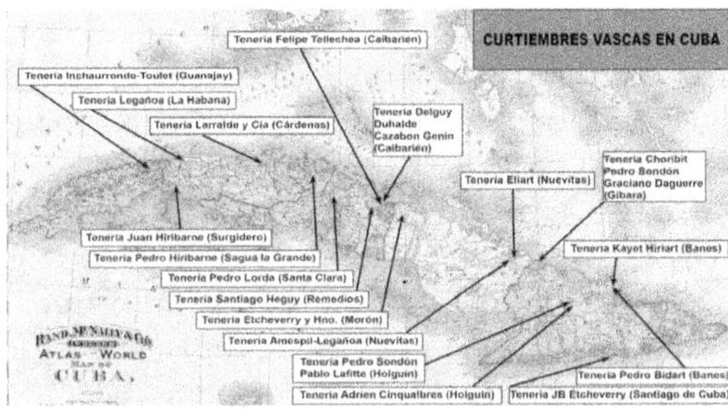

Figure 12.1. Basque tanners in Cuba.

Esteban Delguy (written Delgue before he left Hazparne)[20] also emigrated in the 1850s, and we do not know under what conditions he reached the town of Caibarién, where he opened a tannery in 1860. This establishment has been the longest lasting in the history of tanning in Cuba and is still operating today, 155 years later. It was administered by Basque tanners for more than a century and we give its history below.

Finally we must mention Ignacio Choribit and Pedro Sondón as the last pioneering tanners in Cuba. The former was a member of a family with a great tanning tradition in Hazparne. He was born in 1829 and his name was Jean Baptiste,[21] although he was known as Ignacio in Cuba. He founded a tannery at Gibara, in the eastern part of the country, in 1862,[22] which he later sold to Pedro Sondón, another tanner from Hazparne, born in 1837, and who we will also consider below.

These pioneers paved the way for dozens of tanners from Hazparne and, to a lesser extent, from other towns in the Basque Country where

---

18. Nantes Diplomatic Archive—Centre des Archives Diplomatiques de Nantes (CADN), Registry 33: Inscriptions (1894–1896) and Hazparne municipal archive, H I 74: Census tables for the army and national guard (1855–1888).

19. CADN and Jean Baptiste Lissarrague's diary (Lissarrague family archive). In this travel diary at fifteen year-old boy, the one of a Hazparne tanner, was put in the charge of two tanners on their way back to Cuba after a stay in Hazparne in 1902. They were Etienne Amespil and Arnaud Jaureito, emigrants to Cuba in the 1850s.

20. Civil register. Hazparne municipal archive.

21. Civil register. Hazparne municipal archive.

22. Gibara municipal minutes archive.

hides were tanned, such as Ainhoa, Kanbo, Ezpeleta, Larresoro, and Zuraide.[23]

Some French Basque Tanneries in Cuba

It is of interest to analyze in-depth the history of some of the tanneries set up by French Basques since, as we will see, their foundation and later development were linked to the influential personalities of some of the immigrant tanners such as the Genin and Cazabons at Caibarién, Daguerre at Gibara, and Lafitte at Holguín.

The first we wish to examine is at Caibarién: it is one of the oldest and, as we have said, it is still working today. Caibarién is a coastal city in western Cuba in the current province of Santa Clara, founded in the first half of the nineteenth century. The tannery was established in 1860 by Esteban Delguy, a tanner from Hazparne who settled near the coast where the city's current Parque de la Libertad is to be found. During the same decade, Pascual Duhalde, another French Basque tanner from the village of Zuraide, decided to embark for Mexico to escape military service, which lasted for three years at that time. We do not know under what conditions he reached Caibarién, but Esteban Delguy offered him a job at his tannery and he settled there.[24]

In 1867, Esteban Delguy sold the tannery to Pascual Duhalde in order, apparently, to emigrate to Argentina. In 1873 the tannery was moved to the intersection of Jiménez, Parrado, Alonso, and Agramonte Streets, where it would be for twenty-seven years, until 1910. A further, final move would take it to where it is at present, on the road leading out of the city to Remedios. At that time, rudimentary methods were still used: recently obtained animal skins were hung on stakes in the open air and left for birds[25] to remove the remaining meat before tanning began.

In 1886 and 1890, respectively, Louis and Pierre Genin, Pascual Duhalde's nephews,[26] arrived from France. Louis Genin had married Mathilde Casabonne, Pascual Duhalde married Madeleine Casabonne, Mathilde's sister, and her brother Sauveur Casabonne married Marie Genin, sister of Louis and Pierre Genin. These several marriages consolidated their two Basque families' control of the Caibarién tannery for a century, it becoming known as, sequentially, Pascual Duhalde, Pedro Genin y Cía, Cazabón Genin y Cía, and finally, Curtidora Tanín S.A.

---

23. Not all of those who arrived in Cuba were tanners. From Hazparne, for instance, a total of forty have been identified as having this trade before leaving the town. Agricultural workers and shoemakers who were employed in tanneries in Cuba also emigrated, having some knowledge of the work carried out there as we have seen before.

24. In an interview which Katti Aguirre—the widow of Estebe Aguirre, who was the tannery's technician between 1923 and 1960—she told us a family legend in which the ship in which Pascual Duhalde had embarked was shipwrecked on the coast of Cayo Barién and that was how he had reached Cuba and Caibarién.

25. Aura: a large bird of prey which is very common in Cuba.

26. The Genins' mother was Pascual Duhalde's sister.

In 1908 Jean Baptiste Casabonne, Louis Genin's brother-in-law, came to reinforce the family firm and later, in 1920, 1923, and 1929, Jean Casabonne Genin, Estebe Aguirre, and André Casabonne Genin arrived respectively. The latter had qualified as an engineer at the tanning school at Lyon, France. Jean and André Casabonne were Sauveur's—Salvador Cazabón's—sons. Estebe Aguirre was a cousin of the Casabonne brothers, he learned tanning in Cuba and became an excellent technician, working for the tannery for thirty-eight years. His arrival made it possible to completely mechanize the tannery and start using chrome tanning, a fundamental advance for accelerating the transformation of hides into leather.[27]

The company grew quickly and, during World War II, made some of the leather used to shoe US troops. Its high technology meant it could adapt to all the fashions and, when patent leather was launched in the states, the Cazabons started employing specialized techniques from that country in order to make the right leather for it and the fashion caught on in Cuba as well. Like French Basque tannery owners in other parts of the country, the Genin-Cazabons went to recruit dozens of tanners from Iparralde whom they knew in the towns of Ezpeleta, Larresoro, Ainhoa, and Zuraide. When they arrived in Cuba, they were put up in rooms in the building where hides were salted. Some of them, such as Pierre Telletchea, were later to open their own tanneries in the region.

In 1950, when Alberto Genín, Pedro's son, arrived from France, the Caibarién tannery had around two hundred employees and was one of the most important factories in the country and the largest tannery in Latin America.

During World War II, Jean Cazabón headed the Comité de la France Libre, and his wife was in charge of the women's section. They oversaw collection of donations (money, leather, shoes, etc.) to send to France and, in gratitude, Jean Cazabón was named French consular agent in Caibarién when the war ended.

In 1960 the festivities for the centenary of the tannery were prepared by the whole family, but the Cuban revolutionary government decreed the nationalization of companies and the commemorative ceremonies could not be held.

The second tannery to mention is the one at Gibara, set up in the same year as that at Caibarién, in 1860, but which was closed in 1970. Gibara is a city on the coast, in Holguín province, in the former Oriente province. It was founded in 1817, and its port made it possible to export coffee and sugar from the area until the end of the nineteenth century. The railway between Holguín and Gibara, opened in 1893, becoming the eastern region's main commercial route, and the tannery at Gibara exported part of its production using this means of transport.

27. This information about the Genín and Cazabón family history has been taken from interviews with Katti Aguirre, Estebe Aguirre's widow (given at Larresoro, French Basque Country), with Claudette and Régine Casabonne, André Casabonne, and Henriette Sallaberry's daughters (given in Paris) and with Alberto Genín, Pedro Genín's' son (given at the Etchenica house Zuraide, the house where Pascual Duhalde was born).

The notarial archive at Gibara documents a tannery there in 1861 as well as three shoe factories and, in the 1864 census, the presence of two Frenchmen and a tannery with " three tanners and 328 hides" is recorded. We believe that these two Frenchmen were Carlos Guitay and Ignacio Choribit. The city's notaries' protocols include a document in which these two men and a third, José Clemente Leal, from Holguín, state that they have "formed a company for a tannery which the former two have set up in this city in the Marina Street area."[28]

We have previously mentioned Ignacio (Jean Baptiste) Choribit, born at Hazparne in 1829. His family worked in tanning in the Basque Country and, in 1831, three members of the family were owners of three different tanneries in the town and one of them, Narciso, was a leather salesman, covering part of France and the north of Spain.

Two decades later, the tannery at Gibara was being run by Pedro Sondón Alberiche (Arbeletche), born in 1852 in Aiherra, a town near Hazparne. He seems to have arrived in Cuba around 1870[29] and almost certainly knew Choribit because he arrived at Gibara's port to work in the tannery there. According to his great-great grandson, recounting family legend,[30] he worked for low wages for a long time and, after a few years, the owners of the tannery sold it to him to make up for that. Pedro Sondón then did like everybody else: he brought out other tanners from the Basque Country. This was how Antonio, his brother, immigrated to Gibara, as did Pierre Bidart who, after spending many years in the tannery at Gibara, set up his own in the neighboring town of Banes.

Pedro Sondón prospered and in just a few years he became the owner of a brick factory, a soap factory, and several agricultural properties in the region. This position of ease made it possible for him to buy another tannery in the capital of Holguín province before passing his own on to another immigrant from Hazparne, Graciano Daguerre. The latter reached Cuba thanks to Etienne Amespil, the owner of the tannery at Nuevitas, who had brought him from Hazparne in 1894.[31] He had been born in Malechiatea house in Hazparne in 1874 into a family of farm workers who were, at the same time, shoemakers. His father worked at both jobs, as did many people in the town, and Graciano learned how to tan hides at home. He fled from military service and seems to have chosen Cuba because an uncle of his on his mother's side had immigrated there previously.[32] He spent some time working at Nuevitas but not long because by 1895 he was already at Gibara, working with Sondón and

---

28. Gibara notaries' protocols, 1864, volume 10, sheet 93-2.
29. Data gathered in an interview given in Holguín with Pedro Sondón's grandaughter, Elisabeth Cinqualbres.
30. Interview given in Holguín with Pablo de Armas Lafitte.
31. CADN, Registry 33: Immatriculations (1894–1896).
32. Dominique Londaitzbehere, born in 1835. (Source: Civil and military censuses. Hazparne municipal archive.)

Pierre Darricau, another immigrant from Hazparne and a neighbor who had traveled to the island with him.[33]

We can say that it was Graciano Daguerre who developed the tannery at Gibara, making it one of the most prestigious factories in the area. He installed machines with drums and constructed a building for storing hides and another for housing the workers who came from Hazparne. The Gibara tannery was specialized in making soles for footwear, so the hides to be tanned were hard and thick. Work at the tannery was mostly manual, long hours were spent standing with the workers' feet in water, breathing in air with nauseating smells and selling the products. The hides came from a local slaughterhouse on the other side of the city and were brought to the tannery on carts. After conserving them in coarse salt for a time, the hairs were removed, and the hides were then put into pits filled with water and lime. Graciano Daguerre was familiar with this method because it was the same one used in the Basque Country. On land bordering the tannery they had built lime kilns to produce that prime material needed for removing hairs from the hides. Later Graciano and his workers removed the meat using special knives and the recovered flesh was put through a press before being sold in the United States for glue making. A prime material, of which there was an abundance in Gibara Bay, was used for tanning: the mangrove. The leaves and skin of a particular variety of mangrove pataban"[34] were crushed and the hides were cured for several months in pits filled with water and the powder derived from the plants, which gave them a reddish color. Later they were cut in two to "separate the butt and the head,"[35] before putting them into water again in drums. The final operation was drying by hanging the hides on hooks from the ceiling.

At the moment of its greatest development in the 1940s, the tannery at Gibara had around twenty employees and produced 800 hides each month. Many of the workers had been brought by the Daguerres from Hazparne. They slept in a building which had been constructed for them and had a cook who made their meals. Among the tanners who came from Hazparne, we should mention Pascual Daguerre, Graciano's brother, who immigrated to Gibara around 1903 and worked at the tannery for around thirty years. Another relative of Graciano's emigrated: his nephew Jean Baptiste Hiriart-Urruty. In 1921 Bernard Bacardats and Jean Baptiste Lahirigoyen arrived; the latter was to become Graciano Daguerre's right-hand man when he started to travel to the Basque Country much more frequently to spend part of the year there with his family toward the end of his life. In 1923 it was Adrien Cinqualbres's turn; he reached Cuba at the age of just fourteen. He worked at the tannery for some years before

---

33. Interview given at Gibara by Belkis Daricó, Pierre Darricau's grandaughter.

34. DRAE: (Spanish Royal Academy Dictionary) Patabán: m. *Cuba.* Tree from the Combretaceae family which grows in marshland and gives a hard, dark-colored wood; it is used for making posts and other things. It is a variety of mangrove.

35. Toñito Chacón provided us with this information about the manufacturing process in an interview given at Gibara. He started working in the tannery in 1935.

settling at Holguín where, in 1930, he married Berta Sondón, one of Pedro Sondón's daughters. After having opened his own tannery specialized in fine leather in Holguín, he lost all that he had gambling on cock fights and ended his professional life at Jean Lassalle's tannery. Lassalle was another Frenchman who had settled at Manzanillo, also in the eastern province, and was from Sauveterre de Béarn, near the Basque Country. A further two Basques worked with Graciano Daguerre for several years: Jean Hiriart (known as Kayet), who also opened his own tannery at Banes in the 50s, and Pedro Duhalde, who had been born at Aiherri but who lived in Hazparne for some years before emigrating to Cuba.

During the first half of the twentieth century, Graciano Daguerre became the richest man in Gibara. He owned around a hundred houses in the city, an agricultural estate of 420 hectares, La Gibarita, and was highly respected. He won this respect because he worked just as did his employees in the tannery, trying to help them solve problems. As well as constructing a building to house them, he set up a facility near the tannery for them to play Basque pelota.[36] This paternalistic attitude was very common among tanners and footwear manufacturers.

Graciano Daguerre had married María Crescencia Lamorena on November 19, 1902, and they had eight children of whom two—Nino and Melquiades—worked for him at the tannery. Graciano kept his French nationality and chose to have his children educated in Europe. This meant that the family often traveled between Gibara, Hazparne, and Hondarribia, where Graciano lived for several years. In addition to his strength of will, he brought undaunting faith from the Basque Country and, while the people of Gibara do remember the wealthy immigrant who had arrived without a penny, they recall him above all as a fervent Catholic. He never missed Mass and paid for all the city's children's communion suits. In 1929 he commisioned a factory in Naples to make a bell with his name engraved on it and it still rings from the belltower of Gibara church.

Graciano Daguerre died at Gibara on December 22, 1950, but the tannery carried on, in part through the involvement of his children, but, above all, thanks to Juan Bautista Lahirigoyen's hard work. After the revolutionary government confiscated the tannery, it was closed for some years until reopened with Juan Bautista Lahirigoyen as its head of production. It continued as a tannery until the 1970s, when it was transformed into a footwear factory.

Up to now the various sources consulted in Cuba and in the Basque Country have allowed us to identify eighteen tanneries founded by Basques from Iparralde. Any one of them could have been studied, including the one in Holguín, which belonged to Pablo Lafitte, an exceptional emigant. He had all the characteristics of the Basque tanners in the highly local network from some towns such as Hazparne in the province of Lapurdi. They had immigrated when they were very young to join other tanners

---

36. Interview with Mirtha Gurri Leyva (Pascual Daguerre's god-daughter) given in Gibara.

who had opened tanneries in Cuba and who later passed their businesses onto them. There were not very many (around two hundred altogether, it seems), but they held a particular place in Cuban tanning. When they reached Cuba, they knew that they were going to be able to work in a trade in which they had countrymen, and that would make it easier for them to settle in. Many of them married and had families and, as the only Basque centers were in Havana, some of them joined Spanish associations. Many of them never went back to their birth country. This was Pablo Lafitte's story: although he took over from his father-in-law Pedro Sondón at the Holguín tannery and became a prosperous businessman, he never returned to Hazparne over the following fifty years. A progressive thinker, actively supporting the Spanish Republic and Free France during World War II, he was named consular agent for France in the eastern region of Cuba. When his tannery was nationalized by the revolutionary government, he decided to support the project for a new society on the island completely and took out Cuban nationality.

Bibliography

Albanés Martínez, Juan Rafael. *Historia breve de la ciudad de Holguín.* Holguín: Editorial Eco, 1947.

Arrozarena, Cecilia. *El roble y la ceiba: Historia de los vascos en Cuba.* Tafalla: Editorial Txalaparta, 2003.

Bosco Amores, Juan. *Cuba en la época de Ezpeleta (1785–1790).* Barañáin: Ediciones University of Navarra, 2000.

Chaunu, Huguette y Pierre. *Séville et l'Atlantique (1504–1650).* Volumes 6b–8. Paris: S.E.V.P.E.N., 1959.

Commercial Directory of the American Republics. Government Printing Office, Washington, *1898.*

Cuadro estadístico de la siempre fiel Isla de Cuba. Havana: Oficina de las viudas de Arazoza, impresoras del Gobierno y Capitanía General por S.M., 1829

Cuba Contemporánea: Oriente. Havana: Centro Editorial Panamericano, 1942.

Cuba: Population, History and Resources 1907. United States Bureau of the Census, 1909.

El Libro de Cuba. Havana: Talleres del Sindicato de Artes Gráficas, 1925.

Fernández de Pinedo Echevarría, Nadia. *Comercio exterior y fiscalidad: Cuba (1794–1860).* Bilbao: University of the Basque Country, 2002.

García y Castañeda, José Agustín. *La municipalidad holguinera: Comentario histórico, 1898–1955.* Holguín: Imprenta Hermanos Legrá, 1955.

Hasparren, regards. Baiona: Imprimerie Jean Laffontan, 1997.

Iglesias García, Fe. "Características de la Inmigración Española en Cuba (1904–1930)." *Economía y Desarrollo* no. 2 (March–April 1988): 76–101.

Langlois, Hyacinthe. *Géographie universelle, physique, politique et historique: Rédigée depuis son origine (1800) jusqu'à ce jour*. Volume 3. Paris: Edme et Alexandre Picard Libraires, 1839.

Le Riverend, Julio. *Historia Económica de Cuba*. 4th edition. Havana: Ed. Pueblo y Educación, 1974.

Leyva Aguilera, Herminio. *Gibara y su jurisdicción: Apuntes históricos y estadísticos*. Gibara: Establecimiento Tipográfico de Martín Bim, 1894.

Marqués Dolz, María Antonia. *Las industrias menores: Empresarios y empresas en Cuba (1880–1920)*. Havana: Editorial de Ciencias Sociales, 2006.

Marrero Artiles, Leví. *Cuba: Economía y sociedad*. Volume 4. Madrid: Edit. Playor, 1992.

Moreau, César y Andrzej Slowaczynski. *Annuaire statistique pour 1838 de l'Europe, l'Asie, l'Afrique, l'Amérique et l'Océanie*. Volume 2. Paris: Bureau de la Société de Statistique, 1838.

Pagola, Manex. *Culture basque et urbanisation à Hasparren: Étude ethnologique*. Baiona: Ed. del Autor, 1996.

Roche, Annie. *La tannerie romanaise de 1403 à nos jours*. Die: La Manufacture, 1984.

Sarmiento Ramírez, Ismael. "La artesanía popular tradicional cubana: Del legado aborigen al utillaje mambí." *Estudios de Historia Social y Económica de América* no. 13 (1996): 487–519.

Vidal Rodríguez, José Antonio. *La emigración gallega a Cuba: Trayectos migratorios, inserción y movilidad laboral (1898–1968)*, Madrid: Editorial CSIC, 2005.

13

Basques in Vueltabajo, Cuba: Nineteenth Century

Jorge Freddy Ramírez Pérez, Sergio Luis Márquez Jaca, and
Pedro Luis Hernández Pérez

Immigration into Cuba from different parts of the world was the main factor in the creation of Cuban nationality. In this ethno-cultural amalgamation, which took place over centuries, the Hispanic contribution was paramount due to Spanish ties to the colonizing metropolis. There has been considerable research into Cuba's Spanish immigration, as well as into that of other nationalities, but there are still many roads to explore in this area.

This research has been motivated by the lack of precision about the Basque presence in the historical region of Vueltabajo, to the west of the capital of the island of Cuba. The arrival of the Basques on the island was brought about by various factors, both external and internal: among the former, the Spanish Carlist Wars and their consequences; among the latter, the policy of the island's colonial administration of stimulating the immigration of white people. Due to these factors, the island received a strong influx of European immigrants, mostly from the Iberian Peninsula, whence the Basques came. This chapter is only a starting point for further work on immigration from the Basque Country that will have to be undertaken in the future.

The Basques' ethno-cultural characteristics, in contrast with those of other Spanish regions, are well known. This Basque heritage is very well represented in Cuba by descendants who, in many cases, know nothing of their ancestors. We hope that this modest contribution to illustrating cultural and family connections between the Basque people and their successors in Cuba will be of some use.

The Historic Region of Vueltabajo

The role of geography in the evolution of humanity has been highly significant. Each type of environment has been settled and developed socioeconomically in particular ways. Different migratory movements of groups of people from Europe to Cuba, and the places they settled during the colonial period, are no exceptions. Because of this, and in order to be able to understand the peculiarities of the Hispanic presence in Cuba, including that of the Basques, a neo-historical approach to the region of Vueltabajo is indispensable.

The area where some Basque immigrants settled is known as Vueltabajo and is considered to be a historical-cultural region, lying to the west of the city of Havana. Its boundaries are not strictly those of a political-administrative entity, but rather of reference points (above all during the first colonial period) given by geographers, travelers, surveyors, and other commentators.

Various factors of diverse origin have influenced the configuration of the region. The natural and sociocultural features most commonly taken into account to the east include Lake Ariguanabo and the eastern boundary of the Guanajay municipal area. Economic and sociocultural factors, as well as natural ones, gave it particular characteristics in the broader Cuban context. Our analysis examines the space between the referenced places, as far as Cape San Antonio, the westernmost point of the Cuban archipelago. This regional approach recognizes that immigration and settlement were carried out within certain geohistorical parameters rather than following strictly political-administrative ones.

The vast area between the reference points is made up of various natural subregions, which are: the Guaniguanico mountain range, divided into the Sierra del Rosario and the Sierra de los Órganos; high slate areas in the north, south and center; the Guanahacabibes karst plains in the south and north.

Human activity over the last four hundred years has made a historical impact upon this natural setting. The conquest and colonization of Cuba led to a new form of economic exploitation in Vueltabajo. This geographical area was influenced, to a large degree, by the economic expansion of the city of Havana, where the power groups of Cuban society were based.

During the sixteenth and seventeenth centuries, the region kept its geo-economic unity, livestock estates (herds and enclosed pastures) predominating and being very similar in type throughout the territory. Tobacco was introduced early on, especially on the southern plain. These economic activities did not lead to a considerable increase in population, much less population nuclei.

Changes in means of production, which took place at the end of the eighteenth century and the beginning of the following one, caused a crisis in the primitive livestock economy, which gave way to more advanced forms and more complex social structures. The spead of commercial agriculture, based on sugar and coffee plantations, slowly replaced the former type of economy in the Vueltabajo region.

At the end of the eighteenth century, the northern plain began to be penetrated by the sugar industry, which slowly expanded toward the west beyond Bahía Honda town. This took place at the same time as certain international political events, among others the Haitian Revolution, which led to the forced immigration of skilled people into Cuba who stimulated the island's economy. One of the immediate consequences was the settling in the Sierra del Rosario area, during the nineteenth century, of French and Basque immigrants who increased the number of coffee plantations in the mountains, of which there were now more than one hundred.

Similarly, there were more and more sugar factories and coffee plantations on the southern plain, and there were Basque immigrants there too. It was a time of rapid change on the island, where, in addition to political factors, there were others: the accumulation of capital; the metropolis' change of strategy, above all after the English captured Havana in 1762; the acceptance of the Enlightenment and illustrated despotism; the industrial and philosophical revolutions; and the strengthening of the wealthy creole class.

During the first three decades of the nineteenth century, plantations experienced considerable development; coffee and sugarcane were added to the western Vueltabajo rural landscape. One immediate consequence was a demographic explosion in that part of the region. In the western part, however, livestock farming remained the main activity, while tobacco plantations were growing in number; all of which, due to the type of work involved, meant that there were no considerable demographic changes in comparison with the eastern area.

Because of the above, and taking into account the geographical characteristics of the area in which the mentioned economic-social transformations transpired, we can point out the forming of two large geo-economic or historial subregions in Vueltabajo in the first half of the nineteenth century. The first, based on the plantation economy, was the southern plain and extended westward as far as the Candelaria area, part of the Sierra del Rosario, in the same direction, as far as the San Cristóbal River valley, and part of the northern plain going beyond Bahía Honda. The other subregion, within the eastern limits specified earlier, went as far as Cape San Antonio in which tobacco and livestock predominated. Although within this subregion there were differences between the north and the south as well with regards to topography, demography, population, economic evolution and infrastructure, among other factors.

There were no defined limits between the two subregions other than those imposed by nature. There were transitional strips in both subregions in which different activities could be seen, until one became more predominant that the other. Taking all of these factors into account, we are able to analyze and examine the characteristics of Basque immigration in Vueltabajo.

Causes of Basque Emigation to Vueltabajo

Human migration is a multi-cause phenomenon in which the main factors are economic, connected with food, and natural phenomena. In spite of that, each migratory phenomenon must be researched in its own terms, starting with the migrants' motivations and their impact upon the destinations where they settle: this is the main reason for researching the Basque presence *sui generis* in Vueltabajo. So in order to understand Basque migration, we have to examine its origin, in the emblematic region known as the Basque Country.

Basque emigration to Cuba, and particularly to Vueltabajo, was part of the migratory movements from the Iberian Peninsula. It is known that there were differences among groups of Spanish migrants due to their regions of origin. The phenomenon of migration, above all mass migration, comes with various premises in which the main factors to be taken into account are the existence of a suitable destination for receiving the migrants as well as the conditions for producing and facilitating the emigratory impulse from the country of origin.[1]

Throughout the nineteenth century there were significant socioeconomic transformations in the Basque region, traditional forms of production—based on agriculture and livestock farming—were replaced by a new, industrial society.[2] These changes convulsed the region and led to the two famous Carlist Wars (1833–1839 and 1872–1876), it was the confrontation between the protected "Basque socioeconomic tradition against the liberalism that industrialisation had brought with it."[3] The liberals, who came from urban surroundings, had the final victory and, in this way, the centuries-old Basque rivalry between the countryside and the cities was reawakened. This circumstance led to rural Basque agriculturalists emigrating to Cuba and other countries in America.

Well into the nineteenth century, and as a consequence of the agreement known as the Proclamation of Somorrostro signed by the head of the Spanish government, Antonio Cánovas del Castillo,[4] young Basques became obliged for the first time to do military service, which led to numerous desertions as not all of them were prepared to go to fight in colonial wars in America.

Another factor, which is no less important in causing Basque emigration, was the exponential rise in population during the nineteenth century.

---

1. José Manuel Azcona, "Causas de la emigración vasca contemporánea."

2. Ibid.

3. Ibid.

4. Antonio Cánovas del Castillo (1828–1897), Spanish politician, historian, writer, and Spanish prime minister on several occasions (from December 1874 to 1895) was the main creator of the Restoration political system and the outstanding figure of Spanish conservatism.

This phenomenon was to lead to struggles within families, making the traditional transfer of the farmstead between generations more difficult, a system whereby the person who was given the farm property was always the first-born while the rest of the (often numerous) siblings had no chance of inheriting anything. This meant that they were forced to look for other ways of life, and one means was emigrating to other countries.[5]

Basque Presence in Vueltabajo

During the last years of the eighteenth century the first political-administrative division was created in Vueltabajo; until that time, the area to its west had been administered from Havana. In 1774 Felipe Fondesviela y Ondeano, Marqués de la Torre, set up the Nueva Filipina jurisdiction, naming it after himself; this administration took charge of almost half the historic region of Vueltabajo, its central-western area from Los Palacios River to Cape San Antonio.

In 1819, due to the rapid increase in plantations in the eastern extreme of the Vueltabajo region, the Mariel government delegation was set up, bordering with Nueva Filipina. This development led, in 1847, to a new political-administrative order in this area, giving rise to the jurisdictions of Bahía Honda, Guanajay, and San Cristóbal. This meant that there were four jurisdictions in the Vueltabajo region, set up with the objective of having more effective local administration within such a wide geographical expanse. In 1878 the island was divided into six provinces, one of them, Pinar del Río, including the abovementioned jurisdictions, as well as Nueva Filipina. This restructuring was a considerable change in terms of government administration that would last into the second half of the twentieth century.

As we have said before, the historic region of Vueltabajo is divided into two large areas in geo-economic terms: the plantations and the tobacco-livestock areas. The new economic situation gave the region an exceptional boost, along with considerable demographic growth, above all due to the introduction of slave labor, which affected the whole country.

Despite the prohibition on slave trading in 1820, their supply did not diminish and slave traders even thought that an increase in slavery would help to prevent any attempt at revolution in the country by the creoles in Cuban society. This became an obstacle, at first, for policies favoring white immigration, which had been recommended in 1817 by superintendant Alejandro Ramírez as a strategy to pursue.[6]

In contradictory fashion the period of greatest concern in the Cuban slave-labor-based society was also a time of economic boom that made the island the biggest exporter of sugar and coffee in the world, Santo Domingo having relinquished that distinction. To some extent, this required

---

5. Azcona, "Causas de la emigración vasca contemporánea."
6. Santacilia, *Lecciones orales de la Historia de Cuba*, 57.

an increase in the slave population, the vast majority of them being of African origin, which led to the "fear of blacks."

This stimulated a progressive modification in Cuban demography between 1774 and 1841. The forced immigration of African slaves, which increased exponentially, had a proportional influence on the white population: in 1792 it was 48.8 percent of the total population; in 1817, 43.2 percent; in 1841, 41.5 percent.[7] A glance at these percentages demonstrates the demographic tendency of the black and mixed population to grow with its predominance over the white population increasing.

This demographic situation was a point of interest and worry for the Cuban slave-based society: its wealth increased as the slave workforce increased and so did its concerns about an insurrection such as had happened in Sainte Dominique. Until the end of the first half of the nineteenth century, there was an anxious campaign to encourage white immigration: it is hard to find minutes, memories, projects, or ideas from the Island of Cuba Promotion Board in the 1840s which are not connected with this matter.

Many Europeans arrived in this climate of encouragement of white immigration, most of them from all regions of Spain. The Basques were not to be left out of this process and they became involved in various aspects of the economy. In the Vueltabajera region, the immigrants' backgrounds led to them working in sugar factories, coffee plantations, and trade, in other words, in the eastern part of said territory.

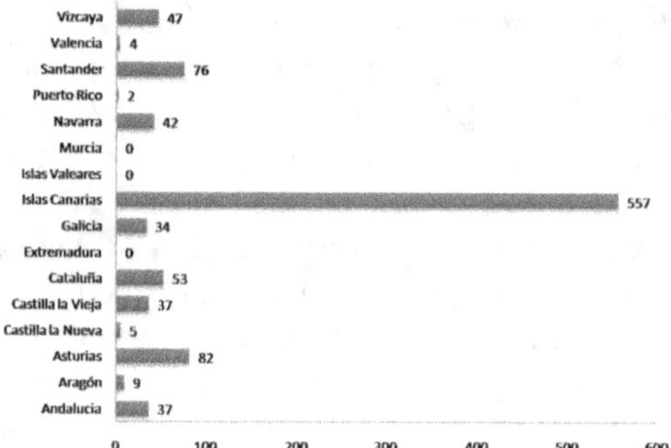

Figure 13.1. Graph comparing Basque immigrants with immigrants from other Spanish regions (Jurisdicción de San Cristóbal, 1855). Source: Pichardo, Geografía de la Isla de Cuba, 335.

With coffee plantations it is symptomatic that, along with the French colonists who had arrived in the region at the start of the nineteenth century, the second most important group was the Basques. More than a hundred coffee plantations were set up in the Sierra del Rosario during that century, many of them by Basques: one distinctive feature of immigrants from the Basque Country is that they founded companies to plant and

---

7. Ibid.

administer these plantations, which is what they did at Liberal coffee plantation in the San Claudio River basin in what is now the municipal area of Bahía Honda.

Statistics from the middle of the nineteenth century, in spite of their imprecisions, give an approximattion of the Basque presence in the region. As can be seen in figure 13.1, the Basques were in sixth place, making up 4.1 percent of the Spanish population in the Nueva Filipina jurisdiction. While the number of Basque people in this jurisdiction was not large, in comparison with immigrations from other Spanish regions, their participation in key posts in the region's development made their presence more important.

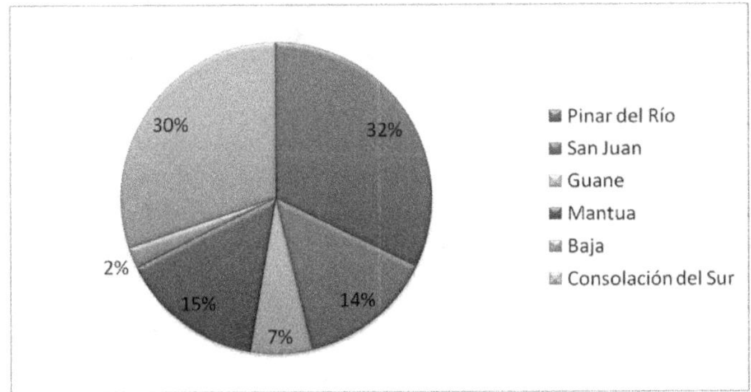

Figure13.2. Percentage distribution of Basque immigrants by local area. Nueva Filipina Jurisdiction. Source: Pichardo, Geografía de la Isla de Cuba, *335.*

It should be remembered that tobacco was the main economic activity in Nueva Filipina, which did not entice the Basques as much as it did people from the Canary Islands. Even so, Basques went to the San Cristóbal plantations juridiction, but, there too, they constituted a lower percentage compared with other Hispanic immigrants.

The total number of Basque immigrants in connection with the areas of the Nueva Filipina jurisdiction can be seen in figure 13.2. Of these, 32 percent settled in the Pinar del Río area, that being the most important jurisdiction; this was followed by 30 percent in neighboring Consolación del Sur; 15 percent in Mantua, which is striking because the land is poor and there is a low population density in general; 14 percent in San Juan y Martínez; 7 percent in Guane; and, lastly, 2 percent in Baja.

If the previous distribution were to be stated in comparison with the total number of Spanish immigrants, the percentages would be different, as is shown in figure 13.3. The place with the highest percentage of Basques was Mantua, with 9.8 percent, which is interesting if we take into account the fact that it was one of the areas with least economic development at the time; it was followed by Consolación with 6 percent; Guane had 4.3 percent; 3.4 percent in Baja; neighboring Pinar del Río had 3.3 percent; and, finally, 2.3 percent in San Juan y Martínez.

In the San Cristóbal jurisdiction (figure 13.4), where coffee and sugarcane plantations predominated, the Basque presence was 5 percent of the total of Spanish immigrants, being in fifth place among the Spanish regions which had contributed most immigrants. This was due to the Basque immigrants' prolixity for economic activities connected with plantations.

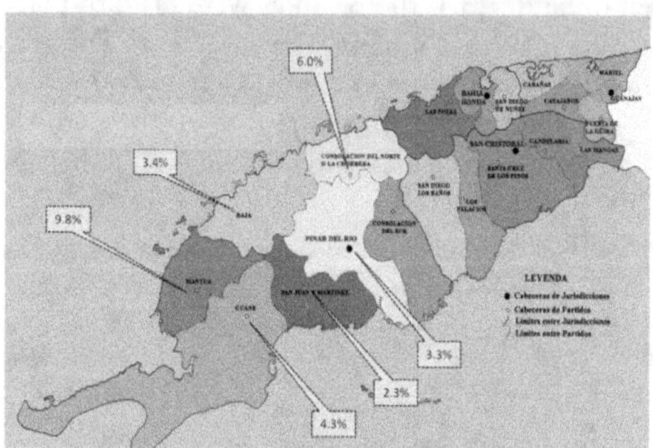

Figure 13.3. Percentage distribution of Basque immigrants by local areas in comparison with the total number of Spanish immigrants. Nueva Filipina Jurisdiction, 1854. Source: Pichardo, Geografía de la Isla de Cuba, *335.*

As far as the San Cristóbal region is concerned, where Basque immigration would make a more considerable economic contribution, the immigration process went on throughout the nineteenth century and even during the first two decades of the following one; they came in waves caused by different factors. What remains of this is the Basque presence among the residents of the region, as can be seen in the surnames[8] of many of the families who settled there to live out their Caribbean dream. Nowdays many of their descendants walk along the street and through the countryside unaware that they have Basque blood.

The distribution of Basques in the San Cristóbal jurisdiction by areas can be seen in figure 13.4. That with the highest percentage of Basques was San Diego de los Baños, with 30 percent of all the Basques in its jurisdiction; 23 percent in Candelaria, where Basque immigration was connected with coffee growing; 21 percent in the neighboring area of San Cristóbal; 17 percent in San Marcos (Artemisa); and 9 percent in Los Palacios.

On the other hand, the percentage distribution of Basque immigrants among all the Spanish immigrants in San Cristóbal jurisdiction can be seen in figure 13.5. The San Diego de los Baños area had the largest percentage at 10.4 percent, which was considerably more than in other areas, the reasons for which have still to be determined; it was followed by Can-

---

8. The best-known surnames include: Soroa, Muñagorri, Bastarrica (or Basterrika), Ugarte, Ganbarte, Berazaluce, Salaberry, Sarriegui, Errasti, Echeberría, Izaguirre, Goenaga, Salabarria (or Salaberria), Arteaga, Belauzaran (or Belaunzaran), Ibarra, Miqueo, Ugalde, Jaca, and Bengoechea, among others.

delaria with 5.4 percent and San Cristóbal with 5.3 percent; Las Mangas followed with 4.4 percent and Los Palacios with 1.5 percent.

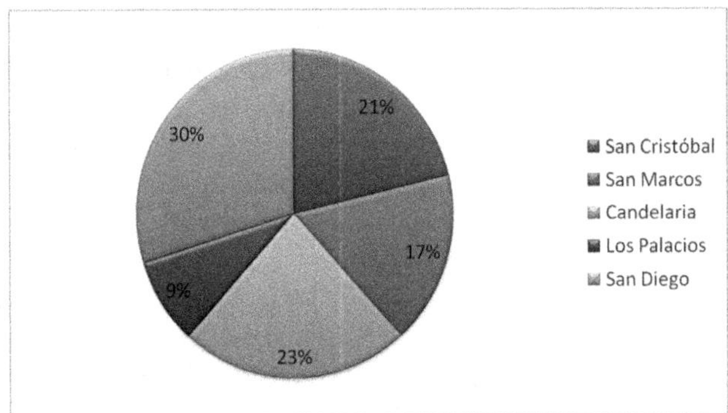

Figure 13.4. Percentage distribution of Basque immigrants by local areas (San Cristóbal Jurisdiction). Source: Pichardo, Geografía de la Isla de Cuba, *335.*

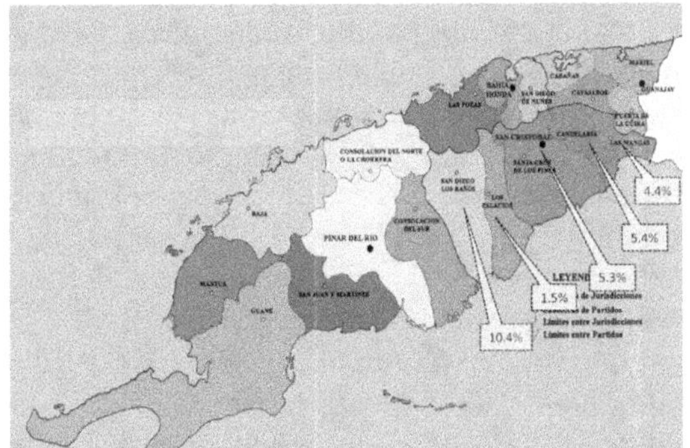

Figure 13.5. Percentage distribution of Basque immigrants in comparison with the total number of Spanish immigrants by local areas (Jurisdicción de Nueva Filipina). Source: Pichardo, Geografía de la Isla de Cuba, *335.*

Two Basque Immigrant Families in Vueltabajo

The Soroa Family

There are places in the world whose names alone conjure up an infinite quantity of memories and emotions: the tourist area of Soroa, in the northeastern part of Candelaria municipal area, in Artemisa province, is one such place. The most varied desires have been satisfied here, from those openly in love in an appropriate environment for their deepest feelings to flourish to the scientist fascinated by the infinite possibilities of demonstrating a hypothesis and wrenching secrets from nature.

In Soroa the human imagination has become reality with the inclusion of tourist resources and other signs of human influence in the landscape. But is more known about this place than just the visual impressions that visitors perceive? Not even the origin of its fine-sounding name.

José Miró Argenter, a war correspondent between 1895 and 1898, found it difficult to trace the name's etymology, not knowing it to be the surname of the first family to settle there or, perhaps, a name derived from the common noun "soroche," a type of anxiety from which which travelers to the steep Andes suffer.[9]

Others have gone much further in their speculations and linked Soroa with an aboriginal chief who lived in the area: this does not seem to be a logical deduction in that the word is in no way connected with the native languages in Cuba when the Europeans arrived there. A more recent oral version mentions a French immigrant called Jean Paul Soroa as the owner of these lands. In spite the best efforts of tourist organizations in terms of publicity, this matter remained far from clear for a long time.

The birthplace of the surname Soroa is the Basque province of Gipuzkoa; the surname is documented from the fourteenth century of the current era in connection with a family of the feudal nobility. In Basque *soroa* means a "field or meadow."[10]

The Soroa family was not just an ancient one, it was also numerous. In the mid-nineteenth century the brothers Lorenzo and Antonio Soroa Muñagorri arrived in Cuba from Gipuzkoa. They were attracted by the search for new economic horizons, life being overshadowed in their native land by the continual wars. The area they chose for their agricultural yearning was the old, demolished livestock farm San José de Manantiales, situated in the Sierra del Rosario, a mountain range in the north-east of Artemisa province, in the Candelaria municipal area.

In 1802, in the context of profound changes in the Cuban economy, the San José de Manantiales livestock farm was divided, each new part being given a different name and being used for growing coffee. This area, which has finally become a tourist destination, in the nineteenth century was made up of the Neptuno, San Luis, La Merced, Remoto, and San Ramón de Aguas Claras coffee plantations, among others. When the Soroa Muñagorri brothers landed, these plantations were in disuse, so it must have been easy for them to acquire La Merced coffee plantation in 1856, their first property. It had various medicinal mineral water springs.

After the Soroa family's pioneers, two of their nephews—José and Ignacio Mujica Soroa from Andoain—immigrated. They, too, began to buy land from among the abovementioned coffee plantations, acquiring their first estate in 1875. One year later they had already added several more to it. At this time Ignacio accumulated a large number of properties.

On November 3, 1882, Antonio Soroa y Muñagorri drew up his will. He died on the seventeenth of the same month and his nephews Ignacio

9. Miró Argenter, *Crónicas de la Guerra*, vol. 3, 158.
10. The word *soroa* is made up of the nound *soro*—field—and the article *a* which means *the*. Basque nouns are not gendered. Since most Basque surnames derive from house names, implicit is that *soroa* refers to "the house next to a field or meadow." See López, *Vocabulario Castellano-Vasco*; and Narbarte, *Diccionario de apellidos Vascos*.

and José were his heirs. At the start of the last decade of the nineteenth century, Ignacio bought additional pieces of land. Little by little the surname Soroa took root in local toponyms and spread with the growth of their properties, which become a large agricultural estate.

By then an old man, Ignacio Mujica Soroa, wrote his will in 1905 and made his wife Rosario Dachs y Laborie his heir. Ignacio, the last Soroa Basque immigrant, died on April 15, 1907, without ever imagining that his surname would live on for ever. The family's presence as landowners for more than half a century meant that people were used to identifying the area with their surname. Furthermore, it stuck as the surname of their numerous slaves and ex-slaves, who had taken it on baptism.

Soroa appears as the name of land from March 28, 1930, when a company with that same name acquired it and replaced the previous names for the area. Then, due to its attractive natural features and the large number of tourists, this Basque surname has become the name of a tourist resort known all over the world, perhaps even in its place of origin.

The Jaca Family

By chance one of the authors of this paper—Sergio Luis Márquez Jaca—is of Basque descent. His research into the Jaca family has enriched the history of immigration of many of the inhabitants of such a distinctive origin and culture. The word Jaca or Jaka means *reed,* a water or humid land plant of around fifty centimeters or more in height.

Francisco Jaca Imaz was born on the cold morning of January 21, 1859, in the Basque farmstead of Sansaetan, a few kilometers from Idiazabal in Gipuzkoa. He was the youngest of José Martín Jaca's and María Imaz's four children. He was baptized in the parish church of Idiazabal a few days later.

Young Francisco's restlessness, along with other political and family phenomena of the time, led to this strong agricultural worker starting his life as an emigrant at just eighteen and, like many at the time, he set off to America to seek his fortune. Francisco was not alone on his new Odyssey: his brother José Vicente crossed the Atlantic with him. After a long voyage they disembarked at Santiago de Cuba in 1878, and his brother continued on his journey to Argentina shortly afterward.

Why Francisco Jaca stayed in Cuba and did not travel on with his brother is a mystery to this day, as is the whole period of his life between his arrival in Cuba and the 1880s, when he appears as an experienced tradesman in San Diego de Núñez town, in the current Bahía Honda municipal area, Artemisa province. He lived there with his wife and two children, Paulino and Isidora. On his wife's death, Pancho Jaca met the young widow María Pérez de Errasti on an estate near Soroa[11] and married her a few months later. María and Vicente Jaca Pérez were the offspring of the marriage.

---

11. María Pérez's first husband had been the Basque immigrant José María Errasti.

*Figure 13.7. Photograph of Francisco Jaca Imaz, taken in a
studio in Havana towards the end of his life.*

By this time Francisco had the wealth that allowed him to buy four
estates in the mountainous Sierra del Rosario property, near the Soroa
family's area, unite them under the name Miracielos and make them into
something like a traditional Basque farmstead. It was there that his nine
children grew up along with María Pérez's offspring from her previous
marriage.

In 1896, with war between proindependence Cubans and the Spanish army raging, the Candelaria Municipal Property Register records that
Francisco Jaca Imaz bought a house and the urban land next to it near the
railway station to the west.

Vicente Jaca Pérez, Sergio Luis Márquez Jaca's grandfather, married
the young María Almeida Montesinos and they had four children: María
Josefa (1925), Rosario (1927), Esperanza (1928), and Carmen (1929). In
1936 grandfather Vicente died of a septicaemia, but María was pregnant
with their so greatly desired male son. Celestino Jaca Almeida was born a
few months later and would never know his father. He is the only one of
the children still alive today.

Having five children, most of them girls, an ancient grandfather and
other half-brothers was a very difficult situation for the widow. She made
the decision to move to the house in Candelaria, but Pancho, the Jaca family patriarch, went to Havana, where he had bought a house for his daughter María. He spent his last years there until the 1940s, when he died from
heart problems typical at his age.

All of Francisco Jaca Imaz's grandaughters had children. The current
generation remembers the way their parents brought them up with much
love and pride in their heritage. In 2000, Sergio Luis Márquez Jaca was
able to make his dream come true and visit the wonderful land where his
great grandfather, Pancho Jaca, had been born and meet the rest of his
family. The Sansaetan farmstead in Idiazabal is intact and has remained as

it was in Francisco's time. Luis was able to see that many Basque traditions are passed from one generation of the family to the next. With regards to food, for instance, his mother used to say "you have to eat all the food and leave nothing on the plate." There was also the caligraphy, religion, and enthusiasm for knowledge, work, and good manners.

Pancho Jaca was never able to return to the Basque Country and, having won his fortune in the time-honored way he left his mark, as did many. There are many things about his life in Cuba and his motivations which are still unknown and should be researched. What is clear is that he left behind his example and the house he owned, where Sergio Luis Márquez Jaca lives today with his family, and where there is a photograph which they all venerate as a symbol of the branch of a line they are proud of because of its origins and because their surname is Jaca. This is a good example of a family history, a line of research which has not yet been deveolped sufficiently regarding Basque immigration in Cuba.

Bibliography

Arrozarena, Cecilia. *El roble y la ceiba: Historia de los vascos en Cuba.* Tafalla: Txalaparta, 2003.

Azcona, José Manuel. "Causas de la emigración vasca contemporánea." Available at: http://www.euskonews.com/0072zbk/gaia7206es.html. Accessed May 24, 2016.

López, Isaac. *Vocabulario Castellano-Vasco.* NP: Ed. España, 1908.

Luengo, Félix. "Los vascos en cuba a finales del siglo xix." Available at: http://www.historiacontemporanea.ehu.es/s0021-con/es/contenidos/ boletin_revista/00021_revista_hc19/es_revista/adjuntos/19_12.pdf. Accessed on April 15, 2013.

Miró Argenter, José. *Crónicas de la Guerra.* Volume 3. Havana: Ed. LEX, La Habana, 1943.

Narbarte, Nicanor. *Diccionario etimológico de Apellidos Vascos.* 6th edition. Donostia-San Sebastián: Ed. Txertoa, 1989.

Pichardo, Esteban. *Geografía de la Isla de Cuba.* 3rd part. Havana: Establecimiento tipográfico de D. M. Soler, 1854.

Ramírez, Jorge Freddy. "Presencia vasca en la región histórica de Vueltabajo, Cuba, siglo xix." In *América Latina en la turbulencia global: oportunidades, amenazas y desafíos,* coordinated by Alexander Ugalde Zubiri, 501–10. Leioa, Universidad del País Vasco, 2013. Available at https:// web-argitalpena.adm.ehu.es/listaproductos.asp?IdProducts=UWLG-SO8540 percent20percent20&page=1&IdTopics=011525&Id=&buscapor=&key1=&Avanzada=&IdTopicsgrupos=&arbol=01.

Ramírez, Jorge Freddy and Fernando Paredes. *Francia en Cuba: Los cafetales de la Sierra del Rosario.* Havana: Ed. Unión, 2004

Rousset, Ricardo V. *Historial de Cuba*. Volume 1. Havana: Ed. Librería
    Cervantes, 1918.
Santacilia, Pedro. *Lecciones orales de la Historia de Cuba*. New Orleans:
    Imp. de Luis Eduardo del Cristo, 1859.

14

Immigration, Basques, and Santiago de Cuba: As Seen from Notaries' Protocols, 1902–1933

Mónica de la Caridad García Salgado and
Maithe Sánchez Garrido

The movement of Basques and Navarrese people across the ocean to America until the seventeenth century was not large-scale. It was not until then that the pace increased with respect to the previous period, more people wanting to "make their fortune in the Americas." This was based, above all, on the Basque maritime skills and tradition in the Basque Country and their trading activities in the Mediterranean and the Atlantic. So, when the Compañía Guipuzcoana de Caracas was founded in 1728, this marked the beginning of a phase in which Venezuela became the main stage for the Basque presence in America, opening paths for Basque emigration to the Americas that was to become more numerous during the following century.[1] Through investigation of the work of prominent figures in different regions, such as missionaries, priests, and/or important groups of traders, the existence of this ethnic group in American lands has become more apparent.

This group's immigration during the nineteenth century was stopped, initially, by factors such as the independence movements in America after 1810 and the Spanish authorities' restrictive emigration policies during the first third of the nineteenth century. However, when the Spanish government and the governments of some American nations—Venezuela

---

1. Azcona Pastor, "La participación vasca en la empresa colonial y migratoria americana," 470–73. Although researchers into the subject have determined that Basque emigration to America in the sixteenth–seventeenth centuries must have been more common than is believed, it is difficult to quantify. However, researchers, such as José Manuel Azcona Pastor, believe that Basque immigrants must have been fewer than the Andalusians and Extremeños during those two hundred years.

and Uruguay—later reached an agreement, this favored the reactivation of Basque migration, which increased throughout the century, especially toward Argentina and Uruguay, reaching what researcher José Manuel Azcona has called "the high point of 1880–1900."[2]

From then onward, and particularly during the first fourteen years of the twentieth century, Basque emigration climaxed. There were different circumstances in the destinations that led to a reduction in this ethnic group's immigration, particularly from the beginning of the World War I until the mid-1930s. World War I was crucial in this, interdicting a substantial amount of the maritime traffic between the Old World and the Americas. The fact that Spain kept out of the war produced an economic boom in the Basque provinces, above all in industry and, to an extent, the demand for its producsts. This increase in industrial activity lasted right up to 1936 and explains, to a large extent, why emigration to America was much less than it had been during the first fifteen years of the twentieth century.[3]

Basque Presence in the City of Santiago de Cuba, 1902–1933

After Spain's defeat in Cuba during the Spanish American War the victors censused the population. This census, titled *The US Military Governor's Register of Spaniards Resident in Cuba*, enumerated those who wished to keep their Spanish nationality after the Treaty of Paris—the period from 1899 to 1900. It is one of the few documents regarding Cuba that lists Spanish residents by their Old World regional origin. It details approximately sixty-seven thousand Spanish residents. This source, in researcher José Antonio Vidal Rodríguez' words, "gives a picture of the regional make-up of immigration which arrived during the last years of the previous century; however, it should be pointed out that other sources detail the same regional structure, with slight variations, throughout the first half of the century."[4]

The 1915 statistics provided by the Board of Emigration are an example of one of the few Spanish sources which gathered information about emigrants' regional origin in a systematic way. According to that source, 44 percent of the emigrants to Cuba that year were from Galicia, 24.5 percent from the Canary Islands, 11 percent from Asturias, followed by people from León, Santander, and Zamora, who made up 3.5, 2.9 and 2.28 percent of the total respectively. On the other hand, people from the other 40 provinces—including the Basque Country—only made up a little more than 11 percent of the emigrants.[5]

So it is possible, using the figures mentioned above, to confirm that the Basque ethnic group was, at the end of the nineteenth century, one of the least numerous regional groups in Cuba. It was to continue to be so during

2. Ibid., 474–76.
3. Ibid., 486–87.
4. Vidal Rodríguez, La emigración gallega a Cuba, 69.
5. Ibid., 68.

the first three decades of the twentieth century, which has been confirmed by the Spanish researcher Consuelo Naranjo Orovio who describes the Basque Country as one of the least represented areas in Spanish migration to Cuba. María del Carmen Barcia, lecturer at the University of Havana, confirms this thesis.

Regions	Spanish citizens	% of total	% males	% bachelors
Galicia	19,088	28.56	98.22	71.0
Asturias	15,853	23.72	98.22	68.0
Canarias	10,509	15.72	95.42	54.0
Old Castile	5,126	7.60	97.56	66.0
Catalonia	3,563	5.33	97.60	59.0
Andalucía	3,185	4.76	91.14	55.0
Basque Country	**1,760**	**2.63**	**96.53**	**60.0**
New Castile	1,225	1.83	93.71	58.0
Valencia	1,047	1.56	97.51	60.0
BalearIc Islands	869	1.32	98.41	49.0
Aragon	780	1.16	95.89	62.0
Navarra	**754**	**1.12**	**94.42**	**70.0**
Murcia	419	0.62	97.20	61.0
Extremadura	384	0.50	98.43	59.0
% of total	66,834	100	—	—

Table 14.1. Regional origin of Spaniards who kept their nationality (1900). Source: Iglesias, "Características de la emigración española en Cuba."

Cuba was Basque emigrants' third most favored destination after Argentina and Uruguay, above all after the second half of the nineteenth century and the first half of the twentieth, and it is surprising that the Basque presence in the country has not been researched better.[6] Perhaps the explanation, in Santiago de Cuba's case, is that they were not the largest group in the region. Researchers' attention has gravitated to groups that were larger in size.

Our chapter does not aim to determine the behavioral patterns of Basque immigrants in the city of Santiago de Cuba; this is merely an overview of their relative numbers and a partial vision at best as the initial basis for future research. Therefore, the timeframe examined encompasses only 1902 to 1933. At the start of this period, which was when the new Cuban republic began, even though Spain no longer exercised political power the island was still within the awareness of Spaniards, not only because it remained a popular destination but also because of a series of laws and projects that favored their continued immigration. At the end of the period, the economic crisis of 1929–1933 led to the Cuban government passing the Work Nationalization Law in 1933, which prevented and/or limited foreigners' access to employment on the island, a factor that influenced Spanish migration.

With respect to this ethnic group's presence in the city of Santiago de Cuba, the data in the *Register of Spaniards in Santiago de Cuba City Hall* of those who wanted to keep their original nationality show that their presence in the province was a lower percentage than on the island as a whole.

---

6. Luengo Teixidor, "Los vascos en Cuba a finales del siglo xix," 237–38.

In this regard, researcher Manuel Pevida Pupo's recent work, based on the Citizen Books, shows that the Basque presence as part of the Spanish contingent in the region of Santiago de Cuba was a minority that oscillated between 2.36 and 1.15 percent, compared with other groups: 20.28 percent from Galicia; a similar percentage from Catalonia; followed by 16.91 percent from Asturias; 11.42 percent from the Canary Islands; 5.54 percent from Andalusia; 4.40 percent from León; 3.99 percent from New Castile; 3.86 percent from Old Castile; and 3.07 percent from Aragón.[7] This data makes it clear that the ethnic group in question was one of the least numerous.

Our account relies on information from the notaries' protocols from the period 1902–1933, although this is by far not the only source for research into this migration. Consequently, this article is no more than an approximation of the Basque/Navarrese ethnic presence as reflected in these documents. They show that most of these immigrants were men. This, we believe, can be explained by the institutionalized social roles for women in those times—generally the men who had the obligation of providing for families whether they were married or not. They were the group most prone to emigrate as they had more opportunities to enter the labor force and thereboy accumulate savings that would allow them to return to their homeland; it should also be considered that some were escaping from obligatory military service.[8]

Our research identified twenty-nine persons, twenty-six of them male and three of them female. It is worth underlining that the majority of the Basque population that settled in the Santiago region was from Bizkaia (thirteen people), followed by Navarra (seven), Gipuzkoa (six), and Araba (three).

Gender	Immigrants	Married	Bachelors	Widowed	Divorced
Male	26	11	13	1	—
Female	3	—	2	1	—
% of total	29	11	15	2	—

Table 14.2. Gender and marital status. Source: Table drawn up by the authors based on notaries' protocols (1902–1933).

They were all single although, from what can be gleaned from the data, there was no great difference between those who remained single and those who married. It must be pointed out that only one of the men was widowed, married, and divorced during the period under study, and because of this he has not been included in any of the variables and, consequently, he has been removed from the total of Basque males present in the Santiago region, but only for the purposes of this analysis. More detailed

7. This data has been taken from the annexes to Manuel Pevida Pupo's doctoral thesis in history, "La inmigración española en la región de Santiago de Cuba entre 1899 y 1936" (not yet presented).
8. The job market open to immigrants included working in the sugar harvest, building railway lines and mining; official work contracts for women offered appalling conditions.

information is given in table 14.2.

Whether they had children or not was not registered. Among the married men, the nationality of only four of their wives was stated: in all cases, the wives were Cuban citizens from Santiago. With regards to children, only one stated that he had any (two children) and they were born outside Cuban territory, in the United States.

With regards to age, there is no reference to that of most of the people in the study: twenty-four immigrants are simply described as being "of legal age." However, basing ourselves on precise information given, the results for different age groups were: between twenty-one and thirty, one immigrant; between thirty-one and forty, two; between forty-one and fifty, one; between fifty-one and sixty, one.

The above information is evidence that the Basque people who settled in the region were of working age, ranging from twenty-one to sixty.

Their Economic Activities

We next determined the profession of the members of the Basque ethnic group resident in Santiago de Cuba. The documents suggest that there was very little diversity in this regard as is showed in table 14.3.

Trades and/or professions	Number of Basque-Navarrese people
Traders	16
Employees	2
Farmers	1
Sugar planters	1
Pharmacist	1
Medical Doctor	1
Engineer	1
Religions	2
Driver	1

Table 14.3. Trades and/or professions of Basque-Navarrese men in the city of Santiago de Cuba (1902-1933). Source: Our data taken from notaries' protocols (1902–1933).

Taking into account the preponderance of men working in commerce, we decided to do some research into their work in this sector and, in addition to that, the role of this activity in the development of the economy in Santiago. In this respect we must underline three commercial sectors.

Merchant Companies

These include the foundation of merchant companies (regular companies, partnerships, and/or corporations) for trading in various products. Of particular interest was the Gipuzkoan Julián Cendoya Echeverría who, in spite of being a US citizen, spent part of his life in Santiago. Examples of his enterprises include:

> Julián Cendoya y Cía.: A regular company set up in partnership with Andrés Duany Suárez, on September 19, 1913, for a period of three years. It traded lumber from the area. Its headquarters were on the Muelle de Luz hills. Both partners were administrators and the com-

pany had capital of $135,000 in American gold, 60 percent contributed by Duany and the rest by Cendoya. It was dissolved in 1920.

E. Giraudy y Cía.: A partnership founded in 1911 for a period of ten years. Headquartered at Cristina Street no. 8, in Santiago's lower district, it traded in general foodstuff, local produce, and candles and engaged in manufacturing and other projects. Cendoya was a silent partner contributing a value of twenty thousand dollars worth of American gold in merchandise, loans, tools, and cash for setting up the company. It was dissolved in 1920.

Compañía Sanitaria de Santiago: This company was founded in 1915 in partnership with José Liñero and Enrique Echeverría for trading in sanitary products, and importing and manufacturing for one year. Its headquarters were in José A. Saco street in the upper area. It was prolonged for three years, its name being changed to Cendoya y Compañía and moving its headquarters to Jagüey, taking up premises at numbers 34, 36, 38, 40, and 42, importing and trading in sanitary products and hardware for two years with an initial social capital of $175,000 from each partner. It was dissolved in 1921 in order to found Echeverría y Compañía with the same characteristics as the former dissolved company.

Julián Cendoya Sons & Company: A company founded in partnership with his sons Julián Cendoya Lane and John E. Cendoya Lane, as well as José F. Valls and Echaniz, in 1919 for a period of two years for trading with ships, docks, and sugar and lumber warehouses. Its headquarters were at Muelle La Luz and it had $181,564 capital. In this case Cendoya senior provided $160,819.49 (contributed as 350 shares in the Santiago Warehouse Company, 153 shares in the Santiago Terminal Company, the house in building no. 13, Cristina Street, which, among other things, served as the company's headquarters). It was dissolved in 1922 and refounded under the same conditions, but for a longer period of three years.

Compañía Azucarera Cendoya: Limited company or corporation founded together with the partners of the previous company, with Julián Cendoya Lane as chair. With headquarters on the Luz, Calzada de Lorraine dock, its mission was to sow, grow, and promote sugar planting and sell the harvest for an unlimited period of time.[9]

Other emigrants also started companies. For instance,

Soteras y Fernández: A regular company founded by Adolfo Fernández Llamas in 1916 for setting up various shops, including a bakery with machinery installed for coffee making and called La Central.

---

9. The Santiago Warehouse Company, Santiago Development Company, and Santiago Terminal Company were companies founded in the United States of America in which Cendoya had shares and he became their representative in the city of Santiago de Cuba.

It was founded with capital of $4,800 of American gold, of which $1,000 was advanced in cash, for a period of 5 years. The company was dissolved in 1917.

Liñero, Sabater y Compañía: a company which traded in hardware with a shop in rented property at Cristina Street no. 50 in the upper district.

Others only declared ownership of trading establishments:

Francisco Pérez Hernandorena: Owner of a trading establishment of the "bodega" type known as Primera Caridad or Sucursal de La Primera Caridad in the house on no. 3 Reparto Ensanche de Fomento Street with all its fittings valued at three hundred dollars worth of American gold.

Real Estate

Julián Cendoya was, once more, the best example in this sector, buying and selling rural and urban properties and sites. Among the former:

He bought the rural estate Limones, Guaninao, in Dos Palmas district, Cobre municipal area, with 46.26 caballerías of land.[10] He split it into lots, almost always of 1 or 2 cabellerías, which he sold off (for example, Benjamín Bonne Blalereau paid $333.30 American gold for 1 caballería); in another transaction Pedro Beatón Arias paid $600 American gold for 4 caballerías.

He also bought the rural estate El Cupeyal del Sur in the municipal area, judicial area and property register of Barreras, Guantánamo, for the sum of $400 American gold; and other pieces of land in Zacatecas district, Caney municipal area ($5,500 gold official currency); Bacuey rural estate at Dos Caminos ($1,500 official currency); La Unión rural coffee estate, Barrio de Dos Palmas, El Cobre ($2,000 American gold), half of La Australia estate, in Alto Songo; a piece of land at Cuartel de Rojas, Jutinicú, Songo; among others.

Meanwhile, with other pieces of land, he carried out similar operations: In Santiago itself his real estate purchases included the purchase of a plot of land on the corner of Santa Rita Street with Clarín Street ($400 American gold); also a single story house at Carril Oeste Street 10 at San Luis with its own land ($1,500 official currency); and a piece of land on Paseo de Concha that he sold for $15,000 American gold; a piece of land on lower San Antonio Street with all its factories, water sources, and so forth that he sold to Enrique Schueg y Chassín, managing director of Bacardí y Compañía ($21,500 gold official currency). The other main player in real estate was José Liñe-

---

10. The caballería is a historic land measurement that was used throughout Latin America. Its origin is that of the amount of land granted to a retiring calvary member. It varies from country to country, in Cuba it represents 13.42 hectares (33.2 acres).

ro Arbaiza who, unlike Cendoya, did not invest in rural properties, concentrating exclusively on urban lots or flat roof buildings, usually in partnership with Emilio Catasús Caldas, from Santiago.

He bought the following urban property: Desiderio Fajardo (previously San Fermín) no. 66, built on its own plot, and no. 75 on the same street ($2,400 and $2,800 official currency, respectively); Salsipuedes Alley no. 16 ($1,190 official currency); San José Alley ($842 official currency); Rey Pelayo Street on San José Alley no. 28 1/2 ($2,800 official currency); two houses on upper San Antonio Street nos. 1 and 4 ($4,000 and $3,250 official currency, respectively); and a plot with factories built on it at no. 1 lower San Ricardo Street on the corner with San Fermín Street ($842 official currency).

Money Lending or Moneylenders

Just as Julián Cendoya obtained the considerable number of rural and urban properties mentioned above, he was also the most significant player in giving loans and mortgages. Their collateral was usually real estate. For example:

A loan given in 1919 to Martín Novellas y Recto of $1,500 for which he mortgaged 4 caballerías of land on the rural estate known a Bacuey at Dos Caminos, which, when the period for repaying the loan came due, he forfeited the property over to Cendoya.

Allocation of rural estate due to a debt of $2,020.92 American gold, with interest of 12 percent paid with a plot of land of 0.55 caballería of land at Cuartón de Rojas, Jutinicú area, Songo.

Loan of $9,000 American gold to Guillermo Hernández Rojas, collateralized by the San Federico rural estate at Carrasco, Santa Cruz del Sur municipal area, Camagüey, of 31 caballerías of land bought for the price of $6,800 American pesos.

Loan of $1,000 American gold to Daniel Arias Arias for which he mortgaged a single story house made of wood and zinc in Carril Oeste Street, San Luis, built on leased land, which is later purchased.

Loan to J. Guso Sobrinos y Compañía, for $52,033.58, for which 1,306 sacks of coffee were given in payment.

Cendoya also acted as a moneylender for government organizations for public works projects in the city of Santiago de Cuba.

Loan of various sums to the Oriente Public Works Department for building the Santiago aqueduct, totaling $19,647.19 American gold and $1,473.52 for the Santiago water supply. To be able to reclaim these sums special powers were granted to the Royal Bank of Canada.

Servants and Housewives: Stereotypes about Women's Work

The situation of women as shown in the documentation is very different. There were very few Basque-Navarrese women in the Santiago region, a fact that is in line with the general tendency for fewer women than men to emigrate. This agrees with the social role that has historically informed to the migration process, in which men are the main players due to the socio-cultural definitions of their gender, and, consequently, their greater influence on the migratory process. So it is not surprising that, coming from a patriarchal society in which women's roles were limited when it came to migrating, among other factors because of their roles as family reproducers and caregivers, that women should be a distinct minority among the arrivals. The very fact of leaving their homes individually, setting their "obligations" to one side, left them open to recriminations.[11]

Due to this, after managing to emigrate and settle, the next obstacle they had to face was that of finding employment, which is where the gender difference would start to be apparent. So women immigrants who settled in Santiago de Cuba took charge of domestic chores at home, as housewives; fewer—only one—assumed other roles: The Reverend Madre María Luisa Erroy Felipe took charge of the Casa de las Siervas de María in Santiago de Cuba.

However, recent research has demonstrated that migration for many women meant scaling the social ladder, achieving economic independence and autonomy, a transformation that only takes place when women enter the job market. Taking on new economic and social responsibilities can lead to a change in women's roles in the family, elevating them from being reproducers and caregivers to positions of greater authority and participation in decision making.[12]

In this sense there was one woman who could have followed this direction because of her stated profession: Mercedes González Luas, pharmacist. While this is in no way a representative sample of an evolution in the thinking that has been outlined above, it can be taken as one of the first signs of change in the invisibility of Basque women, and Cuban women in general, as well as the way to to free them from relegation to subordinate roles.

Regions	Spanish citizens	% of total	% males	% bachelors
Galicia	19,088	28.56	98.22	71.0
Asturias	15,853	23.72	98.22	68.0
Canarias	10,509	15.72	95.42	54.0
Old Castile	5,126	7.60	97.56	66.0
Catalonia	3,563	5.33	97.60	59.0
Andalucía	3,185	4.76	91.14	55.0
Basque Country	1,760	2.63	96.53	60.0
New Castile	1,225	1.83	93.71	58.0
Valencia	1,047	1.56	97.51	60.0
Balearic Islands	869	1.32	98.41	49.0
Aragon	780	1.16	95.89	62.0
Navarra	754	1.12	94.42	70.0
Murcia	419	0.62	97.20	61.0
Extremadura	384	0.50	98.43	59.0
% of total	66,834	100	—	—

Table 14.4. Trades and/or professions carried out by Basque-Navarrese women in the city of Santiago de Cuba (1902–1933). Source: Notaries' protocols (1902–1933).

11. González Pagés, *Macho, varón, masculino*, 103–9.
12. Gaytán Cuesta, "Mujeres cruzando fronteras," 11.

Conclusion

The Basque presence in the Santiago de Cuba region has not been researched previously. Based on an examination of notaries' protocols and citizenship books, this research has determined that the presence was not numerous and mostly regarded men of working age, pursuing positions in commerce and, to a lesser extent, in professions and/or trades. With regards to commercial activity, it should be pointed out that they did not restrict themselves to working with those from their ethnic group, having relationships with people from other Spanish regions and other nationalities (Cubans, Arabs). Julián Cendoya stands out: an influential businessman who traded in various parts of the world and made Santiago his center of operations.

Bibliography

AHPSC. Protocolos Notariales, 1902–1933.

Azcona Pastor, José Manuel. "La participación vasca en la empresa colonial y migratoria americana (1492–1992)." In *Historia general de la inmigración hispana a Iberoamérica*, edited by Pedro A. Vives, Pepa Vega y Jesús Oyamburu, vol. 2, 460–99. Madrid: Fundación CEDEAL, 1992.

Barcia Zequeira, María del Carmen. "Un modelo de inmigración 'favorecida': El traslado masivo de españoles a Cuba (1882–1930)." *Catauro* 12 (2002): 36–59.

Gaytán Cuesta, Andrea Adhara. "Mujeres cruzando fronteras: La feminización de las migraciones y la incorporación de la teoría del género a las teorías migratorias." 2003. Available at www.migrationinformation.org/feature/display.cfm?id=106 (Last accessed February 2, 2012.

González Pagés, Julio César. *Macho, varón, masculino: Estudios de masculinidades en Cuba*. Havana: Editorial de la Mujer, 2010.

Iglesias, Fe. "Características de la emigración española en Cuba." In *Españoles hacia América: La emigración masiva (1830–1930)*. Edited by Nicolás Sánchez Albornoz. Madrid: Alianza Editorial, 1988.

Luengo Teixidor, Félix. "Los vascos en Cuba a finales del siglo xix." *Historia Contemporánea* 19 (1999): 237–38.

Naranjo Orovio, Consuelo. "Inmigración: Análisis cuantitativo." In *Nuestra común historia: Poblamiento y nacionalidad*, edited by Aurea Matilde Fernández Muñiz, Olga García Cabrera, Consuelo Naranjo Orovio et al., 119–36. Havana: Editorial de Ciencias Sociales, 1993.

Pevida Pupo, Manuel. *La inmigración española en la región de Santiago de Cuba entre 1899 y 1936: Principales características sociales*. Ph.D. Thesis (unpublished), 2013.

Vidal Rodríguez, José Antonio. *La emigración gallega a Cuba: Trayectos migratorios: Inserción y movilidad laboral: 1898–1968*. Madrid: Consejo Superior de Investigaciones Científicas, 2005.

15

Overview of the Economics and Business Presence of Basques in Havana, 1901–1930

Michael Cobiella García

The start of the twentieth century brought with it the end of Spanish domination in the Antilles and the beginning of a Cuban republic, proclaimed on May 20, 1902, after a period of US military occupation that began in January 1899. It was a republic with many shortcomings and few strong points, called neo-colonial because of its political and economic dependence on foreign capital, mostly US, as Cuban historiography has suggested and explained since 1959.

The start of the new century saw the arrival and presence of a pluri-ethnical series of immigrants and temporary residents from many parts of the world who settled or had already settled all over the country. This coming together of nationalities from such different places included Basque and Navarrese people among the groups who made up the Spanish multi-ethnical group, which was not without its ethno-historical and sociological contradictions. Although Basque immigration dated from the beginning of the conquest and colonization of the island, it was not until the second half of the nineteenth century that its ethno-demographic presence became more significant. Since then, and at the beginning of the following century, these immigrants' ethno-cultural and economic influence has been felt and their descendents have been increasingly important in Cuban life and society.[1]

From this perspective, this article's objective is to offer a panorama, a first historical approach to the main manifestations of Basque immigrants' economic and financial presence and that of their descendants in the city of

---

1. Guanche Pérez, *España en la savia de Cuba*, 16–18, 46–47, 58–63, and 69–73; and *Componentes étnicos de la nación cubana*, 5–10.

Havana in the period 1901–1930. It is a subject barely explored by Cuban historiography and anthropology. This analysis will take into account the sectors of the Havana economy in which these immigrants' and their direct descendants' business and investments are evident throughout those years.

The decision to study the economic activity of the Basque people and their descendants in Havana is not fortuitous. This city was, not only in this period, but for a long time, the ideal place for the Hispanic communities to carry out their economic, commercial, and even cultural activities; it was also the largest port for the importing and exporting of goods, raw material, industrial products, as well as being the largest population center and urban area in Cuba.[2] Havana was the seat of political and ideological authority (executive, legislative, and judicial) and military power (the three armed forces, the police, and the rural guard), with a complete economic infrastructures (industrial, commercial, public, and financial services). All of these were continually growing and rapidly expanding to the extent that the most advanced capitalism was conquering all at the start of the twentieth century. The country's greatest socioeconomic and cultural development was, in short, to be seen in this great city, an eclectic mixture of the ancient and the modern, of the past and the present, but with its eyes set on the future. Because of this Havana was, and had to be, the most obvious choice as a destination for temporary and permanent immigrants from the Basque provinces and Navarra. This immigration was to integrate into the wider Spanish community and its first and even second generation descendants who had settled in the city in previous times.

The Economic-Financial Presence of Basque People and Their Descendants in Havana

If we base ourselves on the information to be found in financial, industrial, and trade directories; leaflets; guides and magazines; along with certain bibliographical sources that have, recently, examined the creation and evolution of the Spanish Cuban republican business world and bourgoisie during the first three decades of the twentieth century, we can appreciate that the Basque people and their second and even third generations had a distinguished presence, which in some cases was highly significant, in many sectors of Havana's thriving economy at the start of the century.[3] In fact, they took part in all the economic arenas that existed at the time: import-export, commission agents, representatives, wholesalers, retailers, general businessmen, specialists, bankers, and other moneylenders. Their

---

2. *Libro de Cuba*, 444; Pérez de la Riva, *El barracón y otros ensayos*, 309–10; and García Álvarez, *La gran burguesía comercial en Cuba 1899–1920*, 35–36.

3. See *Directorio de Cuba 1927*; *Directorio de información general de la República de Cuba 1916*; *Directorio general de la República de Cuba*; *Guía Comercial e Industrial de Cuba*; *Guía de la ciudad de la Habana y ferrocarriles de la República*; *Guía Directorio del comercio, profesiones e industrias de la Isla de Cuba*; *Guía Directorio de la República de Cuba*; *El Libro Azul de Cuba 1912*; *Libro de Cuba*; and Rojo y García, *Guía Comercial de la Isla de Cuba para los ferrocarriles y servicios marítimos*.

influence was also felt in industrial production and product treatment, both sugar and sugarcane and other parts of the sugar industry; different types of financial activity and areas concerned with public services and values.[4]

Given these sectors' significance in the Havana economy, they must be described, at least in overview, to demonstrate the Basque presence and that of their descendants in each one. Without any doubt, the Basques were mostly in trade, as were Cubans with Basque maternal or paternal forebears. It should be pointed out that retailers—"detallista" was the name for them in Cuba in those years—were the most numerous and more influential in microeconomic terms: the bibliography examined about these three decades always underscores how many Basque people, or Cubans of that ethno-cultural background, were owners of small businesses or food stores: the famous "bodegas" that were popularly associated with creoles and immigrants from Galicia, although also with persons from Asturias and their descendants. The Basques never quite became as well known for retailing as did their Spanish colleagues from Galicia and Asturias. Basques and Navarrese were also involved in other activities, such as owning "fondas" (small establishments which sold food, refreshments, and drinks), bars, cafés, and men's and women's clothes shops.[5] It would be difficult to mention any individual example, or the name of any relevant small association of retailers in this area, because of the continual evolution and renovation in this sector over those three decades.

Import-export, along with working as commission agents or representatives, was another of the livelihoods assumed by Basque people and their Spanish-Cuban descendants. It was, perhaps, the one which gave them the greatest material return and, in general, social prestige during these years, as we will explain below.

The island's remarkable economic activation at the start of the twentieth century enabled the gradual development of trade with other parts of the world—which had previously not existed or only at an insignificant scale, as well as an increase in trade with areas with which Cuba had been trading since the previous century. The reactivation of traditional Cuban agricultural production during the first decade of the century, and the arrival of immigrants, enabled by the investment boom fueled by foreign capital—mostly from the United States and western Europe (Great Britain, France, and Germany) led to the country, and Havana in particular,

---

4. See Dollero, *Cultura Cubana*, 468–74, 476; García Álvarez, *La gran burguesía comercial en Cuba 1899–1920*, 29–34, 78–83, 91–102; Lloyd, *Impresiones de la República de Cuba en el siglo xx*, 425–37, 455; Marqués Dolz, *Las industrias menores*, 99–102, 105–8; and Toro González, *La alta burguesía cubana 1920–1958*, 250, 254–55, 259.

5. *Directorio de Cuba 1927*; *Directorio de información general de la República de Cuba 1912*; *Directorio de información general de la República de Cuba 1914*; *Directorio de información general de la República de Cuba 1916*; *Directorio de información general de la República de Cuba 1918*; *Directorio general de la República de Cuba*; *Guía Comercial e Industrial de Cuba*; *Guía de la ciudad de la Habana y ferrocarriles de la República*; *Guía Directorio del comercio, profesiones e industrias de la Isla de Cuba*; *Guía Directorio de la República de Cuba*; *Guía Directorio de la República de Cuba*; *Guía Directorio de la República de Cuba*.

being flooded with manufactured and handmade goods, primary materials, fuel, investment capital, and a workforce from many parts of the world. The capital's ports were also full of goods from domestic agricultural production ready to be exported and re-exported to the main import markets around the world.[6]

This situation was taken advantage of by numerous import-export traders, commission agents, and bankers; in fact, by the people who were in the best position and had the greatest solvency to be able to invest and increase their volume of business and profits. A few of them became tremendously wealthy, others less so, many did not—only maintaining a certain solvency and modest profits—and some even went broke, were ruined, and disappeared from the records of the city's commercial activity forever.

Basque traders were not excepted from this reality that characterized the capitalist economic model, deformed in itself, imposed on the island by foreign capital, basically from the United States. Although not all of them triumphed or were rewarded socially and in material terms, the hard work, daring and skills of many of the Basques were rewarded over these decades: they managed to take advantage of the new conditions of the Havanan economy. It was in that way that small, medium, and large companies—which could be set up by single individuals or members of a family, father and son(s), uncle and nephew(s), by a widow and her son(s), and so on—flourished. There were also companies founded by groups of shareholders or partnerships in which there were no family relationships; indeed these were the most common types of firms in the city's socioeconomic framework. Many of these businesses had their origins in the previous century and managed to continue or even grow during the boom at the start of the twentieth century.

The acquisition and sale of the country's main agricultural and livestock products, in particular sugar and tobacco, including certain derivatives, as well as coffee, rice, small fruit, meat, lard, and animal hides, and some other natural resources, were typical exports to foreign markets. At the same time, the purchase and sales in towns and even nationally of a long list of foodstuffs, industrial, mineral, and fuel goods that were not obtained or produced nationally were the bases of imports. It was very usual to import foodstuff from Spain—including the Basque provinces and Navarra—which was in such demand from the Spanish community in the capital. They also flooded the Havana market with industrial technique and technology, particularly from the United States and some western European countries such as Great Britain, France, Germany, and Belgium.[7]

---

6. Dollero, *Cultura Cubana*, 440–66; García Álvarez, *La gran burguesía comercial en Cuba 1899–1920*, 27–28, 84–91; Lloyd, *Impresiones de la República de Cuba en el siglo xx*, 311–14, 452–53; Toro González, *La alta burguesía cubana 1920–1958*, 172–73, 176–79, 208–10.

7. *Directorio de Cuba 1927*; *Directorio general de la República de Cuba*; *Directorio de información general de la República de Cuba 1916*; *Directorio de información general de la República de Cuba 1918*; *Guía Comercial e Industrial de Cuba*; *Guía Directorio del comercio, profesiones e industrias de la Isla de Cuba*; Rojo y García, *Guía Comercial de la Isla de Cuba para los ferrocarriles y servicios marítimos*.

A group of Basque traders and their Cuban descendants, helped by all the sociohistorical factors, managed to become what Cuban socioeconomic historians have classified as polivalent and specialized, obtaining high socioeconomic position and class.[8] The former had numerous types of export-import operations in their portfolios, on which they earned commissions or were given allocations and which might include a wide range of products and merchandise; they also offered credit services (no small number opened banks and offered loans in the city), transport services, and were also public bond holders and providers. In other words, everything which their financial resources, investment capacity, national and international contacts with suppliers, and their trading skills allowed them to achieve.

A quick look at the bibliographical sources examined enables us to identify the names of individuals and companies that obtained social renown and economic success in Havana over these three decades, such as Manuel and Jorge de Ajuria, of Jorge M. de Ajuria y Hnos.; Aspuru y Cía., S. at C.; Hilario Astorqui y Cía.; Pedro Basterrechea, of Basterrechea y Hnos.; Pablo Eguzquiza, of Eguzquiza y Osorio; Paulino Gorostiza, of Gorostiza, Barañano y Cía.; José de Lejarza, of Lejarza y Cía., S. en C.; José I. Lezama, of José I. Lezama y Cía.; Julio Lobo Olavarría, of Galbán, Lobo y Cía.; Manuel Otaduy; Gabriel Otaola, of Otaola e Ibarra; Francisco Saralegui; Zabaleta, Sierra y Cía.; Hnos. Zulueta and Ruiz de Gámiz; Juan A. and Marcos Zárraga, of Zárraga, Rodríquez y Cía., S. en C.; among others.[9]

The specialized traders, at the same time, and as their classification suggests, were in the import and later sale on the domestic market of certain products such as comestibles (food and drink), cloth, clothing, glass wear and crockery, wood, building materials, different classes of industrial machinery, different types of motors, vehicles and various accessories, musical instruments, electric devices, chemical and pharmaceutical products, comestics and perfumes, and more. Depending on the vagaries of market prices, they also specialized in exporting certain Cuban products that gave them better profits.

There are significant examples of individuals and names of trading companies with records of the involvement of Basques and their Cuban descendants in the specialized import-export business. The most significants cases

8. García Álvarez, *La gran burguesía comercial en Cuba 1899–1920*, 30–31; Toro González, *La alta burguesía cubana 1920–1958*, 250, 259, and 261.

9. The spelling of surnames used in the sources examined has been used. *Directorio de Cuba 1927*; *Directorio general de la República de Cuba*; *Directorio de información general de la República de Cuba 1916*; *Guía Comercial e Industrial de Cuba*; *Guía Directorio de la República de Cuba*; *Guía Directorio de la República de Cuba*; *Guía Directorio de la República de Cuba*; *Guía Directorio del comercio, profesiones e industrias de la Isla de Cuba*; *El Libro de Cuba 1925*, *Libro Azul de Cuba 1917*; *Libro Azul de Cuba 1918*; *Libro de Cuba*; Jiménez Soler, *Las empresas de Cuba 1958*, 48, 55, 60, 62, 319–21, 335; and Jiménez Soler, *Propietarios de Cuba 1958*, 42–43, 45, 159, 230, 272, 303, 315, 317–19, 344, 471, 504, 577, 541–43); Rojo y García, *Guía Comercial de la Isla de Cuba para los ferrocarriles y servicios marítimos*.

(in alphabetical order by specialization) were: Aranguren, Martínez y Cía., Goitía y García, Zárraga, Martínez y Cía., automobile dealers and importers of auto parts and accesories; Mondragón y Echevarría, Zaballa y Cía., sugar warehousing and fruit sellers; Sebastián Arteta, lumber warehouse; Barandiarán y Cía.,steamship consigner; Guillermo Aldazábal, Braulio Larrazábal, pharmasist ; Luis L. Aguirre, de Luis L. Aguirre y Cía., Mayor y Arzola, arms and ammunition importers; José M. Zarrabeitia, importers of electric products; Estaban Garay, de Capestany y Garay, Pedro Garay y Lucio Zatica, de Garay y Zatica, José Marina, de Marina y Cía., Trueba y Aróstegui, Aniceto Uriarte, importers of hardware; Erviti y Arregui, Loidi, Ervite y Cía., Oriosolo y Cía., S. en C., importers and warehousers of animal feeds; Tiburcio Ibarra, de T. Ibarra y Cía., S. en C., Felipe y Germán Lizama, de Díaz y Lizama, S. en C.-La Filosofía, José Otaolaurruchi, de José M. Otaolaurruchi y Cía., importers of glassware and earthenware; Cosme Manzarbeitia, de Manzarbeitia y Cía.-La Vizcaína, Recalt y Laurrieta, Uriarte, Hormaza y Cía., Urtiaga y Aldama, wine and liquor importers; Eguidazo y Echeverría, S. en C., José M. Gallarreta, de J. Gallarreta y Cía. S. A., Gregorio Luzátegui, Francisco Martín Echevarri, de Víveres Finos Fsco. Martín S. A.-Casa Potín, importers of foodstuff in general and fine foods.[10]

Finance for expanding businesses, or simply to maintain their stability, was a factor to be kept in mind in all enterprises, however safe they might seem. Traders of Basque origin did not neglect this fundamental aspect. A sizeable group of them—who also had their own import-export businesses or were commission agents or representatives—entered the world of finance in order to consolidate their socioeconomic and class position. Furthermore, being a moneylender, or underwriter of another type, was one more way to obtain profits without, in general, having to use as much physical or intellectual effort as in other business activities. Examples of this, some of them paradigmatic, include Hilario Astorqui, Tiburcio Esquerro, Muniátegui y Cía., Francisco Saralegui, and Juan Zárraga, of Zárraga y Cía., who founded their own banks that prospered, many of them linked with trading interests. Then there was that celebrated member of the Basque community, Manuel Otaduy, who represented the interests of the capital's large financial institutions such as the Banco Español de la Isla de Cuba and The Trust Company of Cuba.[11]

Industry was another sector of the Havana economy in which the Basques and their descendants were present and, in some cases, in a very significant way.[12] While the country's industrial development—particularly outside the sugar sector—was very limited and dependent on foreign capitalist investment and supplies, imposed by US economic penetration,

---

10. Ibid.

11. *Directorio de Cuba 1927*; *Directorio general de la República de Cuba*; *Directorio de información general de la República de Cuba 1912*; *Directorio de información general de la República de Cuba 1914*; *El Libro de Cuba 1925*; *Guía Comercial e Industrial de Cuba*; *Guía Directorio de la República de Cuba*; *Guía Directorio del comercio, profesiones e industrias de la Isla de Cuba* (1909); *Libro Azul de Cuba 1917* (1917); *Libro Azul de Cuba 1918* (1918).

12. Ibid.

all was not, to use a popular Spanish expression "black with gray stitching." The manufacturing sector not connected with sugar had its weight in the island's economic statistics during these years. Independently from vagaries of all underdeveloped economic subject to capital investors, technology and even certain foreign prime materials. Various other industrial activities were carried out in which the descendants of immigrants from the Basque Country were involved out of proportion with their ethno-demographic presence in the country.[13]

In Havana, specifically, the manufacturing sector not connected with sugarcane, tobacco and other national products offers the best examples of the presence of members of the Basque community and their Cuban descendants. They often carried out their economic activities with considerable skill and good fortune. Perhaps their presence in so many different sectors, the volume of production and sales, capital invested and profits earned, was only surpassed by the Catalans and their descendants, except for Cuban businessmen and their descendants. Although more in depth research would be needed to confirm this theory.

A glance at the bibliography examined and mentioned above, confirms what we have said. It must be pointed out that rather than setting up great industrial companies, these businessmen founded, acquired—as partners or shareholders—a series of establishments that, by the international standards of the day, would be classified as small businesses or, at most, medium-sized ones; in other words, a series of factories, often workshops, of modest size and production, although for some Cuban owners they could be signs of the sector's gradual development and potential. There were two very significant examples that were highly unusual in the city during those years both in terms of size and production capacity. One was the foundries and machine shops, smithies, and kettle-making workshops belonging to the Viuda de Ruiz de Gámiz, which would later belong to Hnos. Zulueta y Ruiz de Gámiz, their successors and children, with its headquarters at Casa Blanca on the other side of Havana Bay. The other was La Vasconia S. A.'s boilerworks, foundry, and machine shop, specialized in the repair and manufacture of parts and machinery for sugar factories, with its headquarters at Calzada de Puentes Grandes y Aldecoa, on the outskirts of the city.[14] As can be seen, there were two quite unusual examples of attempts to develop a type of metalurgical industry—or rather heavy machinery industry—and make it flourish, closely connected with the sugar industry, its potential client, from what their advertising tells us. However, they were going to have serious difficulties competing with imports for the same sector during these years.[15]

Otherwise production industries mostly focused on furniture, principally beds and metal frameworks; some construction materials; iron and

---

13. Ibid.
14. *Directorio general de la República de Cuba*; and *Directorio de información general de la República de Cuba 1916*.
15. Marqués Dolz, *Las industrias menores*, 36–40.

steel structures; mosaics and crockery; women's shoes and hats; matches; the manufacture and bezelling of mirrors; food production, mostly sweets, syrups, and bakery; providing certain services which could be defined as industrial, such as machine shops repairing different kinds of machinery and manufacturing some of their parts.

As in previous sections, this list included the main players in alphabetical order: Benguria, Corral y Cía., Gómez, Benguria y Cía., Izaguirre y Penabad, Trueba y Aróstegui, Vidaurrazaga, Menchaca y Cía., Vidaurrazaga y Rodríguez, S. en C., Benigno Villadóniga, bed frame and metal bed factories; Diego Gorría, Hechemendía, Víctor Vidaurrazaga, Andrés Zubillaga, women's shoes and hats factory; Joaristi y Lanzagorta, S. en C., steel structures and metal boats; Diego Pérez Barañano, matches factory; Manuel Aramburu, de Cía. Constructora Contratista S. A., Zabala y Aguiar, manufacturer of construction materials; Álvaro Crespo Zabala, de Crespo, García S. A., maker of mosaics and earthenware; Gorostiza, Barañano y Cía., Esperanza Sagastizabal de Pando-La Francia; manufacturer and bezeller of mirrors; Secundino Aldecoa, Duñaveitia y Rico-La Estrella Polar, Salustiano Urteaga, bakery goods, sweets, jams, and syrups; Guitián, Echavarría y Cía., S. en C., Echevarría y Cruz, Alejandro Loyola, turnery and machine shop.[16]

Production and processing industries connected with sugar and tobacco production, although to a much lesser extent, also enabled the Basque businessmen and owners to show their character. With tobacco—including cigarette production, storage and sales of tobacco leaves and cigars—Basque investment was never as large or as well known as that from the previous century onward of immigrants from Asturias, Galicia, and Catalonia and their descendents. However, the vital importance of this industry in the national economy—in fact, for a long time it was the second most important in the country after sugar and related products—led to some Basque immigrants becoming involved in this sector too. The best example was that of brothers Bernardino, Francisco, and José Manuel Solaún, of the company Solaún y Hnos., owners of a tobacco and cigarette factory and, for a time, also partners and administrators or the famous H. Upmann cigar factory, as well as owners of a destemming workshop and a tobacco leaf warehouse. Vicente Arizaga should also be mentioned, as owner of the cigarette factories El Gremio and El Ticket. Then there were the tobacco warehouse owners and tobacco leaf exporters Manuel de Ajuria, Gutiérrez y Zabala, Oyarzún, Sánchez y Cía, and Basarrate e Higuera, operating in

---

16. *Directorio de Cuba 1927*; *Directorio de información general de la República de Cuba 1912*; *Directorio de información general de la República de Cuba 1914*; *Directorio de información general de la República de Cuba 1916*; *Directorio de información general de la República de Cuba 1918*; *Directorio general de la República de Cuba*; *Guía Comercial e Industrial de Cuba*; *Guía Directorio del comercio, profesiones e industrias de la Isla de Cuba*; *Guía Directorio de la República de Cuba*; *Guía Directorio de la República de Cuba*; *Guía Directorio de la República de Cuba*; *El Libro Azul de Cuba 1912*; *El Libro de Cuba 1925*, *Libro Azul de Cuba 1917*; Jiménez Soler, *Las empresas de Cuba 1958*, 485.

partnership with other Spanish immigrants and with Cubans.[17]

Lastly, while the city of Havana—being the largest, most dynamic urban area of Cuba—was never a place for growing sugarcane or manufacturing sugar on a large scale—as happened on the rest of the island—it housed the presence of a series of landowners and sugar producers from the Cuban bourgoisie (including Spanish landowners who had settled in the country), that had set up their commercial offices in the city. Their objectives were clear: Havana, as noted, was the main commercial and financial city, which included its excellent port facilities for exporting so—regardless of the fact that they produced their sugarcane and had their sugar factories and distilleries in the provinces and that a part or most of their products were shipped from ports there—they needed to be represented in the capital. Furthermore, this made producers of sugar and derived products visible to the international market, above all to the United States.

This list of sugar landowners also included a very important group of immigrants from the Basque Country-Navarra and their direct descendants; they made investments and owned properties in this production and manufacturing industry. In fact, Basque investment in sugar had began earlier, being of great note during the nineteenth century. At the start of the twentieth century many of these surnames, now belonging to their widows, children, and other descendants, were still present in this industry, and some of them tried to survive the economic difficulties of the first three decades of the century, in particular the famous banking crash of 1920–1921 which so affected all sectors of the national economy. Some new surnames were added to these older Basque ones, in growing sugarcane and producing sugar over several decades with greater or lesser success.

In this way, with commercial offices and markets established in the city of Havana, there were sugar landlords, most of them absentee, such as: Jorge and Ramón de Ajuria, owners of Santísima Trinidad, sugar estate with offices at 100, Aguiar Street; José Ma. Beguiristaín, owner of María Antonia and San Isidro sugar estate, offices at Oficios Street no. 16 A; Francisco M. Durañona, owner of Toledo sugar estate, offices at Maceo Street, Marianao; Fermín de Goicochea, owner of Mercedita sugar estate, offices at Prado Street, no. 84; José I. Lezama, owner of Limones, Resolución, and Unión sugar estate, offices in Amargura Street no. 2; Antonio and Ramón Larrea, partners in Providencia sugar estate, offices at Salud Street no. 73; Ernesto A. Longa, owner of Mercedita sugar estate, offices at Cuba Street, no. 120; Juan P. Ruiz de Gámiz, partners in Vitoria sugar estate, offices at Marina Street no. 19; Francisco L. del Valle Iznaga, owner of Mapos and Natividad sugar estate, offices at Obrapía Street no. 19 A; Sebastián Zabaleta, owner of La Vega sugar mill, offices at Aguiar Street no. 71; Zozaya y Cía., owners of Adela sugar mill, offices at Escobar Street, no. 12; Hijos de Zulueta y Ruiz de Gámiz, owners of *Álava*, España, Zaza, and Vitoria, sugar estate, with offices at 20, Cuba Street; and

---

17. Ibid.

there were also some sugar estate administrators such as Arturo Iturralde, who was in charge of administering Santa Lutgarda sugar estate, with offices at Habana Street no. 140 and 142.[18]

In the same way, we must also mention a industrial sector very closely connected with the sugar industry: alcohol distilling, liqueurs, aguardiente, and rum, all derived from the sugarcane production and refining process. The Basque and their Cuban descendants were also involved here from early on. They included Ramón Otamendi, owner of El Tívoli distillery at Zanja Street no. 88, and Pedro Oyarzábal also owner of an unnamed distillery at San Ignacio Street no. 87, just to mention two of the best-known propietors at the start of the century. At the same time—although the sources examined do not provide information about this—we have no doubt that at some point during these three decades these leading companies in this sector had commercial offices in the capital, especially the manufacturers of aguardiente, liqueurs, and rum such as Echeverría y Cía., S. en C., with its famous Cárdenas distillery and J. Arechabala S. A., owned by the very well-known Bizkaian Arechabala family, both with their headquarters in the city of Cárdenas, Matanzas province, and a history in the sector going back to the nineteenth century. Also the signatures of José Ma. Beguiristaín, mentioned above as a notable sugar landowner, who, at the start of the century, was the owner of a distillery in the city of Sagua la Grande, Las Villas, and the famous San Juan distillery in the city of Matanzas.[19] The reasons for their presence have already been explained in this article and they are connected with Havana's fundamental importance as an economic and financial center independently of where the production was geographically.

Some Final Considerations

Given the characteristics of this research—which is rather a first approach to the little known subject of the economic and business presence of Basque people and their Cuban descendants in Havana—we believe it inappropriate to draw definitive conclusions. For this reason we have decided to finish with some considerations which seem more appropriate in this case and which can lead—and, indeed, should lead—to further research into this subject from a historical and anthropological point of view.

As we have seen, during the first three decades of the twentieth century the presence of Basque people and their Cuban descendants in the first and even second generations was far-reaching and, in fact, multifaceted. The members of these Hispanic groups in the city were able to adapt well

18. *Directorio de Cuba 1927*; *Directorio de información general de la República de Cuba 1916*; *El Libro de Cuba 1925*; Jiménez Soler, *Las empresas de Cuba 1958*, 48, 55, 62, 64–65, 72–74, 83, 104–5, 152–53, 369, 377, 379); Rojo y García, *Guía Comercial de la Isla de Cuba para los ferrocarriles y servicios marítimos*.
19. *Directorio general de la República de Cuba*; *Guía Directorio del comercio, profesiones e industrias de la Isla de Cuba*; Jiménez Soler, *Las empresas de Cuba 1958*, 72, 396–97; Rojo y García, *Guía Comercial de la Isla de Cuba para los ferrocarriles y servicios marítimos*.

to the new sociohistorical conditions at the start of the century when Spanish colonial power finally collapsed and a bourgeous republic was set up, marked by the gradual penetration by the United States of the country's economic and sociocultural spheres. Their work in terms of socioeconomic success and prestige—although we are dealing here with a class-based elite rather than all the Basque immigrants and, furthermore, further research is needed—was highly significant, above all compared with that of representatives of other Spanish ethnic groups in Havana during the same period. This success and eminence was achieved, in several cases, by the following generations of Basque Cubans.

Trade of all types was the sector in which their presence and preponderance was most felt, especially in social and microeconomic terms thanks to their participation as retailers. Second, they stood out as warehouse owners, commission agents, importers-exporters, and representatives, in other words, wholesalers. Third, they were both specialists and generalists. They also held some distinguished roles in finance, although this was always closely connected with the main activity of trade. Industry was the other area of the economy in which Basque influence and that of their Cuban descendants was particularly felt. Their presence was more visible and discernable in sectors not connected with the country's most traditional industries—sugarcane and tobacco—although, over the years, they managed to stand out and compete there too. So many important surnames from the Basque Country-Navarra were associated from early times with the production of various household goods, construction materials, food, machinery repair services, and manufacturing certain machiney parts, to mention the main industrial sectors in which they worked.

Today, at the start of the twenty-first century, we can only bring to light, remember and keep this ethno-cultural legacy which so many Basque people left us when—whatever their various personal, family, socioeconomic, or political and ideological motives—they risked leaving their homeland and took the hard route of emigration, crossing the Atlantic and making the biggest island in the Antilles their new home, settling there for the rest of their lives and making it the base of their dreams for the future.

Bibliography

Directorio de Cuba 1927. Havana: Editorial Schneer, S. A., 1927.
Directorio de información general de la República de Cuba 1912. Havana: Imprenta Rambla, Bouza y Cía.
Directorio de información general de la República de Cuba 1914. Havana: Imprenta Rambla, Bouza y Cía., 1914.
Directorio de información general de la República de Cuba 1916. Havana: J. A. Borges del Junco, editor, 1916.
Directorio de información general de la República de Cuba 1918. Havana: No publisher, 1918.
Directorio general de la República de Cuba. Havana: Imprenta Rambla y

Bouza, 1907–1908.

Dollero, Adolfo. *Cultura Cubana*. Havana: Imprenta El Siglo XX, 1916.

El Libro Azul de Cuba 1912. Havana: Imprenta de Solana y Cía, 1912.

El Libro de Cuba 1925. Havana: República de Cuba, 1925.

García Álvarez, Alejandro. *La gran burguesía comercial en Cuba 1899–1920*. Havana: Editorial de Ciencias Sociales, 1990.

Guanche Pérez, Jesús. *España en la savia de Cuba: Los componentes hispánicos en el etnos cubano*. Havana: Editorial de Ciencias Sociales, 1999.

———. *Componentes étnicos de la nación cubana*. Havana: Editorial Adagio, 2008.

Guía Comercial e Industrial de Cuba. Havana: Imprenta La Prueba, 1926.

Guía de la ciudad de la Habana y ferrocarriles de la República). Havana: J. J. Higuera, editor, 1919.

Guía Directorio del comercio, profesiones e industrias de la Isla de Cuba. Madrid: Bailly-Bailliere e Hijos, 1909.

Guía Directorio de la República de Cuba. Barcelona: Bailly-Bailliere-Riera, S. A., 1920

Guía Directorio de la República de Cuba. Barcelona: Bailly-Bailliere-Riera, S.A., 1924

Guía Directorio de la República de Cuba. Barcelona: Bailly-Bailliere-Riera, S. A., 1926.

Jiménez Soler, Guillermo. *Las empresas de Cuba 1958*. Havana: Editorial de Ciencias Sociales, 2004.

———. *Propietarios de Cuba 1958*. Havana: Editorial de Ciencias Sociales, 2006.

Libro Azul de Cuba 1917. Havana: No publisher, 1917.

Libro Azul de Cuba 1918. Havana: No publisher, 1918.

Libro de Cuba: Cincuentenario de la independencia 1902–1952. Havana: No publisher, 1954.

Lloyd, Reginald. *Impresiones de la República de Cuba en el siglo xx: Historia, gente, comercio, industria y riqueza*. London, Lloyds Greater Britain Publishing, 1913.

Marqués Dolz, María A. *Las industrias menores: Empresarios y empresas en Cuba (1880–1920)*. Havana: Editora Política, 2002.

Pérez de La Riva, Juan. *El barracón y otros ensayos*. Havana: Editorial de Ciencias Sociales, 1975.

Rojo y García, Francisco. *Guía Comercial de la Isla de Cuba para los ferrocarriles y servicios marítimos*. Havana: Imprenta Avisador Comercial, 1907.

Toro González, Carlos del. *La alta burguesía cubana 1920–1958*. Havana: Editorial de Ciencias Sociales, 2003.

16

Francisco Ulacia's Cuban Novel

Cecilia Arrozarena

Pancho: A War Child

Francisco Ulacia was born on August 11, 1864,[1] at Santa Clara, Cuba, to a Basque father and Cuban mother. His father, Domingo Ulacia, was from Bilbao and his mother, Eloísa Veitia, was from a comfortably-off family from Villa Clara. There were five siblings: Juan, Ramón, Blanca, Francisco, and Amalia. From an early age they called their fourth child, Francisco, Pancho.

Pancho's father, Domingo Ulacia Maiz, was the owner of the Villa Clara gas company. Gas lighting had spread from Havana in the 1840s[2] and the city council signed contracts for this with Compañía Española, Sociedad Echevarría, and Ruiz y Compañía among others. Later, limited companies were set up to install and run gas lighting in Santiago de Cuba, Matanzas, and Cárdenas. In Villa Clara service started in 1859. Jacobo de la Pezuela remarks on it in the fourth volume of his dictionary:

---

1. Manuel Vitoria gives his date of birth as May 14, 1868, in a well-informed article, "Vida y obra del doctor Ulacia." Koldo San Sebastián and José Luís de La Granja give the same date. Some reference sources, such as Enciclopedia Auñamendi, state that he was born in 1863. Jon Juaristi gives 1864. In fact, the inter-parochial archive of the city of Santa Clara records that Francisco Ulacia was born on August 11, 1864, and was baptized in the Cathedral of Santa Clara of Assisi on December 2 with the name Francisco Teodoro Ulacia Veitia. His father, Domingo Ulacia Maiz, was from Bizkaia. His mother, María Feliz Eulogia Veitia Gutierrez, was from Santa Clara. His paternal grandparents were Ramón and Josefa; his maternal grandparents José Manuel and María Eufracia.

2. There is information about a project in the Havana newspaper *El Faro Yndustrial* on December 4, 1841: "which the Royal Promotion Board gave news of last year and Joaquín Arrieta, according to the memories of Sociedad Patriótica, requested permission to install this lighting."

The main streets and towns in Villa-Clara are gas lit, the others being lit by oil lamps and both types of lighting being paid for by municipal funds. A company with liquid capital of 65,000 pesos was founded in 1859 for providing public lighting and, in particular, of the former type. It has been working successfully since 1860."[3]

Later the family was involved in the sugar industry, which was connected to gas in that the first permanent gas lighting systems in Cuba were installed in sugar mills with the objective of lengthening night shifts and obtaining continual production.[4]

Carlos Manuel de Céspedes's proindependence insurrection—which began on October 10, 1868, in Bayamo—started a war which was to last ten years. It spread steadily from Oriente to the center of the island and changed the life and future of the Ulacia Veitia family.

Various sources name the gas factory as one of the conspirators' meeting places, for instance Migdalia Cabrera in his research into the insurrection in Villa Clara:

> The Santa Clara conspirators held their exchange meetings in Miguel Gerónimo Gutiérrez's house; he was a public attorney who visited the businesses of the main property owners in the jurisdiction. They also used the gas factory and, above all, La Salud Pharmacy, owned by Juan Nicolás del Cristo, opposite the Plaza Mayor.[5]

On February 6, 1869, shattering the apparent calm in the center of Cuba and led by Miguel Gerónimo Gutiérrez,[6] there was a rising in the Las Villas area. Around four thousand rebels rose in Camarones and Ranchuelo, which meant that Sancti Spíritus, Remedios, Villa Clara, Cienfuegos, and even Sagua became war zones. By February 2 many of the inhabitants of Santa Clara had abandoned their homes, which led to the newspaper *El Alba de Villaclara* publishing an article titled "¿Por qué se van?" (Why do they leave?):

> So many families have left the city during the last four days that most of the houses have been closed up and Villaclara, which used to be so lively, looks sad, silent, and dark.

3. Pezuela, *Diccionario geográfico, estadístico, histórico de la Isla de Cuba*, 115.

4. On page 28 of the second volume of *El ingenio*, Manuel Moreno Fraginals explains that: "The increase in grinding as a result of fitting horizontal presses connected to steam engines meant that a continual, 24-hour cycle was called for. And gas lighting made that possible. At the end of the 1820s English firms provided efficient gasometers which could be adapted for Cuban sugar mills and toward 1840 this type of lighting was usual in the large semi-mechanized mills in the Havana-Matanzas area."

5. Cabrera Cuell, *La guerra del 68 en Villa Clara*, 13.

6. The Ulacias may have been maternally related to Miguel Gerónimo Gutiérrez, who presided over the Villa Clara Revolutionary Board, which had been set up at the start of the insurrection. Miguel Gerónimo Gutiérrez, born in Villa Clara in 1822, public attorney, writer in the press from the age of eighteen, poet, who had proreform ideas and, later on, markedly proindependence ideas, took part in the founding meeting at Guáimaro and was elected vice president of the Representatives' Chamber. Captured after being betrayed on April 19, 1871, he was murdered by the Spaniards at Monte Oscuro, Sancti Spíritus. There were also the brothers Veitia, proliferation officers at Santa Clara.

The Ulacias were one of the families that fled from the war at the start of 1869. They went to Bilbao, where the father was from, and arrived in the Zazpi Kaleak with their black woman servant. Paradoxically, they fled from one war and found themselves in another. In April, 1872, Carlos María de Borbón—pretender to the Spanish crown—ordered a rising and numerous Basque factions declared for him; this was the start of the Second Carlist War, which lasted until 1876. The city of Bilbao, which was on the Liberal side, was subjected to a harsh siege from February 1874 onward.

The Ulacia family spent the three months that the siege of Bilbao lasted in Castro Urdiales. They seemed to identify themselves as Liberals in terms of the duality which Miguel de Unamuno describes in his extraordinary novel about the siege, *Paz en la guerra*: "Carlist tinsmiths ('ojalateros') emigrated to Baiona and Liberals to Santander." The word "ojalatero" in this case did not come from the Spanish word *hojalata* ("tin"), but from *ojalá* ("if only"). Although the Ulacias decided to take refuge in Santander, Francisco Ulacia did witness the war as he admitted himself in a article titled "Recuerdos de la Montaña" (Memories from the Mountain) published on May 1, 1891, in *El Noticiero Bilbaino:* "the scenes of war and desolation which I saw were indelibly engraved in my mind." For the children they were recreation days, as Unamuno wrote: "with every new bombardment there was a new life, some fine days for playing as there was no school."[7]

After the siege, the Second Carlist War went on for a further two years, until 1876, while the First Republic had been founded in 1873 and the monarchy returned in 1874: the start of the Restoration regime. After the bloody defeat of the Carlists, the Basque territories were occupied during the last part of the war, followed by the traumatic removal, in 1876, of what remained of the foral institutions (Fueros) and customs in Araba, Bizkaia, and Gipuzkoa, and a state of siege there which went on until the summer of 1879.

Miguel de Unamuno also remembers the Bilbao of his childhood and youth in another book: *Recuerdos de niñez y mocedad* (Memories of childhood and youth) and we would like to point out certain similarities between his life and that of Francisco Ulacia. They were both born in 1864; they both went to the Instituto Vizcaíno secondary school; they both died in the terrible year of 1936.

Francisco de Ulacia: Doctor, Politician, and Novelist

Toward 1883, while Francisco Ulacia went to Barcelona to study medicine, his elder brothers Juan and Ramón returned to Cuba to look after the family businesses. Ramón Ulacia was kidnapped in 1886, a pause between

7. Unamuno, *Paz en Guerra*, 188.

wars in Cuba and in which banditry was common. Juan and Ramón managed the sugar estates Santa Catalina and Ulacia, partnered with Eduardo González Abreu at Santa Catalina and with Manuel Gutiérrez Quirós at Ulacia.[8] They were also proprietors of a tannery which they rented from Santiago Heguy Arreguy[9] and they gave their siblings Francisco and Amalia financial support: the latter lived without generating income.

After qualifying as a doctor, Francisco Ulacia returned to Bilbao and worked with Enrique Areilza, but soon left the profession to engage in politics and literature on a full-time basis.

With regards to politics, the abolition of the fueros and anti-Basque policies in Spain led to the Basques reacting by defending their language and culture, as well as taking a radically new view of the question of nationality. Francisco Pi y Margall, briefly the president of the Spanish First Republic in 1873, and author of the essay "Las nacionalidades" (The nationalities) in 1877, and one of the few politicians to understand the latent problem of nationalities in the Basque Country, Catalonia, and Cuba, had warned about possible events:

> After defeating the Basques, the current effort is to remove their exemption from military service and taxes. If this happens, will they become more Spanish? Will they share our ideals and feelings to a greater extent? Is the antagonism that exists between them and us not the natural result of being different races? If they work together a little—in line with the various theories about nationalities—I believe that one would have to be in favor of Basque independence. Would Spain allow that?[10]

In 1876, the Sociedad Euskalerria (The Basque Country Society) was founded from the Partido Liberal Fuerista (Liberal pro-Fueros Party) and was to be the precedent for many other pro-Basque organizations. Francisco Ulacia, due to pro-Catalan influence and his feelings for Cuba, began to embrace a pro-Basque, republican ideology and, at the same time as the War of Independence in Cuba, he adopted the radical proindependence positions of his friend Sabino Arana, the founder of the Basque Nationalist Party (EAJ-PNV).

Francisco de Ulacia, who was a republican and openly anticlerical, did not fit in very well with Sabino's devout beliefs. However, he joined EAJ-PNV. He was even elected to the Bilbao City Council in the 1901 elections

---

8. It is easy to come across the name Ulacia in the center of Cuba. With regards to place names, there is a Ulacia on the Villa Clara railway between Santo Domingo and Sagua la Grande, twelve kilometers from the former and seventy-nine from the latter. The sugar mill once known as Ulacia is now called Carlos Baliño.

9. Juan Ulacia Veitia's sons—Juan and Eduardo Ulacia—were rich landowners in Havana when the revolutionary forces won in 1959. Juan Ulacia Fernández had been a basketball player and had married Raquel Uriarte, their children being called Raquel and Juan Miguel, and living at Avenida Boulevard no. 1905 between the first and fourth floors, in the Country Club district.

10. Pí y Margall, *Las Nacionalidades*, 157.

and took an active part in the hygiene campaigns in the city's proletarian districts in tandem with the socialist councilor Facundo Perezagua. His work as councilor was ended by government reprisals: Ulacia was one of the EAJ-PNV councilors suspended for having received a delegation from the Argentine Navy without wearing his Spanish patriotic insignias. After being restored to his position, in 1904 he resigned giving an extraordinary pretext: he wanted to stop being Spanish as he had the chance to take out Cuban citizenship.

In spite of having spent only very short periods in Cuba, Francisco Ulacia claimed his right to become a citizen of the newly founded Republic of Cuba, the land of his birth. Giving up his Spanish nationality may have been motivated by his Basque nationalism, and a firm rejection of Spanish impositions, but there is no doubt that Francisco Ulacia's Basque nationalism was influenced by his Cuban nationalism.

He had already had bitter ideological disagreements with fellow party members over religion. During the following years he published several anticlerical, proliberal nationalism articles in *Euskalduna*. For instance, there is his article "Nacionalismo religioso" (Religious nationalism), in *Euskalduna* on February 14, 1906, signed by Maiz'tar Franzesko, a pseudonym he often used in the press. In line with this proindependence republicanism, Francisco de Ulacia took part in the attempt to found a left-wing Basque nationalist party between 1909 and 1913. This organization was called Partido Nacionalista Liberal Vasco at first and, after January 1911 Partido Republicano Nacionalista Vasco and, from April in that year—in imitation of a similar Catalan initiative and believing that they had founded a model to be followed—Unión Federal Nacionalista Republicana.[11] In January 1911 the Centro Nacionalista Republicano Vasco (Basque Republican Nationalist Center) was opened, and this led to violent disagreements with members of EAJ-PNV. From February 1911 Ulacia and his fellow members also published a magazine called *Askatasuna, Patria y Libertad* (Freedom, Homeland, and Liberty).[12]

With regards to his literary work, Francisco de Ulacia was a poet, novelist, playwright, and author of travel books as well as a writer of articles. After a first volume of poems, entitled *Pasionarias* and published in Bilbao in 1894, he wrote the novels *Don Fausto* (Mr. Fausto, 1905), *¡Nere biotza!* (My heart! 1907), *Martinchu ta Matilde* (Little Martinchu and Matilde, 1907), *Las gatitas rubias* (The blonde kittens, 1908), and *El Caudillo* (The Leader, 1910).[13]

---

11. In Catalonia, at the same time, the three pro-Catalan republican parties fused into the Unión Federal Nacionalista Republicana—UFNR: Republican Nationalist Federal Union—and it won a great victory in the municipal council elections in May 1910.

12. After the dictatorship of Miguel Primo de Rivera, during the Second Republic, Francisco de Ulacia was a firm supporter of autonomy for the four Basque provinces, while not abandoning the utopia of independence. He died of a heart attack in April 1936, a few months before the military uprising which led to the Spanish Civil War.

13. Francisco de Ulacia later wrote the following books: *Cervantes mentalista* (Cervantes

El Caudillo, Cuban novel

Francisco de Ulacia wrote *El Caudillo: Novela cubana* (The leader: a Cuban novel) in Bilbao between November 1909 and May 1910 during a "sad, misty winter," and published it at the end of 1910. It is a story filled with Cuban scenery, customs, and characters. It was a tale of the redeemed Cuba that had begun to exist thanks to the independence that had been wrested from Spain in 1898.

The newspaper *El Liberal* published news about the novel on January 6, 1911, along with the transcription of its last chapter. Its appreciation of the work was favorable in general:

> *El caudillo* is, above all, a clearly, deeply Cuban novel, perhaps the first of these dimensions and ambition, and in which the author has managed to give an impression of the real Cuban character, life on the island, which we miss out on through our own fault, and its scenery, so beautiful and full of charm. The soul of its women, the very model of women in love and of mothers; the way of thinking of men for whom life and money are the ultimate and who, whether honorable or shameless, take being gentlemen and nobility as their motto; the endless affection of servants who adore their masters as if they were their parents, who would give all their blood for them; all of them are portrayed by a master in *El Caudillo*. For whoever has lived in Cuba, for whoever has enjoyed its hospitality, the sincere affection of the children of the land which is born so soon and is erased so late, for whoever has spent happy nights in the immense countryside in which the sky pours its poetry, Ulacia's novel will surely be a book of indescribable tranquility and pleasure.

The novel was also well received in Cuba. On September 10, 1911, the Havana weekly *El Fígaro* gave the "Cuban author living in Bilbao" its cover and said of his new work:

> *El Fígaro* is pleased to offer the portrait of and news about Mr. Ulacia on its most prominent pages. Although he has not been in Cuba for years, he has not stopped being Cuban and it is only fair for his homeland to celebrate the intellectual triumphs of one of its sons abroad, working on novels with enthusiasm, an area in which there are so few names in Cuba's bibliography.

The commentator praised his warm, enthusiastic paint brush and said that: "This book alone would be enough to make the name of the author of *El Caudillo* respected in contemporary literature, if it were not already."

The novel, as well as being well received in Cuba, was also widely read. The critic from Guanajay, Joaquín N. Aramburu, wrote about it in

mentalist, 1924), a speech read on May 6, 1916; *Ernesto* (1925), play written around 1914; *Cuentos de Euzkadi* (Stories of the Basque Country, 1929), short stories; *Bajo un cielo azul* (Beneath a blue sky, 1930), travel writing; *Hacia Oriente* (Toward the Orient, 1930), travel writing; *Moros y cristianos* (Moors and Christians, 1931), travel writing; *Los tres golpes de Pascual* (Pascual's three blows, 1932), short stories.

Diario de la Marina: "It is a picture of customs in Tierra Adentro because the characters and the situations are from Villa Clara."

And José de Armas, who was also known as Justo de Lara, wrote about the novel:

> Dr. Ulacia, a very distinguished Cuban who has written an interesting Cuban novel titled *El Caudillo*, full of love for Cuba and heart-felt descriptions of our country's character and customs . . . On the brilliant pages of this book, full of local flavor, there are sweet memories of the absent homeland and the Cubans' generous soul is painted.

It is a nineteenth-century novel. In spite of its uniqueness, it has some features in common with other nineteenth century-novels. Albert Camus used to mock the beginnings of classical novels, saying they always started with something like: "On a beautiful May morning, an elegant horsewoman riding a superb chestnut horse rode along the flowered paths of the Bois de Boulogne." It is impossible to say that *El Caudillo* does not start like that. The beginning, in fact, is in the month of April when, under the tropical sun whose incandescent rays burn the savannah, a carriage with enormous wheels and steered by a black driver carries two ladies . . .

Tropical Countryside

Francisco Ulacia's language is flowery and it is inevitably connected with the island's countryside. When the main character—Jaime Aguirre—comes back to Cuba from the United States after his mother's death, one reads that:

> After the wide, sun-burned plain they had to go through the shadowy jungle, exuberant and rich with climbing plants which prevented the riders from going forward. Belisario proceeded, machete in hand, to clear the path of the swamp's undergrowth. Trees of all sizes— from small papayas and mysterious guaos to enormous ceiba trees and elegant palm trees—rose into the air to heights which tired our eyes, forming the jungle's solid scaffolding. And at the foot of these trees climbing plants threaded together, climbing up the branches, jumping up to the top, leaping from coconut trees to guazumas, from guavas to mameys, forming caves, arches of greenery and thick nets of green leaves, small white flowers and innumerable *bejucos*, some thin, like fine wire, and others thick, like cables which reach the highest parts of gigantic trees.
>
> At times Spanish limes link their branches with those of annonas, bijas and sibacus, forming thick curtains of flowers, leaves and fruit, which had to be mercilessly ripped asunder with the sharp blades of machetes.
>
> But Belisario was not enough for the job and Mr. Ramon and Jaimito, who were walking behind him, also had to use their wide, sharp blades in order not to be tied up by the foliage all around them.[14]

---

14. Ulacia, *El caudillo*, 48.

This exuberant countryside is striking as it featured in an article titled "Del otro mundo" (From the other world), published in *El Noticiero Bilbaino* on March 4, 1892, in a report about a recent visit to his homeland:

> I looked toward the east and saw a light, tenuous clearly in that direction and that began to spread across the horizon like a smooth, rosy mist.
>
> It was dawn, full of beauty and charm, appearing as it always does in tropical regions.
>
> The moon and the stars, put to shame by that splendor, hurried to retire, quickly gathering up the delicate, pale blanket woven by their weak rays, to cast it like a transparent, luminous gauze over the dome of the sky and the face of the earth.
>
> The rosy mist which spread across the horizon changes color into scarlet.

One cannot help connecting this descriptive abundance with the theory of marvelous reality which Alejo Carpentier was to propound many years later. He explained it in this way to Pierre Bleiberg in *Nouveau Clarté* in 1978:

> I hold that the features of what is marvelous to be found raw around every corner in Latin America due to the clash of races, the survival of natural syncretism, the presence of the highly imaginative Indian race, the buildings' baroque appearance, and certain incredible features of everyday life. This is the marvelous and it has been my task to express it.[15]

With regards to scenery, it is José Lezama Lima who said, in a well-known text, *La expresión americana* (The American expression), that scenery leads us "acquire a point of view":

> Scenery is one of man's forms of dominating, like Roman aqueducts, a sentence from Lycurgus or the classical triumph of the flute. Scenery is always dialogue, reducing nature to the stature of man. If we accept Schelling's sentence—"nature is the visible spirit and the spirit is invisible nature"—we can easily reach the conclusion that the visible spirit of what is most enjoyed is dialogue with man; and that the dialogue between nature-revealing spirit and man is the scenery. First, nature has to win the spirit; then man will set out to find it.[16]

There is a detailed relationship with tropical nature throughout the novel with picturesque references such as that to guao[17] when the illness affects the doctor himself:

> The swelling of his face had completely covered over his eyes. His nose was puffed up, like an elephant's trunk, his lips thick, like shapeless lumps of bruised flesh, his cheeks edematous and ample

---

15. *Bleiberg*, "Le réel merveilleux d' Alejo Carpentier," 65–71.

16. Lezama Lima. *La expresión americana*, 27.

17. There are two bushes in Cuba called *guao*: one is called guao de sabana (*comocladia dentata*) and the coastal guao tree (*metopium toxiferum*). They can both cause allergic contact dermatitis.

and his ears like elephants', standing out like enormous fans to either side of his gigantic cranium.[18]

Strange nature, mysterious bush that defies science and exposes the expert medic to ridicule:

> The young doctor, with his words mumbled due to the enormous swelling of his lips, insisted that it was not because of guao but had been caused by linfangitis erysipelatous, which he had had before, and he said he would not put up with ignorant people giving him lessons in medicine.[19]

Francisco Ulacia's admiration for tropical scenery could be compared with José Martí's in his last diary *De Cabo Haitiano a Dos Ríos*. The language in the novel is quite florid, in line with modernism, which was just beginning to echo, and what Alejo Carpentier was to call baroque sensitivity. As he explains in the dedication, Francisco Ulacia wanted to be in tune with the "rich plasticity" and "warm tones which the luminous atmosphere of the tropical zone always gives all its people and countryside."

Plasticity of Language

In addition to the plasticity of the countryside and the visual, there is also admiration for the unexpected in the languages employed in Francisco Ulacia's Cuban novel. The peculiar language used on the island is explained in an introductory note along with a vocabulary of Cuban words. In this short glossary readers from other places can find words they may not have known such as *aura, batey, bohío, ceiba, cuje, fuete, guanábana, guano, guarapo, guataca, majá, maloja, quiquiribú, sinsonte, tonga, yaya,* and *zafra.*

The note warns, "however, in this novel we will not copy the Cubans' peculiar phonetics literally except when locals talk, people who make a most evident use of that special pronunciation and a considerable number of local idioms."[20]

In the text, it is black people who talk in dialect,[21] for instance the fat black women who talk holding onto the railings on the windows of the secondary school:

> Éte sí que é un muchacho como no le hay otro en Cubanacán. Naide mejó que él pa casase con Candita. Disen que se quieren como her-

---

18. Ulacia, *El caudillo*, 236.
19. Ibid.
20. Ibid., 3.
21. With regards to heteroglossia, and the literary creation of dialect models with political intentions, Jon Juaristi's book, *El chimbo expiatorio*, is of interest when looking at Bilbao. With regards to forming Latin American creole language, from a more linguistic point of view, Germán de Granda's work in the twenty-third volume of *Thesaurus*, is a good introduction: "Sobre el estudio de las hablas criollas en el área hispánica," "La tipología criolla de las hablas del área lingüística hispánica," and, above all, "Materiales para el estudio sociohistórico de los elementos lingüísticos afro-americanos en el área hispánica."

mano, pero á mi se me figura que Jaimito la mira con los ojo muy tiernesito. Ademá, cuando Pepe Luí platicó ante con Candita, le ví ponese pálido... Mira, ahora á Chucho bailando con una de la de Mendoza. No he vito muchacha má chispoleta... Ese siempre va á lo más distinguío. Ya se conose que ha sío malojero. Y tiene la cara como un camarón cosío...[22]

[That was a boy, all right, like none other in Cubanacán. None better to marry Candita. They say they love him like a brother, but to me it seems that Jaimito looks at her with pretty sweet eyes. Better yet, when Pepe Luí talked before with Candita, I saw him get pale . . . Look, now Chucho dancing with that one from Mendoza. I've never seen a bigger flirt . . . She's always after the one who is all that. Now you know she sold the *maloja*. And has a face like a boiled shrimp.][23]

Dialect was widely used by European poets and playwrights in the Renaissance and Baroque periods. In Cuba it was employed in writing by popular poets such as Manuel Cabrera Paz, from Artemisa; Bartolomé José Crespo, Gangá, from Ferrol; and throughout Bufo theatre. Esteban Pichardo, in the prologue to the fourth edition of his *Diccionario provincial casi razonado de vozes y frases cubanas* (Provincial dictionary almost reasoned with Cuban words and phrases), published in Havana in 1875, explains graphically that:

> Another relaxed, confused language is heard throughout the island every day, among the BOZALES black people, or those from Africa, as happened with CREOLE French on Santo Domingo: this language is common and identical among black people, from whichever nation they come, and which they conserve for ever, unless they arrived at a very young age: it is disfigured Spanish, clumsily spoken, without harmony, declination, conjugation, the stong R, S and D at the end of words, Ll often being replaced with N, E with I, G with V, etc.; in short, a sub-language which is the more confusing the more recent the immigration; but that any Spaniard can understand except for some words, common to all, which have to be translated.[24]

The Chinese man ill with leprosy in the hospital also speaks in his own, peculiar way: "Yo tá mu malo, Jaimito, mu malo; mañana ñau, ñau..."

Esteban Pichardo writes of the Chinese people's way of speaking Spanish:

> The Chinese or Asians, of whom there are many, mostly in Havana, have not formed their own dialect, nor have people taken more than a few strange words from them, Chao-chao Tabacúa: they pronounce

---

22. Ulacia, *El caudillo*, 107.

23. This translation is provided to so that the non-Spanish reader will have an idea of what is being said. It does not particularly reflect the African Cuban Spanish that is used in the passage.

24. Pichardo, *Diccionario provincial casi razonado de vozes y frases cubanas*, vol. 1, 17.

Spanish words clearly, and learn them quickly, although with a creole accent similar to that of the Yucatecos, replacing rr and sometimes r with d and l, a sound they use too often.[25]

Nowadays Cubans still sustain that the Chinese came up with "aló con flijole" to say "*arroz con frijoles*" (rice with beans).

Cubanacán and Its Characters.

The novel is set in the center of the island, in Las Villas. Cubanacán, in Francisco Ulacia's novel, is the name of an imaginary city which can be identified with Santa Clara, the author's home town.

The name Cubanacán has a native resonance as it is the name that the chroniclers of the conquest and colonization of the island gave to the chieftainship in the center of the island. It also has a patriotic resonance as in the 1820s the secret organization Soles y Rayos de Bolívar conspired to set up the República de Cubanacán on the island. Those first conspirators for the independence of Cuba planned a popular rising for August 17, 1823. It failed because one of the members informed the authorities and the organization was broken up; but separatist ideas began to be developed from then onward.[26]

It is well known that in 1607, with a population of twenty thousand, the island was administered by two governors: the eastern part was directed from Santiago de Cuba and the western part from Havana, with a large area between the two not dependent on either between 1607 and 1721, when Philip III consigned Trinidad, Remedios, and Sancti Spíritus to the Havana captaincy. In the middle of the nineteenth century the territory of six of the thirty-two jurisdictions was called Las Villas: Cienfuegos, Remedios, Sagua la Grande, Sancti Spiritus, Santa Clara, and Trinidad, in alphabetical order. During the Ten Years' War political-administrative areas were adapted depending on military needs and a six-province system was set up, the province of Las Villas or Santa Clara being between those of Matanzas and Puerto Príncipe.

Santa Clara was founded in the seventeenth century, and in the middle of the nineteenth century it was a very important town with a settled population and road links with Cárdenas, Trinidad, and Puerto Príncipe. It is near Cruces, Lajas, Cifuentes, Encrucijada, and Camajuaní, sugarcane producing areas, with a trained labor force, and many ancillary services for the sugar industry. The town of Santa Clara was also the place of residence for many of the landowners in the area.

The landowners and traders in Las Villas did not suffer as much as those in Oriente and Camagüey during the Ten Years' War and tried to

---

25. Ibid., 18.

26. There is a poem by Gabriel Aresti, published in the third number of *Kurpil*, in 1975, that uses the place name: "*Siboneitik Kubanakanera/goajiro honek/egunero janen dut/ nire arroz-aranke pizka.*" (From Siboney to Cubanacán, that Guajiro will eat his rice with herring every day.)

avoid being affected by incendiaries and slave risings. Many of them—above all those who had come from the Peninsula—saw their fortunes increase thanks to the destruction and seizures that took place during the war. The abolition of slavery, later on, led to a process of modernization in the sugar industry with a salaried labor force.

Potrerito, the place where the Aguirres had their estate, is a common place name in Cuba. The slopes of Siguanea could be seen from there with its exuberant vegetation and blue summit. The river was called Arimao. The journey could be replicated. While he made up some of the names of the most important places, the author of *El Caudillo* took the trouble to make very clear where and when things transpired. This is how nineteenth-century novels were set: the idea was to reflect a stable, credible reality, which anybody could experience, trying almost to reflect the commonplace.

In line with this realism, the names of the streets of Cubanacán were connected with independence linked with a patriotic feat: one street is called Calixto García, previously known as Santa Rosa; another is Coliseo, previously known as Buen Viaje; another has been renamed Baire. The central park in Cubanacán takes the name of the novel's main character. Francisco Ulacia simply reflects what happened to streets on the island when the Cubans, after defeating Spain, took charge of the symbols of the territory by renaming them, erasing colonial domination from the collective memory and establishing their own signs of identity. It is what Francisco Calcagno suggested to his neighbors in Güines: "Today we have no need for the names of heroes because today Cuba has its own history and it is our unavoidable duty to honor the memory of those who fell to give us our homeland."[27]

In Cuba street names were not changed by the initiative of the government but due to local, large-scale, simultaneous initiative at the end of 1898 and the beginning of 1899. In Sagua la Grande, for example, Cánovas del Castillo Street became José Martí Street; Tacón Street, Carlos Manuel de Céspedes Street; Cruz Street, Padre Varela Street; and González Osma Park became Parque de la Libertad.

It was not only imaginary place names which had meanings and matched the context in an almost archetypal way. The characters in the novel also tend to represent reality. Plantations as socioeconomic units—the patriarchal economic regime—formed shared ways of life reflecting the people's culture and character. Sugar barons had a highly pragmatic idea of business and life, different from that of livestock and coffee landowners. They were highly dependent on the international market and developed a very cosmopolitan view of the world and its markets. From a very early age they had to follow the price of African slave and Chinese coolies. Later on they had to follow variations in sugar prices and the development of new technology.

---

27. Ulacia, *El caudillo*, 33. Changing street names is one of the "decolonizing" factors examined in Utset, *Las metáforas del cambio en la vida cotidiana*, 153.

Another feature of the Las Villas landowners was their absenteeism. Worries about the abolition of slavery and separatist insurrections led to many investing in other places or, quite simply, the diversification of their business interests meant it was more suitable for them to live in Havana. They left managers and tenants in charge of their properties and lived from a distance on the rent. While the main character in the novel cannot be accused of this, his rival was a negligent absentee landlord. Nor should it be forgotten that, like many of his origin, the author of the novel himself could be classified in this group of cosmopolitan absentee landlords in Tierra Adentro.

The novel's five thousand–strong livestock, with mares bearing two hundred colts a year, are impressive. In any case, Jaime Aguirre, the novel's main character, is an archetypal good landowner, the opposite of an absentee one, a landowner who is very much present and concerned about the prosperity of his holdings.

His surnames also reflect real ones and reinforce the archetype of the hard-working landowner—honest and patriotic. Jaime Aguirre Agramonte's first surname is not unconnected with the many Aguirres who formed part of the army of liberation, nor is Agramonte. José María Aguirre, for instance, a Havanan who took part in the Ten Years' War, was captured in 1877 and imprisoned in Ceuta. He also took part in the Little War and, finally, in the war of '95, leading to a rebel landing on the island on November 9 of that year. He finally dies of pneumonia at Las Escaleras on December 29, 1896. As it happens, the biographies of José María Aguirre mention his participation on March 26, 1875 in the combat at Potrerillo, Las Villas. Other Aguirres who died fighting for Cuban independence: were Daniel Aguirre, Marcos Aguirre, Pedro Aguirre, Carlos Aguirre, Eladio Aguirre, among others.[28]

The novel's main character's second surname was probably in memory of Ignacio Agramonte. In a letter to José Manuel Mestre, this combatant said: "A country's independence would not be so valuable if its conquest did not involve such great difficulties to be overcome: Cuba will be independent whatever it takes."[29]

There was also an Agramonte from Las Villas in the war of 1895, Frank Agramonte, a rebel captain, an expert in Mambisa artillery, who landed on the eastern coast from the ship *Honor* and who was imprisoned in Morro de Santiago castle. The story is told that when the military governor visited

---

28. But there were also Aguirres on the Spanish side, such as General Ernesto Aguirre y Bengoa, the commandant general of Las Villas at the end of the War of Independence in 1898. There were even Aguirres in the US army of occupation: Valentín Aguirre, for instance, had been born in a farmstead on the slopes of Sollube and was a merchant navy sailor employed by Naviera Sota who had fled to New York in 1895 to avoid being called up to the Spanish army and sent to Cuba. Paradoxically, in order to earn the right to live in the United States, he was obliged to join the crew of one of the US battleships that, in 1898, destroyed the Spanish fleet at Santiago de Cuba.

29. Pastrana, *Ignacio Agramonte, su pensamiento político y social*, 62.

the prison, he was the only prisoner in the yard who did not take off his hat, which infuriated the Spanish soldier. "Take your hat off!" the governor ordered him. "Take yours off first!" answered Agramonte. "Bufoon!" the Spaniard shouted "You're more of a buffon!" answered Agramonte. The military governor ordered him to be shot. As he had been educated in the United States and had US citizenship, the US consul saved his life.

Although there are revolutions and events, the novel takes place in a settled, stable world. Society is based on transmission and the continuity of customs. Very settled in ethnically, each person sees his/her roots in terms of their ancestors and in an extremely hierarchical way.

Later we will deal with other characters: we will now consider Jaime, the son of Ramón Aguirre, a rich landowner from Las Villas. Jaime was the grandson of a Basque who had come to Cuba from a small village at the foot of the Aralar mountains. Because of his mother's illness, Jaime had spent six years of his childhood in the village in Gipuzkoa from which his ancestors had come. It was a quite peaceful place whose inhabitants were hard-working, honest farm workers and their herds. It is where Jaimito—dressed in a blue sailor's suit and cap—played with other children—wearing their berets—surrounded by green fields, while his mother keeps alive his homesickness for the island.

> During the sad, rainy days of November memories of his homeland filled his spirit with melancholy. He missed the blue, golden sky and the warm touch of the beloved sun of the tropics. And, with Jaimito sitting on her lap, his mother's dreamy eyes staring at the village's grey horizon she would tell her son, as she held him tightly to her heart, the thousand stories and legends of her beloved homeland. She recounted the feats of Güije, a mysterious being—half-man, half-bird—who walked along the slopes of Singuanea every night and, when he heard a child crying, went up to the shack and, stretching out his long neck, sunk his beak into the child's belly.[30]

She also told the boy the more real stories about Mamita Lola, even the most unhappy stories full of her homesickness:

> Other times she told him about the runaway slave whose father, to keep him on the estate, had often had to chase him with man-hunting dogs and catch him with a lasso.[31]

He used to spend the summer in the village in Aralar and the winters in Donostia-San Sebastián and Baiona, where he went to school. One of Jaimito's happiest times was when his father arrived in summer and brought with him a large box full of sweets and fruit from the island of Cuba and so he could give his friends—secretly—guayabas and zapotes:

> He would go with them to stand under some oak trees and give them sweets there. How all the children licked their lips! How good it tast-

---

30. Ulacia, *El caudillo*, 33.
31. Ibid.

ed, how sweet it was! They used to eat a lot! They spoke in Basque. Jaimito understood them and also spoke a little in the sweet local language.[32]

The Siboney Myth

When Francisco Ulacia created the main characters, Jaime and Candita, he made them descendants from the Siboney Indians on their mothers' side. At the start of the novel about Candita's mother:

> That noblewoman was descended, on her mother's side, from one of the last Siboney families, Cuban indigenous people, who had lived in isolation and as nomads for many years on the slopes of Sigua-nea. Her grandmother, who had belonged to those tribes, had been kidnapped at the age of fifteen by a colonist from Las Villas who fell madly in love with her and later made her his wife. And Mummy Juana remembered the story of the Siboneys which her mother had told her. The chief was the source of authority in the tribe—good, brave Cumanayagua—and he always kept its independent spirit in-tact by remaining nomadic. They were peaceful, good people who tilled the land, fished and kept livestock, retaining their own religion and customs. They still remembered Hatuey, the leader of the Sibo-neys on the island, as a venerated idol. But these tribes no longer existed in the mountains and all that remained were some mixed families such as Juana's.[33]

Jaime Aguirre was the grandson of a Basque but was also an Indian on his mother's side. Here is a description of what he looked like: "The young man's face was strange and attractive, he looked like his grand-mother Juana and her family, but even more like his Siboney ancestors."[34]

His ill mother secretly worshipped a wooden idol in a darkened room. "It was a strange figure, roughly carved from a piece of wood. It was like a monstrous animal, deformed, a type of Shuar pig, sitting on its hind legs, its snout squashed, large fangs and an enormous belly."[35]

And she offered the idol sweets and fruit, a glass of milk and a cup of coffee. It was the great Semí, the protecting god of her ancestors. His mother told Jaimito about the twin meaning of her veneration:

> They were descended from the Bohitos, great chieftains of the Sibo-neys, possessors of the secrets and who spoke with the Semís for them to cure illnesses, bring rain or wind. And that Semí, that protecting god in the small darkened room, was her ancestors' main idol. They had to respect him, so he didn't get upset, he didn't get furious. That was why she took him sweets and fruit. Ah! Many of her problems,

---

32. Ibid., 35.
33. Ibid., 6.
34. Ibid., 20.
35. Ibid., 37.

above all the illness which was eating away at her, might come down to having abandoned good Semí for many years. But she wasn't going to forget him any longer and Jaimito had to respect him in order to avoid many calamities.[36]

With regards to the Semí,[37] current Cubans live with Elegguás, fetishes that are supposed to have been brought from the west coast of Africa by the slaves, and they understand Lola's relationship with the Semí: "The Christian education she had been given and the Catholicism she had practiced all her life were not strong enough to expunge the weight of this formidable tradition and the influence of atavistic laws from this good lady's soul: they were invincible even in the heart of modern civilization."[38]

Jaime, too, goes into the darkened room with a bag full of sweets for the Semí, lights a candle before it and begs it to cure his mother. When she dies, he avenges her by hitting the fetish with a lit candle, and then throws it into the dining room fire and watches it burn.

With regards to the Siboney genealogies in the novel, they are a nineteenth-century Cuban myth. The real natives disappeared in the sixteenth century, as José Juan Arrom explains:

> Few people have met such a cruel destiny as the smiling Tainos who received Columbus and his followers on the welcoming Antillean beaches in 1492. The people who had arrived in peace soon waged an unjust war against them. In a few years, overwhelmed by the inequality of arms, decimated by forced labor, hunger and illnesses, stunned by their loss of identity as a people, the few survivors were quickly assimilated by the victors. Little survived that tragic collapse: the growing and making use of certain plants, the way of building rural housing, some domestic tools, words for land, flora and fauna, the vague memory of their songs and some distant information about the gods they believed in and trusted.[39]

Siboneyism was part of the Indianist tendency which arose in the nineteenth century in the Americas, probably influenced by Romanticism's exaltation of natural, savage man, and also connected with nationalist politics. José Fornaris, from Bayamo, was the main figure of Siboneyism with his *Cantos del Siboney* (Siboney Songs, 1855). José Fornaris and Joaquín Lorenzo Luaces founded the weekly publication *La Piragua* in 1856, which gave birth to a whole movement dedicated to praising the life of the original, if no longer present, inhabitants of the island. Another notable poet in this school was Juan Cristóbal Nápoles Fajardo, known as El Cuculambé, above all renowned for his book *Rumores del Hórmigo* (Rumors

---

36. Ulacia, *El caudillo*, 38.
37. Semí, a supernatural being and idol of the indigenous people of the Antilles, also written *Cemí* and *Zemí*. It is a word recorded by all the first historians of Cuba.
38. Ulacia, *El caudillo*, 39.
39. Arrom, *Mitología y artes prehispánicas de las Antillas*, 11.

from El Hórmigo). Siboneyism was a literary movement in the second half of the nineteenth century in Cuba that became very popular thanks to Cuban anti-Spanish sentiment.

Siboneyism has later been questioned. Marcelino Menéndez Pelayo, writing from a Spanish point of view, despised it. But the fallacy of its supposedly nationalist intentions has also been brought to light by modern historians such as Manuel Moreno Fraginals: "There can be no indigenism without black people. Our landowners were Siboneyists because there were no Siboneys. If there had been, rather that writing poems to them and making them into heroes they would have discriminated against them and exploited them as they did black people."[40]

We will talk about blacks later on. It is enough to say, for the moment, that Siboney symbolism colors the main characters' daily life in the novel.

The Fight for Cuban Independence

Francisco Ulacia is interested, above all, in politics and love. On the one hand, he seeks national identity and prosperity, on the other, an amorous relationship. These two threads meet in *El Caudillo*, a political story that dignified a people through proindependence revolution and hard work, and a love story between the hero and a girl, "his first and last love, which absorbed his senses and intoxicated his soul."

Politics is very important in the novel. What Francisco Ulacia wrote about his first novels in the prologue to his *Nere biotza!* can also be applied to *El Caudillo:*

> Any novel which takes place in Bizkaya must, if it is to give an idea of current events, involve politics to a greater or lesser extent. Today, in our country, politics occupies everything: it is the motive for and incentive behind all great thoughts and great actions.[41]

The same is true of his Cuban novel. However, it is of interest to examine the political ideas reflected in it, and one of the main ones, of course, is independence. Jaime's take on the '95 insurrection is frankly separatist:

> Jaime, upright and austere, worshipped that land that, with a little effort from its children, helped by honest public administration, could become the richest country in the world; he had passionate feelings about the revolutionary movements which were awakening in the country.[42]

However, he didn't dare go into the jungle (as a rebel) because he did not want to hurt his father. Generally, people born in the peninsula were

---

40. Moreno Fraginals, *José Antonio Saco*, 9. Regarding this subject Le Riverend's article is interesting, "El indigenismo en la historia de las ideas."
41. In his letter-prologue to *Don Fausto*, Arturo Campión says, in his sole criticism of the book, that the novel's weak points are due to "the explanation of political ideas—the queens and ladies of this novel—that are not always connected with the events."
42. Ulacia, *El caudillo*, 58.

not in favor of independence, but those born on the island were. Of his
father:

> He was a peaceful person who was only concerned with the conser-
> vation and prosperity of his estates, looking upon anything which
> might disturb public order and so harm his interests with horror; he
> opposed the revolution, not because he was unsympathetic toward
> it but because of the harm and horror of a war with no foreseeable
> end.[43]

Then the dominant Spanish authorities' repression changed things:

> One morning troops commanded by a Civil Guard captain, Ramón
> Aguirre, appeared at Santa Dolores sugar estate. It had been report-
> ed and they had an order to search it. They examined his office and
> found various compromising documents. There were receipts signed
> by the local revolutionary leader and certifying that the owner of
> Santa Dolores sugar estate had paid taxes to the provisional revolu-
> tionary government in order to pay for war expenses.[44]

The summary court was immediate and the death sentence passed
was carried out in a barracks' yard twenty-four hours later by an infantry
firing squad, his son's desperate attempts coming to nothing. Jaime recovered his father's body and buried it at Cubanacán next to his mother.

The following day, Jaime, riding a magnificent Arabian horse, a machete on his belt and a rifle on his back, gathered the workers at the sugar mill and proclaimed a rising. With their enthusiastic support, the first
thing the band did was to burn down the outbuildings, the sugarcane, and
then go into the jungle as an army of liberation: "That improvised squadron of revolutionaries of all colors and castes, including some people from
the Peninsula and from Gran Canaria, went through the thick smoke of
the incendiary for the jungle, heading for the north coast. As they went
through the fields, many peasants joined them."[45]

Jaime is forced into the swamps by his visceral resentment of the people who had executed his father and also in the hope of a beautiful Cuba
thanks to its children's patriotism. A Cuba without black vomit and with
rationally organized agriculture, with land on which everybody could
be smallholders, without any domination from the metropolitan power:
"They could not go on under the current domination. At first, he had been

---

43. Ibid., 54.

44. Ibid., 55. During the Ten Years' War it became general Spanish practice to require landowners to contribute money or men to the war effort. Property owners were forced to collaborate, whether they were separatists, Spanish loyalists, or neutral. The insurrectionists, for
their part, also made general demands for contribution, usually economic. In the '95 War
this remained a common practice. For example, when in October 1895 the insurrectionists
nearly defeated Spain through the destruction of the export economy and prohibited that
sugar mills process sugar, Néstor Aranguren's men killed the landowner Sebastián Ulacia for
not obeying the Mambí orders.

45. Ibid., 36.

in favor of autonomy, but then he changed his mind. Why depend on anybody? Weren't they an intelligent race?"[46]

Jaime walked in front of his troops with the incalculable legitimacy of his Siboney ancestry: "Was he not one of the most legitimate representatives of the true owners of that land, of the indigenous Siboneys? And in the streams, in the blue pools in the swamps, in the green waters of the Caribbean, he looked at his Indian effigy with pride."[47]

And he remembered Hatuey, the Indian chieftain who had fought against the conquistadors: "Poor natives, persecuted and hounded like rabid animals! They had been overcome by the barbarian invaders' tyranny, which was much more barbaric than they were themselves, unlucky children of the virgin forest, whose ancestral peace and happiness had been disturbed by unworthy adventurers' brutal advances."[48]

Almost all of Jaime Aguirre's rebel troops were colored, most of them black: "It was because of how much those descendants of African slaves— the most powerful tool for exploiting Cuban soil—liked him."

But they were motivated by the kindness with which their leader had always treated them. They were the working basis for the country's prosperity, but they were fighting because of their loyalty to their good landowner:

> They had made Jaime their idol, a type of god-protector for the warriors who would lead them to conquest and glory.
>
> All of them offered him their services; their greatest pride would have been to sacrifice their lives for that of the young patriot.
>
> They were happy as they swung their machetes, chopping into the reeds closing the way to them in the swamps. They laughed at anything, showing their snow-white teeth and rolling their great, dark, African eyes. Some of them, descendants of fierce tribes from central Africa, had faces like tigers on the watch for prey, ready to pounce and devour.[49]

So it was the sons of the earth who took part in the fight. But there were also sons of the Peninsula who loved justice, above all men from the Canary Islands. There is also a Basque called Josechu, who takes part in the insurrection because of his friendship with Jaime and also because of his ideals for the freedom of his own country:

> There was honorable Josechu, a young man from the small village in Aralar, a childhood friend, who did not want to abandon him during the campaign. He often called for him and they went for long walks in the leafy tamarind wood. It was a vivid pleasure to talk with a man who reminded him of his happy childhood years. He liked hearing him speak in Basque, the sweet language of the Basque mountains,

---

46. Ibid., 27.
47. Ibid., 37.
48. Ibid., 38.
49. Ulacia, *El caudillo*, 65.

from those green, peaceful mountains where his grandparents' generations had been born.

He remembered many Basque words and he was profoundly moved when Josechu, with his fine baritone voice, tore the air with his country's sweet songs. Ah! In the Basque lands, too, there were ideals for freedom, and Josechu's soul was moved as he gave voice to expressions which were as painful as they were enthusiastic.[50]

The war was long and cruel.

And he went on with that tenacious, unending struggle until the campaign finished, always on the move, doing unexpected things; sometimes with few resources, starving, eating bits of hutia or sugarcane; other times with ample provisions from expeditions to the north. But they were always enthusiastic, full of energy, in the grip of patriotic fever, the indescribable desire for freedom, for their country's honor. And when the Cuban and American flags were flying at Morro Castle, Jaime, at the head of his troops, reached Cubanacán.[51]

The Love Triangle

In the same way that the scene is chosen—a specific place and time, a stable reality—the characters are selected as well. Most of them are upper class. This was an unwritten law, perhaps connected with the readers' psychology that the main roles in novels should be played by characters with a certain social position. The landowners' three sons make up a love triangle: Candita, Jaime, and Pepe Luís. Being poor was either banal or picturesque and left for secondary characters.

Love is an essential part of the plot in almost all of Francisco Ulacia's novels. In *Nere biotza!* Juanito Madariaga reflected on the wonder, ingratitude, and injustice of love:

Which strange psychological laws regulate and control the wretched human spirit? –Juanito Madariaga thought after Teresa's death.

How unfair love is! It pierces hearts like a fiery sword, blinds our minds, enthuses and abuses our souls and destroys the most sublime affection, the most delicate feelings, the headiest tenderness from our consciousness.[52]

In his prologue to that novel, Francisco Ulacia even gave his theories about why love was such a lasting theme in literary works:

No acts of passion have been dealt with as much by novelists as that extraordinary feeling of love; however, it is something so all-encompassing in individual and collective life that it always pro-

---

50. Ibid., 65.
51. Ibid., 82.
52. Ulacia, *Nere biotza!*, 7.

vides authors' imagination with plentiful, powerful factors to use in the development of their work.[53]

In a question that he responded to for *Nuestro Tiempo* magazine, Francisco Ulacia replied: "Love is, unquestionably, the poetry of life; it has always been the soul of narrative in novels and eroticism, which is love's passion, and is, to a large extent, what makes reading novels a pleasure."[54]

Candita is the love object of both men. A descendent of the extinct Siboneys on her mother's side and daughter of a landowner, which gives her double legitimacy in the novel:

> Candita, a sixteen-year old girl, with a pretty face and a slim figure, one of those strange beauties who attract and recall things. Her dark eyes, innocent and with candid gazes, were also slightly slanted. Her straight nose, like that of a Greek Venus, her slightly thick lips like rubies, contrasted with the pale color of her oval-shaped face. Her shiny, jet-black hair was brushed to either side in two great waves which went over her forehead, held at the back by a blue silk ribbon.[55]

Francisco Ulacia's novel is a living witness to the period, a demonstration of the role that society gave women, and how courting and marriage were seen in that society. Women's roles were, above all, biological reproduction and passing on sentimentality. The main character, who we already know, is Jaime Aguirre, the heroic revolutionary soldier, savior of Candita and her mother, with a square in the center of Cubanacán named after him. He, too, has Siboney ancestors on his mother's side and is not only the son of a landowner but also in charge of the property himself:

> His healthy color, browned by the sun. As he passed his hand over his forehead, brushing his thick hair back, the long, deep scar he had there was visible. He didn't have a little finger or a ring finger on his left hand and also had a slight scar on his right cheek.[56]

The novel's antagonist is Pepe Luís Heredia, a Creole, "a young waster, who had thrown away his parents' wealth, didn't care for work and was degraded by all sorts of vices," particularly chasing women and was the seducer of a young girl, in fact, of the "apple of the eye" of the main character. Pepe Luís is an incorrigible idiot, like his brothers and sisters, who order suits from Paris and underclothes from New York, often goes

---

53. Ibid., 8.
54. To the question of what should be the moral imperative of the novelist, he responded: "If speaking of traditional morals, this imperative consists in respecting the state of consciousness of the community for whom the writing is done; if speaking of absolute morals, they cannot mark limits and the writer must work to fix the ideas that the writer's culture administers, that is, to help its truth." And he added, "Morality! How can it be? We do not know it, because we do not know we will never know the absolute truth, and not knowing that we can neither know where they are and how how abstract morality and justice should be."
55. Ulacia, *El caudillo*, 6.
56. Ibid., 29.

to Havana and to Acera del Louvre.[57] While his estate was only producing eighty thousand sugar sacks, Pepe Luís used to spend more than ten thousand centenes on chasing girls, contributing to the family's ruin.

All three are sons of landowners, but only Jaime, as well as being a revolutionary hero, is a real landowner. Pepe Luís is squandering his father's fortune, a perfect antihero.

Francisco Ulacia develops consistent characters with basic, predictable psychological mechanisms. The would be suitors clash violently. It is possible to imagine the tragedy which a rejected lover can cause, above all if he has additional justifications and reasons:

If the enormous misfortunes weighing on Jaime's heart had not taught him to suffer, perhaps the pain he felt on seeing his whole search for love thwarted would have driven him to extremes.

> But, beaten by suffering, he became serene and self-sacrificing, like all beings who have come to know and control themselves by the use of willpower. Examining himself, being aware of all his passions, and, so, being able to master them.
>
> Even so, there were moments in which, in an atavistic way, irresistible impulses of hate and vengeance broke out in his heart. The drops of Indian blood in his veins burned his brain in waves of fire. He was a complex character with features from a primitive people combining with traditional and progressive things from other, old European roots.
>
> In any case, his tropical temperament, passionate and fiery, with the aggression of daring hearts, placing him in circumstances difficult to resolve in which there is not enough time to use the inhibiting force of reason, could make him fall into terrible, passionate convulsions.[58]

Love of the Land and Agricultural Modernization

Jaime Aguirre loves the land deeply, but his feelings are connected with a rational project of national industrialization and modernization:

> He loved that land with the intense feeling of a grateful son. But he didn't love it for selfish reasons, as a farm-worker does, anxiously waiting for its produce. What Jaime loved was that exceptionally fertile nature, which was on a higher level, an intellectual love, a deep

---

57. Acera del Paseo del Prado between San Miguel and San Rafael, opposite El Louvre café, was the meeting place for bohemians in Havana. In 1925 Gustavo Robreño published a very interesting novel titled *La Acera del Louvre* about those friendly, bohemian and sometimes rebellious young people who, from 1862 onward, used to go there: a noisy group of gentlemen. Womanizers and quarrelsome, a old song called "El Taco" seems to be about them: "*Soy el rey de los placeres/¿Quien puede toserme a mí?/Las más preciosas mujeres/me adoran con frenesí.*" (I'm the king of pleasures/Who can tell me anything?/The most beautiful women/Love me madly.)

58. Ulacia, *El caudillo*, 191.

feeling. In his chest he could feel generations of his ancestors, all of them peasants, who had worked to fertilize the land with the sweat from their honorable brows. He, too, would rest with them, in the heart of their beloved land. It was his mother, and the mother of grandmother Lola and grandfather Ramón, and the mother of all the people of the island, to whom it had given its rich substance and fertile flow. And he had loved it since adolescence, brought up on the land he rode over hungry for freedom. And when blood had to be spilled for it, he shed it with pride, like a person who wants to express his gratitude with eloquence. And now, more than ever, he turned his eyes to the fertile land.[59]

His relationship with the land was not just intellectual and sentimental. If agrarian romanticism exists, it is enlightened and very open to technical innovations, modernization, and progress: "All the innovations which might help his lands, Jaime wanted to bring them without delay. He was more and more pleased about his father's decision to send him to Philadelphia Agriculture School."[60]

The plantations in Las Villas were rural and agro-industrial estates that were also socioeconomic units. *El Potrerito* was a large estate of more than thirteen hectares, almost all of which could be farmed, and Jaime rented them out to several colonists, except for a piece of hilly land which was kept for cattle and mares.

The housing and other buildings on the estate were mostly around the mill. As sugar agriculture and industry called for a lot of workers, there was a village in which most people were slaves. Next to the slaves' barracks there were luxurious homes for the owners.[61] The owner of the plantation lived there permanently, as did Jaime Aguirre, or just occasionally, or almost never.

In any case, an administrator was needed, as was a group of foremen and technicians. Josechu was the general estate manager with power to rent land out, sub-let or fire colonists.[62] Soon Josechu, too—the noble, hard-working son of a village in Aralar—would become a rich landowner thanks to the island's incredible fertility. In contrast to the Basque Country—always cultivated with difficulty and self-sacrifice—land in Cuba could produce up to three harvests of maize and a well-worked tobacco plantation could produce up to a thousand pesos each year.

---

59. Ibid., 195.

60. Ibid., 89.

61. An excellent book about Brazilian society hints at the proximity and antithesis of the two types of buildings: *Casa-grande* and *senzala* (Big house and slave house) by Gilberto Freyre, published in Spanish in Buenos Aires in 1943 by Emecé. The book's subtitle defines the economic regime well: Forming Brazilian families in the patriarchal economy.

62. The word *colono* (colonist) started to be used in this sense around 1880. In Cuba, sugar-cane agriculture and the sugar industry were generally in the hands of the same landowners. But with the abolition of slavery, and a scarcity of workers, in Las Villas and other parts of the island part of the sugar production was handed over to *colonists* or small-scale renters or owners of land.

One thing which differentiates Jaime and Josechu from some of the colonists is how little some of the latter work:

> The hero of Cubanacán went from cabin to cabin greeting his colonists. Sometimes, seeing them sitting at the door of their horse-soiled huts, he would shout at them from afar, reproaching them for their idleness: "Wake up, you idle man! Don't come to me crying about your bad luck because you've lost the harvest. If instead of sitting there like a boa constrictor after a meal you got down to taking the leaves off the tobacco, your land wouldn't go to waste. The land can't do everything, you have to put your back into it too."[63]

And if any of the colonists, with respect for his military discipline, invited him to a coffee and called him "general," Jaime was upset:

> He didn't want them to call him that. There weren't any more generals now that the island was independent. The young republic, having thrown off the yoke of the monarchy which had enslaved it, needed peasants to tend its lands, where an extraordinary treasure lay waiting. So now the Cubans shouldn't take their pride in pompous titles which, although the republic had the good taste to grant as honors, would always bring memories which had nothing to do with the desire for permanent peace, which was so much needed for the country's prosperity and glory.
>
> He liked to see the generals with hoes in their hands, feeling honored to earn their living through their effort just as before they had been proud to spill their blood for that beloved land, to achieve their independence.
>
> It caused him great pain to see some small and large landowners and many colonists giving up their estates to go into politics and pursue their destinies in public office. The Spaniards' addiction to holding positions had taken root in the Cubans' hearts. Living off public money, driving along the Prado in Havana, going to the Casino, gambling their monthly salary on a single card and then taking advantage of a friend's generosity to get out of a scrape . . . that was what many of the country's sons aspired to, thinking themselves more dignified and noble living like bohemians, corrupted by the city's vices.[64]

As Cuba was an agricultural country, Jaime Aguirre did not approve of landowners sending their sons to the city to get professional qualifications they could boast about, which desolated the countryside:

> They had to realize that the republic would become great if they developed agriculture. In Cuba, being a peasant should be taken as the greatest of honors, they were the ones who generated the country's wealth, and much more now that the governments took care to train people in the country and give them modern culture.
>
> Nowadays a country person could become educated without leaving his estate. Wherever there were four shacks together, a school

---

63. Ulacia, *El caudillo*, 197.
64. Ibid.

was set up with well-paid teachers whose teaching skills had been properly tested.

There was a growing number of farms and, on them, the sons of the country found ways to improve their knowledge of agricultural work. True patriotism meant giving up all the honors won during the revolution and getting down to work. Having fought for independence with the premeditated idea of living from positions and politics did little to honor the liberators' patriotism.[65]

Dignifying rural areas and developing agriculture is suggested, but Jaime Aguirre—and, through him, Francisco Ulacia—was not opposed to the city and industrialization, quite the opposite:

He had fabulous dreams for his country. When he gazed over an infertile plain, he imagined it becoming a highly-populated city, with all the comfort and beauty of the main European cities, surrounded by wide gardens and leafy wooded areas. He also imagined projects for numerous irrigation canals into the center of the island. With just a little work, it would be possible to open irrigation canals from Arroyo Grande to fertilize the nearby plains and guarantee harvests on good agricultural land.

The network of roads and railways was spreading in every direction and, in just a few years, communication between even the most distant shacks would be easy and fast. But people were needed and they had to pass an immigration law to make it easy for workers to come into the country. And then tobacco and sugar would not be the island's only sources of wealth, there would also be large-scale production of other goods of indisputable importance. You could already see large woods of orange trees and henequen plantations; coffee, cocoa, and other food products would follow and, as a consequence of this great agricultural development, industry would grow considerably.[66]

Francisco Ulacia gives a moving description of Santa Dolores sugar plantation, founded by Ramón Aguirre and run by Jaime Aguirre now, in the fifth year of peace, and the second year of milling using all the mechanical and chemical advances. Agriculture was the basis for the country's development, and it was from those plantations which converted sugarcane into gold that the large, comfortable cities would come, with their manufacturing industries and the fine arts.

The Villa Clara sugar harvest in 1901 was enormous, 41 percent of the whole Cuban sugar harvest of 655,000 tons. In 1903 the sugar harvest, which reached a million tons, Villa Clara's contribution was 39 percent. And in the 1904 sugar harvest, which was also more than a million tons, Villa Clara contributed 37 percent.

---

65. Ibid., 199.
66. Ibid., 201.

The Myth of the Republic of Racial Harmony

With regards to the Cuban sugar industry, it should be remembered that these plantations and mills were worked with slave labor until 1886 and, after that, with a salaried workforce. According to the 1861–1862 census—and we go back a few decades because these figures are significant if we are to understand the structure of society at the start of the twentieth century—Cienfuegos, Remedios, Sagua la Grande, and Santa Clara had a total population of 200,409: 123,444 were white and 76,965 colored, of whom 50,238 were slaves. In other words, a quarter of the population were still slaves.

Nor should it be forgotten that abolition did not mean liberation for that social sector. The patriarchal relationship between the inhabitants of the barracks and their owners was still there. In the worst cases, for many slaves, the abolition of slavery and their freedom led to being unprotected rather than being free. Of course the slaves became salaried workers, agricultural workers, railway workers, unskilled crafts workers, or day laborers. But many slaves preferred to keep up their patriarchal relationship with the landowner because, when it came down to it, the working conditions were still appalling.

The first Free Cuba Constitution, in 1869, had specified that all the inhabitants of the planned republic would be free and equal. In his speech for the foundation of the nation, José Martí even said that there were no races, speaking of races was "a sin against humanity." Having taken part in the war of liberation enabled many black people to take on positions of leadership, reinforcing the idea that independent Cuba would be more inclusive and egalitarian. However, after the revolution society was still hierarchical, stable, and discriminatory. Skin color and hair type still marked people's identity. There was little progress in comparison with the roles for black people before the revolution, not even compared with before abolition.

So the racial democracy project became a myth to the extent to which the ways to achieve it were blocked and such ideas were not reflected in reality. Many black people, uncomfortable about their true situation, thought that the republic of racial harmony which José Martí had planned had not been achieved yet, so they asked for real equality and participation on equal terms. But Marti's antiracist discourse could be manipulated and, in fact, it was radically distorted. Afro-Cubans' attempts to demand "racial" equality were described as being racist and antinational with regards to republican society: wasn't talking about race a sin against humanity?

In Francisco Ulacia's novels, black people still serve their masters, now motivated by innate loyalty, and still call their sons "my master." Black people talk in their own way, not pronouncing "s" before stop consonants. The blacks' primitive innocence is always underlined: "In general they were big children who were still as primitive as their whole race."

Generally. However, the black's fate was the darkest in the new society, the worst. There is a significant episode in the novel in which Pedrín, the

little mulatto, disappears, being kidnapped by a black witch doctor called
José María Batita:

> It was he who had kidnapped him. Having used all his resources to
> cure his neighbor from Cubanacán, and afraid of losing his prestige
> as a curer, he made use of the wise precepts of Carabeli witchcraft
> as a last resort. He consulted with another old witchdoctor called
> Mónico, who was venerated by those who believed in witchcraft, and
> recommended that, to save his patient, the only remedy was the ten-
> der heart of a young mulatto crushed with a pestle and mortar, with
> snakeskin powder and guinea-fowl eggs.[67]

The episode in which the child is kidnapped and the gruesome ritual
ceremonies—until the black witchdoctors are finally detained by the rural
police—has a comic side to it too. It is a simple reflection of the clichés
about black people who ritually sacrificed kidnapped children, a sinister
nightmare for some people, a picturesque anecdote for others, which was
still used dishonestly at particularly decisive moments, such as when the
massacre of the Independientes de Color was manipulatively provoked
in 1912.

In fact, it would be unfair to say that Francisco Ulacia is hostile to
black people in his novel. To the contrary, he shows affection toward that
social sector, praises them, although in their position of subjugation.
There is no racist rejection in the novel, quite the opposite: paternalistic
comprehension of black people and Chinese. But, at the time the novel was written, blacks were still strongly discriminated against in Cuba.
Reality was considerably crueler to black people than in Francisco Ulacia's book. It should be remembered that the "fear of blacks" that existed
in nineteenth-century Cuba—that deep social fear, after the abolition of
slavery—carried on and led to the merciless repression of the Independientes de Color,[68] from which some events should be remembered. On
August 7, 1908, in Havana, the Agrupación Independiente de Color was
founded, an organization that aimed to claim rights for the black population, which was still secondary in economic, social, and political terms in
the new society and politics between the Partido Liberal and the Partido
Conservador. Its program included reforms that would benefit not only
blacks and half-castes, but also all marginalized people, such as an eight-
hour working day, the sharing out of state-owned land and free, compul-
sory education. They were opposed to selective immigration, which aimed
to "whiten" the country, and the death penalty, to which black people were
much more often condemned than whites. Aware of government corruption and continual discrimination against black people, the Independien-

---

67. Ulacia, *El caudillo*, 230.
68. For information about Cuba and Independientes de Color, the following books are highly recommended: Ortiz, *El engaño de las razas*; Portuondo Linares, *Los Independientes de
Color*; Fernández Robaina, *El negro en Cuba 1902–1958*; and Castro Fernández, *La masacre
de los Independientes de Color*.

tes de Color thought that they would be better able to defend their interests with an independent party than through the Partido Liberal or the Partido Conservador. General Enrique Fournier wrote from Santiago de Cuba in the *Previsión* newspaper on October 15, 1908, that the race was still being mistreated, and that not even the black leaders from the Army of Liberation were properly treated by the new society, not even being accepted as municipal employees:

> They do not love us, that is how we are rewarded for our sacrifice in freeing so many ungrateful people. It is my belief that the only recourse available to us now is to unite under a single flag which represents all our aspirations and defends—with new, vigorous energy—all the rights which we were able to conquer with arms and for which we shed a lot of blood.

The reaction was quick, especially from the Partido Liberal. *Triunfo* newspaper, which represented the liberal coalition, sounded the alarm on October 23, 1908, over attempts to found a black party: "Black people are a danger to the survival of the Cuban nation." The Independientes de Color was savagely attacked by *Diario de la Marina*, *El Mundo*, *El Comercio*, *Unión Española*, and provincial and local newspapers in a ferocious press campaign peppered with worrying pieces of news about the kidnappings of white children and the rape of white women by black men who were not illiterate but who wanted to live in idleness while endangering civilization. The Independientes de Color tried to explain in vain that they were not racists, nor did they want black supremacy over whites: quite simply, they did not accept white supremacy over blacks.

In February 1910, Martín Morúa Delgado, a black congressman for the Liberal Party, presented an amendment to the election law which, under the pretext of avoiding racial conflict in Cuba, prevented the Independiente de Color party from taking part in elections. Martín Morúa argued that the constitution recognized the equality of races, ignoring the abyss between the legal statement and reality, saying that racial, class and regional parties should be avoided at any cost. Martín Morúa, who was black, and a firm supporter of egalitarianism, paradoxically became the intellectual author of a terrifying massacre.[69] The Independientes de Color's armed protest began in May 1912, while the authorities of the Republic were carrying out an unprecedented repression, inflamed by an atavistic "fear of blacks" and backed up by huge collective hysteria. For around fifty days there was a cruel hunt for blacks that, according to the lowest calculations, led to more than five thousand deaths, mostly in the eastern provinces of Guantánamo and

---

69. It was practically the last thing that Martín Morúa—the mulatto son of a baker from Bizkaia and a black slave—did, and he did not even see the horrific consequences of what he had done, passing away on April 28, 1910, at Santiago de las Vegas, putting a final bitter touch to his biography, whose main purpose had been to work for the emancipation of the black population and working people in general.

Santiago de Cuba. The massacre—which the leaders of the Liberal and Conservative parties and their press celebrated with champagne—cast the black population, including those who had not taken part in the the rising, into a deep terror of claiming their rights and created a long-lasting abstention from politics.

The New Nation and Autocratic Government

From the May 20, 1903, Cuba was officially represented by its flag, coat of arms, and national anthem, which had all been consecrated during the war for independence; but the constitution had an appendix known as the Platt Amendment that, essentially, put limits upon the country's independence. In fact, the Cuban rebels had not taken part in the discussions and decisions in the Treaty of Paris between the United States and Spain, so the republic was founded with the defects of continued dependence and a semi-colonial status. The United States dominated the island's politics and economy, but allowed the Cubans to have their representatives and administer their affairs. These representatives included heroic, decent people who kept up the fiction that the new republic favored its citizens' well-being. However, unscrupulous politicians soon took over the most important posts, people who had earned prestige in the army of liberation and then won power by taking bribes and adapting to the numerous possibilities for corruption which administering power afforded them.

José Miro Argenter—a Catalan by birth and Antonio Maceo's chief of staff during the war of independence—wrote an extraordinary book titled *Crónicas de la Guerra* (War Chronicles), published for the first time in 1909, and a novel called *Salvador Roca,* published in 1910. The young republic's problems are reflected in this novel—which takes place in Havana when José Miguel Gómez was president. In agreement with the thoughts of Jaime Aguirre—he was hurt that landowners and colonists should leave their estates to go into dirty politics and live off public money in the capital—José Miró's character, Salvador Roca, explains:

> I'm not frightened by the explosion of dynamite bombs; the more powerful they are, the better, and the more massacre of tax-payers there are, the finer the dance will be. What I would be ashamed of is—after having called myself a rebel and shot at our adversaries, blown up trains using dynamite and loving dynamite in the countryside, won victory for the revolution-and then having returned to the city, re-creating the disputes which took place under the old regime, imitating its procedures and codes.[70]

After the end of Spanish domination in 1898, military and civil figures from the revolution organized themselves under the US intervention government's administration and, while they built gigantic sugar plantations, the figure of the caudillo arose nationally and at the provincial level. The

70. Miró Argenter, *Salvador Roca,* 73.

first part of the history of the republic of Cuba is characterized by both phenomena: dependence on the US and the political monopoly of caudillismo. We would like to discuss this, not just because of being called caudillo himself, but rather because the character in Francisco Ulacia's novel reflects some of such figures' characteristics, and perhaps not in a critical manner.

The word *caudillo* is connected with military leadership, to protecting troops, leading them during times of war and also peace. One of them was José Miguel Gómez, born at Sancti Spíritus in 1858 and who died in New York in 1921, fought in the Ten Years' War, reaching the rank of Major General in the war that lasted from '95 to '98, and who then led the liberals. Making use of his time in government, he accumulated considerable properties and a fortune. When he passed away, the deeply conservative newspaper *Diario de la Marina* published "Ante el cadáver" (Looking at the corpse) on June 19, 1921, the rhetoric of the editorial helps us understand how the autocratic government system sustained itself:

> The people love it deeply, even more so those who use it, those who understand it. And the people know that Major General José Miguel Gómez had a stable, exact concept. The people always knew that under the old chief's leadership—both in peace and in war—they were on a straight path to obtain their intimate desires, their national aspirations. The people's hero might make mistakes on occasion, as is only human, in tactics or the routes taken, but those mistakes were never of a personal type, never a bad sign of personal gain, because the leader—in his thoughts and actions—always represented the people's plans. That is the reason why his mistakes were so few and so slight, and his triumphs and glory will be legion in the pages of history. Because the soul of the people was affected by all his generosity and sincere expressions of his clear, simple ideology. And very seldom is such an infinite, harmonious spiritual relationship between individuals and collective groups to be seen; that was what there was with this leader that the people have lost today, and today the people are crying over his death.

The long, hard wars against Spain, and the final triumph, imbued the senior officers of the Cuban army with the mysticism of heroism and sacrifice. It being impossible to consecrate dozens of thousands of combatants, a group of the high-ranking officers took advantage of this feeling and practically monopolized the politics of the first decades of the republic. Politicians who had not fought could only become part of the war leaders' client groups. All of this was sociologically logical and—according to historian Joel James Figarola's widely held interpretation—historically beneficial bearing in mind US interventionism, irrespective of the behavior of many of these leaders—which was far from heroic.

They were generally from rich, well-educated families. They had studied in the United States and were in favor of abolition because they saw slavery as a dead weight, and they paid close attention to the technical and commercial vicissitudes of the sugar industry. They had hated Spanish political imposition and hoped that the independent republic would bring stability and prosperity with it. They were not unaware of the dependent nature of the Cuban sugar industry, which did not refine its own sugar: the final process for making white sugar was carried out in US refineries.

Spanish and US magnates soon found the way to safeguard what mattered most to them, becoming *clients*[71] of the the leaders who could best defend their interests. In fact, most of the caudillos were from the families of modest sugar estate owners or well-off traders; in other words, they had always been powerful or were soon to become rich. At the end of the day, they all defended their interests as wealthy people and agreed over the main issues. For them, the prime concerns were racial harmony, ensured in bloodthirsty ways on more than one occasion; control of the working class and revolutionary organizations, being strongly opposed to communism; keeping up mutually beneficial, subservient relations with the United States. The rebel leaders—men who had shown heroic generosity and firmness on the battlefield—now floated above their clients using the power they had over the country's voters: their interests were now much less patriotic and much more egoistical.

José Martí had warned that it was important to differentiate between leaders and leadership, the greatness of a leader not residing in the person himself but rather in the extent to which he served the greatness of the people. One of his objectives on founding the Partido Revolucionario Cubano was to "organize the indispensable war in the Antilles in such a way that, after the victory, our American republics are not disrupted by the leadership and confusion which existed previously and which, by imitation, still exist today."

However, the republic was a series of autocratic governments. And they led, for example, to the government of Gerardo Machado, who was closely connected with Laureano Falla Gutiérrez[72] and his group of Spaniards and Cubans, and who tried to bring the leaders and magnates together under authoritarian democracy which, finally, led to a bloody dictatorship.

A Novel about Things that Happened during His Time

On the pages before the novel, in his dedication to a Cuban woman called Esther Plá,[73] Francisco Ulacia explained his intentions in this area:

---

71. *Client* as in Latin: in Roman society *client* was the word used for plebeians who were protected by a patrician.

72. León Ichaso, *Don Laureano Falla Gutiérrez, su vida y su empresa* (Havana: Cultural S.A., 1930). In fact, León Ichaso—born in Durango, Bizkaia, in 1869 and who died in Havana in 1938—had a life that was not parallel to Francisco Ulacia's: in fact, it was completely opposite. He arrived in Cuba as a soldier in the colonial army, stayed in the island after independence and, as a journalist and writer, worked at the *Diario de la Marina*, becoming a crusader for the most pro-Spanish, conservative ideology. He was one of the founders of CEDA (Spanish Confederation of Autonomous Rightest Parties) in Cuba and campaigned for the "nacionales" during the civil war.

73. Carlos H. Ulacia—Francisco Ulacia's great-nephew—has written in an unpublished personal testimony about this person's identity: "My mother Carmen Ulacia's sister, who had a

> Having written this novel in this corner of Europe, and during a misty, sad winter, it would not be surprising if it did not have the rich plasticity and warm tones of the luminous atmosphere which the tropics always give all their scenery and characters. However, if my modest work does not achieve the right tone or the real color I would like it to; with regards to Cuba, its characters and customs, it will at least be an eloquent witness to my affection for my mother's homeland, the land where I was born, the young republic whose prosperity I so much desire and of which I am one of the most loyal citizens.[74]

There can be no doubt that the novel is an eloquent witness to Francisco Ulacia's affection for Cuba. There is plasticity and there are warm tones in the way he describes the Cuban countryside and characters, but the reality of Cuba is also there: the conflict.

It is a realistic novel in the sense described by Arturo Campión in his letter-prologue published in the pages at the start of *Don Fausto:*

> Painting and reproducing contemporary life cannot be done using the series of adventures which interested readers half a century ago. The prose surrounds us like water around fish. The dissemination of the scientific spirit urges us to seek the truth, which is the objective of science, even in the agreeable field of literature, looking down on beauty, which is also the truth, and of an even higher type. The public asks for reality and writers try to give them reality, and serve it up for them, and, due to the rapport between these two ideas, they try to serve it with a certain type of beauty. You wanted to give us reality, Francisco, and that you have given us.[75]

In the prologue to *Las gatitas rubias,* Francisco Ulacia wrote, "Today's novels are scientific and historical, which is what makes them real. The novelist's mission is to focus on a portion of nature with his perception machine and print it on his sensitive photographic plate; what must be recorded includes not only the external form of things and living beings but also the characters who are going to take part in the work's most intimate ways of thinking and feeling."[76]

We could say that this is an old novel: it was written 105 years ago. It is a type of novel that suffered difficulties during the first decades of the

---

lot of contact with Pancho, always told me that he was a small, short, ugly man, but very well educated and agreeable, who took "street women" home with him; he was very successful with women, except for with a Cuban woman he liked a lot, Esther Plá . . . Esther ended up marrying Manuel Fernández Silva, my maternal grandmother, Ramón Ulacia's wife's brother. That must have been a sad thing for Pancho because Esther and my great-grandfather Manuel, who was also a doctor, came to Europe on their honeymoon and they liked the Basque Country so much that they settled in Hernani; he became an expert jai alai player and he did not go back to Cuba until forty years later, after the civil war . . . They were both vocational doctors. But Manuel Fernández Silva was a one-meter ninety athlete, blond and with my mother's same incredible green eyes."

74. Ulacia, *El caudillo*, 1.
75. Ulacia, *Don Fausto*, 3.
76. Ulacia, *Las gatitas rubias*, 5.

twentieth century, above all between 1920 and 1930. That was when James Joyce's *Ulysses*, Marcel Proust's *À la recherche du temps perdu*, and Franz Kafka's *The Trial* were published.

But it is a novel with insight into what happened at the time and what was to happen later. The countryside, characters, and events are recorded with affection, nostalgia, and almost veneration. Francisco Ulacia's book—which falls between realism and romanticism, reality and desire—tells us of the Cuba between two centuries, and it is so realistic and faithful that it even contains many of the prejudices of the time.

Bibliography

Amezaga, Elías. "Un médico de almas: Francisco de Ulacia." *Muga* 60–61 (1987): 124–33.

Cabrera Cuello, Migdalia. *La guerra del 68 en Villa Clara*. Santa Clara: Editorial Capiro, 2005.

Fernández Robaina, Tomás. *El negro en Cuba 1902–1958*. Havana: Editorial de Ciencias Sociales, 1990.

Granja, José Luís de la. "Francisco de Ulacia: Biografía política." In *Nere biotza!*, Francisco de Ulacia, 9–81. Bilbao, El Tilo, 1998.

Granjel, Luis S. *Médicos novelistas y novelistas médicos*. Salamanca: Real Academia de Medicina de Salamanca, 1973.

Iglesias Utset, Marial. *Las metáforas del cambio en la vida cotidiana, Cuba 1898–1902*. Havana: Ediciones Unión, 2003.

Ichaso, León. *Don Laureano Falla Gutiérrez, su vida y su empresa*. Havana: Cultural S.A., 1930.

James Figuerola, Joel. *Cuba 1900–1928, la república dividida contra sí misma*. Santiago de Cuba: Editorial Oriente, 2002.

Juaristi, Jon. *El chimbo expiatorio: La invención de la tradición bilbaína, 1876–1939*. Bilbao: El Tilo, 1994.

Mees, Ludger. "La izquierda imposible: El fracaso del nacionalismo republicano vasco entre 1910 y 1913." *Historia Contemporánea* 2 (1989): 249–66.

Moreno Fraginals, Manuel. *El ingenio*. Havana: Editorial de Ciencias Sociales, 1978.

Pezuela, Jacobo de la. *Diccionario geográfico estadístico histórico de la isla de Cuba*. Madrid: Imprenta de Mellado, 1863–1866.

San Sebastián, Koldo. "Francisco de Ulacia: laicismo, autonomía y República." *Arbola* 10 (1987): 77–78.

Scott, Rebeca J. *Slave Emancipation in Cuba: The Transition to Free Labor, 1860–1899*. Princeton: Princeton University Press, 1985.

Ulacia, Francisco de. *Don Fausto*. Bilbao: Tipografía de Astuy, 1905.

———. *Nere biotza!* Bilbao: Tipografía de Astuy, 1907.

———. *Martinchu ta Matilde*. Bilbao: Imprenta y Librería de Manuel Fuentes, 1907.

————. *Las gatitas rubias,* Bilbao, Imprenta de José Rojas Núñez, 1908.

————. *El Caudillo*. Bilbao, Imprenta de José Rojas Núñez, 1910.

Vitoria, Manuel. "Vida y obra del doctor Ulacia." *Asclepio* 25 (1973): 337–50.

17

David and Goliath: The Affair of Father Iñaki de Azpiazu and Franco's Representatives in Venezuela and Cuba

Alberto Irigoyen Artetxe

Background

Born on February 1, 1910, at Azpeitia, Iñaki Azpiazu Olaizola was ordained in 1933. In 1934 he graduated in social and political sciences at Lille, France.

During the Spanish Civil War he was arrested and held at the concentration camp at Miranda de Ebro, from where he was liberated in April 1937. He wrote about these experiences in his book *7 meses y 7 días en la España de Franco* (7 months and 7 days in Franco's Spain).

Exiled in France, he used to visit the camp at Gurs[1] and became the unofficial chaplain there.[2] He also worked at the camps for refugee children that the Basque government established in the northern Basque Country.

When the Nazis invaded France he helped people persecuted by the Gestapo, for which he was awarded the French Croix de Guerre.

At the end of the war he joined the Sagrado Corazón de Jesús de Bétharram order. After a short stay at Sagrado Corazón parish in Buenos Aires, he became a secular member of the clergy in the Buenos Aires archbishopric, serving as vicar at the parish of San José de Flores. A year later Monseñor Copello named him Chaplain General of the National Penal Institutes.[3]

---

1. An internment camp near Pau where the French government held refugees from Franco's Spain—including many Basques.
2. Chueca, *Gurs, el campo vasco*, 45.
3. Óscar Álvarez Gila, "Azpiazu Olaizola, Iñaki," in "La Contribución europea a la iglesia en el Río de la Plata: La presencia religiosa vasca (1835–1965)" doctoral thesis attachments, 117–18.

His considerable experience in prisons led him to found the Christian Aid Secretariat for Prisons and the House for Liberated Prisoners.

He was an active Basque nationalist and had connections with the exiled Basque government, being a point of reference for Basque people in the Americas.

In 1959 he went on a extensive tour of prisons in Chile,[4] Brazil,[5] Uruguay, Peru,[6] Ecuador, Venezuela, Mexico, and Cuba, during which he came up against representatives of the Franco regime in Caracas and Havana.

Father Azpiazu in Venezuela

During his stay in Venezuela—and introduced by the Argentine ambassador Yacante Molina—he gave conferences in various prisons.[7]

His denunciations of the Franco regime and defense of Basque freedoms led to the Spanish ambassador Cañal y Gómez Imaz taking steps with the Argentine embassy to silence him. He sent letters and telegrams to the archbishopric with the same aim.[8]

Frustrated by the lack of echo (approbation of his communications), the Spanish ambassador sent a list of questions to the the Argentine ambassador about the priest's background; but, as the answers to the questions were of no use to him, he manipulated them and sent them to the press,[9] to which the Argentine ambassador, justifiably indignant, issued a communiqué denouncing what had happened.[10]

Azpiazu himself forwarded to the media a communiqué denouncing the ambassador's lies:

> My activities have never had a political nature . . . But by political is understood defending human liberties, proclamation of respect for different cultures and setting forward the principles for healthy coexistence, then I fulfil my duty as a priest by working in favor of those noble policies, which is why I condemn with holy indignation the attacks against man, against culture and peaceful coexistence which dictators carry out, whether in Hungary under the communist regime or in the Basque Country under the Franco regime.
>
> When I denounce the crime of genocide to which my people are being subjected, I am not abandoning my priestly duties, nor am I part of a "separatist movement." I work for justice and defend my

---

4. Oficina de Prensa de Euzkadi, Paris, October 13, 1959, 4.

5. Salgado Araujo Franco, *Mis conversaciones privadas con Franco*, 279.

6. Oficina de Prensa de Euzkadi, Paris, October 20, 1959, 4.

7. Fundación Sabino Arana, Archivo del Nacionalismo (FSA. AN)-EBB-381-1, "Me escandaliza que Eisenhower haga visitas de cortesía a Franco," *El Nacional*, Caracas, December 5, 1959.

8. Oficina de Prensa de Euzkadi, Paris, December 7, 1959, 3. AGA. AMAE, 54/05367.

9. "El embajador argentino tiene razón," Oficina de Prensa de Euzkadi, Paris, December 16, 1959, 4.

10. "Comunicado del Señor Embajador de la República Argentina," *El Universal*, Caracas, December 6, 1959, 14.

people, no more than that.[11]

In addition to the growing criticism of Franco and the later scandal as a result of his inflexible attitude, the dictatorship's representative had to put up with the favorable light in which the priest was seen. For instance, the newspaper *La Esfera* stated with undisguised sarcasm:

> We listen to Iñaki Azpiazu . . . If all Catholic priests were like him, Catholicism would be incredibly strong. The strength of democratic conviction . . . Catholicism is as Iñaki says it is. Otherwise it is not Catholicism. Catholicism is democratic. Catholic dictatorships are aberrations. Monstrosities. Mystifications . . . Iñaki was a breath of fresh air from the Spanish clergy. Why not bring more Iñakis?[12]

Far from dying down, the commotion reached the ears of Venezuelan politicians, who also spoke out against the Franco regime.

For example, César Rondón Lovera, member of parliament for Acción Democrática:

> The presence of reverend father Azpiazu in our country, from the point of view of the struggle against the Franco regime, must lead— even bearing in mind the differences of all types—to a powerful stimulus for those of us—Spaniards and others—who want to see Spain freed from the grips of the tyrant. This proves that the idea that the Church is completely behind Franco is not entirely true; there is at least one enlightened priest who fights bravely in his own name, in that of the dignity of his position, in that of his people, the Basque people.

Member of parliament Rodolfo Cárdenas, of the Partido Social Cristiano COPEI, stated:

> Franco's current ambassador has mistakenly believed that Spanish diplomats have power over the Argentine government and the diplomatic service. That is why he has been politically clumsy enough in Caracas to break the most basic rules of respect toward his colleagues, having tried to use even the senior member of the diplomatic corps.

And Eduardo Machado, of the Communist Party, said:

> It seems that Franco's ambassador thinks over here we're still all colonies of Fernando VII, and that he can plot and ask for Spanish citizens to be deprived of the benefits of democratic rights and civil rights reconquered from the claws of the dictatorship which, of course, was so friendly with Franco's regime.[13]

---

11. FSA, AN-EBB-38-1, "Remitido: El Embajador de España está violando la verdad," Press release not identifying any media, undated.

12. Cienfuegos, "Política de Altura," 14.

13. "Repudio total a la actitud del embajador de Franco," *El Nacional*, Caracas, December 8, 1959, 40.

Peli de Irizar, president of the Foreign Board for the Basque Nationalist Party in Venezuela said:

> Father Iñaki has been carrying out very important work over these two weeks, appearing in the press, on the radio, television and at conferences about social and penitential problems, always making reference to the different nature of the Basques, and criticizing dictators harshly. He has had the Spanish ambassador reacting to him and looking ridiculous: Franco's representative came into the ring and wanted to stop father Iñaki's conferences and stop him from speaking on the radio and television, but both the ecclesiastical authorities and the ambassador of Argentina proved not to be docile servants. The "affair" became public knowledge and all social and political classes are against the ambassador and behind our priest. The ambassador thought that by privately complaining to the acting archbishop and to the Argentine representative that he would get his way, but all he has garnered is everybody's disdain.[14]

It was no exaggeration to say that Cañal had looked ridiculous, to such an extent that he was mocked in the humorous magazine *Martín Garabato* which satirized him and wrote poems about his "idiotic allusion" to the Basques having "a narrow mentality."[15]

But the truth is that Cañal did not believe his own statements, saying that:

> I do not think I am wrong in saying that the Basque separatists are the people who do most harm to our homeland around the world and particularly in Hispanic America. More than love for their region, they hate the rest of Spain. By hard work they have achieved a good economic situation in those countries and prestige in religious, social, and political circles. They are very well organized in America and, from what I have been told, have a highly efficient information service in Spain.[16]

La Esfera de Caracas expressed its satisfaction because the events had served to demonstrate the "unbreakable rectitude" of the religious authorities; the government's position in rejecting foreign interference; the Argentine ambassador's uprightness "on rejecting the Franco regime's clumsiness" and the cordiality of the ministry of justice in receiving Azpiazu.[17]

Iñaki Azpiazu in Havana

From Caracas Azpiazu traveled to Cuba where he visited various prisons,

14. FSA. AN-EBB-74-5, "Carta de Peli de Irizar a Jesús de Solaun," Caracas, December 2, 1959.
15. "Al Marqués," *Euzko Gastedi*, Caracas, 5
16. AGA. AMAE, 54/11861. Informe No. 47, Caracas, February 2, 1960.
17. "La ofensiva franquista contra el P. Iñaki," *Tierra Vasca*, Buenos Aires, January 15, 1960, 3

gave interviews and conferences and had meetings with Osvaldo Dórticos and Fidel Castro.

The busy program of activities which he carried out those days included the interview with him broadcast on Mundovisión in which "he condemned the Franco regime in Spain, saying that there was no individual freedom, freedom of the press, trade unions, political parties or academic freedom and human rights were not respected."[18]

Meanwhile, having failed in his efforts with the Apostolic Nuncio and the Argentine ambassador, Spanish ambassador Pablo Lojendio awaited an opportunity to discredit Azpiazu.[19]

This cautiousness was due to the regime being afraid that Mexico's recent recognition of the Spanish republican government-in-exile would be followed by other South American countries. In fact, Lojendio was losing control, which can be seen in the report he sent to Madrid warning that the republican's had an organization which was increasingly dangerous.[20]

The opportunity which Lojendio had been waiting for arrived when Azpiazu left Cuba:

> he organized the Spanish friars to do something which was beneath their dignity: appearing to support Franco's highly Catholic regime and expressing deep love for the cause which the Leader represented . . . Some of the friars had been tricked into going to the embassy under the pretext of a cocktail party at the start of the year and they were later invited to sign a declaration that Lojendio himself had drawn up; one of them was the head of the Franciscans, who was against it all, but he signed along with all the others and then retracted, which caused a real stir in Cuban public opinion.[21]

According to this document, not all the men of God wanted to sign the document, but they had to give way to the ambassador's threats: "He told the friars that they had to do something to hurt the Basque priest or he would harm them in Madrid."[22]

Among them was Friar Balenciaga, who stated that Azpiazu's statements about the Spanish state not respecting human rights and that the Church did not support Franco still held because the document had tried to justify Franco's rebellion as a result of the excesses committed not before the rising—which the relgious men said—but after it.

And he added:

18. "Trasfondo de un suceso. La maniobra franquista en Cuba". *Euzko Deya*, Buenos Aires, March 30, 1960. 3.

19. AGA. AMAE, 54/5367, Informe reservado No. 1, Havana, January 2, 1960.

20. Manuel de Paz Sánchez, "Resumen de prensa del consejero de información y prensa de la embajada de España en Cuba, Jaime Caldevilla, del 2 de enero de 1960," *Zona de Guerra: España y la revolución cubana (1960–1962)*. Workshop of the Historia del Centro de la Cultura Popular Canaria, Canary Islands, 2011, 101–2.

21. Arteche family archive, letter of Margarita Imaz, secretary to Iñaki de Azpiazu, to Pedro Arteche. Buenos Aires, January 27, 1960.

22. Ibid.

but let us imagine—leaving to one side monarchist and military plots to overturn the republic from its very foundation—that crimes committed under the republic justified Franco's rebellion which, in itself, must be provisional and cannot go on for ever."[23]

Panic at the Embassy

The diplomatic information office's strategy is clear in the report which Jaime Caldevilla sent to Madrid and in which he said that

> The Basque priest Ignacio Azpiazu, during his stay in Havana, tried to follow the [Cuban] government's line on things and made statements in favor of the revolutionary government; he also denied that it was subject to communist influence and gained official and public support that helped his declarations against our Regime.

These were aired during a television debate in which he made the well-known accusations; but when he began to stray from his previously approved text, the chairman of the broadcasting company halted transmission. Two Spanish Agustinian priests—fathers Mendoza and Morales—went to the television studio and wanted to protest publicly; however, the interruption of the broadcast thwarted their patriotic intention.

The O.I.D (Diplomatic Information Office) prepared the priests' meeting thoroughly, and it was held at the Spanish embassy. Fifteen bishops and major superiors of the Spanish religious orders based in Cuba met for an hour. At the end of the meeting the ambassador was handed a "joint declaration" that had caused a great stir and should be distributed all over America and even in Spain.

> Around a hundred Spanish priests were with the bishops and major superiors and the meeting's atmosphere was movingly patriotic and religious.
>
> Until the present, this meeting has only been criticized in print by the Communist newspaper *Hoy* and in the philo-Communist paper *Diario Nacional.*
>
> It seems strange that the newspaper *Revolución* has not published an article attacking it.
>
> Given Franciscan fathers Mendizábal and Biain's (delicate) situation, it would be best to take steps for the Holy See to move them to Spain or another nation not in Hispanic America.[24]

Far from being an isolated case, the persecution of religious people who did not support the Franco regime was continual in the countries to which the dictatorship's long arm reached. We have found documentation

---

23. "Los frailes franquistas y el método Ollendorf," Oficina de Prensa de Euzkadi, Paris, January 28, 1960, 4.

24. "Resumen de prensa del consejero de información y prensa de la Embajada de España en Cuba, Jaime Caldevilla, del 9 de enero de 1960 (AGA. Asuntos Exteriores, C-5360)," in Paz Sánchez, *Dos momentos cruciales en las relaciones entre España y Cuba,* 103–4.

about this at the general administration archive of the Ministry of Foreign Affairs at Alcalá de Henares, among other things reports against Capuchins, Trinitarians, Laterans, and Dominicans in Argentina; missionaries of the Immaculate Heart of Mary in Brazil; Jesuits in Venezuela; Carmelites in Colombia; and Capuchins in France and the Philippines.

Lojendio's Document

Caldevilla was referring to the episode provoked by his ambassador in which, with the excuse of bringing together the Spanish religious orders established in the island, he made them sign the "Joint declaration of senior religious representatives in Cuba."[25]

In it the priests declared that, in spite of being far-removed from politics, they denounced

> that, under the republican-Marxist government, not even the most basic human rights were respected in Spain, as, sadly, can be seen in the following information: Between April 1931 and April 1939 twelve bishops, more than sixteen thousand priests and other religious people and more than seven thousand members of the Catholic action youth movement were martyred under the sign of the hammer and sickle. In nine dioceses 80 percent of the clergy disappeared; in Malaga 90 percent of the priests and religious people disappeared.

They added that neither property nor freedom of the press or of worship had been respected, so that "given such outrages by the republican-Marxist government, the Spanish people and its army rose in arms against the barbarism that was destroying the homeland in a mostly religious war that Pope Pio XI classified as a National Crusade":

> This Crusade is at the origin of the current Spanish state, governed by a wholly Catholic man, Generalisimo Francisco Franco Bahamonde.
> We are satisfied to recognize the excellent understanding between the Catholic Church and the current Spanish state, protected by the best concordat between the Holy See and Spain in recent years.[26]

Along with the text of the declaration, the newspaper also published Lojendio's speech and that of Aristónico Ursa, the vice head of the Claretians in Cuba. In this document—after making statements such as that generalisimo Franco was the most Catholic man in the world and that Spanish legislation was, both socially and in penitential terms, one of the best and most advanced in the world—he attacked the Basque priest and said that "Stating, as he recently has, that human rights in Spain are not respected by the Spanish government, is to be unaware of reality or twist it

25. "Declaración franquista de los religiosos españoles en Cuba," *Euzko Deya*. Buenos Aires, March 30, 1960, 3.
26. "Superiores religiosos hispanos en Cuba recuerdan los crímenes de los comunistas en España," *Diario de la Marina*, Havana, January 8, 1960, 1.

so mendaciously and with so much scorn for those of us who feel ourselves to be Spanish."

The Spanish ambassador talked about the Basque priest saying that nobody should "pay any attention . . . to the sad voices (of) travelers that are no more than echoes of personal failures and resentment."[27]

But far from achieving the result which he had hoped for, his efforts helped to make Azpaizu better known. With regards to this the representative of the Basque government wrote:

> Father Azpiazu was "the man of the day" during his stay here. I was able to see how much people like him on two occasions in public places when I was with him: he is recognized (due to the television), and was given tokens of affection, above all because of his defense of the Cuban revolution.[28]

"But They Bring Something More . . ."

Ten days later the magazine *Bohemia* gave a detailed account of what had happened on January 7 at the embassy, mentioning the most important participants:

> the Claretian Aristónico Ursa, the Franciscan José Mendizabal, the Jesuit Ceferino Ruiz, the Dominican José Romero, the Capuchin Antonio Vegemian, the Salesian Rafael Mercader, the Vincentian Gregorio Subiñas, the Piarist Antonio Parredón, the Marist Pablo de la Cruz, the Agustinian Antonio Medina, the Redemptorist Antonio González. They were accompanied by more than a hundred friars.
> . . . They come to greet (Lojendio) for the New Year.
> But they bring something more . . .

Because the journalist thought that something more sinister was happening behind the embassy gates and he explains it in this way:

> There was an important side to the problem that was connected with the Cuban situation. Cuban Catholic leaders saw the appearance of the renegades Aguirre and O'Farril[29] as an indirect attempt to provoke the revolutionary government. They wanted the spokespeople of the July 26 Movement to speak against the Spanish senior clergymen's support for Franco so that they could then accuse the island's governors of intolerance and antireligious persecution.
> A letter sent from Miami by Eduardo Aguirre—Díaz Lanz' self-exiled friend—to the newspaper *Avance* and published on Friday the eighth could have been directly linked.

---

27. "Superiores religiosos hispanos en Cuba recuerdan los crímenes de los comunistas en España," *Diario de la Marina*, Havana, January 8, 1960, 1–2.
28. FSA, AN-PNV-82-5, Havana, letter of José Luis de Garai the the Oficina de Prensa de Euskadi. Havana, January 15, 1959.
29. It is a reference to the flight to Miami—in December 1959—of the priests Eduardo Aguirre and Juan Ramón O'Farril.

Neither Christian nor Ecclesiastical in style, the insolent letter was addressed to R. P. Biain, editor of the Catholic weekly magazine *La Quincena*, which had gained widely held respect in Cuba because of its reasoned and persistent support for the revolution. It started by reproaching him for supporting the Spanish republic in the past and then argues further.

This is why you are so at ease with the new communists in Cuba; this is why you protest that priests in Cuba speak too much. Your case is unique and exclusive: neither Cuban nor Spanish, without any recognized homeland (because Basque nationality has never been recognized by the concert of the world's nations), you unfoundedly join the choir of official slanderers of the [Spanish] government."[30]

Azpiazu in Mexico

From Mexico the priest promised to return to the island immediately to face up to Lojendio. Meanwhile, he was interviewed by the newspaper *Novedades,* gave a telephone interview to *Bohemia,* and wrote in *Eusko Deya* where, in an article titled "Religiosos españoles a las órdenes de un embajador" (Spanish priests under the orders of an ambassador), he wrote:

> Breaking down chronological order, mixing events with different social origins and motivations, is trying to confuse other people and leads to one's own loss of prestige. That is what happened to the signatories of the declaration.
>
> . . . The signatories' social morality is broken by the document that was given to the Spanish ambassador in Cuba when they say that the Spanish Civil War was mostly religious. Such a statement twenty years after the end of the bloody conflict and with the people of Spain still cruelly deprived of their liberty, falsifies history and compromises the Church seriously.
>
> . . . What could be the religious basis for a war that led to such a catastrophe, which was the indirect cause of the crimes committed in the government area and that carried out the execution of thousands behind the Franco lines, without even mentioning the million casualties at the front and the terrible hate created between brothers of a same nation? That war was not based on religion, unless the Spanish priests in Cuba meant the totalitarian religion, which has no Christian contents.
>
> . . . The Basques know that their clergy defends man's legitimate liberties against all political and economic oppression, wherever it may happen, in Hungary under communism, in the Basque Country and in Spain under Franco; the Basques know that we fight for respect for cultures and we oppose whoever tries to destroy them using international imperialism or right-wing empires such as Franco's;

---

30. "Pero traen algo más . . . ," *Bohemia,* January 29, 1960, 61–2, 80.

the Basques know that as priests we do not go along with earthly regimes and that we would never use violence to spread Christianity because we have internal values in the Church. That is why we do not have problems in the Basque Country.

But being human and priests makes us look at reality in Spain and make use of principles and behavior that will allow future generations to live without the bitter memory of the past, ready to create a history of forgiveness, tolerance and liberty.[31]

"Las verdades del Padre Aspiazu"

Days later Friar Sudupe wrote about the contents of the joint declaration in *La Quincena*:

> it is not a matter of working out if the republican regime was responsible for the crimes it is accused of but of whether the current regime respects fundamental human rights as individuals and as members of social groups. Father Azpiazu's categorical, irrefutable answer is that it does not.[32]

He then relentlessly picks apart the falsehoods in the declaration one by one, stating that the military uprising:

> was not the result of a spontaneous flash, bursting out from the ashes of a people subjugated to excesses—as they wanted to convince us— but rather a plot which was nurtured and prepared with tenacious persistence and in a systematic way in military circles unhappy with the regime from the very start of the republic.

Lojendio's Failure

A report sent by the embassy confirms that Lojendio got involved in a worse problem, as Capdevilla points out:

> As a result of the Spanish priests' visit to our embassy and the document signed by their bishops and major superiors, a violent campaign against the ambassador, the press officer, and the chief of staff has been started. The press officer has been accused of writing a letter that the Cuban priest P. O'Farril wrote and published against prime minister Fidel Castro.[33]

The newspapers *Revolución* and *Hoy* did indeed criticize them and accused the embassy civil servants Jaime Caldevilla and Alejandro Vergara of being spies; a group of intellectuals—including Guillermo Cabrera Infante, Néstor Almendros, Heberto Padilla, Rafael Fornés, Alejo Car-

---

31. "Religiosos españoles a las ordenes de un embajador," *Euzko Deya*, marzo, 1960, 3.

32. E. Sudupe, *La Quincena*, Havana, January 16, 1969, 34–36.

33. "Resumen de prensa del consejero de información y prensa de la Embajada de España en Cuba, Jaime Caldevilla, del 16 de enero de 1960 (AGA. Asuntos Exteriores, C-5360)," in Paz Sánchez, *Dos momentos cruciales en las relaciones entre España y Cuba*, 104–5.

pentier, Nicolás Guillén, and Wilfredo Lam signed a manifesto rejecting the priests' document, describing them as "false priests," "Nazi-fascist agents," "natural, spontaneous enemies of the people of Cuba."[34]

But this declaration displeased the Basque Franciscans in two ways because while they had expected criticisms from the left, they were surprised that both the Basque government and the Basque workers' trade union (ELA/STV) signed it.[35]

Far from dying down, the accusations against the ambassador grew to such an extent that, a few days later, Fidel Castro himself stated them on a television channel that—according to the Basque Franciscans—was the corollary of Father Iñaki's actions.[36]

We are referring to Lojendio's untimely interruption in a television studio when Castro was giving a conference. This situation took place when the prime minister, after talking about the priest's meeting at the embassy, read a letter which was said to have been written by Pedro Díaz Lanz's brother-in-law,[37] in which he accused the Spanish embassy of a plan for helping members of the Catholic opposition to the regime to leave Cuba through the US embassy,[38] an accusation that Lojendio decided to deny personally by going to the studios and shouting for the right to reply and declare his innocence and that of his country in the matter.

During this confrontation—of which there are videos on Internet—Castro reproaches Lojendio: "How can the ambassador of the greatest dictatorship in Europe talk to me about democracy!" As is well known, this outburst led to Lojendio being rapidly expelled from the island and the Cuban ambassador in Madrid was recalled for consultations.[39]

With regards to this event, José Luis Garai, the Basque government's representative in Cuba, told President Aguirre:

> In fact, the whole country is nervous about Franco's ambassador's extraordinary behavior. Editorials in the newspapers, comments, violent accusations from everybody, even the ultra pro-Franco newspaper *El Diario de la Marina*.[40]

But he also told him—with surprising foresight—that he was convinced that, in spite of the diplomatic incident—the relationship between Cuba and Franco's regime would not change significantly:

---

34. Uria, Iglesia y revolución en Cuba, 359.

35. Xabier, "Instantáneas," *La quincena*, Havana, January 30, 1960, 36.

36. "15 días en la nación," *La quincena*, January 30, 1950, 22.

37. Pedro Luis Díaz Lanz (Havana, 1926–2008) head of the Cuban revolutionary air force until 1959, when he was relieved from his position by Fidel Castro. In exile in the US, he carried out a continual antirevolutionary campaign.

38. "Da el gobierno veinticuatro horas de plazo al embajador," *Diario de la Marina*, Havana, January 21, 1960, 1, 12.

39. "El grave incidente provocado por el embajador Lojendio" (The serious incident which ambassador Lojendio caused), *Bohemia*, undated press clipping.

40. FSA, AN-PNV-82-5, Havana; Letter from José Luis de Garai to José Antonio Aguirre. Havana, January 22, 1960.

Now there will be interviews and so on, but I do not think there will be a complete break in relations, although the only change could be ambassadors not being sent, trading continuing and, furthermore, sending Chargés d'affairs.

Yesterday thousands of Cubans demonstrated in front of the Spanish embassy; among other people, a Spanish republican spoke, and hard, strong criticisms of Franco's regime were made. There was a mass of people in the street in front of the balcony of the Spanish embassy; people climbed onto others' shoulders and put the Cuban and Spanish republican flags on it. Obviously, we did not go there because we do not know what is going to happen and perhaps it will all end in nothing, and withdrawing from positions can be a little disagreeable.[41]

Azpiazu Returns to Havana

The decision to go back to Havana to defend the Franciscan friars gave Azpiazu an opportunity not only to speak out against the Franco regime's falsehoods but also to take part in various unprogrammed activities such as going to Raúl Castro's house on January 28, along with Monsignor Evelio, to pay homage to José Martí,[42] and, on January 22 and 23—in other words, the two days after the expulsion of the Spanish ambassador—taking part in a tour of the island to visit some agricultural cooperatives. On the trip he was accompanied by a varied international group consisting of the French essayist Roger Caillois, the Ecuadorian politician Benjamín Carrión, the Mexican journalist Fernando Benítez, the Guatemalan novelist Miguel Ángel Asturias, the Venezuelan journalist Fabricio Ojeda, the Haitian novelist René Depestre, all of whom were members of the jury for the Casa de las Américas prize that year.

After visiting Pinar del Rio, the travelers reached Rancho San Vicente at dusk where, at supper time, they had a surprise visit from Fidel Castro, who they had not been expecting until the next day. In what the journalist described as a "long, intimate monologue," Castro talked about his consumption cooperatives projects, the national People's Shops chain, help for retailers, school cities, and the new cities which had been planned.

During this conversation he also talked about Lojendio's expulsion, of which he said:

> Well, the marquis has left, alive and without any problems, but discredited. I'm glad: he was a type of purgative I had to take every once in a while. He deserved a slap, but Cuba would have come out losing and that would have led to a call to attack us. We had to protect him because people would have killed him.[43]

---

41. Ibid.

42. Uria, *Iglesia y revolución en Cuba*, 434.

43. Lisandro Otero, "Punto de Mira: Notas de un viaje con Fidel," *Lunes de revolución*, February 1, 1960, 17–19.

End of the Journey

After his long trip around America and Europe, Azpiazu's journey terminated in Paris where, on March 22, 1960, a few weeks after his arrival, he was surprised by a piece of news that froze the hearts of thousands of Basques all over the world: President Aguirre had died. Along with other mourners, Iñaki went with his President's body to its resting place at Donibane Lohizune, spending a night on the way at Poitiers where, at dawn the following day and before the last stage of the procession, he said mass before the president's body.[44]

After his tour Azpiazu went back to Argentina where, like some biblical character, he never ceased in his unstoppable fight against the Goliath who held his country's will in chains because, as he said himself, he was always ready to serve this cause as far as was humanly and Christianly possible.[45]

Father Iñaki, who the Buenos Aires press called "an integral, complete man, who always fought for freedom and human dignity" died in the capital of Argentina on March 29, 1988.[46]

Bibliography

Álvarez Gila, Óscar. "Azpiazu Olaizola, Iñaki." In "La Contribución europea a la iglesia en el Río de la Plata: La presencia religiosa vasca (1835–1965)." Doctoral thesis, Universidad de Navarra.

Chueca, Josu. *Gurs, el campo vasco*. Tafalla: Txalaparta, 2007.

Cienfuegos, César. "Política de Altura: Iñaki." *La Esfera*, December 6, 1959.

Paz-Sánchez, Manuel De. *Dos momentos cruciales en las relaciones entre España y Cuba: enero de 1959 y enero de 1960: Notas y documentos*. ULPGC: Biblioteca universitaria, 2010.

Salgado Araujo Franco, Francisco. *Mis conversaciones privadas con Franco*. Barcelona: GeoPlaneta, 1976.

Uría, Ignacio. *Iglesia y revolución en Cuba: Enrique Pérez Serantes (1883–1968), el obispo que salvó a Fidel Castro*. Madrid: Encuentro, 2011.

---

44. "La democracia mundial rinde homenaje al presidente de Euzkadi," *Euzko Deya*, Buenos Aires, March 30, 1960, 6–7. Letter from Iñaki Azpiazu to Manuel Irujo, London, June 15, 1960. At www.euskomedia.org/fondo/12244.

45. Letter from Iñaki Azpiazu to Manuel Irujo, London, June 15, 1960. At www.euskomedia.org/ fondo/12244.

46. *La Prensa*, Buenos Aires, March 30, 1988.

18

Incursions in Cuban Franciscan Territory *La Quincena* and the 1959 Revolution

Miel Anjel Elustondo Etxeberria

Contemporary Franciscan Javier Arzuaga's description reads:

> First of January, nineteen fifty-nine. Old Havana. Cuba. I do not remember the time I left home or the noises in the street, whether it was raining or there was a clear sky, nor the mood I was in. I do not even remember if I knew at that time what had happened a few hours earlier, at midnight: the dictator Fulgencio Batista had fled with his family and closest associates leaving a temporary vacuum—lungs without air, heart without blood—in Cuba, the reaction of the rebels in Oriente and Santa Clara, the people's explosion of joy. I suspect it was walking around Old Havana, on my way to the boats at Casa Blanca, that I started finding out about what had happened, what was happening at that time, the avalanche of events which were going to affect us over the following hours. The first page of a new history—capable of burying under its weight the equivalent of a hundred of the one which had just died—was being improvised. I am sure that many of the faces on the Casa Blanca docks looked like question marks, with uncertainty and even fear in their round eyes.[1]

Javier Arzuaga was the parish priest at Casa Blanca, the district of Havana at the feet of La Cabaña military fortress. He had acted as chaplain at La Cabaña Prison during the first months of 1959, up to the first week of June. He used to visit the prison yard every day and, from the early morning of January 29 onward, witnessed "the gallery of death." He was a Franciscan friar, and he accompanied fifty-five people sentenced to

---

1. Arzuaga, *La galera de la muerte*, 17.

death by firing squad. The last Basque Franciscan we spoke with in Cuba, Pedro Ángel García Chasco, says that most of the brothers only carried out pastoral work. Others, a smaller number, got involved in the work of building a new society and a new Cuba. Some of them did so as part of university movements. Others took refuge in different houses that the Franciscan order ran for people persecuted by the authorities. Some, who went even further, hid arms temporarily in San Antonio de Miramar in Havana, or acted as couriers between the revolutionaries in the Sierra and the cities in Oriente when there were baptisms or Mass in the villages in the mountains. Some friars also intervened to try to stop some of the people arrested for being involved with the revolution from being executed. Others were involved in the singular process of change promoted on the pages of *La Quincena,* a magazine edited by the Franciscans.

La Quincena was the third transformation of the magazine that the Franciscans had published since 1910. Their first publication was *San Antonio* (1910–1938), followed by *Semanario Católico* (1938–1955), and, finally, *La Quincena* (1955–1961). Their involvement in Cuban society was based on the slogan "A Christian response to today's problems."

This desire to give a Christian answer to daily problems led to all the copies of two of the 1958 editions being thrown into the sea, as well as the removal of the section *Quince días en la nación* (A fortnight in the nation), that was followed by *Quince días en el mundo* (A fortnight in the world) during the periods of "state of suspension of constitutional guarantees."

La Quincena can been regarded as the Franciscans' official voice on the island. The publication affected Franciscan opinions throughout Cantabria province[2] and beyond. The magazine was edited by Father Ignacio Biain.

The Triumph of the Revolution in *La Quincena*

The Franciscans brought out a double issue of *La Quincena* about the revolution. A close-up photograph of Fidel Castro takes up the whole cover. There are 112 interior pages and around 30 articles.

> Page 1 shows Fidel Castro's entry into Havana in a jeep. Under the photo there is a short text in two columns stating that "The revolution's victory over Batista's dictatorship culminated with Fidel Castro and his troops' triumphal entry." And, at the end of the text, the following congratulation: "*La Quincena* joins with the Cuban people in their joy and offers its collaboration to make Liberty triumph over tyranny once and for all, justice over fraud and crime, Peace over fear, Christian charity over hate and the lack of love."

---

2. Since 2002 the Franciscan province of Cantabria has been one with that of Arantzazu, and the friars on the island of Cuba were under its jurisdiction. The Franciscan province included not only Franciscan convents and friars' houses but also groups of people under the care of junior friars, Poor Clares nuns, Franciscan youth, the Third Order Regular of St. Francis of Penancem Franciscan children, and all of their churches.

On page 3 there is an article by Fernando Díaz de la Rionda under the title "The night is left behind," in which he describes Batista: "Arrogant, conceited satyr who, to satisfy his devilish vanity did not hesitate to bomb and flood with innocent blood his own country and who now flees like a coward."

Between pages 4 and 8 there is a long interview with Franciscan father Lucas Iruretagoyena. Its title: "The 'bearded' friar who was taken to the mountains by a cyclone." In the interview the idea that the revolution had been based on Communist ideas is denied. There are also photographs of the interviewee and a copy of Jesuit father Ángel Rivas's appointment and that of Lucas Iruretagoyena as chaplains of the Revolutionary Army, signed by Raúl Castro and with the stamp of the Second Eastern Front.

Page 8. Article by the Jesuit father Ángel Rivas, "With the Rebel Army," explaining the values and events that took him into the mountains.

Pages 10 to 16. "Catholics in the triumphant revolution," an article by Manuel Fernández about Catholic militants' and priests' part in the years of struggle against Batista. It includes various texts and a list of the casualties as well as Catholics' role at the front and in the rearguard. The text starts by stating that "In all Hispanic America there may not be a case of such a committed Catholic collaboration with a revolutionary movement as that in Cuba in the fight against Batista's dictatorship." The extended article has various different subtitles and sections. The last section says that "we must underline reverend father Ignacio Biain OFM's unending work to maintain *La Quincena* as an ideological trench in opposition to tyranny. If you leaf through the magazine since it was first published with its current name, you will find things which it is incredible to think were published under the worst conditions of oppression."

Page 20. "The Revolution and Charity," a testimonial article by Father Hilario Chaurrondo—and with photographs secretly taken by Father Ángel Gaztelu during their mission to the prison on the Isla de Pinos—about the Daughters of Charity of Saint Vincent de Paul on the Isla de Pinos with the prisoners and their families during the years in which the Castro brothers and other combatants from Moncada were serving their sentences there.

Page 31. "Censorship on the press," an article by Father Mariano Errasti celebrating the end of censorship tells us about the reality and the repression to which *La Quincena* was subjected during Batista's regime:

> Until March 1958 *La Quincena* was watched over in a relatively benign way. It was able to skillfully avoid the red pencil by being

ambiguous, for example by condemning the French army's torture of the Algerian rebels so that attentive readers could realize that we were condemning the brutal methods used by the Batista police .

In March 1958, one of our editions was confiscated. But the bloodiest blow was received in July that year when the edition for the first half of the month was taken and destroyed; not even Havana's cardinal secretary's intervention was able to prevent that from happening. In that martyred edition we told certain home truths about the tension of war and the atmosphere of terror in the country. A specific censor was appointed for the magazine and, as punishment, the following edition, which was completely "uncensorable," was held back for some time . . .

La Quincena, continually mutilated by censorship, had to refrain from any comment that referred to Cuba's problems. We filled various pages with stories about space travel and articles about medicine and psychoanalysis . . . The censors removed sentences, articles, headlines and even, on one occasion, ordered the type used to be changed in order for certain statistics not to stand out . . .

Page 33. On the following pages, under the headline "About tyranicide. ¿What happened on the Thirteenth of March . . ." mentioned the assault on the presidential palace on March 13, 1957.

Pages 34–35. M. Azcoaga, Father Mariano Errasti's pseudonym, appeared beneath the short article "The Strangest Warriors in the World." Just a few words accompany the five really curious photos. In one there is a bearded man with four rosaries, eight medallions, a relic . . . In another, there are four bearded men kneeling for communion in front of Father José Luis Sarrigoitia and Brother Father Simón Larrañaga. The caption is telling: "The 'bandits' and 'communists' which Batista propaganda talks about are extremely sincere Christians, as devout as children. Here are four heroes kneeling down before the God of Victories at Manzanillo parish church.

Pages 41–43 and 72. "My Experiences in the La Cabaña prisons," report by Father Javier Arzuaga.

Page 44. The article by Father Luis Zabala, "The Fatherland Redeemed," recounts waking up after a terrible nightmare about Batista tortures and crimes.

The days after the fall of the tyrant were days of exaltation and jubilation, genuine collective elation. It was as if we had suddenly woken up from a terrible nightmare. The ominous circumstances had so oppressed the soul of the people, the terror had been so intense and worrisome, the infamy and blood had covered over people's sensibility, without ever really getting comfortable with the daily record of crimes, torture, imprisonments and all types of humiliations we were so used to them that the sudden and radical transition from the darkness to light we felt blinded, suspended in a pure daze, hardly daring to believe the miracle which, despite having been long awaited and hoped for, took us by surprise.[3]

Page 45. Father Moyua (the usual pseudonym of the magazine's editor, Ignacio Biain) wrote a column headed "In a Few Words" about revolutionary justice: "When the world knows about the terrible things which have been happening in Cuba over the last six years, executing a few hundred guilty men will seem like a benign punishment. Until present nobody in the capital has been shot and there are around 600 men in prison. In Santiago all the men executed belonged to the defeated army, the police and Dr. Masferrer's sadly infamous private army. No civilians or politicians have been shot."

Pages 46–47. Rodolfo Riesgo, accompanied with photographs, deals with the most gruesome tortures and murders perpetrated by the tyranny.

Pages 48–51 and 61. Father Ignacio Biain, signed the editorial titled "Balance of Marxism and the Destinations of a Revolution." In it, Biain goes over the regime's disasters since Fulgencio Batista's coup d'état on March 10, 1952. He argues that "the social doctrine of the Fidel revolution can easily be placed in the context of Social Christianity."

> It is the decisive, only time for making such urgent social reforms. If the revolution does not succeed in this area, we will see rampant Communism take advantage of the vacuum left by the revolution . . . Let us give them that social justice and Communism will be unnecessary . . . We cannot live in this state of revolutionary fervor every day, in the mystic exaltation of recent days. We have to return to the everyday rhythm, the slow duty of every hour . . . This is the most difficult moment of the revolution, the time to restructure the institutions . . . the time to replace the battle front with the urban front . . . We Catholics cannot remain in the rearguard, waiting for mistakes as an excuse to bite and criticize. The correct guidance of the terrestrial order is a previous condition for a Christian society . . . Everything except for egoistical reserve with regards to the revolution's various possible directions.[4]

---

3. *La Quincena*, year 5, 1-2 (January 1959), 42.
4. Ibid., 49.

Pages 56, 57. This is followed by an entertainment page written by M. Azcoaga (Mariano Errasti): "Callen cartas y hablen barbas."

Pages 58, 59, and 62. The *15 días en el mundo* section includes photo taken by Xavier (Estanislao Sudupe), mostly about events in Cuba as seen from abroad and in defense of the revolution: "The guns of international journalism point toward two objectives: the 'blood baths' and summary executions . . . Christian moral principles and the legal system do not object, at least in principle, to the use of capital punishment."

There are many more articles, a great number of which are of a similar type and others of which are specifically religious, along with advertizements in the 112 pages of this extraordinary edition of *La Quincena*.

The Franciscan magazine celebrated the victory of the revolution over Batista's dictatorship from the first moment. Very soon, however, the firing squads were set up and that cooled the enthusiasm of some of the most enthusiastic brothers. Father Javier Arzuaga, chaplain at La Cabaña and mentioned above, witnessed them. Father Arzuaga talks about fifty-five executions by firing squad at La Cabaña fortress during the first five months of 1959. He brought accounts of what he had seen into the convent in Old Havana. *La Quincena* was to talk about more than two hundred people condemned to death in Santiago before January 13. Prisoners at different prisons on the island were sent to the wall, which created a cruel atmosphere far-removed from the charity which the Franciscans preached from the pages of *La Quincena*. The public cries of "Shoot them, shoot them!" made the Franciscans increasingly uncomfortable about the deteriorating situation.

Agrarian Reform in La Quincena

In April, Rodolfo Riesgo wrote in *La Quincena* about his opposition to US pressure to prevent agrarian reform in Cuba. In particular, he dealt with the US senate's agreement to suspend aid to any country that confiscated US property. Likewise, the editorial staff criticized the United States and its media, which were accusing the Cuban regime of Communism.

There is no doubt that agrarian reform was one of the most important measures adopted by the revolution during its first phase. The First Law of Agrarian Reform (May 17, 1959) confiscated all properties of more than four hundred hectares to give them to Cuban peasant smallholders. While there were few Basques among those benefited by the measure, several Basque families did lose property as a result of it.

La Quincena supported the First Law of Agrarian Reform, although it also set out the inherent dangers in applying such drastic legislation. For example, there was the long editorial in *La Quincena* "El espíritu de la reforma agraria" (The Spirit of the Agrarian Reform)[5] in June 1959 with the following footnote: "Passed by Mons. Evelio Díaz for publication." The editorial justifies this state intervention "as a transitory measure."

On July 26, 1959, there was a large gathering of peasants in Havana. *La Quincena*, in its section "Quince días en la nación," published Rodolfo Riesgo's reflections on the subject.

> The sight of 500,000 peasants wearing their traditional "guayabera" shirts and straw hats, gathering in response to the Triumphant Revolution's call to support the Agrarian Reform, was the definitive support for this fair measure.
>
> On July 26, 1959, with the same faith in the future, the same conviction about the ideals of freedom, recovery, justice and integral humanism, 500,000 peasants were the leaders at the start of the most splendid social, economic and human revolution on our continent.[6]

By July the Cuban revolutionaries had already tried to enter other countries to carry on fighting to liberate "brother nations," as *La Quincena* describes them, and which, after praising the revolution's achievements, gives those who want to export the revolution to other countries a warning.

> Foreigners who visit Cuba have to think that public order in Cuba is wonderful. This order cannot be found lacking at any moment, not even during the first days of the revolution. At the moment, it is as perfect as any politician could wish. The public demonstrations—of which there are many, and very well attended—have been orderly and correct, without any looting, thievery, or murders. The revolutionary government has scrupulously respected the human dignity of those who were so recently its enemies . . .
>
> The international scandal about the executions—between 500 and 600 in total—was caused by a lack of knowledge of the Cuban situation and, furthermore, there was a radical change in Cuba in this respect . . .
>
> There is a sensitive issue with regards to the revolution: its international facet.
>
> We are referring to the Cuban revolutionaries who have set out on an adventure to recover the dignity trampled on by the neighboring dictators, and who are interfering in problems which are not their own. Much as we would like all dictatorship in America to disappear, we think it would have been better for these groups to have remained here to consolidate our revolution, perhaps waiting for a more opportune moment. The revolution is going through its most difficult period, consolidating itself against innumerable domestic and foreign enemies and it does not need difficulties of this type.[7]

---

5. *La Quincena*, year 5, 11, (June 1959), 30–32.
6. Rodolfo Riesgo, "La reforma agraria," *La Quincena*, year 5, 13, (July 1959), 29.
7. Ibid., 31–32.

The National Catholic Congress

The National Catholic Congress began on November 27, 1959 with opinions and perhaps positions divided in terms of the ideology and ideas being adopted by the revolutionary government. Perhaps for that reason, a multitude of people came to the congress from the center of the island, filling up Catholic schools and houses in Havana. The congress finished on the night of November 28 and there was an enormous gathering of people in spite of the rain. The warmth of the meeting later caused Mons. Pérez Serantes to conclude, in a subsequent pastoral address: "We want a Catholic Cuba."

The image of the Virgin of Charity had been flown into Havana from her sanctuary at Cobre in Oriente province. Given that many people might see the large crowd as a challenge to some of the government's measures, Fidel Castro made an appearance at the Plaza Cívica, where he was acclaimed by the multitude, doubtless because many of them took Fidel's appearance to express his support for Cuban Catholicism.

Javier Arzuaga tells us about that night, at which he was present:

> At almost midnight, when the act was about to start, Fidel Castro, accompanied by some of his commanders—Juan Almeida and Víctor Bordón Machado, among others—came onto the stage-altar, where, a few moments earlier, the image of the Virgin of Charity— Cuba's protectoress—had been placed.
>
> The commander-in-chief—owner of Cuban lives and properties by this time—was not invited to take a distinguished place on the stage. He would have loved to steal the show from no less than Cachita, the Virgin of Cobre. I saw them and went down to greet them. The crowd's shouts of "Charity! Charity! Charity!" crushed the night and the square. They also made it difficult for me to talk with Fidel and his people. The comandante shook his head up and down and from left to right, his cap pulled over his eyes, his jaw wanting to eat his upper lip, extremely nervous, as if he were swimming in a sea of threats and trying, in a panic, to escape them. It looked as if he were about to explode. And so he did, and he started shouting: "What charity is that? And when is it going to be justice's turn?" He wasn't asking me: it was a rhetorical outburst in the style of Cicero. ("*¿Quousque tandem, Catilina, abuteris patientia nostra?*"). But I answered his question. "Comandante, there can be no charity without justice, that's true, but remember that where there is not charity there can never be justice either." Almeida butted in and asked me to leave, not to get in the way.

On May 7, 1959, Father José María Layuno wrote in his diary:

> I see that we friars are divided about the revolution. And the people are too.
>
> Were we right or not? I don't know. Those of us who supported the revolution had their reasons. It was the revolution of the humble. We

Catholics were not wise during that revolution. We wanted to "get our bit." And our contribution should have been humble, sincere, profound service. But we preferred to use everything to our advantage. I believe that was a mistake.[8]

1960, the Confrontation

At the end of 1959 the Spanish clergy issued a declaration in defense of the Franco regime and against Father Iñaki Aspiazu,[9] a Basque Jesuit priest who lived in Argentina at the time and had given a series of conferences revealing the oppression that the dictator Franco was carrying out in Spain. The senior clergy in Havana, most of whom were Spaniards, had been summoned to sign the declaration. Xavier (Estanislao Sudupe), in *La Quincena* in January 1960, wrote in defense of Father Iñaki Aspiazu.

In February, 1960, *La Quincena* published an article by Father José Luis Albizu—who signed as Vasco de Barra, as on his articles in *Diario de la Marina*—which was titled "La expansión de la URSS en Havana y la realidad soviética" (The Expansion of the USSR in Havana and Soviet Reality) in which he talked about "concentration camps with 15 or 20 million guinea pigs in them."

From May 10 to 12, 1960, the senior Cuban newspaper, *El Diario de la Marina,* was attacked at night by a dozen armed men who broke windows, pillaged the premises, and destroyed printing presses. Father Biain wrote an article titled "El Diario de la Marina" in which he gave his opinion about the attack and the paper's closure: "The hundred-year-old *Diario de la Marina* was attacked by journalists and graphics workers. We confirm this event and also express our revulsion over it: it was not Pharisaical but very sincere . . . I believe that the attack on *Diario* has harmed the revolution."[10] This newspaper's disappearance is not an isolated event and, during September, fifteen national Catholic organizations would sign a letter of protest about the removal from the airwaves of two hours of Catholic radio and television.

In a July issue, on the cover, there is an article titled "Catolicismo y comunismo frente a frente" (Catholicism and Communism Face to Face). It examines the Christian idea of man, society, and the world and also explains Communist methods for infiltrating countries, "which are highly revealing."[11] The attacks on the clergy this year will receive a lot of pop-

---

8. Layuno, Experiencias de un misionero, 289.

9. Father Iñaki Aspiazu was a Basque Catholic priest who escaped from a Franco prison during the Spanish Civil War and, following his bishop's advice, took refugee in Argentina. Leo Huberman and Paul M. Sweezy in their book *Cuba, anatomía de una revolución* (Cuba, anatomy of a revolution) (Buenos Aires: Palestra, 1961), 102, include an article written by Father Aspiazu titled "Justicia Revolucionaria" (Revolutionary justice) written on February 8, 1960, in which he says that to understand the revolution it has to be seen from within the island, not from abroad.

10. Padre Ignacio Biain, "El diario de la Marina," *La Quincena*, year 6, 12 (July 1960).

11. *La Quincena*, year 6, (July 1969), 1.

ular support and will focus, among other things, on Catholic centers of education and, in particular, the Catholic University of Villanueva. On November 27, 1960, Fidel justified the war against the Catholic colleges by saying that the counterrevolution had taken refuge in private schools and in the University of Villanueva.

Declaration of War: The Bishops' Pastoral

As García Chasco states, two documents were to set the tone during 1960. In May, Monsignor Pérez Serantes's pastoral against communism and, on August 7, the Cuban Bishoprics' Collective Circular, which was signed by all the bishops and concluded with these words:

> So remember our children and tell all Cuba in a loud voice that the Church has nothing to fear from profound social reforms as long as they are based on justice and charity, because the Church seeks the people's well-being and celebrates it but, precisely because of that, because it loves the people and wants its well being, it can do no less than condemn Communist doctrines. The Church is and always will be in favor of the humble, but it does not agree and never will agree with Communism.
>
> So nobody should ask Catholics—in the name of a misunderstanding of citizens' union—to silence their opposition to these doctrines, because we could not do so without betraying our fundamental principles. The majority of the Cuban people is opposed to materialist, atheist Communism, and could only be led into a Communist regime by deceit or coercion. May the Most Holy Virgin of Charity never allow this to happen in Cuba.[12]

In the August 31, 1960, issue of *La Quincena,* in its section "Nuestros lectores opinan" (Our readers Give Their Opinions) there is support and congratulations for the article, but also opposing opinions. The editorial staff of *La Quincena* also accuses those who have tried to divide Christians with regard to the bishops' collective pastoral: "Some people have prevented it from being read in churches or have stood at church doors pressuring and insulting." *La Quincena* published the entire pastoral and commented on the points in which the Church expresses its support for social reforms. Finally, the Franciscan magazine expressed its fear of what it calls anti-Cuban and antihuman things which have been included in the revolutionary ideals.

Luis Zabala, a member of the editorial staff, wrote an article in 1962 titled "La persecución religiosa en Cuba" (Religious Persecution in Cuba) about Fidel Castro's reaction to the pastoral. The subtitle is eloquent: "La declaración de guerra" (Declaration of War):

> Fidel Castro gave an explosive speech about the publication of the pastoral in which he threatened: "We give the bishops time to retract

---

12. García Chasco, *Franciscanos en la Cuba de Fidel*, vol. 1., unpublished manuscript, 39.

what they have said in their Letter. Otherwise, they will have to face the consequences." Naturally, there was no such retraction. To the contrary, a few weeks later the bishops published another letter in which they said that the prime minister had avoided answering their position and in which they defended the vilified clergy.

Meanwhile, the campaign of insults and attacks against the Church was still incandescent . . . in the context of the general collapse of the press, *La Quincena* had survived, having shortly earlier abandoned all uncertainty and disorientation about the revolution's mistaken and disastrous ways and having adopted a homogeneous line of opposition to the regime; following the collective pastoral, this critical posture became even more accentuated and became—amidst the general silence—the brave, determined and energetic voice of Catholicism.[13]

The situation did not improve and the government-Church relationship grew increasingly tense, positions being more and more in conflict with each other and with no signs of any possible agreement.

The Survival of *La Quincena*

The magazine published a short note in its August issue: "Clarification: The bishop of Pinar and Father Biain have reached an agreement, with the head of the order's approval, for Father Biain to do missionary work in Pinar and also to prepare a radio program about Christian doctrine and Catholic social doctrine which will soon be broadcast," and in November Father Mariano Errasti is listed as the editor of *La Quincena*, which led to some readers protesting in "Nuestros lectores opinan." One reader stops subscribing to the magazine "because you have silenced Father Biain and sent him to Pinar." Many readers do not believe that the change of editor at the magazine has been the result of an agreement.[14] For example, in October 1960, a group of women attacked the magazine for "the antirevolutionary campaign it has been running since Father Biain left the editorial board."

In short, the country was in a difficult situation at the end of 1960. The exiles, helped by the United States, were preparing for a war against Fidel Castro's regime. Father Biain wrote in *La Quincena* about the evils of a possible war, saying it would be terrible for the people of Cuba. Permits to travel abroad also became harder to get. According to *La Quincena*, in October, "several conditions have been imposed for any citizen who wishes to travel abroad."

---

13. Luis Zabala, "La persecución Religiosa en Cuba," *Cantabria Franciscana* 17 (1962): 22.
14. García Chasco states that "after half a century, we, too, have trouble believing it, knowing that Father Biain, who passed away in Cuba in 1963, used to reply to those who said to him that he had been completely taken in during those key years or told him 'this is Communism': 'So what?'"

The Last Issues in 1961

La Quincena did not publish either of its numbers for January 1961 "for various circumstances," according to those in charge of it. The first issue published that year was on February 15, with a portrait of Martí taking up the whole cover. On the first page, the editorial staff of *La Quincena* apologized for not turning up at its fortnightly meeting with the readers.

> Various circumstances and, in particular, repair work being done in the print shop at which *La Quincena* was printed made it impossible to print the two January issues. We trust that our readers and advertizers will value the reasons behind these shortcomings as fits: they were beyond our control.

If those in charge of the magazine in Cuba avoided making any public comment, the answer to what had happened came from the head of the Franciscans in Cuba, their provincial representative, Father José Agustín Mendizábal, in a letter sent on January 21, 1961, to his superior, the provincial minister of Donostia-San Sebastián:

> On December 3 a group of 35 women soldiers—not militia members—came to us with the order to occupy the terraced roof of the church and they settled in there, also making use of the stairs beside the sacristy, the whole landing and adjacent bathroom. From the 4th they stood sentry at the gates of the convent and at the church door on Cuba Street; the entrance from Amargura had been bricked up for some time . . . On some days there were up to 50 young women in the convent. Their presence forced us, or made it seem wise, not to do any work on the large press—the noise it makes can be heard all over the house—in case they got curious and decided to inspect it and, so, give them an opportunity to take some decision about the magazine. The next issue, which will be on February 15, will have 30,000 copies: there is an enormous demand for it.

This issue of the magazine focuses on Martí, which an extensive supplement titled "Was Martí a Communist?" by Alex Ferrán, as well as Monsignor Eduardo Boza Masvidal's article "The Homeland Martí Dreamed Of." In another section, Monsignor Boza Masvidal publishes a note titled "Terrorism and the Death Penalty" and objects to them both.

Another of the strong men and habitual collaborators of the magazine, Rodolfo Riesgo, lists a series of events which are taking place in his section *15 días en la Nación*: political crimes are the cause for being laid off; salary freezes; the continual "voluntary collections"; the suppression of the Minimum Salaries Commission; work being paid for with tokens which can only be used in the so-called People's Shops; the need to join the PSP in order to find work; the need to join the Young Rebels Association in order to access improvement courses, and so on.

Monsignor Pérez Serantes's pastoral denouncing outrages against churches and priests and reporting on the general malaise among the working classes "only lessened by the faith which they had had in the revolution of January 1, 1959, and by the tension about the foreign aggression against our homeland which has been announced."

In his *15 días de televisión* section, G. García Valencia tells us how—since January 3, this year, 1961—"using the excuse of the official government news of a soon-to-happen invasion, the 'Great Chain of Liberty' has been set up." From then onward the same news will be broadcast on almost all channels and, later, all programing will be unified. "The state is expected to take complete control . . . We do not agree with the idea—as we have said on other occasions—that being a state company and the state's opinion means that the people are giving their opinion."

The February 15 issue of the magazine reports on the Church's struggle with the state and the magazine's head-on opposition to the government. In fact, the March 31 issue also came out, the second of the year.

Father Mariano Errasti, who had been editor of *La Quincena* for six months, states they they printed another issue, for April, which was when Playa Girón was invaded and there was a large-scale arrest of friars, who were locked up in their places of residence or other places around the island. This created an atmosphere of terror, making bringing out another issue unthinkable. It was dangerous to even keep the thousands of copies printed at Aguiar convent in Old Havana. Mariano Errasti was to say years later that "It was an enormous job to guillotine the copies into shreds one-by-one as the print-run had risen to several thousand, around 30,000."[15]

The magazine management was forced to get rid of all the copies of *La Quincena* which had been published until then.

That was how the Franciscan publication—which had been set up in 1910 with the name *San Antonio de Padua*, later being called *Semanario Católico* and, in its last seven years of life *La Quincena*—came to an end.

The presence and involvement of some priests—especially Spaniards—in the failed attempt to invade the island at Playa Girón gave Fidel even more excuses for dismantling churches and Church institutions. Members of religious orders, priests, and committed members of the Church were subjected to home arrest or imprisoned. The hundred odd Franciscans living on the island were controlled and their parish homes, convents, and residences were systematically attacked. Father José A. Mendizábal, the Franciscans' provincial representative in Cuba, described the situation:

> Everything started unexpectedly. It was the day the disaster started, in which the horror and violence exploded. More than 500,000 people on the island were detained those days and locked in the most un-

---

15. García Chasco states that the number of subscribers to the magazine had increased sharply during 1960, partly because it was the only publication which dared to express opinions opposed to the revolution and, also, because many Cubans had got closer to religion, the immense majority of them having been harmed by the measures taken by the government and its various institutions.

likely places; it was all frenetic and hysterical. It was also the day they broke into and searched all the churches and convents on the island, with greater or lesser degrees of hostility and sadism depending on each group leader.[16]

It was the beginning of the end and led to all members of religious orders being expelled from the island. The handful of them who stayed in Cuba could no longer continue to carry out any of their usual, daily activities. The convents were closed. March 1961 saw the end of *La Quincena* and the Franciscan religious community on the island—131 people—was expelled six months later, in September.

Bibliography

Amores, Juan B. *Cuba y España, 1868–1898: El final de un sueño.* Iruñea-Pamplona: Eunsa, 1998.

Arzuaga, Javier; *Biografía de un sueño.* Santo Domingo: Impresora Carlos, 1998.

———. *La galera de la muerte: Cuba, 1959.* Puerto Rico: Carta de Cuba, 2006.

Arrozarena, Cecilia. *El roble y la ceiba: Historia de los vascos en Cuba.* Tafalla: Txalaparta, 2003.

Barandiaran, A. "Uste zuten ni nintzela Castroren kapilaua." *Berria, Igandea* supplement, July 13, 2008, 12–13

Cantabria Franciscana. Volume 17, 1962.

Céspedes, Carlos Manuel de. *Pasión por Cuba y por la Iglesia: Aproximación biográfica al padre Félix Varela.* Madrid: BAC, 1998.

Elustondo, Miel A.; "Javier Arzuaga: Che justizia-egilea ezagutu nuen, edonor hiltzeko gauza zena," *Argia,* November 2010, 11–14.

———. "Javier Arzuaga: Cheren kapilaua izan nintzen, baina inori ez diot esperientzia opa." *Berria, Igandea* supplement, February 2010, 10–11

———. "Che Guevararen kapilauaren pausoan." *Berria, Igandea* supplement, June 2011, 8–9.

García Chasco, Pedro A. *Del bello sueño a la tiranía: Franciscanos en la Cuba de Fidel.* First volume. Unpublished manuscript.

Huberman, Leo y Paul M. Sweezy. *Cuba, anatomía de una revolución.* Buenos Aires: Palestra, 1961.

Intxausti, Joseba. "XX. mendeko euskal frantziskotarrak. Historialari hasi berrientzako ohar batzuk." In *Gogoz, hitzez eta egitez: Pello Huiziri eskainitako lanak,* edited by Kepa Korta and Jesus Mari Larrazabal, 211–49. Leioa: University of the Basque Country, 1961.

Larrúa Guedes, Salvador. *Cinco siglos de evangelización franciscana en*

---

16. Mariano Erraste; "La Comisaría Franciscana de Cuba bajo la persecución Fidelista," *Cantabria Franciscana,* vol. 17 (1962): 8. This is undoubtedly the most complete document about the events which took place in 1961. In his report, Father Mariano Errasti looks at each Franciscan house on the island from the invasion in April until the last expulsions in September, basing himself on information given by the members of each brotherhood.

Cuba. Volumen II, 1887–1998. Puerto Rico: No publisher, 2004.

———. *Grandes figuras y sucesos de la Orden Franciscana en Cuba.* Puerto Rico: No publisher, 2006.

Layuno, José María. *Experiencias de un misionero.* Burgos: Monte Carmelo, 2001.

Moradellos, Enrique. *El oficio de historiador.* Madrid: Siglo XXI, 2008.

La Quincena, 1959–1961.

Pérez-Stable, Marifeli. *La Revolución Cubana: Orígenes, desarrollo y legado.* Havana: Colibrí, 1998.

Thompson, Paul. *The Voice of the Past: Oral History.* Oxford: Oxford University Press, 1935.

19

Hemingway and the Basques
Edorta Jiménez

Ernest Miller Hemingway was born in 1899. His father was a doctor and he was the second of six brothers. They lived in Oak Park, a suburb of Chicago. He died in 1961 in Ketchum, Idaho after a self-inflicted wound. In 1954 he was awarded the Nobel Prize for literature thanks to the success of his short novel *The Old Man and the Sea*. The reason I started to read Hemingway's work has a lot to do with that book. I am from Mundaka, a small town on the coast of the Basque Country in which everybody knows everyone else, so when I found out that a fellow townsman, Father Andrés, had been a close friend of the writer's, I started to research their relationship. On doing so, I found out that Ernest Hemingway had several other Basque friends as well as Don Andrés. As a result of my research, I wrote a book in Basque telling the life stories of Hemingway's Basque friends and their relationship with him. The original Basque title is *Hemingway eta euskaldunak zerbitzu sekretuetan* (Hemingway and the Basques in the secret service). Although the book has more than five hundred pages, I will try to summarize some parts of it and, at the end of this text, I will also try to give my opinion about the relationship between Hemingway and the Basque Country and its people. But, before proceeding, we need to ask, which Basque Country do we mean when we talk about Hemingway's?

Discovering the Country

In 1917 Hemingway started to work as a reporter on the newspaper *Kansas City Star*. The following year, he was a volunteer ambulance driver at the front in Italy, where he was seriously wounded and also decorated twice for services rendered. He went back to the United States in 1919 and married in 1921. In 1922 he was sent to report on the Greco-Turkish War and, after two years, decided to give up journalism and write fiction. He settled in Paris and renewed his friendship with other ex-patriot Americans such as Ezra Pound and Gertrude Stein.

This summary of the first years of Hemingway's life has been taken from the "About the Author" of one of his books.[1] It positions us at the start of this narrative as it was during these years in Paris that he visited the Basque Country for the first time. He went to Iruñea-Pamplona via Hendaia, a French-Basque town on the Franco-Spanish border. That was in 1923. Some years later, he published *The Sun Also Rises*, the novel that led to his becoming famous.

In that novel, the Basque Country is not just the setting, it is perhaps also something more, so I will not discuss the book in itself but rather the protagonist Jake's perception of the country.

The narrator says Jake tells the reader that after leaving Baiona he finds himself in a special place, which is perhaps exotic or simply different, but definitely special.

> We passed some lovely gardens and had a good look back at the town [Baiona], and then we were out in the country, green and rolling, and the road climbing all the time. We passed lots of Basques with oxen, or cattle, hauling carts along the road, and nice farmhouses, low roofs, and all white-plastered. In the Basque country the land all looks very rich and green and the houses and villages look well-off and clean. Every village had a pelota court and on some of them kids were playing in the hot sun. There were signs on the walls of the churches saying it was forbidden to play pelota against them, and the houses in the villages had red tiled roofs, and then the roads turned off and commenced to climb and we were going way up close along a hillside, with a valley below and hills stretched off back toward the sea. You couldn't see the sea. It was too far away. You could only see hills and more hills, and you knew where the sea was.
>
> We crossed the Spanish frontier.[2]

Ernest Hemingway was aware that although he was in France the country he was traveling through was really part of the Basque Country and, on getting there, you reached the frontier with Spain. However, this borderland was not the real Spain. Real Spain lay farther beyond the frontier.

In *The Sun Also Rises*, Jake travels in a taxi through the mountains to Iruñea-Pamplona. "For a while the country was much as it had been; then, climbing all the time, we crossed the top of a Col, the road winding back and forth on itself, and then it was really Spain. There were long brown

---

1. Hemingway, *The Garden of Eden*, 248.
2. Hemingway, *The Sun Also Rises*, 74.

mountains and a few pines and far-off forest of beech trees on some of the mountainsides."[3]

And then there was Iruñea-Pamplona, with what would become one of Ernest's favorite hangout, the Café Iruña, the city's famous café—and then the town of Burguete. The narrator goes to Burguete by bus and the passengers are Basques.

> A Basque with a big leather wine-bag in his lap lay across the top of the bus in front of our seat, leaning back against our legs. He offered the wine skin to Bill and to me, and when I tipped it up to drink he imitated the sound of a Klaxon motor-horn so well and so suddenly that I spilled some of the wine and everybody laughed. He apologized and made me take another drink."[4]

After a day of trout fishing near Burguete, we're in Iruñea-Pamplona again, "Basque and Navarrais dancers and singers, and afterward the Val Carlos dancers in their costumes danced down the street in the rain."[5]

So for Hemingway, or for his alter-ego Jake, the narrator of the novel, the people there are Basques or Navarrese, or both. This is important because it reflects Hemingway's perception of the country, which was similar to everybody's at the time. As some of you will know, the national identity of Navarra—we should bear in mind that Lower Navarre is on the French side of the border—is one of the main issues in current politics.

The people in the novel speak in Spanish, but at that time the language spoken in the north of Navarra was Basque. However, Hemingway says nothing about the Basque language. Nobody speaks in Basque in the novel. However, it is possible that the only difference between those Basque and Navarrese singers was the language in which they sang. The famous Navarrese *jota* was only sung in Spanish until a few years ago (now it is also performed in Basque). But what did Hemingway know about Basque?

We know that during his years in Paris Hemingway tried to learn Italian, French, and Spanish as he moved around, meeting all sorts of people and speaking with them. We know that he bought grammar books of various languages, including a Basque one. Which book was it? I do not know its title but I do know that it is in the Hemmingway Collection of the JFK Library in Boston. This means that Ernest was aware that the Basque language existed and had some interest in it.

One curious detail is that both Brett and Mike wear Basque berets in the novel. And, after his years in Paris, Ernest Hemingway used to wear a beret and typical Basque footwear.

In short, we can say that Hemingway saw Navarra—the Navarra in the novel—as part of the Basque Country. But was Iruñea-Pamplona part of real Spain or not? This is a very good question. I do not think he paid attention to this historical issue; simply describing Iruñea-Pamplona's at-

---

3. Ibid., 75.
4. Ibid., 83.
5. Ibid., 136.

mosphere as perceived in their present by him without taking into account any characters.

At the end of the novel, the narrator is in Donostia-San Sebastián, at the other end of the Basque seacoast and there he did feel he was in real Spain, although he writes: "There was a bicycle-race on, the Tour de Pays Basque, and the riders were stopping that night in San Sebastian."[6]

It seems that Ernest Hemingway did not have very clear ideas about territories and frontiers.

After publishing *The Sun Also Rises*, Ernest Hemingway kept on traveling to Paris, the Basque Country, and Spain almost every summer, until the Spanish Civil War broke out and everything changed.

Civil War and Exile

In July 1936 a group of generals and officers, some groups of Fascists, other right-wing parties and most of the Roman Catholic Church started a long civil war. After three years of blood and tears, the rebel band—which was aided by Hitler and Mussolini—won the war. From the outbreak, Ernest Hemingway was on the side of the legitimate republic, usually called the republican band. In fact, at the end of the day Ernest Hemingway was one of the exiles. The US expatriate became another Spanish exile. Spain had become his second country and he would not be able to return there for a long time.

Paradoxically, many of Ernest Hemingway's friends were with the rebels, supporting Fascism. Almost all of his esteemed bullfighters were with them.

And then Ernest Hemingway, the eternal expatriate, decided to live in Cuba, another Spanish-speaking country, near Florida. He had known it for years through fishing, but what led him to settle in Cuba was his exile from Spain. So in 1940 he bought Finca Vigía. Before buying the estate he wrote *For Whom the Bell Tolls* at the Hotel Ambos Mundos in Cuba. *For Whom the Bell Tolls* is set in the Spanish Civil War just before the fall of Bilbao.

Hemingway met several Basques in Cuba. Curiously, some of them were political exiles like him. Others were jai alai or pelota players who had lived in Cuba for years, since before the Civil War.

As we have seen, Ernest Hemingway had known about the Basque Country since his years in Paris. In March, 1937, he was sent to Madrid to cover the war for the North American Newspaper Alliance (NANA). In Madrid he met Robert Capa, who had photographed the bombing of Bilbao during the rebel offensive to take Bizkaia. He also met Noel Monks, who was one of the first international journalists to reach Gernika on the evening of April 26 after the Condor Legion destroyed the Basques' spiritual capital.

---

6. Ibid., 189.

Hemingway did not cover the bombing, but on April 30 he wrote that the Fascists needed to "restore the international prestige they had lost since then with a new victory, and eliminate the embarrassment the self-styled Red-destroying general suffers when bombing and the killing Basque Catholic Nationalists."[7]

A few weeks later at the *American Writers' Congress*, held in New York on June 4, 1937, he said: "It is one thing to destroy Guernica and another to fail to take Bilbao.[8]

He was not a prophet, for Bilbao fell and the Bizkaians had to flee, first to France and then to America. Among those Basques who got away to Cuba, some were to become friends of Hemingway's. And they were Catholics.

The Crook Factory and Operation Friendless

It has been said that Hemingway set up an espionage network in Havana known as the Crook Factory. I would only like to say a couple of things about it. Firstly, almost all of its members were Basques. Second, previously these Basques had belonged to the Basque government-in-exile's Basque Information Service and had collaborated with the Allies (France and the United Kingdom) from the start of the World War II. Later, when the United States entered the war, they had also worked with the FBI. There are 834 declassified FBI dossiers about the Basque Information Service (BIS), which was the FBI's name for it. One of them clearly explains the cooperation between Hemingway and some Basques. These people were his friends. The BIS decided that it would be more practical for these Basques to carry on in the Crook Factory rather than being part of the BIS. There is a long chapter in my book with an in-depth examination of this matter.[9]

Thanks to having a special relationship with the American embassy, in the summer of 1942 Hemingway was able to propose an idea that many FBI agents thought was senseless—Operation Friendless.

The operation consisted of fitting out Hemingway's fishing boat *Pilar* with guns and hand grenades and a crew specifically trained for hunting German submarines. His idea was that once a submarine detected the boat it would rise to the surface and, once surfaced, the *Pilar*, the boat could attack it. The objective was to make the submarine useless by throwing grenades down its hatch from a certain distance. The grenades were to be thrown by jai alai players using their hand-baskets. I am not going to say much about this operation either: I describe it in detail in another chapter in my book. However, Hemingway wrote his own book about hunting submarines, the third part of *Islands in the Stream*.

---

7. Braasch, "Hemingway's Spanish Civil War Dispatches," 37.
8. Bruccol, *Conversations with Ernest Hemingway*, 194.
9. Jiménez, *Hemingway eta euskaldunak Zerbitzu Sekretuetan*, 115–20.

Islands in the Stream is the title of Ernest Hemingway's eighth and longest novel. It was also the first to be published (1970) after his death in 1961.

Islands in the Stream was not acclaimed by the critics, but it was on the *New York Times* bestsellers' list for twenty-four weeks. Apparently, Hemingway's original idea had been to include most or all of *Islands in the Stream* in a trilogy of novels about the sea, which would form part of a larger trilogy that would include: a novel about the earth and another about the air. *The Old Man and the Sea* was the first of the three parts of the sea novel and other manuscripts with the provisional title sea novel were to make up the second and third parts. These were brought together and published as *Islands in the Stream*. The novels about the air and the earth, to the contrary, were never written.

So *Islands in the Stream* is fragmented, divided, and made up of unequal parts that have little in common. Furthermore, it is striking that the protagonist Thomas Hudson (again Hemingway's alter ego) is introduced as the main character in all three parts as if they were separate stories.

The third part, "On the high seas," has 135 pages and is divided into twenty-two chapters. Its action transpires during two or three days in 1944. The wind had been blowing uninterruptedly for fifty days, which is the period of time between the end of the second part and the start of the third. "On the high seas" is about how Hudson and his crew of just eight men search the Camagüey archipelago for German submarines.

Let us examine the eight-man crew. Who were they?

Norberto Fuentes, basing himself on Gregorio Fuentes's memoirs, gives us a good description of them. Gregorio, in fact, is our best source as he himself was a member of the crew on the *Pilar* as Antonio in the novel. Then we have Hudson, Hemingway's alter ego. Third, there is Winson Guest, a polo player and close friend of the writer—Henry Wood in the book. Fourth, a US navy officer called John Saxon in charge of communications on board. There are three other characters who, in principle, are not connected with real people. They are Peter, Gil, and George.

We learn that George is Basque in this paragraph: "'Mi capitán,' said George, who was a taller Basque than Ara and a good athlete and fine seaman, but not nearly as strong as Ara in many ways."[10]

So who are the other two characters, Ara and Juan? Ara is Francisco Ibarluzea (Paxtchi or Pachi Ibarlucia), a former jai alai player and a close friend of the writer. He appears in Ernest's famous "First Poem to Mary in London," written for his future wife Mary Welsh in 1944 or, just after the submarine hunt described in the third part of *Islands in the Stream*.

> Then I am homesick for Paxtchi who took the armour from his cockpit so she would trim better in the sea and never dropped the drums of gas he sat on when we closed. For Wolfie standing on the flying bridge the muscles jumping in his cheeks. Saying, "Papa it's all right

---

10. Hemingway, *Islands in the Stream*, 387.

with me. Don't worry For a moment Papa it's all right with me."[11]

"Where are you, Wolfie now? Where are you Patchi?"[12] Juan is Juan Duñabeitia (Sinsky, Sinbad), a sailor from Bilbao. This other close friend of Hemingway's used to spend long periods at Finca Vigía. Their friendship is recorded in a painting by Jose María Uzelay, a painter from Bizkaia, an Anglophile and another good friend of Ernest's.

As I have said before, I am not going to talk about the plot of the book: I will concentrate on what Hemingway says about these Basques. There is a clear reference to Basque in the book.

> "Krauts eat 'em plenty codfish now on in," Willie said.
> "What language is that?"
> "My own," Willie said. "Everybody has private language around here, like Basque something. You got an objection if I speak mine?"
> "Tell me the rest."[13]

This means that the Basques on the *Pilar* used to speak with each other in Basque. But there is more: Hemingway was aware of another characteristic of Basque speakers, which was that they did not speak Spanish correctly.

> "Willie had learned that horrible Philippines Spanish, but they had no problem understanding each other. That is partly because Ara, too, is Basque and speaks Spanish badly."[14]

It could be no more than a cliché, but it is a true cliché.

The Bells Toll for Jai Alai

In 1945 the magazine *Cancha*—the jai alai magazine published in Mexico for many years[15]—had an interview with Hemingway written by Félix Ermua, one of the best pelota players of the time. When he asked Hemingway about the Basques, he replied:

> "The Basques are good people. Very noble, but also very noisy when the atmosphere gets lively. I've had some great times with them. They like having fun. He also says that if Basque pelota players were to behave in the court as they do around a table, all the games would end 29 all."[16]

As we have seen, in *Islands in the Stream* Hemingway mentions two main clichés about the Basques: communicating in Basque and speaking bad Spanish. In this interview you can see more clichés about the Basques. As it says, the Basques are considered to be good people, noble people,

---

11. Gerogiannis, *Ernest Hemingway*, 104.
12. Ibid.
13. I quote the original to show how Hemingway imitates Basque phonetically. Hemingway, *Islands in the Stream*, 380–81.
14. Ibid., 447.
15. Cancha: http://urazandi.euskaletxeak.net/vol1/dvd09/Cancha/htm/port2.htm.
16. Areitio Ermua, "Las companas doblan por el jaialai," 23.

honest, funny when the situation is right, they like food, drink, and sports. But there is more still.

In 1947 Hemingway's second son, Patrick, suffered a serious mental illness. His Basque friends immediately became Patrick's support group. The clearest evidence for that is an unpublished letter from Ernest dating from 1947. The letter says:

> You will be given extensive information about Patrick. For the moment we can say that he has had a nervous breakdown as the result of a car crash and he has been like this for more than 70 days, but this is no more than a passing thing and he will make a full recovery. From the first day of his illness there was a team to look after him— Papa, Sinbad, and the Champion (Roberto Herrera)—and permanent helpers, Félix as a helper when available, Don Andrés and the group's excellent butcher: given the scarcity of meat, he has brought us some from Melena del Sur every week.[17]

The letter is signed by all of those mentioned in it and it was sent to Paxtchi, who was in Mexico by then. That unfortunate illness showed Hemingway another cliché about the Basques: their generosity and sense of friendship. That Don Andrés was the Mundaka priest I mentioned at the start of my essay. And he was the reason why I started researching the relationship between Hemingway and the Basques.

Conclusion

An expatriate is a person who lives in a country other than their own. An exile is somebody who has been exiled, somebody who is forced to live outside their own country, especially for political reasons. An emigrant is somebody who has left their country to go and live in another. All three have one thing in common: they live in foreign countries.

In Cuba, Hemingway was an American expatriate and his Basque friends were exiled political advocates—such as the priest Don Andrés and the sailor Juan Duñabeitia or simply emigrants such as the jai alai players. But the jai alai players, too, were involved in politics.

In my opinion, one of the things which formed such a close link between Ernest Hemingway and his Basque friends was that they were all living in another country, Cuba. The Basques could speak the language and form a social network thanks to the colony of Basque traders, businessmen, and clerics who had been there previously, not to forget the jai alai players. In short, there was a Basque community in Cuba, with an official Basque house (Euskal Etxea), Basque restaurants, and also a Basque atmosphere in certain places—places that Hemingway loved. Hemingway, too, knew Spanish, had a circle of Cuban and US friends, but he was an expatriate and liked to live as such. By that I mean that he liked to live

---

17. Museo Hemingway; San Francisco de Paula (Provincia de Havana), Cuba.

without the daily distractions of a writer living in his own country: politics, interviews, conferences, and so on. From this point of view, Hemingway had a very useful relationship with the Basques. This is one of the conclusions of my book.

Another is that his perception of the Basques, although full of clichés, was perfectly in line with the people he knew. In fact, his relationship with the Basques lasted until the end of his days.

Hemingway never gave his opinion about the political situation in Spain and in the Basque Country after the Civil War. Perhaps that was because he wanted to go back to Spain. And, in fact, in 1953, the year in which an agreement was signed to open US military bases in Spain, he did go back. This agreement meant opening the dictatorship up to the United Nations. That year Hemingway went back to Spain, but under the condition of not talking about politics. This year, 1953, was also the year that the dictatorship signed an agreement with the Vatican. Thanks to the latter, Don Andrés, the priest from Mundaka, could also go back. It was the end of two different exiles, that of the writer (Hemingway) and of the priest (Don Andrés). And it was also the year that many Basques, who would otherwise have had to wait for Franco to die, went back to their land.

Bibliography

Areitio Ermua, Félia. "Las campanas doblan por el jaialai." *Cancha*, November 15, 1945.

Braasch Watson, William. "Hemingway's Spanish Civil War Dispatches." *Hemingway Review* 7:2 (1988 Spring): 13–92.

Bruccoli, Matthew J., ed. *Conversations with Ernest Hemingway*. Jackson: University Press of Mississippi, 1986.

Gerogiannis, Nicholas, ed. *Ernest Hemingway: Complete Poems*. Lincoln: University of Nebraska Press, 1992.

Hemingway, Ernest. *Islands in the Stream*. New York: Charles Scribner's Sons, 1970.

———. *The Garden of Eden*. New York: Scribners, 2003.

———. *The Sun Also Rises*. Hemingway Library Edition. New York: Scribner, 2014.

Jiménez, Edorta. *Hemingway eta euskaldunak Zerbitzu Sekretuetan*. Zarautz: Editorial Susa, 2003.

20

Contemporary Economic, Institutional, Social, and Cultural Relations between the Basque Country and Cuba

Alexander Ugalde Zubiri

In memory of my friend and university colleague Joseba Macías Amores (1961–2013)

"We have enormous respect for the Cuban people, we respect their capacity for decision and doing things, and the people of Cuba's respect of the Basques' capacity for deciding and developing and controlling our destiny ourselves."
—Lehendakari Juan José Ibarretxe (Prime Minister of the Basque Government), interview in the newspaper *Granma*, Havana, April 12, 2002

On the basis of a historical substratum begun at the start of the colonial period and maintained over the centuries,[1] during the last years of the twentieth century and the start of the twenty-first century the links between the Basque Country (Euskal Herria or Euskadi) and Cuba have multiplied.

This chapter's objective is to explain and evaluate the current relationships between both parties in economics (exports and imports, business exchanges, etc.) and institutional ties (contacts, agreements, and cooperation between the Basque and Cuban governments and other institutions: foral provincial governments and municipal authorities), social and cultural terms (activities carried out by the Basque-Cuban community on the island and Cuban residents in the Basque Country, the Euskadi-Cuba Association, NGOs and other cooperation groups, collaboration between education centers and universities, artistic events, etc.).

I am going to use a dual hypothesis during my analysis: (1) Based on a consistent historical pillar,[2] there are currently many links between the Cuban and Basque people and their various organizations; and (2) these

---

This article is from a speech in the series of academic work carried out by the University of the Basque Country Research Group: "Descentralización del sistema internacional y acción exterior del Estado de estructura compleja: desarrollos teóricos y experiencias prácticas" (code IT861-13).

1. Some of Christopher Columbus's first crew were Basque. Bilbao, *Vascos en Cuba*.

2. The bibliography about the various dimensions of the historical Basque-Cuban relationships is growing. In addition to the other papers in this book, I submit my contribution to Ugalde Zubiri, coord., *Patria y Libertad*, footnotes 92–153, 191–207.

relationship could be increased and further developed, both in quantity and quality.

I am going to concentrate on contemporary relations, by which I mean the last decade until the present day. For previous periods, see my work presented in March 2001, "Las relaciones País Vasco-Cuba desde la perspectiva de la acción exterior vasca," at the fifth Basque Sociology Congress in Bilbao; and October 2011, "Las relaciones políticas, económicas y sociales entre Cuba y el País Vasco," at the ninth European Studies International Conference at the Centro de Estudios Europeos in Havana.[3]

Institutional Relations: Basque Government

We consider institutional relations to be those between different political-administrative levels in the Basque Country, the Basque government, foral provincial governments, and municipal authorities, with their equivalents in Cuba, the Cuban government, people's provincial powers, and municipal authorities.

In the first place, because of their importance, I deal with the highest level relations between the Cuban and Basque governments. They should be situated as Cuban foreign policy (which, since the 1990s, has cooperated with non-central or intermediate governments); and Basque international and foreign action policies (similar to those of Scotland, Flanders, Catalonia, Quebec, São Paolo, etc.).[4]

These links involve the Basque lehendakari's visits and those of ministers (people in charge of departments and ministries), Cuban ministers and high-ranking officials' visits, and the opening of the Basque commercial office in Havana, among other things.

Formal contacts began at the start of the '90s. The trips of Rosa Díez—minister for commerce, consumerism, and tourism—in 1991 and 1993, at the time of the Havana International Fair, stand out. She traveled with business and Chamber of Commerce people. In 1991 she met Fidel Castro and, on both occasions, several ministers.

The final touch was the two visits that lehendakari José Antonio Ardanza made in 1997 and 1998; they were political and economic missions, in support of Basque companies and the setting up of joint ventures.

In June 1997, Ardanza led a delegation that included Javier Retegui, the minister for industry. There were meetings with Fidel Castro, head of state; José Ramón Fernández, vice president of the cabinet; Carlos Lage,

---

3. A synthesis in Ugalde Zubiri, "Las relaciones País Vasco-Cuba desde la perspectiva de la acción exterior vasca," 1.392–1.404.

4. The Basque Country Autonomous Community—to give it its formal name—has had international policies since the 1980s and this is coordinated by the General Secretariat of Foreign Action, which is part of the Presidency Department of the Basque government. This consists of going on trips and receiving visits; opening delegations abroad; transfrontier cooperation; cooperation in the development of countries in Southern Europe; belonging to interregional associations and worldwide networks; attending the needs of Basque communities and their centers abroad, among other things.

vice president of state council; Roberto Robaina, minister for foreign affairs; and Ricardo Alarcón, president of the national assembly. They visited projects financed with Basque participation.

In September 1998, Lehendkari Ardanza made his second visit and was again received by high-ranking officials, including Fidel Castro. Minister Javier Retegui met with ministers Marcos Portal (basic industry), Ignacio González Planas (iron and steel), and Ulises Rosales del Toro (sugar).

The main objective of the visit was the opening of the commercial office of SPRI the Sociedad para la Promoción y Reconversión Industrial (Company for Industrial Promotion and Reconversion) in Havana.[5] This has played a key role in promoting economic-commercial exchanges, supporting the presence of Basque companies, assisting in the creation of joint ventures, and giving advice to Cuban companies about training and business management. Among the first initiatives was the 1999 agreement with Unión del Níquel (equipment renovation); the program began in 1999 and gave training to Cuban production and service company managers; and, from 2000, credit for exports was made available to Basque companies which were suppliers for the Plan Urgente de Renovación Energética (Urgent Energy Renovation Plan) for the Cuban hostelry sector (PURE). The office was closed in 2013.[6]

Several ministers traveled over the following years: Josu Jon Imaz, industry, commerce, and tourism (1999, with managers from the Basque Energy Organization and the Chambers of Commerce); Javier Madrazo, Housing and Social Affairs (2002, he reviewed development cooperation); and Joseba Azkarraga, Justice, Employment and Social Security (2002, he signed agreements with the People's Supreme Court).

Visits were also received from Ricardo Sánchez, vice minister for technology and the environment (1998, collaboration in the development of wind energy, recycling waste materials and innovation management); Néstor Gutiérrez, head of production of the pharmacological industry (1999, "Medi-Cuba" campaign for the acquisition of prime materials for producing medicines); Alberto Juantorena, vice minister for Sports (1999, investigating collaboration with the Basque sports federations for training techniques); Carlos Pablo Dotres, minister for public health (1999, signing an agreement); Adelaida Guevara, pediatrician (2000, health collaboration and appearance before the commission for foreign action in the Basque parliament); Isabel Allende, ambassador for Cuba in Spain (2001, interview with president Ibarretxe and presence at the event "Cuba: Business Opportunities for Basque Companies"); José Ramón Fernández, vice president of the cabinet (2001, finalized the framework for a cooperation agreement); Carlos Lage, vice president of the State Council and secretary

---

5. SPRI is a public agency that depends on the Basque government and one of its sections promotes the internationalization of the Basque economy.
6. It was not the only one, in 2013 the SPRI Foreign Network offices in San Francisco and Philadelphia were also closed, as was that in Silesia, Poland.

of the cabinet, and Marta Lomas, minister for foreign Investment and Economic Collaboration (2002, interview with president Ibarretxe and visits to Zamudio technology park and Mondragón cooperative corporation); and Rubén Remigio Ferro, president of the People's Supreme Court (2002).

Various agreements were reached during those years: "Memorandum of Understanding" about cooperation between the Cuban government's ministry for health (MINSAP), the Basque energy organization (EVE), and the Basque health service (1999); collaboration agreement between the Cuban government and the Basque Country's energy sector (2001);[7] "Development and Cooperation Collaboration Protocol" between the Basque government and the ministry for foreign investment and collaboration (2002); and "terms of reference" for promoting the "Libertad Educational City's science complex campus network" between the Basque government's department of housing and social affairs, the ministry of education, the ministry for foreign investment and economic collaboration and the Higher Pedagogical Institute (2002).

One of the most interesting experiences was the founding, in 2001, of Maitek (the office of shared technological services), with various R&D and innovation projects being started up by scientific, technological, and business organizations.

Institutional relations were at their most active after president Juan José Ibarretxe's visit in April 2002. He had meetings with Fidel Castro, president of the Councils of State and the cabinet; Carlos Lage, vice president; José Ramón Fernández, vice president of the cabinet; Felipe Pérez Roque, minister for foreign affairs; Ulises Rosales del Toro, minister for the sugar industry; Fernando Acosta, minister for the iron and steel industry; and Alfredo López, minister for fishing. Meetings with Monsignor Emilio Aranguren, bishop of Cienfuegos and secretary of the Episcopal Conference; and José Ramón Balaguer, member of the Communist Party politburo, among others. And visits to Old Havana (urban rehabilitation projects receiving Basque aid), the genetic and biotechnological engineering center and the Latin American School of Medical Science.

The Protocol of Intention between the Basque Country and Cuba was signed. It was a very important framework agreement: it set out the basic lines of cooperation between Cuba and the Basque Country for a decade, led the way for later sector-wide developments and set up a mixed commission for following up the agreement. Signed on April 10, 2002, by President Juan José Ibarretxe and the vice president of the cabinet of the Republic of Cuba, José Ramón Fernández Álvarez.

The Cuba-Basque Country Intergovernmental Commission for Economic and Scientific-Technical Collaboration met annually, the venue alternating, and was coordinated by the Basque government's general sec-

---

7. For greater dynamism, in 2002 the energy cluster of exporters to Cuba (Gececuba) was founded; over the following years it was to collaborate with various ministries and the Cubanacán tourism company.

retariat for foreign action (SGAE) and the ministry for foreign investment and collaboration. Around twenty people for each country took part, coming from the Cuban ministries and Basque departments and other public bodies most involved. The meetings' minutes—of which I have copies—reflect the wide range of collaborations (economy, health, education, culture, technology, justice, etc.) This organ functioned between 2002 and 2008. Later, during the term of office of President Patxi López, it stopped meeting. During this period, as I say, Basque-Cuban institutional collaboration was at its height. Later it was diminished considerably, and has not yet to be given renewed force.

Under this framework-agreement, other sector agreements were reached with the Basque government: ministry of public health (2002); people's supreme court, Cuban UNESCO lawyers' national union and commission (2002); United Nations development programme (UNDP) to reinforce the local human development program (PDHL) at Holguín, Guantánamo, and Old Havana (2004); ministry of justice (2007); Cuban people's supreme court (2007); and the ministry for sugar (2008).

Ministers Joseba Azkarraga (justice and social security, 2008) and Gabriel Inclán (health) (2008) visited Cuba.

From Cuba, Ricardo Sánchez Sosa, diplomat and regional director for Latin America and the Caribbean of the United Nations environment programme (UNEP) (2004); Alberto Velazco, ambassador (2005 and 2006); Ricardo Alarcón de Quesada, president of the national assembly of the people's power (2005); Otto Rivero Torres, vice president of the cabinet (2006); Orlando Requeijo, vice minister for foreign investment and economic collaboration (2006); José Luis Toledo Santander, president of the commission for constitutional and legal affairs at the national assembly of the people's power (2007); Ricardo Guerrero Blanco, vice minister for foreign investment and economic collaboration (2008); Elio Gámez, vice president of the Cuban institute for friendship with countries (2010); Olga Salanueva and Adriana Pérez, the wives of René González and Gerardo Hernández—two of the "five" imprisoned in the United States since 1998, accused of espionage and conspiracy—who explained their case to the Basque parliament (2010).

Cuban ambassadors to Madrid have paid regular visits to the Basque Country, for instance Alejandro González Galiano (2011 and 2012) and Eugenio Martínez Enríquez (June 2014)—where he was received by president Iñigo Urkullu and Basque parliament speaker Bakartxo Tejería—and December 2014.

Institutional Relations: Foral Provincial Governments

The contact between the three Basque foral provincial governments and Cuba have not been continual and have been limited to specific collaborations except for cooperation and development funds, of which Cuba is one of the countries that has benefited most.

As an example of some of the contacts in the past, the presentation in 2001 to the province of Havana and other institutions of the "Declaration of Bizkaia on Human Rights Regarding the Environment" by María Esther Solabarrieta, member of the Bizkaian Parliament for the environment and territorial action. The public organism BEAZ (Bizkaia European center for companies and innovation), with the provincial government's financial support, has taken part since 2002 in restructuring sugar factories.

At present the provincial government most involved with Cuba is Gipuzkoa. In 2014 Cuban ambassador Eugenio Martínez Enríquez held meetings with high-ranking Gipuzkoan officials, including Martín Garitano, the head of government. Some of these relations are bilateral and others are part of the work carried out with countries in the Bolivarian alliance for the peoples of our America (ALBA). In June, 2014, the ambassadors from these states paid a visit with political and commercial aims. Other Cuban officials who have visited Gipuzkoa include Fidel Castro Díaz-Balart (scientific advisor to the state council and vice president of the academy of the sciences) who was received in the provincial government and visited various installations (Nanogune research center, specialized in nanotechnology).

In November 2014, a delegation from Gipuzkoa's provincial government—led by Jon Peli Uriguen, member of parliament for innovation, rural development, and tourism—and representatives of the chambers of commerce, as well as Gipuzkoan companies, were present at the Havana international trade fair (FIHAV). Meetings were held with the ministry for foreign trade and foreign investment and the Cuban chamber of commerce; there was a visit to the Mariel thermoelectric plant.

Institutional Relations: Municipal Authorities

An increasing number of local administrations plan activities with foreign dimensions to them. In the Basque Country, a high proportion of these involved Latin America and the Caribbean (behind Europe). Municipal authorities travel, receive visits, reach agreements and twin with other authorities, set up funds for cooperating with development, encourage cross-frontier cooperation, and join international associations and networks for culture, technology, tourism, and other areas.

There is not a considerable number of intermunicipal cooperation agreements with Cuba compared with other countries. Various twin-city agreements were signed several years ago. In 1998, after a visit to the city of Havana from a delegation from various Basque municipal authorities, documents were signed linking Santurtzi with Old Havana; Barakaldo with Diez de Octubre; and Trapagaran with Plaza de la Revolución. At present, in practical terms, they have no common programs.

In 1998 links were formed between Donostia-San Sebastián and Havana, and actions were taken in the tourism, urban planning, cultural, and sports areas. However, the planned twinning was not formalized and the relationship fell into disuse.

The relationship which has been most consolidated over time is that signed by Pasaia and Mariel in 1996. Funds for development have been set up for various projects and there have been exchanges in the fishing and professional training arena (Mariel maritime fishing institute). With this precedent, there is currently a dynamic relationship between the Oarsoaldea area (Pasaia, Lezo, and Oiartzun) and the people's power in Mayabeque province (a subdivision of the province of Havana). The technical support given by the Oarsoaldea local development agency to the "Osvaldo Sánchez community Playa Rosario Evacuees Integration" project stands out. Carried out since 2006, when Hurricane Wilma hit, it involved moving people within the Güines municipal area. This involved Cubans (drawing up the plan, providing land, urban planning, workforce), the Basque government (funds for buying equipment and materials), and the Elan Euskadi NGO.

Cuba is one of the places prioritized by Euskal Fondoa/Association of Local Basque Cooperatives Organizations, made up by the foral regional governments and that works on international cooperation by co-financing the members. Since its foundation in 1988, it has supported projects in San Miguel de Padrón, Guanabacoa, Boyeros, Cotorro, Mariel, and Matanzas, among others. Currently being carried out: Building protected housing for the elderly (Havana); support for the care for the elderly program (Havana); support for the national care program for children with brain and/or physical-motor disability; and remodeling and enlarging the Vicente Álvarez old people's home.

At various moments a large number of municipal authorities have made official pronouncements about Cuba. The most common agreements have been in opposition to the US blockade. The most recent (October and November 2014) are requests for the three remaining Cubans from the group called "Los Cinco," prisoners in the United States, to be released. The campaign—which had been going to continue—was suspended when Gerardo Hernández, Ramón Labañino, and Antonio Guerrero were freed on December 17, 2014. At that moment the motion had been supported by twenty-five municipal councils in the Basque Country and Navarra.[8]

Economic and Commercial Relationships

Current commercial relationships began at the start of the 1990s at the same time as factors such as Cuba's partial economic opening up to the

---

8. Those councils were: Anoeta, Aramaio, Arbizu, Astigarraga, Atarrabia, Ataun, Eskoriatza, Etxarri-Aranatz, Larrabetzu, Larraun, Leitza, Lekeitio, Lesaka, Lizartza, Ondarroa, Oñati, Ordizia, Orexa, Otxandio, Unzueta, Usurbil, Zaldibia, Zaralegi, and Zestoa. The text read: "(1) We demand that the president of the US make use of his executive powers to impose a solution which will lead to the end of the unfair situation by freeing these prisoners . . . ; (2) We are sending these agreements to the Cuban embassy, the embassy of the United States of America and the ministry for foreign affairs."

outside world; Basque companies' internationalization plans; and the support of the Basque government and the foral provincial governments for the projection of the Basque economy into other countries, especially via the activity of small and medium-size companies.

This work included other factors: the opening, in 1998, of the commercial office of the Industrial Restructuring and Promotion Association (SPRI) in Havana; since 1999, the presence of Basque companies (usually between thirty and forty), with the support of the Basque chambers of commerce, at the Havana international Trade Fair (FIHAV), with a specific Basque pavilion;[9] and the founding, in 2000, of the Kubako Euskal Enpresarien Elkartea (Cuban association of Basque business people).[10]

The following data give an idea of Basque exports to Cuba: in 1994, exports were worth 40 million euros; in 1999, 81 million; in 2007, 163 million; in 2012, 143 million; and, in 2013, 152 million.[11] At present Cuba is the twenty-sixth on the list and the fourth leading customer in Latin America (after Brazil, Mexico, and Venezuela).

Import figures from Cuba are lower. In 1994, they were worth 1 million euros; in 1999, 10 million; in 2007, 10 million; in 2013, 20.5 million. Cuba is fifty-fifth on the list, tenth in Latin America.

At present there are around 40 Basque companies on the island, and around 130 Basque Country ones that export there. They are mostly small and medium-sized companies as well as cooperatives and social economy companies. The main products are machines and mechanical devices, electric materials, foundry products, and iron and steel.

At the latest FIHAV (2014) there were twenty-three companies (energy, engineering, services, machine tools, etc.).[12] Institutional support included the presence of Miren Madinabeitia, the director the SPRI International Department, and a delegation from the Gipuzkoa provincial government. The Basque pavilion was visited by René Mesa, the Cuban minister for construction, and Alfredo López Valdés, the minister for energy and mines, among others.

There have also been a few Cuban visits to events in the Basque Country at which Cuban business groups and ministries have explained opportunities for trading and investing in the island.

---

9. In 2005 the Basque pavilion was named the best technological installation at the fair and awarded the Giraldilla prize.

10. At the end of 2014 the association of Basque business people in Cuba (AEVC) has twenty-five member companies. Not all the Basque companies on the island are members. In November, 2014, it became part of the association of Spanish business people in Cuba (AEEC).

11. I use data from various sources, principally Eustat the (the Basque Statistics Institute) and Eusko Ganberak (Basque Chambers of Commerce).

12. Aceros LST Bilbao; Grupo Berotz; Bezabala Cables y Elevación; Boj Olañeta; Cesyta (Compañía de Estudios, Servicios y Tecnologías Aplicadas); Grupo Ugao; Compañía Elaboradora de Caucho Coeca; Consorcio Industrial Shesga; Cotransa; Covertrade; Edelnort; Ebi Talleres Electrotécnicos; Electra Vitoria; Ferretería Unceta; Grupo Automoción Mutauto América; Industrias Goini; Industrias Metálicas Soroa; Ininser; Inkug-Idurgo, Kondia; Metrología Sariki; Miesa; Novaexim; Rodabilsa; Roydex; Talleres Guibe; Tor Panel/Panelfisa; Tubos Reunidos Industrial; Viroex; Zubiola.

Development Cooperation

The Basque administrations (government, provincial governments, and municipal authorities) have been, with their limitations, one of the most advanced models in the world in terms of financial commitments, percentages, norms, management, and so on, since the 1990s. The largest quantities are sent to Latin America and the Caribbean.

At the end of the 1980s—which is when this activity began in the Basque Country—and at the beginning of the 90s, Cuba did not receive any type of aid because this type of financing had not yet been accepted there. In 1993 two projects were passed and in 1995 a further one. From 1996 onward, with seven active projects (worth 1.6 million euros), Cuba became one of the main receivers of this type of Basque aid.

This dynamic increased in 2006 when the Basque government passed the "Strategic Country program for Cooperation" that made Cuba a priority—along with Guatemala.[13] This was approved in Cuba by signing a collaboration protocol for particular sectors (sugar industry restructuring; agriculture and livestock production; industry, science, and technology; biotechnology; health; etc.)

During 2008 and 2010, for instance, Cuba was the second destination (after Peru) with a total of 9.5 million euros (7.8 percent of the total funds).

Since the Basque development cooperation agency began to function in 2011, Cuba has been one of the twenty-two priority countries. Recently its percentage has been reduced somewhat, but over the years it is still between third and fifth place among all the destinations.

The types of projects are varied in terms of objectives, sectors, quantities, stakeholders, etc. To give two examples of this: "The reinforcement and optimization of the productive capacity of sustainable production materials for the rehabilitation of the heritage and housing stock in Old Havana," backed up with 364,128 Euros of finance, presented by Fundación Tecnalia Research & Innovation[14] and the "Program for training and technical assistance for agro-industrial restructuring and the development of food self-sufficiency in the east of Cuba," with a payment of 250,000 Euros managed by Fundación Mundukide Fundazioa.

Cuban organizations taking part include the Oficina del Historiador de Ciudad de Havana, Instituto Cubano de Investigaciones Azucareras (ICINAZ), Asociación Nacional de Innovadores y Racionalizadores (ANIC), Instituto Superior Politécnico J.A. Echeverría (ISPJAE), Centro

---

13. Cuba was chosen for being one of the countries with greatest cooperation with the Basque Country; the number of Basque NGO's and other organizations (foundations, technological centers, etc.) working with equivalent Cuban bodies; inter-institutional relationships; among other reasons.

14. For information about Basque involvement in the "General plan for the complete revitalization of Old Havana," see Piñero et al., "Influencia del requerimiento social en la metodología para el proceso de priorización en la rehabilitación de estructuras degradadas del Centro Histórico de Havana."

de Química Farmacéutica (CQF), Complejo Científico Ortopédico Internacional Frank País, among many others.

Sums of money have also been made available for humanitarian aid in circumstance of natural disaster on the island, mostly for immediate aid after hurricanes.

Mutual Support Relationships and Social and Cultural Links

Showing the extent of the social, political, cultural, and relationships of mutual support with documentary back-up is impossible in such as short text. Not even giving a summary of it is viable. So I will just present a few thoughts.

One of the social dimensions from the Basque Country to Cuba is support for the revolutionary, transformative process. This includes organizations such as the Asociación Euskadi-Cuba, Askapena, Komite Internazionalistak, other groups, and NGOs. This has been seen in activities for promoting awareness (conferences, exhibitions, etc.); donations (sending sanitary material, educational material, etc.); supporting development cooperation projects; and organizing work groups (groups of people who have spent time at agricultural or other productive installations and who have been able to become familiar with the Cuban daily reality rather than just having the contact which tourists have). Some of this has been organized through the Instituto Cubano de Amistad con los Pueblos (ICAP). The names of some of the initiatives taken are significant: "Gora Kuba Askatuta: Sin Cuba ya nada sería igual" (Long live free Cuba. Without Cuba nothing would be the same), "Euskadi-Kubaren alde" (The Basque Country with Cuba), "Blokeoaren 50 urte . . . Cuba pa'lante" (50 years of blockade . . . go Cuba!'), "Libertad 5 presos cubanos en EE.UU: Obama, bostak askatu!" (Freedom for the five Cuban prisoners in the US: Obama, free the five).

The work carried out by the Asociación Euskadi-Cuba—founded in 1989 and which had its twenty-fifth anniversary in October 2014—must be underlined. It has always been the key social organization in support of the revolution. It has led the most important campaigns with the support of other organizations, political parties, trades unions, and Basque institutions. The most outstanding of its current initiatives, in my opinion, is the making of the website Cubainformación with the slogan "A gap in the media blockade."[15] It has become one of the best digital information pages about Cuba, based on news items, videos, documentaries, interviews, radio programs, and more. Other media use its materials and quote it regularly. It receives financial support from the Basque Development Cooperation Agency (Basque government) and from the Gipuzkoa provincial government.

---

15. The link to Cubainformación is www.cubainformacion.tv/.

In Iparralde (the Basque area of France), Cuba'ko Etxea. Casa de Cuba. Maison de Cuba, with offices in Baiona. The Pays Basque/Bas Adour committee is part of the France-Cuba association.

Education is a good area for establishing links, from grammar schools to universities. One of the recent initiatives has been the twinning of twenty Basque schools with schools in the east of Cuba.[16] The relationship began with the Cruzada Teatral Guantánamo-Baracoa (2011), after which the children began to correspond. The materials (letters, greetings, drawings, etc.) were collected in "Friendship Books" that were exchanged. The Basque children learned the song "Guantanamera" and the Cuban children learned the Basque song "Uka, uka, keinuka." At the suggestion of the drama school Kurkuluxetan Antzerki Eskola, and with the collaboration of the Comité de Artes Escénicas del Oriente de Cuba, the Keinuka Mugaz Gaindi . . . Un guiño, Un sueño, project was started to make a film about human values (friendship, mutual support, etc.) The actors were the children who had planned the film and then shot it. The technical side was organized by Ibaizabal Telebista and the Instituto Cubano de Arte e Industria Cinematográfica (ICAIC). In June 2014, the film was shown at various playings in Bilbao and at the 26 de Julio city school in Santiago de Cuba.[17]

There have been several cinematic coproductions. We will mention one of the most successful: *Maité*, which came out in 1994. A comedy about two almost ruined businessmen who believe their way out is an easy piece of business: taking a load of elvers to Cuba and bringing back Cuban cigars. It was directed by Eneko Olasagasti and Carlos Zabala, with the collaboration of Senel Paz with the script. The Cuban actors included Jorge Perugorría, Natalia Herrera, and Adela Legrá. In 1998, using this film as its basis, Euskal Telebista (Basque public television) filmed the sitcom *Maité*. One of the businessmen and a Cuban girl get married and live in the Basque Country and have several adventures. Produced by Ángel Amigo, directed by Carlos Zabala and Eneko Olasagasti, the scripts were by Patxo Telleria, Aizpea Goenaga, and Teresa Calo. The actors included José Ramón Soroiz and the Cubans lleana Wilson Gross, Caridad Rosa Llinas, Lilian Kourí, Idelfonso Tamayo, and Carlos Acosta.

The romantic drama *Valeria descalza* came out in 2011. A coproduction financed by the Cuban Cinema Art and Industry Institute (ICAIC) (30 percent) and Sendeja Films and Basque television (ETB) (70 percent), subsidized by the Basque government and the Ibermedia program. It was shot in Bilbao and Havana, directed by Ernesto del Río and with the script by Luis Eguiraun and Xenia Rivery. The cast included Gabriela Griffith, Aitor Mazo, Maiken Beitia, and Rubén Breña.

---

16. The Cuban schools are in Santiago de Cuba, Guantánamo, La Clarita, Arroyo del Medio, Los Naranjos, Casimba, Palenque, etc.; the Basque schools are in Bilbao, Lemoa, Derio, and Etxebarri.

17. The film (1 hour, 20 minutes), can be seen at www.youtube.com/watch?v=59EQ1FSlGs0.

There have been various audiovisual productions. I will discuss a particularly interesting one: the making of historical documentaries about Basques in Cuba. The Haziak Denboran/Semillas en Tiempo project is led by Ángel González Katarain. One of the series is about the Seven Streets of Havana (paraphrasing the name for the historical center of Bilbao), identifying street names that are connected with the Basque Country. Aranguren, Ayestarán, Belascoaín, Goicuría, Espada, Loynaz, and Zulueta. Three documentaries have been made so far: *Belascoaín: La calle de los pelotaris* (The pelota players' street), *Zulueta: Azúcar moreno* (Brown sugar), and *Espada: Ser y hacer sobre el lecho de un volcán* (Being and doing on the bed of a volcano).[18]

There are numerous connections in the world of music and they cannot all be listed here. Just a few examples.

First it should be pointed out that Cuban musicians and performers tour the Basque Country on a regular basis and play all sorts of styles. These have ranged from Compay Segundo to Silvio Rodríguez, Pablo Milanés, Los Van Van, Bebo Valdés, Familia Valera Miranda, Elíades Ochoa and Cuarteto Patria, Vicente Feliú, and much more. More recently, Gente de Zona and the Reggaeton-player El Micha (Michael Fernando Sierra), among others, and in 2014 the excellent singer Laritza Bacallao visited us.

The accordionist Kepa Junkera worked with the pianist Ronaldo Luna in Havana in 2009 to record the compilation: *Fandango Habana Sessions: Cuba y Euskadi sonando juntos* (Havana Fandango sessions: Cuba and the Basque Country playing together). They played together in 2010 and 2011.

Cuban musicians Ricardo Riverón, Daxon Rodríguez, Amaury Ortega, Miguel Arboleda, and Aida Diez live in the Basque Country and in 2012 they formed Grupo Havana 537. During their performances they play traditional music (son montuno, boleros, guarachas) and give it a modern touch.

There is a mixed group called La Jodedera formed by Jon Txorromorro, Jon Oiartzun, Mandi Cienfuegos, and Oscar Havana. They sing in Spanish and Basque, and some traditional Cuban songs have even been translated into Basque.

The last example I will mention is the duo Las dos D, sisters Danieuris and Daniellis Moya Ávila. They have played in Cuba and in the Basque Country, where one of them lives. As with the previous group, their personal and artistic connections with the Basque Country have led them to include pieces in Basque in their repertoire.

The Contemporary Basque-Cuban Community

As I said in my talk in Havana in January 2013 at Colegio Mayor de San Jerónimo, I believe that the Basque-Cuban community or group on the

---

18. The website Semillas en el Tiempo: www.semillaseneltiempo.com/index.html.

island includes three types of people: those who have Cuban nationality and are children or descendants of previous generations or Basques who moved there for social reasons (a better life) or political reasons (various periods of exile); Basque citizens who live there, whether temporarily (professional people, cooperativists, etc.) or permanently (for reasons of work, having formed families, retired there, etc.), whether voluntarily (the majority) or being forced to (exiles deported in the 1980s);[19] and those Cubans who are not direct descendants of Basques but who have Basque surnames (Zulueta, Aranguren, Goitisolo—or Goitizolo—Arrieta) being descendants of slaves brought from Africa in the nineteenth century and who adopted the surnames of the owners of the plantations where they worked. I should underline that these people, in addition to their Cuban and Afro-Cuban identify, must have full rights to join Basque-Cuban societies if they feel themselves to be Basques as well.

This is a product of history. Since colonization there have been Basque-American communities with their various associations and brotherhoods. The Real Sociedad Bascongada de Amigos del País promoted forming groups in Santiago de Cuba (1787) and Havana (1792).

They were founded in the nineteenth and the beginnings of the twentieth century: in 1868 the Sociedad de Beneficencia de Naturales y Descendientes de las Provincias Vasco-Navarras (Matanzas); in 1877 the Asociación Vasco-Navarra de Beneficencia, AVNB (Havana); and in 1908 the Centro Euskaro, later known as the Centro Vasco (Havana).

The most important is the AVNB (one of the main American euskal etxeak, the third eldest, following Montevideo and Buenos Aires). The members were from throughout the Basque Country (French and Spanish states). They gave immigrants considerable help. Its activity decreased after 1959.[20] In 1979 its document archives were catalogued.[21] During the 1990s a small group of people promoted the Basque society Zazpiak Bat, but it was not a success.

From 2002, efforts were made to reactivate the AVNB, and it was given official recognition by the Basque government in February 2006, and included in the register of Basque centers worldwide. After a crisis in the organization, in 2012 its board of directors was renewed and new plans were undertaken: setting up the euskal etxea, increasing the number of members, holding regular activities, celebrating Aberri Eguna (Basque Homeland Day) and other festivities, organizing conferences and, above

---

19. Documentary *Los Deportados, la historia de tres ciudadanos vascos en Cuba* (The exiles, the story of three Basque citizens in Cuba, 2013), En Boca Cerrada Producciones, directed by Lupe Alfonso, https://vimeo.com/68348295.
20. Various of its members' experiences—whether born in the Basque Country or in Cuba, and who are currently of considerable age—have been recorded in Lauredo, *Los puentes de la memoria*.
21. Work supported by the Donostia-San Sebastián city council, Eusko Ikaskuntza, and the Spanish Cultural Center. The results can be seen in: Various Authors, *Memoria documental de los vascos en Cuba*.

all, trying to have its own headquarters or premises. This is probably its main challenge. It has 370 members at present. Between 2013 and the start of 2015 efforts went on to consolidate the organization, having received financial support from the Basque government for this purpose.

The Cuban Community in the Basque Country

There is not a large group of Cubans living in the Basque Country. The Basque Autonomous Community's population—excluding Navarra—was 2,188,849 in 2014. Of this total, 140,917 of them were registered foreigners (6.4 percent of the total). Further subdivided, 50,847 are Latin American (2.3 percent of the population). There are exactly 1,721 Cubans (0.07 percent of the population). There are 1,026 women and 695 men.

To look at it another way, they are 1.2 percent of the people from other countries. Cuba is number twenty-three on this list of donor countries.[22] Those not registered would have to be added to the 1,721 registered Cubans, but I believe that the figure would not increase substantially.

Although most of them have medium or high-level training and education in comparison with immigrants from other places, the current economic situation means that they are working in diverse positions, whether as employees in shops and hostelry, self-employed (bricklayers, hairdressers, etc.) and postgraduate university students. Some have Basque living partners and have even formed mixed families. In these cases they often have Spanish passports.

Most of them keep up their contacts with the island and, when time and money allow, travel there. They are looked after by the Cuban embassy in Madrid's "itinerant consulate," whose employees spend some days each year in the Basque Country carrying out administrative tasks for their citizens (renewing passports, foreign residence permits, issuing certificates, etc.)

Some Cubans have organized their own groups: Asociación Sierra Maestra Euskadi (founded in 2008); and the Asociación Cubano Vasca "Desembarco del Granma" (2011). They carry out various social and cultural activities.

In December 2014, on Immigrants' Day, a delegation of Cuban residents went to an official reception held by president Urkullu at the Basque government headquarters.

Conclusion

The historical links between the Basque Country and Cuba from previous centuries are essential as the basis for current relations. Now in the twenty-first century, the high degree of connection between the people of Cuba and the Basque Country and their various organizations can be seen

---

22. Data from Ikuspegi (Basque immigration observation), 2014.

in the institutional, socioeconomic, and cultural areas and in other social spheres.

Valuing the positive nature of these contemporary links is no obstacle to saying that they could be improved in terms of quantity and quality. This will depend, to a large extent, on the wills of both parties and, in particular, on the institutions (governments and administrations at different levels) and all types of organizations (associations, NGO's, companies, foundations, universities, etc.) involved.

I believe that in the institutional area relations were at their most active between 1997 and 1998—Lehendakari Ardanza's visits—and, in 1998, the opening of the Basque Commercial Office—dependent on the public company SPRI—in Havana was key in this. This was consolidated in 2002—president Ibarretxe's visit. High-ranking officials of the Cuban government also visited the Basque Country. The best period was between 2002 and 2008, thanks to the framework-agreement between the Basque Country and Cuba known as the "Protocol of Intentions," signed in April 2002. Actions taken were followed by a mixed commission—"The Cuba-Basque Country Intergovernmental Commission for Economic and Scientific-technical Collaboration." The level of collaboration decreased from 2009 onward as this body stopped meeting, plans were not revised and sector agreements were no longer renewed. And, finally, closure of the Commercial Office in 2013 was not a good decision, either politically or economically.

I believe that both parties—the Basque government and the Cuban government—should look into different ways to restart the relations and collaboration which existed until a decade ago. For one thing, it would be positive for Cuba in its current situation of transformation and economic opening to the outside world. For another, it would help the Basque Country to meet a series of requisites to be considered worthy of the Strategic Internationalization Framework (adopted in 2014).

In the same way, there could also be proposals, plans, and initiatives for improving and reinforcing the other types of links briefly mentioned in the previous pages.

In short, and as explained in previous academic papers, Cuba is one of the countries with the greatest potential with regards to the Basque Country's internationalization.

Bibliography

Bilbao, Jon. *Vascos en Cuba, 1492–1511*. Buenos Aires: Ekin, 1958.

Lauredo, Aurelio Francos. *Los puentes de la memoria: Vascos en Cuba*. Vitoria-Gasteiz: Basque Government, 2011.

Piñero, Ignacio, et al. "Influencia del requerimiento social en la metodología para el proceso de priorización en la rehabilitación de estructuras degradadas del Centro Histórico de Havana." In *Diálogos para el estudio de América Latina en el siglo XXI*. Coordinated by Alexander Ugalde Zubiri, 405–19. Leioa: University of the Basque Country, 2014. Available at: https://web-argitalpena.adm.ehu.es/listaproductos. asp?r=i1.

Ugalde Zubiri, Alexander. "Las relaciones País Vasco-Cuba desde la perspectiva de la acción exterior vasca." In IV Congreso de Sociología Vasca minutes, March, 1–3, 2001. Bilbao, Asociación Vasca de Sociología, 2005, 1.392–1.404.

Ugalde Zubiri, Alexander, coord.. *Patria y Libertad: Los vascos y las guerras de independencia de Cuba (1868–1898)*. Tafalla: Txalaparta, 2012.

Various Authors. *Memoria documental de los vascos en Cuba*. Havana: Centro Cultural de España en Havana, 1999.

Index

About the Contributors

Haizpea Abrisketa is a PhD student at the University of Pau et les Pays de l'Adour and the University of the Basque Country. Haizpea is currently working at Kontseilua (the Council of Basque Language Social Organizations) with responsibility for project development.

Joseba Agirreazkuenaga is professor of contemporary history at the University of the Basque Country. Author of numerous books and articles, his interests include crisis in the Ancien Regime, Basque foral history and issues surrounding Basque political independence, and social movements in Bilbao and the Basque Country. He directs the Consolidated Research Group Biography & Parliament (IT-658-13). (Joseba.agirreazkuenaga@ehu.es).

Félix Julio Alfonso López has a doctorate in history from the University of Havana a masters in inter-disciplinary studies on Latin America, the Caribbean, and Cuba, graduate in history. His bachelor degrees are in social anthropology and public administration. He is a lecturer at San Gerónimo University College, Havana. He is also the author of various articles and books about history and culture in Cuba.

Óscar Álvarez Gila is doctor in history and lecturer on the history of America at the University of the Basque Country. He is a specialist in subjects related with Basque emigration to America in the nineteenth and twentieth centuries. He has authored dozens of articles and books. He was the Basque Visiting Professor at the University of Oxford, 2008–2009; the William Douglass Distinguished Scholar at the Center for Basque Studies,

University of Nevada, Reno, 2010–2011; and the Elena Díaz-Verson Amos Eminent Scholar at Columbus State University, Georgia, 2013–2014.

Juan Bosco Amores Carredano is doctor in history (1993, University of Sevilla). He is a lecturer in the history of America at the University of the Basque Country, specializing in the history of Cuba, eighteenth and nineteenth centuries; political, social and cultural history. He is the author of more than 70 publications, including *Cuba y España, 1868–1898, El final de un sueño*, 1998, and *Cuba en la época de Ezpeleta (1785–1790)*, 2000. He is also the voice for Lo Vasco en Cuba, *Enciclopedia Vasca Auñamendi*.

Urko Apaolaza Ávila is a graduate in history from the University of the Basque Country and journalist at the magazine *Argia*, where he is in charge of history contents. His research work has focused on two areas: firstly, the Civil War in the Basque Country, about which he has published several books; secondly, groups of Basque collectivities in the Americas.

Cecilia Arrozarena is a troubadour and is the author author of a novel titled *Examen suspendido* and a historical examination of Basque presence in Cuba, *El roble y la ceiba*, published in 2003.

Mónica de la Caridad García Salgado is a graduate in history, University of Oriente (2005); master in Cuban and Caribbean studies (2008). She is currently completing a structured doctoral program for non-residents in the history of Cuba, America, and the Caribbean (University of Havana, 2008). She also has served as an assistant lecturer in the history department at the University of Oriente, Santiago de Cuba, since 2005.

Michael Cobiella García is a doctor in historical sciences. He is also an anthro- pologist, researcher, and the chief editor at the Fernando Ortiz Foundation, Cuba. In addition, he is a lecturer at the University of Havana. He specializes in research into immigrations and ethnic groups settled in Cuba and, in particular, in the city of Havana in the twentieth century. He has published articles and other pieces about these matters, and about other cultural anthropology subjects, in Cuban and international publications.

Beñat Çuburu-Ithorotz is a lecturer at the Université de Pau et des Pays de l'Adour (France) and writing a thesis about emigration to American from the French Basque town of Hasparren (1830–1930).

William A. Douglass is a doctor of social anthropology (U. of Chicago, 1967). He founded the Basque Studies Program of the University of Nevada System (1967) and directed it for 33 years. He has published two dozen books and 200 articles—including *Amerikanuak: Basques in the New World* (1975) with Jon Bilbao.

Miel Anjel Elustondo Etxeberria is a researcher into the Basque diaspora. His recent books include *Western Basque Festival, 1959, 2007), William A. Douglass: Mr. Basque*, 2011. He is also a well-known journalist and photographer. He publishes articles in the Basque press. He is writing a PhD about the Franciscans in Cuba.

Miliada Hernández García is a graduate in history (2006) and master in historical studies and Cuban sociocultural anthropology (2010). She is a lecturer in ancient history and the history of Cuba at the University of Cienfuegos "Carlos Rafael Rodríguez" (2006–2013). She has published the book *Vascos a la Cuba Colonial: en el vórtice de Cienfuegos (1860–1898)*, 2011.

Pedro Luis Hernández Pérez is a graduate in history, MSc. He has published numerous scienti c articles and around twenty books, mostly about geohistory, nature, and Hispanic migration to Cuba. He is a member of the Unión de Historiadores de Cuba and the Unión Nacional de Escritores y Artistas de Cuba.

María Cristina Hierrezuelo Planas is a graduate in history and holds a doctorate in historical sciences. She is a lecturer at the Department of History in the University of Oriente, Cuba. She has published the books *Las olvidadas hijas de Eva*, 2006, and *Tumbas para cimarronas*, 2013.

Alberto Irigoyen Artetxe is a Uruguayan historian and novelist. He has published *Laurak Bat de Montevideo, primera euskal etxea del mundo*, 1999; *El Centro Euskaro de Montevideo, and dialéctica del ser*, 2003; *La hora vasca de Uruguay: Génesis y desarrollo del nacionalismo vasco en Uruguay*, 2006; *La Sociedad de Confraternidad Vasca 'Euskal Erria' de Montevideo (Uruguay)*, 2007 (with Xabier Irujo Ametzaga); *La Asociación Vasco Navarra de Beneficencia de Havana y otras entidades vasco cubanas*, 2014, among other books. He has been awarded the Andrés Irujo prize twice.

Edorta Jiménez Ormaetxea is a Basque writer. He is author of *Hemingway eta euskaldunak Zerbitzu Sekruetuetan*, 2003. His fiction and essays have been translated into several languages.

Sergio Luis Márquez Jaca is a doctor of medicine, anthropologist, and archaeologist, lecturer at the Faculty of Medicine in Artemisa province. He has published various articles and books whose main subjects are anthropology and history.

Hilda Otero Abreu is a graduate in history at the University of Havana. She is a technician at the National Archive of Cuba, 1989–1995. She is also a lecturer at the Department of History and the House of Superior Studies Fernando Ortiz at the University of Havana, 1996–2000. She received her doctorate in history at the University of the Basque Country, 2006. She is currently a researcher connected with the consolidated investigation group Biography & Parliament at the University of the Basque Country. She is the author of the book *La diplomacia de los vencidos*, 2012).

Jorge Freddy Ramírez Pérez is a graduate in history and a doctor of geography. He has published numerous scientific articles and around twenty books, mostly about geohistory, nature, and the Hispanic migration to Cuba. He is a member of the Unión de Historiadores de Cuba, the Cuban Academy of History, and the Unión Nacional de Escritores y Artistas de Cuba.

Jon Ander Ramos Martínez is a graduate in history (2004) and PhD student in history. He is a lecturer in the history of America at the University of the Basque Country. He specializes in contemporary Basque migrations. His publications include: *Víctor Mendizábal, un faro en la tormenta*, Ordizia, 2013 (with Marcelino Irianni); and is co-author (with Ó. Álvarez Gila and A. Angulo Morales) of *Devoción, paisanaje e identidad: Las cofradías y congregaciones de naturales en España y América (siglos XVI-XIX)*, 2014.

Maithe Sánchez Garrido is a graduate in education, specializing in Marxism-Leninism and history at the "Frank País García" Higher Institute, University of Oriente (2003); and master in Cuban and Caribbean studies (2008). She is an assistant lecturer in the Department of History at Oriente University, Santiago de Cuba since 2005. She teaches subjects such as African and Middle Eastern history and history teaching methodology.

Alexander Ugalde Zubiri is a graduate in history; doctor of political science, and lecturer in international relations at the University of the Basque Country. His publications include coordinating the work: *Patria y Libertad: Los vascos y las Guerras de Independencia de Cuba (1868–1898)*, 2012. E-mail: alexander.ugalde@ehu.eus.

Mikel Urquijo is professor of contemporary history at the University for the Basque Country. His work has been carried out in the framework of the Biography and Parliament Research Group (IT-658-13), recognized by the Basque Government. His main lines of research are the analysis of elites using collective biographies and prosopographic analysis and contemporary Bilbao. He has eighty publications including books, book chapters, and articles.

www.ingramcontent.com/pod-product-compliance
Lightning Source LLC
Chambersburg PA
CBHW070752240726
48654CB00007B/44